Y0-ALH-415

WITHDRAWN

THE RISE AND FALL OF THE SINGAPORE NAVAL BASE, 1919–1942

CAMBRIDGE COMMONWEALTH SERIES

Published in association with the Managers of the Cambridge University Smuts Memorial Fund for the Advancement of Commonwealth Studies

General Editor: E. T. Stokes, Smuts Professor of the History of the British Commonwealth, University of Cambridge

Roger Anstey
The Atlantic Slave Trade and British Abolition, 1760–1810

T. R. H. Davenport
South Africa: A Modern History

B. H. Farmer (editor)
Green Revolution? Technology and Change in Rice-Growing Areas of Tamil Nadu and Sri Lanka

Partha Sarathi Gupta
Imperialism and the British Labour Movement, 1914–1964

Ronald Hyan and Ged Martin
Reappraisals in British Imperial History

W. David McIntyre
The Rise and Fall of the Singapore Naval Base, 1919–1942

B. R. Tomlinson
The Indian National Congress and the *Raj*, 1929–1942
The Political Economy of the *Raj* 1914–1947

John Manning Ward
Colonial Self-Government: The British Experience, 1759–1856

Further titles in preparation

THE RISE AND FALL OF THE SINGAPORE NAVAL BASE, 1919–1942

W. David McIntyre

1979
Archon Books

© W. David McIntyre 1979

All rights reserved. No part of this publication may be reproduced or transmitted, in any form or by any means, without permission

First published 1979 in England by
THE MACMILLAN PRESS LTD
*and in the USA as an Archon Book
an imprint of*
THE SHOE STRING PRESS, INC.
*995 Sherman Avenue,
Hamden, Connecticut 06514*

British Library Cataloguing in Publication Data

McIntyre, William David
    The rise and fall of the Singapore Naval Base,
    1919–1942– (Cambridge Commonwealth Series)
    1. Singapore Naval Base
    I. Title   II. Series
    359.7   VA459.S5

MACMILLAN ISBN 0-333-24867-8

ARCHON ISBN 0-208-01835-2
LCN 79-65821

Printed in Great Britain

Contents

List of Maps	vii
List of Plates	viii
Preface	xi
INTRODUCTION	1
1 'THE NAVAL KEY TO THE FAR EAST', 1919–24	19
2 'SOMETHING LESS THAN THE WHOLE', 1924–26	39
3 'A BAIT TO CATCH SOME MONEY', 1923–28	53
4 'GUNS v AIR', 1921–28	69
5 'SLOWED DOWN AS MUCH AS POSSIBLE', 1929–32	86
6 'THE WRITING ON THE WALL', 1932–35	103
7 'THREATS AT BOTH ENDS OF THE EMPIRE', 1935–39	123
8 'SO MANY VARIABLE FACTORS', 1939–40	144
9 'KITH AND KIN', 1940–41	165
10 'A CLOSE RUN THING', 1941–42	188

POST-MORTEM	210
Bibliography	231
Notes	250
Index	275

List of Maps

1	Trade and strategy in the East	8
2	Singapore and Malaya	12
3	Choosing the site	26
4	The first proposals of 1922	33
5	The truncated scheme of 1926	33
6	First coastal artillery proposals, 1923	73
7	Main fleet and air force routes	79
8	Gun-sites and airfields approved in 1935	121
9	Australia, New Zealand, Fiji and the Pacific Islands	142
10	Japan moves south	145
11	Initial dispositions – Percival's analogy	197
12	Outline of the campaign	200

List of Plates

1. Admiral of the Fleet Lord Jellicoe
2. Normanton Oil Fuel Depot
3. A 15" naval gun adapted for coastal defence
4. David, Lord Beatty
5. The Earl of Cavan
6. Hawker *Horsley* (proposed torpedo-bomber)
7. Sir Hugh Trenchard
8. Air Vice-Marshal Arthur Tedder; Air Vice-Marshal Richard Williams
9. The big guns practising
10. Loading a 15" gun
11. Vickers *Vildebeeste* torpedo-bomber
12. Bristol *Blenheim* fighter-bomber
13. Sir Maurice Hankey
14. Sir Leopold Savile
15. Stanley M. Bruce
16. Richard G. Casey; Robert Menzies
17. Lieutenant-General Sir Webb Gillman
18. Sir Arthur Jackson
19. The floating dock under construction at Wallsend
20. Admiral Sir Ernle Chatfield
21. Sultan Ibrahim of Johore
22. Sir Thomas Inskip
23. Contractor's photograph, July 1931
24. Guide to dockyard photographs
25. Looking south-west through the dock entrance
26. *Seabelle II* cuts the tape
27. Looking north-east to dock entrance
28. The completed dock in 1940
29. Progress on the wall by December 1931
30. HMS *Norfolk*, dressed for the opening
31. Progress by November 1932
32. The half-finished Stores Basin in 1938

List of Plates

33　HMS *Prince of Wales* at the Naval Bäse
34　HMS *Repulse* leaves the Johore Strait
35　Air Chief Marshal Sir Robert Brooke-Popham
36　Admiral Sir Tom Phillips
37　General Sir Archibald Wavell
38　Lieutenant-General Arthur Percival
39　Major-General Gordon Bennett
40　Percival signs the surrender document
41　Victor and vanquished

Preface

Since the fall of Singapore in 1942 at least two books a year, on average, have been published about the disastrous Malayan campaign. It is not my intention to add to the number. Only one chapter of this book is devoted to the campaign. I want instead to tell why Singapore became a target and why the great naval base was built in the first place. I have attempted a study of British Commonwealth naval strategy east of Suez from the closing years of the 1914–18 War until the opening months of the Pacific War.

The book was conceived in the late sixties, during the controversy over Britain's withdrawal from east of Suez. Ironically, the same government which accelerated that withdrawal facilitated study of the earlier period by adopting the thirty year rule for access to archives. Thus, when the editor of the *Journal of Southeast Asian History* asked me to contribute to an issue commemorating the 150th anniversary of the founding of Singapore, I decided to investigate the strategic significance of Singapore. I soon found myself confronting a fascinating mirror of Commonwealth history between the wars.

In 1968 the naval base was handed over to the Government of Singapore and a wry joke was heard in Wellington: 'Do we ask for our million pounds back?'. For the British gave away an asset which, in a real sense, had been created as a collaborative Commonwealth venture. Not only had the New Zealand taxpayers contributed, but those of Singapore itself and the Federated Malay States made substantial contributions. The Colony of Hong Kong and the Sultan of Johore also gave money. Although Australia did not help to pay for the base its defence depended on the Singapore strategy. And during the campaign an Australian division, five RAAF squadrons and a RAN destroyer took part. The Government of India did not provide funds either, but the army and air force reinforcement schemes for Singapore had long looked to India. In 1941 over 40 per cent of the garrison were from India.

Many writers have alluded to the symbolic impact of the fall of

Singapore – Britain's worst disaster since the loss of the American colonies. Until recently few looked at the background, although a very useful study by an American, Eugene H. Miller (*Strategy at Singapore*, New York, Macmillan) was published only a few months after the disaster. Most writers on the Malayan campaign sought to apportion blame on either the commanders in the field or the strategists in London, Washington or Canberra. However, Major-General Woodburn Kirby, author of the United Kingdom official history of the campaign, later wrote his own 'unofficial' history (*Singapore: the Chain of Disaster*, London, Cassell, 1971), in which he concluded: 'It can be truthfully said that the naval base was at least theoretically lost before the first sod had been turned ...'. My book may be read as an extended comment on this judgement. Whether or not General Kirby's view can be accepted, I leave readers to judge for themselves.

I want to thank all those, in three continents, who have helped generously in the production of this book. The Council of the University of Canterbury granted me paid leave to visit Australia and Singapore in 1968 and Singapore again in 1973, to visit Britain in 1970 and in 1973-4. The staffs of the following record offices and libraries have always been helpful: in London – the Public Record Office, the National Maritime Museum, the India Office Library, the Labour Party Archives (Transport House), the British Museum, the School of Oriental and African Studies Library, the Institute of Commonwealth Studies, and Chatham House; in Canberra – the Australian Archives Office, the National Library of Australia, the ANU Library, and the Ministry of External Affairs; in Wellington – the New Zealand National Archives, the Alexander Turnbull Library, the General Assembly Library and the Ministry of Foreign Affairs; in Singapore – the National Library, and the University of Singapore Library. Photographs were provided by the Public Record Office, the Imperial War Museum, the Australian War Memorial, the Royal Artillery Institution, Woolwich, the Institution of Civil Engineers, London, G. Maunsell and Sons, Sembawang Shipyard Ltd, the State Library of Victoria and the Christchurch *Press*. Every effort has been made to contact all the copyright holders but if any have inadvertently been missed the publisher will be pleased to make any necessary arrangements.

I would also like to express my gratitude to a number of individuals who shared their knowledge. My colleagues Dr S. A. M.

Preface

Adshead and Dr N. R. Bennett read the whole of the first draft and made valuable suggestions. Dr I. J. Catanach helped me through the India Office catalogues. Dr John Cumpston, formerly historian of the External Affairs Department in Canberra, arranged access to Australian material and in Wellington Ian Wards, of the Historical Publications Branch, and Dr John Henderson, then of the Ministry of Defence, gave advice and criticism. Dr Geoffrey Rice assisted with photocopying. David McDine, the Fleet PRO, Far East Fleet, took me round the naval base in 1968 in the twilight days of Royal Navy control when there was still an aircraft carrier and a commando carrier on station. Mr R. A. Hooker, of Sembawang Shipyard, showed me a transformed dockyard in 1973 by which time the residual ANZUK fleet was confined to the old Stores Basin. Major-General L. E. Beavis, of Melbourne, talked about the siting of the big guns from his experience on secondment in the War Office in the 1930s. Mr J. W. Hunter (whose father figures in the story too) told me about the rush to complete the wharves in 1940 when the word was: 'we'll just about finish it in time for the Japanese'. Mr John Reid of G. Maunsell and Son introduced me to a splendid cache of contractor's photographs in Penge and Bernard Sunley and Sons Ltd provided some material on Sir John Jackson Ltd. The inter-loans, photocopying and photographic departments of the University of Canterbury must be thanked for efficient service and good humour. Mr T. M. Farmiloe and Mrs P. A. Marshall gave sympathetic editorial advice.

Finally, special words of thanks to Merilyn Johnson for her meticulous typing; to my dear wife Marion, who as usual helped to read the proofs without interrupting her knitting; and to my five children, who always keep me on my toes.

April 1979   W. DAVID McINTYRE

Introduction: Why, Where and How?

I

The Singapore Naval Base was built so that the Royal Navy could dock its largest warships in the Far East. There was no dry dock east of Malta which could take a battleship with the anti-torpedo 'bulges', which were fitted from the end of the First World War. If it were to contemplate a major fleet action east of Suez, the navy required an up-to-date dockyard somewhere in the region.

Singapore was mooted as the appropriate site in 1919. The decision to build the base was made in 1921, but the first funds were not voted until 1923. In the following year, soon after site preparations began, the first Labour Government announced the cancellation of the project. This did not, actually, halt the preparations and a Conservative Government pressed on with the scheme – at a reduced level – in 1926. The main engineering contract was let in 1928. This meant that when the second Labour Government tried to call a halt once more, in 1929, it found that the project – like the later *Concorde* – had achieved a momentum of its own. Cancellation had become more costly than continuance. The work was kept going, but expenditure on machinery to make it usable and defences to make it secure was withheld. It took the Manchuria and Shanghai crises of 1931–2 to prompt the National Government to complete the project. Then, with the coming to power of the Nazis in Germany, in 1933, the Singapore base was subsumed within the wider endeavours of British rearmament. The dockyard was formally opened in 1938, but it was far from finished. Construction work was still proceeding in 1940–1, on the eve of the Pacific War.

Although the seemingly technical decision to provide a dockyard was really a strategic decision of momentous import, the twenty-year construction period might give the impression that it was not treated urgently. This was by no means true for the service advocates of the base. But they were not the final decision-makers, and the project itself cannot be separated from the context of the events in which it was conceived.

II

The original proposal in 1919 arose from a post-war reappraisal of strategy, in which the British defence planners found themselves in a paradoxical predicament. With the elimination of German naval power the only rival navies were those of Britain's allies the USA and Japan. This meant a shift in the centre of concern, from the Atlantic to the Pacific – from seas close to well-established home bases to a distant ocean where the Royal Navy had never been securely established. Although the Pacific naval powers were allies, their navies became rivals for the supremacy of the seas. It was, therefore, not unnatural for the British Naval Staff to begin to think of a 'Two Power Standard' of strength to match them.

If they had been able to adopt a purely theoretical and rational, as opposed to a traditional and realistic approach to naval policy in 1918, the Government might have called, first, for an assessment of commitments and strategy in relation to risks and resources. From these considerations might have emerged a picture of the appropriate size of the navy; the shape of its *matériel*; the best form of organisation, system of supply; and the right spread of bases. But such an approach is rarely, if ever, possible. It was certainly not to be contemplated in 1918. The strategic reappraisal of the post-war years arose directly from an existing situation.

The Royal Navy had just emerged from a war, in which a threat to its centuries-old sea-supremacy had been successfully checked – albeit with the aid of allies. Britain had worldwide commitments involving the defence of the Dominions, India and many other colonies and territories. The senior defence staff, born in mid-Victorian times, had devoted their lifetime careers to maintaining the increasingly tenuous fabric of Britain's world power. 'Imperial Defence' – which for some meant just the defence of the Empire, but for others a form of unwritten alliance between Britain and the King's overseas governments – was the Royal Navy's chief *raison d'être*.[1] Yet imperial defence had for some time involved an element of shared responsibilities. The lion's share of the burden was still borne by the mother country, but for thirty years the Dominions had been making small contributions in the form of naval subsidies and expeditionary forces and so had won a modest, consultative, voice in decision-making. Australia and Canada had created their own small navies. New Zealand and the Federated Malay States had each paid for capital ships for the Royal Navy. In 1918, it was not a case of taking a fresh look at strategy, but of picking-up 'unfinished business' from pre-war days. As the vast, inflated, wartime navy, which in 1918 surpassed the rest of the world's navies put together,[2] was demobilised and decommissioned, and the immediacy of wartime operations ended, the Admiralty had to take-up some of the 'loose ends' of imperial defence. These problems were highlighted by the shift in centre of gravity from Atlantic to Pacific.

To start with the Admiralty was presented with questions, not of strategy, or ships, but of organisation. During the Imperial War Cabinet of 1917 there had been complaints from the New Zealand representatives, 'Bill' Massey, the Prime Minister, and Sir Joseph Ward, his wartime coalition deputy, that pre-war naval arrangements had not been honoured in the Pacific. Massey, who hoped that the British Empire would last until the Day of Judgement, envisaged New Zealand as the centre of a vast British island federation with a great maritime future. Ward, who believed in imperial naval unity, moved a resolution favouring Dominions' control over their own naval forces. He withdrew it in favour of the version by Sir Robert Borden, the Canadian Prime Minister, calling on the Admiralty to work out, as soon as the war ended, the most effective scheme of Empire naval defence.[3]

The Admiralty did not wait for the war to end. When the Imperial War Cabinet reconvened in 1918 the Dominion leaders were treated to a proposal from the First Sea Lord, Admiral Sir Rosslyn Wemyss, reasserting the Admiralty's faith in the 'ideal of a single Navy'. Control of strategy and operations was to be vested in an Imperial Naval Authority. The 'partner nations' of the Empire would appoint Local Naval Boards to take charge of dockyards, recruiting and training. Dominion naval ministers might occasionally sit on the Imperial Naval Authority. It was clear that the naval staff still cherished the traditional doctrine of one sea, one empire, one navy. The Dominion leaders did not. All, bar the premier of Newfoundland, agreed with Borden that, while the strategic argument was 'strong but not unanswerable', the single navy was not practicable. Instead they asked for a highly qualified naval authority to visit the Dominions in turn and advise on naval policy.[4]

Soon after the Armistice in November Sir Joseph Cook, the Australian Defence Minister, sounded Admiral Jellicoe, the former First Sea Lord, who agreed to take on the task. Since the Dominion Governments were suspicious of any schemes smacking of imperial unity, and Jellicoe was likely to advocate such schemes, the framing of his instructions needed care. In one draft Sir Oswyn Murray, the Secretary of the Admiralty, suggested spelling it out that Jellicoe must take Dominion proposals seriously and not merely use them as a means of carrying on a crusade for the Admiralty scheme. In the end a more tactful formula was evolved. Without compromising on their doctrine of central control, the Admiralty recognised that the promotion of 'uniformity' could be given as the main goal. Jellicoe was told to advise the Dominions' and Indian Governments whether, in the light of wartime experiences, the scheme of naval organisation 'which has been adopted, or may be in contemplation', required reconsideration, and to suggest how best to evolve, in the light of their local needs, 'the greatest possible homogeneity and cooperation between all the naval forces of the Empire'.[5] Jellicoe sailed on his Empire mission on 21 February 1919 in HMS *New Zealand*, the battle-cruiser donated in 1909 by the Dominion. Promotion to Admiral of the Fleet from 3 April gave him an added touch of authority.

III

With Jellicoe on his way the naval staff continued to consider the wider problems of sea-power, empire co-operation, and the practical problems arising from the post-war situation.

The next issue to come up concerned naval bases in the Pacific. On 26 April 1919 the Plans Division of the Admiralty produced a paper which was prompted by Australian and Canadian enquiries as to what dockyards they should develop and by the problem of the future of the small dockyard at Hong Kong. These questions could only be decided in the light of general strategy in the Pacific, where the navy might have to operate far from existing bases. If Japan were to be the enemy, a base in western Canada would be too far away, but Hong Kong would be too vulnerable. Preparations for war against either the USA or Japan would require primary imperial bases at Sydney and Singapore and rapid military reinforcement of Malaya from India. Offensive operations against Japan would require advanced bases in Chinese or Korean waters. This document raised bigger issues than bases. The assistant Director of Plans, Captain Kenneth Dewar, wrote that if the Admiralty could adopt a policy for the Pacific, some of the outstanding questions relating to bases could be settled.[6]

The naval staff remained uncertain as to the best locations for bases. Hong Kong was generally believed to be too vulnerable, Sydney was secure, Singapore not quite so certain. But the deputy Chief of Naval Staff, Rear-Admiral Sir James Fergusson, was shocked by the whole tenor of the discussion. To build a main fleet base at either Singapore or Sydney would, he felt, be 'rattling the sword', whereas development at Hong Kong could be taken as the normal growth of a base important for commerce and prestige.[7] Before this argument could be resolved the naval staff decided they must study the basic strategy to be followed in the event of war with either Japan or the USA so that war orders could be prepared for the commanders-in-chief of the eastern stations.

As well as the questions of organisation, bases and contingency plans there was the problem of new warship construction. And all these decisions hinged on the central issue: What policy would the Government adopt in the great issue of 'the supremacy of the seas'? This question was placed squarely before the Cabinet by the First Lord of the Admiralty on 13 August 1919. For 300 years, he argued, the navy had maintained supremacy at sea. Germany had been eliminated as a rival. France and Italy were allies. Japan was an ally. The only navy which might surpass the Royal Navy was that of the United States, which was building sixteen new capital ships under its 1916 programme and had plans for sixteen more. A decision as to whether to match this challenge was needed.[8]

The British Government was more concerned at this moment with economy than strategy. Two days later, without considering the Admiralty paper, the Cabinet made its first major defence decision of the post-war era. It laid down the rule that in framing the service estimates it should be assumed that the British Empire would not be involved in a major war for the next ten years. Changes in the standard of naval strength were not to be made without Cabinet approval. New warship construction was to cease. Annual naval expenditure was given a ceiling of £60 million; the army and the air force were to share £75 million. The Admiralty Board assumed that by this move the Cabinet intended to prevent them using comparisons with the American fleet to establish the size of the RN.[9]

Soon after this, the staff studies set off by the naval bases question bore fruit in a paper on 'Imperial Naval Defence' approved by the Admiralty Board on 25 September 1919. Hypothetical wars with a European power or the USA or Japan had been studied. In the case of a European war operations would be concentrated in the North Sea, Atlantic and Mediterranean; an Anglo-American war was regarded as a remote possibility – opposed to the fundamental interests of both parties. The case of war with Japan was regarded more seriously. If Japan took the initiative, as was likely, Hong Kong, Malaya, Australia, New Zealand and the Pacific Islands might be threatened.

> In order to meet the probable Japanese plan of campaign, it is essential that the Imperial fleet should be provided with a secure base well to the southward of Hong Kong, and no more suitable position can be suggested than Singapore.[10]

Singapore was far enough from Japan to make attack upon it difficult. It was in an excellent position for a fleet 'covering' the vital Australasian and Indian trade routes. It already had a defended commercial dockyard long used by the navy, and at Selat Sinki, southwest of Singapore, there was an anchorage suitable for twenty-five capital ships. Finally, if a fleet superior to Japan's was to be assembled and the invasion of Japan or Korea, or a blockade of Japan, contemplated, a fleet anchorage would be needed at Hong Kong and a mobile naval base and fuelling organisation needed further north. These recommendations pointed to the actions needed if the Government decided to make preparations for a war against Japan. The Admiralty sent them to the Committee of Imperial Defence as embodying its view on the 'broader aspects' of imperial naval defence; detailed studies could be made when Jellicoe came home.[11]

It is clear from this sequence that the idea of the Singapore Naval Base arose during the post-war discussions about naval bases in the Pacific, which, in turn, arose from the possibility of a war with Japan. For the next twenty years British naval planning for the Far East was based on the simple sums of seapower strategy: How many battleships would Japan have – How many British ships were needed to meet them?

IV

The assumption that Singapore was the most suitable place for the dockyard was subjected to surprisingly little debate among the naval staff at the time. There was subsequently a public debate both about the need for a new dockyard and about its location, and several retired Admirals weighed in at this point,[12] but initially it seems that Singapore was simply taken as the obvious spot. This assumption may be explained by reference to three other, largely unspoken, assumptions. First, the requirements of the fleet in the East would not be met completely by the new dockyard. Sydney, Hong Kong, and Trincomalee (in Ceylon) would all still be needed.[13] It was not a question of one-or-another, but of where to put the *new* facilities. Secondly, Singapore's geographic position was a 'central' one in relation to India, Hong Kong, Australia and New Zealand. Its position by the mouth of the Straits of Malacca was at a 'gateway' between the Indian Ocean and the Pacific. It was the leading commercial port in Southeast Asia, at the 'cross-roads' of trade routes between Suez, the Cape and India, and China and Japan. It also had a large entrepôt trade with British Malaya and the Netherlands East Indies. Thirdly, it had been British territory for just a century since Stamford Raffles had occupied the then almost uninhabited island in 1819. This important landmark had, itself, been a by-product of an earlier transition in British trade and strategy.

Britain's valuable eastern trade had grown from the East India Company's activities in India, Southeast Asia and China, which had expanded rapidly from the middle of the eighteenth century. With the defeat of the French in India; the conquest of Bengal; Captain Cook's great explorations in the Pacific, and the growth of the Canton trade, there was a 'Swing to the East' in British commercial aspirations, which pre-dated the loss of the American colonies in 1783.[14] This loss, in turn, had prompted the search for a new penal colony and new sources of naval stores and led to the founding of New South Wales in 1788. In the Napoleonic Wars, strategically-based French and Dutch colonies along the sea routes to India and China were captured. Of these the Cape of Good

Hope, Mauritius, Ceylon and Benkulen (in Sumatra) were kept after the war, while the rest of the East Indies were returned to the Dutch in the interest of good relations with a close European neighbour. However, by this time the British East India Company had acquired its own outposts in the region – known as the Straits Settlements. Penang Island, off the west coast of the Malay Peninsula, had been occupied in 1786 and Raffles acquired Singapore in 1819.

Some of these new possessions became springboards for widespread expansion. From Australia, the British moved on to the Pacific, annexing New Zealand in 1840, Fiji in 1874, and acquiring protectorates in New Guinea, the Solomon Islands, Samoa, Tonga and many smaller island groups. The attractions of the China trade pushed the British on from the Straits Settlements to the South China Sea. Hong Kong was annexed in 1842 and Labuan (off the north coast of Borneo) in 1846. Privileges were also obtained in a

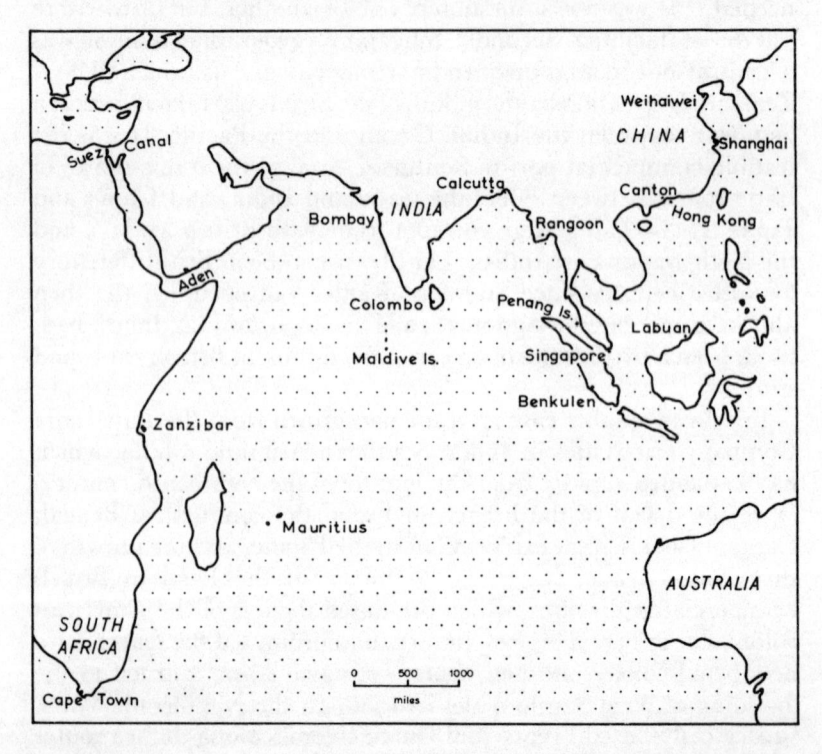

MAP 1. Trade and strategy in the East

Introduction: Why, Where and How?

series of Chinese ports, especially Shanghai, and in 1898 Weihaiwei (on the Shantung peninsula) was leased for a small naval base. India was the *core* of this Eastern Empire; China remained an ever-elusive *goal*, but the by-products – in Southeast Asia, the South Pacific, even the Persian Gulf and East Africa – were far-reaching (see Map 1).

Singapore – at the 'crossroads' – became the capital of the Straits Settlements in 1826. The other settlements were Penang, to which Province Wellesley on the mainland opposite had been added, and Malacca (on the west Coast) which was exchanged with the Dutch for Benkulen in 1824. These were the only territories under British sovereignty in Malaya. After the transfer of the Straits Settlements from control by India to the Colonial Office in 1867 and the opening of the Suez Canal in 1869 Singapore prospered as a port. By 1901 it had a population of over 200,000, 72 per cent of whom were Chinese. As a Crown Colony it had an undemocratic constitution. The Governor's Executive Council (or 'official cabinet') consisted of five senior civil servants, the GOC of the army garrison, and three 'unofficials', who represented local (mainly business) interests, and one of whom was Chinese. In the Legislative Council, which made the local laws, officials and unofficials were exactly balanced, but the Governor retained a casting vote. Most of the unofficials were Europeans, but there were three Chinese, a Eurasian, an Indian and (from 1924) a Malay. Since 1899 the Colony had contributed up to 20 per cent of its revenues towards the costs of the local garrison.[15]

Because of its geographical location and its growing importance as a commercial port Singapore had long had a modest role in the pattern of imperial defence. There had even been intimations of bigger things to come. In 1869 Sir William Jervois, the Inspector-General of Fortifications, had suggested defences to meet a cruiser attack on the port or an uprising of the local populace. For the former he recommended some shore batteries and torpedo boats, and for the latter the maintenance of Fort Canning as a place of refuge and defence. The main defence was the 'deterrent' provided by the Royal Navy. To assist its deployment Singapore was designated a defended port and coaling station from the 1880s. Local proposals that it might become the site of a large naval dockyard in the 1880s and 1890s were turned down. Similar ideas were mooted in the years 1906 to 1912, at the time of the Anglo-German dreadnought race, when the British battleships were withdrawn from the Far East under Admiral Fisher's concentration scheme. His idea that a separate British Empire Eastern Fleet, contributed jointly by Australia, Canada, New Zealand and South Africa also implied the need for a new base.[16] But nothing came of the project. The navy was able to dock ships in the five graving docks controlled by the Singapore Harbour Board. 'King's Dock', the largest, was 873 feet by 93 feet in area and could take vessels up to 33 feet draught, but a damaged battleship might draw up to 45 feet. Thus, if Singapore was to be the post-war base, new dockyard facilities would certainly be needed.

V

In the light of this century-long development it is understandable that Singapore would seem a natural focus for naval thinking. Whether the naval staff ever thought beyond Singapore, and considered the relationship which a new naval base would have with British Malaya, is more doubtful. Yet once the project became a real possibility, the problems of its 'linkages' to the Peninsula were unavoidable. A causeway was being constructed to link the mainland railway system to the port: Would this conflict with fleet movements around the island? Defences for the naval base might need to be constructed on the landward side: Would this be allowed in a protected Malay State? Reinforcements to the army and air garrisons might become necessary: Would these require rail transit from Penang, or air staging through landing-grounds in the Peninsula? Even though the naval base and its defences might be conceived, to begin with, as something almost independent from the wider problems of British rule in the region, Malaya as a whole could not be ignored.

Yet Malaya's relationship with Britain had evolved quite differently from that of Singapore and the Straits Settlements. There were three different categories of Malay State. The four states lying across the middle of the Peninsula were part of the administrative union known (rather inappropriately) as the Federated Malay States. In the middle years of the nineteenth century alluvial tin deposits in the west coast states of Perak, Selangor and Sungei Ujong had attracted thousands of Chinese migrants, who threatened to overwhelm the administrative capacities, even the very populations, of the small Malay sultanates. Therefore, partly to keep order between rival Chinese secret societies and the Malays, partly to mediate in Malay dynastic disputes and partly to make sure no other western powers stepped in, British officials from the Straits Settlements began to intervene in the 1870s. Officials, known as 'Residents' were accepted by the Malay rulers, who agreed to act on the Residents' advice in all matters except Malay custom and religion. Under the fiction of 'government by advice', modern colonial-type administration and economic development proceeded. Pahang, on the east coast, was brought into the system in 1889, and the new administrations were unified by an FMS secretariat, at Kuala Lumpur, from 1896.[17]

To the north of the FMS lay the Malay/Thai border states of Perlis, Kedah, Kelantan and Trengganu, which retained much more of their Malay character and were more loosely tied to Britain. Until 1909, indeed, they were tributary states of Thailand, and, as such, had become a source of anxiety to the British. Rumours were rife in the 1890s that a rival European state might seize the Isthmus of Kra – that narrow neck of Thai territory which joins the Malay Peninsula to the Southeast Asian mainland. To overcome this problem the British Government made a secret agreement with Thailand in 1897 recognising Thai 'suzerainty' in the four northern states in return for the promise that no third party would be admitted without consultation with the British. Later, the Thai Government agreed to fill positions of 'Adviser' to local rulers with British officials. Then, in 1909, Thailand transferred its rights to Britain. The way was then opened for the British to extend the Malayan system. The 'Advisers' were seen as similar to the 'Residents' in the FMS, but not the same. The British trod more carefully in the north and the Sultans cherished their autonomy.

At the southern tip of the Peninsula, adjacent to Singapore (in fact partly surrounding some of the possible sites for the naval base) lay the State of Johore, at once the 'closest' to the Colony and also the most 'independent' of the States. Its economy was closely tied to Singapore. But the first Sultan, Abu Bakar (reigned 1862–95), had carefully modernised his state along partly western lines, without allowing it to be drawn into the FMS system. His successor, Sultan Ibrahim (reigned 1895–1959), however, soon became a well-known Edwardian playboy, renowned in three continents for his extravagance, womanising and interest in the turf. He, too, cherished his independence but, after some minor administrative scandals, even

Johore was forced to accept a 'General Adviser' on the eve of the 1914–18 war.[18]

With the four 'federated' states, five 'unfederated' states and the three Straits Settlements, 'Malaya' consisted of no less than ten different administrations, most of which were not under British sovereignty (see Map 2). What uniformity there was came at the

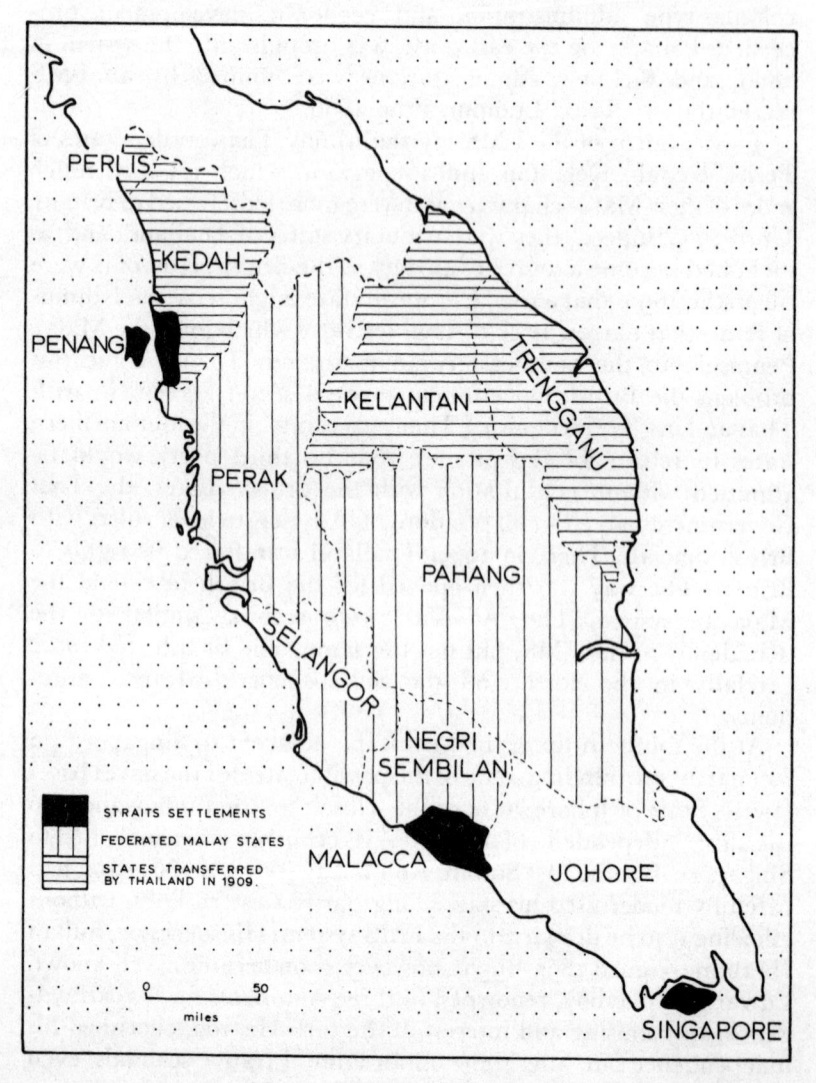

MAP 2. Singapore and Malaya

top, through the Governor of the Straits Settlements, who was also High Commissioner for the FMS and the UMS. (The Sultan of Johore insisted on addressing the High Commissioner as 'Governor of the Straits Settlements'. Labuan, off the coast of North Borneo, was part of the Straits Settlements, and the Governor and High Commissioner was also Consul-General for Sarawak, Brunei and British North Borneo.) Uniformity was also facilitated to some degree by the movement of officials in the Malayan Civil Service, which liked to regard itself as a cut above the better-known Indian Civil Service.[19] The map-makers, of course, made their own contributions, in that the whole of Malaya was 'unified' in school atlases by the famous imperial-red printers' ink.

For all its political anomalies, Malaya was, economically, one of the success stories of British imperialism. The tin, which drew the Chinese miners in the 1850s, eventually attracted large, highly capitalised, dredging companies. By the turn of the century Malaya supplied over half the world's tin. Rubber trees, from experimental cultivation after 1877, were available for commercial planting in the 1890s. By the time of the motoring boom of the 1920s Malaya was supplying over half the world's rubber. For labour the new industry recruited migrant Tamils from South India and Ceylon. Yet for its size (equal to England and Wales) the country still had a small population. In 1911 it totalled only 2.5 million – 53.5 per cent Malays, 34.5 per cent Chinese, 10 per cent Indians and 2 per cent others, including Europeans. In contrast to India, Burma and Ceylon there was very little in the way of nationalist stirrings, since there was no 'nation' to act as a focus.[20] This may have seemed an attraction to those who sought a secure naval base. But Malaya's multi-cultural population, combined with its subtle gradations of administrative control, would make for difficulties if ever clarity and speed in decision-making were necessary.

VI

Loose co-ordination, bureaucratic complexity and rival interests were not, of course, confined to Malaya. They were the most noticeable characteristics of the British Commonwealth, and nowhere were they more evident than in Whitehall. If ever a naval base was to materialise under the tropical skies and quaint polities of Malaya, the project would have to win support on the political, military and civil service battlefields of London.

The idea of the naval base arose in the Admiralty. For the twenty-year construction period the emerging dockyard was a project of the Division of the Civil Engineer-in-Chief. But, from the start, it became a vital element in all the thinking of the Plans Division of the naval staff. Although the Admiralty – grand strategy department *par excellence* – was the main advocate throughout, the War Office and Air Ministry had to be consulted about the defences. They thus found themselves drawn into one of the great bureaucratic battles of the day. This concerned the relative merits of artillery and air defences. The naval staff believed (rightly in 1919) that battleships could only be deterred by big guns and that they were quite safe from bombers. The infant air staff, seeking to establish the role of the air force as a *substitute*, rather than a supplement, to older forms of defence, preached the virtues of the torpedo-bomber. The generals at first sided with the admirals, until they discovered that the gunners missed their targets, and so a compromise mix was worked out. For more than ten years, however, Admiralty House and Adastral House reverberated to the flak of the 'Guns v Air' war, and decisions about the defences of Singapore were held up by one of the classic cases of inter-service rivalry. As a tragic and lasting memorial to this grand tournament of bureaucratic jousting, the hulks of two great capital ships lie at the bottom of the South China Sea forlornly displaying the White Ensign.[21]

As the services required land in Singapore, the Colonial Office was drawn in at an early stage. The Governor of the Straits Settlements, ever sensitive to the feelings of the Malay rulers, insisted that the unpredictable Sultan of Johore (whose palace would overlook the naval base) had to be consulted. The Treasury, the most powerful department in Whitehall, applied its customary dampener as soon as it was consulted. Treasury officials found it incredible that the services should be planning to go to war with an ally, and they argued that the country's finances could not stand the expense.

The costs of construction and the imperial dimension of the scheme led rapidly to the question of sharing the burden. From its inception the Singapore base was the subject of consultation with the Dominions, India and other Colonies and Protected States. Broad hints were dropped that the various Empire and Commonwealth governments might be invited to help. The Colonial Office, the Dominions Office (after 1925) and the India Office were

Introduction: Why, Where and How?

increasingly brought into the scheme. The naval base was discussed at every Imperial Conference between the Wars. Indeed, it was for this reason that the years 1921, 1923, 1926, 1930, 1935 and 1937 each marked minor landmarks because the need to clarify policies, to put to Dominions' and Indian representatives, was one of the most important spurs to action in London. There was an element of irony in this procedure. Although the prospect of financial or military support was an incentive for courting the Dominions, there was also a fear that their democratically-minded leaders could not be trusted with too many secrets. In 1925 and 1937 there were charges of information leakages in Dominion delegations.[22]

The co-ordination of these inter-service, inter-departmental and inter-imperial endeavours, and the preparation of soundly-based recommendations for decision by the Cabinet, were tasks for the Committee of Imperial Defence. Founded in the years 1902-4 to co-ordinate matters 'naval, military, political,' the CID was designed to 'survey as a whole the strategical military needs of the Empire' for the Cabinet. The service ministers, the Foreign Secretary and the Chiefs of Staff met under the chairmanship of the Prime Minister or his deputy. After a somewhat chequered career up to 1915 it was suspended for the rest of the war. It was revived in 1920 and came to play a central role under the secretaryship of Sir Maurice Hankey, the former Royal Marines captain, who had joined the CID as assistant-secretary in 1908. As Secretary of the Cabinet and the Privy Council, as well as the CID, Hankey came close to being *de facto* Secretary-General of the Commonwealth.[23] Dominion representatives were able to attend the CID when the interests of their countries were discussed. The CID was that part of the Whitehall hierarchy where the Singapore Base was most frequently discussed. For the details of its defences the Overseas Defence Subcommittee was called upon. Wider matters of defence policy (especially the air v artillery issue and overseas emergencies, like the Manchurian, Ethiopian and Czech crises) became the province of the Chiefs of Staff Subcommittee founded in 1923. It was able to draw on the services of specialised bodies, such as the Joint Planning Subcommittee (made up of the Directors of Plans of each service), the deputy Chiefs of Staff Subcommittee and the Joint Intelligence Subcommittee, which emerged in the 1930s. In this committee structure the ramifications of the Singapore strategy continuously were sifted and refined. All the Committees however, were advisory, not executive.

Decisions were made by the Cabinet. But on numerous occasions the Singapore Naval Base and related naval expenditure questions were passed to Ministerial Standing Committees, or *ad hoc* committees, chaired by senior ministers, or the Prime Minister. Similar special committees discussed the Singapore base during the Imperial Conferences of 1930 and 1937. Finally, in the 1930s, after the Ten Year Rule had been waived and rearmament was under consideration, an interesting mixture of service staff, civil service and political representation was given oversight of defence spending.

Beginning with the Defence Requirements Committee of 1933 which consisted of the three Chiefs of Staff and two civil service department heads chaired by the Secretary of the Cabinet, the problem was passed (such was the ethos of the day) to the Ministerial Committee on Disarmament, which was renamed, more appropriately, the Ministerial Committee on Defence Requirements after the Geneva Disarmament Conference collapsed in 1934. In the following year it became the Defence Policy and Requirements Subcommittee of the CID. Soon there was also a Ministerial Committee for war planning, the Defence Policy (Plans) Committee, and there was considerable overlapping.[24] In 1937 they were both reorganised under CID auspices, but the habit of *ad hoc* Committees continued. The Strategic Appreciations Committee of 1939 was a notable example. In that year, an impatient civil servant, alarmed about Britain's own security, dubbed the CID the 'Committee for Impeding Defence'.[25] The Singapore base did survive the political and bureaucratic delays, but the fleet demanded by the naval staff in the late 1930s was never approved.

The political-military-bureaucratic committee structure was never without its critics. The Labour Governments were particularly sensitive to the problems of civil service inertia, but they were not often able to overcome them. In 1925 Philip Noel Baker and Arthur Ponsonby MP, who had been Parliamentary Under-Secretary for Foreign Affairs in 1924, wrote a note for the Labour Party Executive recommending the abolition of the CID on the ground that it had achieved a quasi-constitutional position, making it a rival of the Cabinet. They suggested, in its place, a Standing Cabinet Committee on Defence.[26] When Labour returned to power in 1929 they did create a Ministerial Fighting Services Committee (from which the Cabinet Secretary was excluded), but the CID and

COS Subcommittee were retained. Others, notably Winston Churchill, wanted a Ministry of Defence, but the only changes were the appointment of a Minister for the Co-ordination of Defence in 1936 (who was charged with rationing rearmament funds) and the splitting of the civil and military secretarial duties of the Cabinet Office on Hankey's retirement in 1938.

There were also some misgivings in the Dominions about the role of the CID. South African representatives rarely attended. Many autonomy-minded Canadians (who always had the thinnest constitutional skins) feared the CID and the COS would work for imperial unity by the back doors to the corridors of power. The External Affairs Department in Ottawa resented correspondence and intelligence-sharing between the British and Dominions' defence staffs. Canadian High Commissioners in London were forbidden to attend tea-parties and briefings for Dominions' representatives.[27] At the other extreme – constitutionally and hemispherically – the Australian Government worked on the principle: 'If you can't beat them, join them'. In 1923 it appointed an External Affairs Liaison Officer, who was located within the CID Secretariat and saw all British Cabinet papers which related to Australia. He could thus alert his Prime Minister by cable if policy changes seemed likely. On top of this device, the Australians had, as High Commissioner in London from 1933 to 1945, no less a figure than Stanley Bruce, a recent Prime Minister with impeccable personal contacts from his Cambridge, rowing, business and army days. Bruce did not hesitate to play on his easy entrée to the British élite in Whitehall, the CID offices and Downing Street, among civil servants, politicians and the COS, to press for Australia's interests, which included the Singapore base.[28]

Perhaps the most interesting aspect of the British defence planning bureaucracy and the Commonwealth consultative system was that the advocates of the Singapore base in the London service departments and the CID secretariat were able to line up support among their opposite numbers in the Dominions, especially in Melbourne and Wellington. They, in turn, could urge their respective premiers to persuade, criticise or plead with the Prime Minister of Britain. Similarly, carefully organised offers of financial support for the Singapore base from various parts of the Commonwealth and dependent Empire were deliberately orchestrated to ensure joint commitment to the project so that cancellation by the British Government would become politically and financially unlikely. The Singapore base was designed for imperial defence. The 'imperial lever' became a useful source of pressure in the strategic and financial battles, waged by the civil-military bureaucracy, to get it built.

1 'The Naval Key to the Far East', 1919–24

I

The idea of the Singapore Naval Base emerged during the post-war discussions about naval bases in the Pacific. These arose from the suggestion that the naval staff should prepare for hypothetical wars with Japan and the United States. To deploy a battle fleet in the Pacific the navy would need dockyard facilities greater than anything then available at Trincomalee, Singapore, Hong Kong or Sydney. All the requirements of an operational fleet would have to be provided; graving docks, so that ships' hulls could be regularly scraped clean of marine growth; wharves adjacent to workshops and cranes capable of lifting the heaviest equipment like engines and gun turrets; more wharves with quick access to stores; temperature-controlled magazines for ammunition storage; homes for the permanent staff, and barracks, recreation facilities and hospitals. A first-class base was a mixture of dockyard, headquarters complex and home-from-home for the sailor. In the Far East this presented particular problems for Britain. Japan's bases were on its home territory. The United States built a large graving dock at Pearl Harbor, in Hawaii, between 1909 and 1919.[1] Britain had no major dockyard east of Malta.

II

That the naval staff should have been contemplating contingency plans with an eye to matching Britain's allies may now appear bizarre. Partly it can be explained by the traditional tendency of naval planners to think in terms of the supremacy of the seas; of planning to match the strength of their largest rivals. In the case of Japan, however, the matter went deeper.

Japan was a naval partner by virtue of the Anglo-Japanese Alliance. Yet the Singapore base was mooted in the context of plans for a war with this ally. That the naval staff should contemplate this can be explained by the history of mutual suspicion, which had grown up during the 1914-18 war, over Japanese expansionism, notably the twenty-one demands on China; and also by the growing fear among imperialists that Japan's status as a major power symbolised the rise of 'Asia for the Asians'.[2] It seemed a deliberate challenge to the British Empire. It was obvious, however, that this sort of future planning could not go on without a political decision. The naval staff needed to know whether the Anglo-Japanese Alliance would be renewed in 1921.

This question was put to the CID in a paper on 'The Naval Situation in the Far East' compiled at the end of October 1919. In this the naval staff expected that the Government would be reluctant to 'prolong an Alliance which might cause them to be embroiled with the United States'. If this was so, the situation in the Far East would be completely changed. Preparations for a war with Japan would have to be made. As it was unlikely that a fleet equal to Japan's projected eight battleships and eight battle-cruisers would be available in the Pacific in peacetime, a period in which Japan would have a free hand was possible. Existing British naval forces in the Far East would have to be withdrawn to 'the probable port of Assembly of the Main Fleet, which may be assumed to be Singapore'.[3] The loss of Hong Kong would be permanently damaging for British prestige, but it could only be made secure if an adequate fleet were maintained in the Pacific, or if defences were provided strong enough for a long siege.

As this paper made the rounds of the naval staff the urgent importance of a decision on the future of the Anglo-Japanese Alliance became more and more evident.

> The strategical centre of gravity may be said to have shifted from the North Sea to the Pacific, and future Naval policy depends on our relations with Japan. The sooner, therefore, the intentions of the Government are known in regard to the renewal or otherwise, of the Anglo-Japanese Alliance, the better.

These were important questions, wrote the deputy Chief of Naval Staff Vice-Admiral Sir Osmond Brock: 'I am afraid they will be most unpalatable to the new Cabinet'.[4] As if to rub it in, the Far East paper also coincided with one on the level of naval expenditure possible under the Cabinet's 15 August ceiling, which seemed to require the abandoning of naval supremacy. For the present the RN held approximate numerical equality with the USN. With twenty capital ships in commission, Britain could still match the United States with its eighteen dreadnought-type battleships. But HMS *Hood* was Britain's only post-Jutland super-dreadnought, and when the sixteen modern capital ships of the American 1916 building programme were completed the USN would be supreme on the seas, technically as well as numerically.

Within a year of the end of the 1914–18 war, then, the Admiralty found itself in the awkward position of planning to match the naval strength of Britain's two major allies. Unpalatable questions for the Cabinet indeed. Yet, at this very moment, still more unpalatable business presented itself in the shape of Jellicoe's Australian report. The First Sea Lord saw it on 31 October 1919 and noted that Jellicoe had 'entered into a sphere never contemplated by the Admiralty and far beyond his terms of reference'.[5]

III

Jellicoe, who had undertaken to tour the Empire as the technical servant of political masters had, in fact, taken it upon himself to do the Admiralty's job. He saw his task not simply as one of advising the overseas governments on their own naval defence. He gave them a coherent strategic framework for the whole region from the east coast of Africa to the west coast of America. And this, to Jellicoe, meant one thing: preparations for a war against Japan. He had already given a blatant indication of his thinking when he sent home his report on the Indian navy in May. 'Japan is as much a bogey to India as it is to Australia.' He warned that, before long, a major dockyard would be necessary in the Far East.[6] Although Jellicoe did not know it, of course, the naval staff were already seriously thinking of Singapore for this role.

In Australia Jellicoe went much further. On the day following the British Cabinet's decision on the Ten Year Rule he had presented his report to the Australian Government.[7] He sent it off on 21 August to the Admiralty, where it arrived in October, just as they were preparing their papers on Pacific strategy and bases. Without any knowledge of these discussions, nor of the financial constraints imposed by the Cabinet, Jellicoe had told the Australian Government that, in order to counter Japan's '8:8' fleet, the British Empire would have to build the equivalent. In a secret section of the report, entitled 'The Naval Situation in Far East Waters', he argued that it was unwise to trust to the Anglo-Japanese Alliance; that it was 'almost inevitable that the interests of Japan and of the British Empire will eventually clash'.[8] To counter this threat he proposed and this was published, that a new British Empire Pacific Fleet should be built consisting of 8 battleships, 8 battle-cruisers, 4 aircraft carriers, 10 cruisers, 40 destroyers, 36 submarines and a full complement of auxiliaries. Its annual cost would be close to £20 million and he suggested that this should be met in the proportions UK 75 per cent, Australia 20 per cent and New Zealand 5 per cent, according to a formula based on his assessment of their respective populations and commerce. Canada, India and South Africa might contribute some naval units. This fleet would be under imperial control. It would require a dockyard, anchorage, and headquarters. These he would locate at Singapore, which was, he said, 'undoubtedly the naval key to the Far East'.[9]

This grandiose proposal was received with shock and embarrassment. The First Sea Lord felt the Australian Government would have to be told that in strategic matters Jellicoe was stating personal views. However, a précis of the report prepared in the Local Defence Division of the Admiralty went to the core of Jellicoe's scheme and noted that the strategic requirements caused by Japan's strength were serious and that a dockyard at Singapore capable of servicing any British warship was necessary. It was also agreed that Jellicoe's assumption that capital ships would be sent to the Far East, as soon as 'we can afford to send them out', was reasonable.[10] Further embarrassment attended the arrival of the New Zealand report early in 1920. Jellicoe had repeated his secret section on the inevitability of a clash with Japan and had also repeated the proposal for a new Pacific Fleet. To make matters worse the Dominion Government had published large sections of the report (but not the secret section) as a White Paper, including the details of the fleet.[11] At the Admiralty, Captain Barry Domvile, of the Plans Division, felt that the references to a major fleet controlled from Singapore could only refer to Japan. It was hardly tactful to publish such material.[12] It almost seemed as if Jellicoe was trying to commit the British Government to a contribution of £15 million towards a Pacific Fleet which the Cabinet had not heard of.

Jellicoe went on to visit Canada, the United States, and the West Indies. He missed out South Africa and reached home at the beginning of February 1920. Unrepentant in his conviction that his task had required him to state the possible source of danger to the Empire, he said everything pointed to Japan. Sooner or later, a major fleet would have to be sent to the Pacific. The deputy Chief of Naval Staff somewhat ruefully noted on this that it probably would have been better to have postponed Jellicoe's mission until the size of the post-war fleet had been settled![13]

Until this critical question of the peacetime naval standard was decided the Admiralty had to stick to practical and immediate tasks. The staff drew up *War Memorandum (Eastern) 1920*, a series of standing instructions for naval units in the event of war with Japan, which stressed that it was 'absolutely essential' to hold Singapore, that 'an attack on the Malay Peninsular and the subsequent capture of Singapore would be disastrous to the British Empire'.[14] The Admiralty also approved the idea of holding periodic meetings of flag officers to co-ordinate the contingency plans of the East Indies, China, Australia and New Zealand Stations. These activities, generated within the naval planning bureaucracy, set Britain on the path which led to Singapore well before the politicians had made up their minds about the shape of the post-war navy.

It was for the Government to decide who the likely enemies were, and who were the likely allies, so that defence planners could proceed to allocate resources to particular tasks and build the right ships to fulfil them. The naval staff and Lord Jellicoe agreed on some things, but not others. Both accepted the need to make plans for a war against their ally Japan. They differed as to method. Jellicoe wanted a complete new British Empire fleet in the Pacific; the Admiralty thought in terms of sending the main fleet to the Pacific in an emergency. These methods of countering Japan were, of course, quite different in their implications, but both required a new naval base and dockyard. Singapore was accepted as the right place and the Admiralty set about finding an appropriate site.

If the Admiralty was beginning to plan for a Singapore base, the Government had yet to decide on the shape of the navy. The Ten Year Rule and the halt on new warship construction provided constraints but left the basic question open. In November 1919 the vigorous, handsome and popular Admiral, David, Lord Beatty became First Sea Lord and for the next eight years the case for seapower was relentlessly pressed. It was also clear that Britain would either have to make a warship limitation agreement with the United States or indulge in a cripplingly expensive naval building race. As an interim policy the First Lord was allowed to announce, when he presented the 1919 navy estimates, that the navy would not fall behind its largest rival – a one power standard. But it was not until December 1920 that the basic question of the size and purpose of the navy was considered by ministers and naval staff together in the Committee of Imperial Defence.

Lloyd George, the Prime Minister, led off the debate by ruling out a war with the United States or an Anglo-American naval race, which 'might in the end ruin us'. He suggested an agreement whereby each might be supreme in its own seas. Winston Churchill, the former First Lord, who was now Secretary of State for War and Air, spoke out for traditional naval supremacy. It would be 'a terrible day', he said, when Britain gave up its sea supremacy. If the existence of the Anglo-Japanese Alliance was responsible for the American naval building programme they should consider revising the terms of the alliance. When Lloyd George appeared to change tack and suggest that the bellicose attitude of the United States might drive Britain into a defensive alliance with Japan, Churchill replied that, if Britain and Japan combined against the United States, the Dominions would be antagonised. There could be 'no more fatal policy' than that of basing the navy on a possible combination with Japan against the US. Lord Curzon, the Foreign Secretary, put the view that it would prudent to renew the alliance, which the Japanese desired. Beatty brought the discussion down to brass tacks by insisting that unless new battleships were built Britain would not only lose its first place but fall to third. Bonar Law, (the Lord Privy Seal) thought the wise course would be an arrangement with both Japan and the United States to prevent a new battleship race. No decision was reached. The Foreign Office was to sound the Americans about a possible agreement, and technical studies were to be made as to whether the battleship had a future in war.[15]

The basic question of the size of the navy remained unanswered. But by the beginning of 1921 three themes which were to recur throughout the inter-war years were evident. First, relations between the British Empire, Japan and the United States would be the decisive elements in naval strategy. Britain was, indeed, facing one of the critical dilemmas of the century: should it choose the USA or Japan as an ally, or – as it seems from the viewpoint of the naval staff papers – would it decide on Japan or the USA as the enemy?

Could it, as the Foreign Office suggested, have a tripartite pact?[16] Secondly, there was an appreciation of the two-ocean predicament. As the First Lord put it on 25 January 1921:

> should hostilities be necessary between Great Britain and Japan, we should not only have to send a superior Fleet to the East at the outbreak of war, but should have to retain some portion of our forces in European Waters in order not to leave our shores wholly uncovered.[17]

Thirdly, the old question of Dominions' subsidies for imperial defence was revived in the new form of possible contributions to the Singapore base. In January 1921 an inter-departmental committee, chaired by Leo Amery, the Under Secretary of State for Colonies, began to assemble materials for the first post-war Imperial Conference. The question of the future of the Anglo-Japanese Alliance and the Jellicoe reports were obvious items, and the Admiralty suggested that the Singapore base was a project in which parts of the Empire could be invited to share.[18]

IV

While these questions of strategy, alliances, the size of the fleet, expenditure and organisation were being studied for the benefit of the CID, the Cabinet and the coming Imperial Conference, the naval staff pressed ahead with its plans for a Singapore base. Although no decision had been taken to establish it, the proposal was given some urgency from the middle of 1920 because an unexpected hitch suddenly appeared. The causeway between Singapore and Johore, which was being built for the Federated Malay States Railways, was going to block permanently the Strait between Singapore Island and Malaya. When the Admiralty was first consulted on this in 1917 it had offered no objection to a bridge or causeway across the Strait.[19] But on 8 July 1920 Rear-Admiral Sir Frederick Learmouth, the Hydrographer, suggested the matter should be reopened in view of their present search for a fleet anchorage and site for a dockyard.

Some of the naval staff were sceptical. Captain Frank Larken, Director of the Local Defence Division, did not want to reopen the question because the rail link to northern Malaya was strategically vital. Captain Gerald Dickens, deputy Director of Plans, argued that if they really needed to send the fleet round the Strait they would have to build something like the Forth Bridge.[20] Yet the causeway issue could not be brushed-off: it highlighted the question of the site for the new naval base. Singapore had been a 'defended port' for forty years and the Admiralty had long used facilities at Keppel Harbour – the port of Singapore. So far discussions had centred on the waters southwest of Singapore, and west of Blakang Mati Island, as a suitable fleet anchorage. But a costly breakwater would be needed and therefore interest was shifting north to the Johore Strait. A survey ship, HMS *Merlin*, was due to reach Singapore in October 1920 to make soundings (see Map 3). The Chief of Naval Staff was alerted to the causeway problem by Admiral Brock, who suggested that a gap of 600 feet might be left in the causeway and filled by a pile bridge which might later be converted into a swing bridge. 'Very unfortunate' was Beatty's comment. The Colonial Office was told about the possibility of a

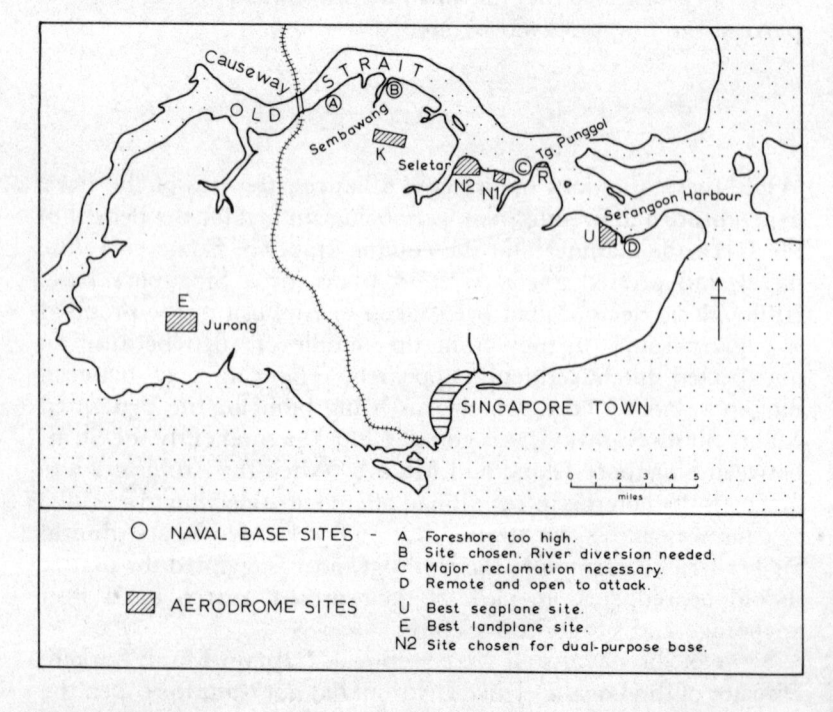

MAP 3. Choosing the site

fleet anchorage in the Strait, and the Secretary of State for Colonies accordingly informed the Governor of the Straits Settlements of the Admiralty's plans.[21]

In December 1920 a conference was held in Singapore between colonial and naval representatives and Sir Maurice FitzMaurice, the consulting engineer. The latter rejected Admiralty ideas for a pile bridge or for a removable span floating on barges, but said a bascule bridge could be built for £750,000. As this would increase the cost of the causeway to £2½ million and the Admiralty would have to find the extra money, this decided the matter. The chance of needing to send the fleet right round Singapore was now 'exceedingly remote'. After a meeting with FitzMaurice when he got back to London, the Admiralty dropped its objections to the causeway in February 1921.[22]

The causeway issue had, however, cleared the air in several important respects. First, it became clear that the 'Old Strait', between Singapore and Johore, would provide the fleet anchorage and this narrowed the area of choice for the dockyard site.[23] Secondly, the final choice would depend to some extent on local defence needs, over which the War Office had to be consulted. Its immediate reaction to this question – highly ironical in view of later recriminations – was that the most important requirement was securing 'the land front' in Johore. At the least it would be necessary to hold a thirty-mile perimeter to form a bridgehead in front of the causeway, the town of Johore Bahru and the Johore River. Such defences would be needed against forces which might land on the southeast coast of Malaya. To test the practicability of such landings the GOC Singapore was instructed to make a reconnaissance; he was also asked to investigate the best place for a defensive line and the matter of rail reinforcements to Malacca and Penang on the west coast.[24] The army certainly began with the right ideas.

By now planning was sufficiently advanced for a full study of the defences of Singapore to be formally requested. At the CID on 2 May 1921 the Admiralty presented the case for the strategic significance of Singapore as the 'gateway' to the Far East and Australasia, and the matter was referred to the Overseas Defence Subcommittee (ODC). There were allusions to the view, still held by the 'defensive school', that Sydney should be the main base in the Pacific, but it was made clear that the naval staff rejected this. Indeed, a decision about Singapore was wanted before the Imperial Conference met in the following month.[25]

The third matter which came out (somewhat as an afterthought), was the need to maintain the goodwill of Malay rulers. As officials of the Straits Settlements Government consulted with naval men about the causeway and the fleet anchorage the Governor asked if he could let Sultan Ibrahim of Johore know what was afoot before his suspicions were aroused. Ibrahim had long been the most independent – indeed obstreperous – of the Malay rulers, but his realms would undoubtedly be affected if the strategy of the Pacific became focused on his foreshore. The Secretary of State for the Colonies let the Governor use his discretion, but pointed out that the Admiralty wanted to keep its plans from the Japanese as long as possible. The Sultan was duly informed about the project and volunteered the information that during the 1914–18 war Japanese fishing boats had been seen taking soundings in the Old Strait and (more significant perhaps) that 30,000 acres of land in Johore were leased to Japanese interests for rubber. (He claimed, indeed, that every Japanese employee was a trained soldier.)[26] This question of Japanese land holdings in the vicinity of the proposed Singapore base was not new. It had already been raised at the ODC and would be a source of recurring anxiety over the next twenty years. It appeared that nothing could be done to prevent normal land transactions in view of Britain's commercial treaty with Japan.[27]

V

The Admiralty were determined to get a decision about the Singapore base in time for the Imperial Conference in June 1921, so that they could solicit Empire support. Before then they had authoritative endorsement for the plans, when, in mid-May, an advance copy of the proceedings of the flag officers' conference arrived. Under the chairmanship of Vice-Admiral Duff, Commander-in-Chief, China, the commanders of the East Indies advance copy of the proceedings of the flag officers' conference study the Admiralty *War Memorandum (Eastern) 1920*. Accepting the doctrine that Singapore was the 'key' to the British naval situation in the Pacific, they assumed that it would be made 'impregnable' – a word often heard in later years. The commanders added the suggestion, however, that distance from the Admiralty dictated that a 'Higher Command' should be set up in the Far East and that Singapore was the 'only site suitable' for it. They also called for the establishment of a Pacific Naval Intelligence Centre adjacent to the headquarters. Finally, in view of the three months it was expected that the fleet would need to reach Singapore, they recommended that 'two modern Battle Cruisers of high speed and large endurance should be allotted to the Pacific *now*'.[28] This idea of sending a pair of capital ships to Singapore would crop up time and again before 1941.

By 7 June 1921 the ODC had completed its full report on the naval staff proposals. It estimated the cost over eight years at £4,892,000. However, the Treasury member E. W. H. Millar entered the strong reservation that, until the future of the Anglo-Japanese Alliance had been resolved, the plan was 'somewhat premature'. Based as it was on the hypothesis that in the near future Japan, 'our ally', might consider it worthwhile to challenge the British Empire, the man from the Treasury found the notion 'almost incredible'. Because of the post-war financial situation he felt they had no alternative but to face the risks and 'rely on diplomacy to obviate them'.[29] This report went before the CID on 10 June, when the scheme's importance as a pledge to the Dominions was emphasised. At the meeting on 13 June it was agreed to recommend the project to the Cabinet, with the proviso that, as large expenditures were not possible in the near future, the greater the assistance which could be got from the Empire, the sooner the base could be finished.[30] Balfour, chairman of the CID's Standing Defence Subcommittee, introduced the matter in the Cabinet on 16 June and stressed the importance of being in a position to say something positive on defence at the Imperial Conference, which was then forgathering. This, he felt, was more important than actually starting construction. The Cabinet decided, accordingly, that the Dominions should be told that a new base would be built at Singapore when funds became available, and that the Dominions should be invited to contribute.[31]

Having got their decision the Admiralty were at pains to stress, when the CID turned to discuss the Anglo-Japanese Alliance next day, that renewal would not obviate the need for the base. Sufficient naval force to neutralise the Japanese navy could not be kept in the Pacific if the main fleet was in European waters. The new policy was designed to facilitate the transfer of the fleet to the Pacific in an emergency.[32]

The Dominion and Indian representatives were told of the Cabinet's decision on 28 June during the Imperial Conference debate on the Anglo-Japanese Alliance. After Lord Curzon, the Foreign Secretary, had put the diplomatic case for renewal, Balfour spoke on behalf of the CID. He declared that with the growth of the US navy in the Pacific 'it is a fact that if we had not Japan on our side we should be second or third Power in the Pacific' after some years. It was impossible for financial reasons to keep the main fleet in the Pacific; what was required was an ability to bring it out quickly. Therefore, the British Government had decided that:

> Singapore should be made into a place where the British Fleet can concentrate for the defence of the Empire, of our interests in the East, our interests in India, our interests in Australia, our interests in New Zealand, our interests in the smaller Possessions there, and that for that purpose it is absolutely necessary to undertake works at Singapore. Those works cannot be finished in a day.

They were going on? asked Massey of New Zealand. 'Not yet' said Balfour. The matter had 'only been taken in hand quite recently' – which was much more truthful than the Dominion leaders can have known. Until Singapore was ready as 'a place of concentration, a place of refitting and refuelling' it was essential to stay on good terms with Japan.[33]

VI

A decision had been made in principle. The site now had to be selected. On the day before the Cabinet decision Captain Domvile, the Director of Plans, suggested that the Johore Strait was acceptable as a fleet anchorage, but the dockyard, headquarters and airfield sites, would depend on the local defence scheme. As soon as the decision was secured, therefore, arrangements were made for the study of sites and security. The ODC had been asked to prepare a defence scheme, but it pleaded delay until the ground reconnaissances were completed.[34] As major operations so far from home bases were being contemplated for the first time in British history elaborate supply arrangements were also necessary. Expenditure on 2 million tons of fuel oil reserves along the route to Singapore were authorised as part of an oil storage provision equivalent to one year's supply. The Plans Division called for 'inconspicuous surveys' of four possible fuelling anchorages on the Suez and Cape routes at Kamaran Bay, in the Red Sea, and Horsburgh Attol, Addu Attol and Diego Garcia, in the Indian Ocean.[35] In November 1921 a committee made up of Admiral Learmouth, the Hydrographer, Sir Lawrence Power, the Director of Dockyards, and Leopold H. Savile, the Civil Engineer-in-Chief, with Wing Commander Hewlett as RAF adviser, left for Singapore to select the sites. They were instructed to find anchorages for 12 battleships, 8 battle-cruisers, 26 cruisers, 80 destroyers, 30 submarines and 70 auxiliaries – 226 vessels in all – virtually the entire main fleet. The repair base was to be on the lines of that at Invergordon in Scotland, but capable of expansion into 'a first class dockyard'. Space was needed for storing 400,000 tons of fuel oil, housing for 2000 men and for a hospital and recreational grounds.[36]

By the time the sites committee had done its work the strategic situation had been considerably clarified as a result of the Washington Naval Conference. The Anglo-Japanese Alliance was ended and superseded by the vague Four Power consultative Treaty signed on 13 December 1921. The United Kingdom, Australian and New Zealand representatives at the Imperial Conference earlier in the year had favoured renewal, but the Canadian Prime Minister had (as on so many occasions) upset the chance of imperial unity and sparked off a bitter argument. Canada with its undefended border with the USA had genuine fears. It forced the conference to consider the need to reconcile imperial strategy with Anglo-Saxon unity. And in trying to come to terms with the dilemma the Prime Ministers had some frank and highly secret discussions in which Beatty gave a forceful exposition of the naval view. Standing before a map to stress the vast distances involved Beatty dismissed the notion that the Dominions could rely on the United States for security. The Japanese could get to Hong Kong in five days. The USN, without a major base in the Philippines, could not operate in the western Pacific. The British fleet would get there in six weeks, but better facilities were needed at Singapore to operate the latest vessels.

Finding themselves discussing what would happen if Japan went for the Philippines, and then the plans for war with Japan, the premiers suddenly became embarrassed at the implications and agreed to permit the making of only one copy of stenographic notes.[37] They turned with relief to more general defence matters, until a way out of the strategic dilemma became possible with the receipt of President Harding's invitation to Washington on 10 July 1921.[38] The Singapore project had not, of course, been presented as a condition of renewal or otherwise of the Anglo-Japanese Alliance. The naval staff called for it on general defensive lines. In fact the Five Power Naval Limitation treaty, which was signed in Washington on 6 February 1922, was in part conditional on Japan's acceptance of Singapore.[39] The *status quo* area in which new fortifications were debarred ended in the west at longitude 110°, so that Singapore was specifically excluded.

The ending of the Anglo-Japanese Alliance and the limitation of capital ships gave the Singapore base *added* importance. The tonnage ratios in the treaty were designed to give, after replacements, the following capital ship totals after twenty years:

British Empire	United States	Japan
525,000 tons	525,000 tons	315,000 tons
15	15	9

It meant accepting parity with the United States but it maintained the margin of 50 per cent superiority over Japan (three British ships to two Japanese) insisted on by the naval staff.[40] In order to make this valid in the Pacific, the Singapore base was essential.

The Director of Plans in the Admiralty summarised the strategic effect of the Washington treaties in an influential paper, which was frequently quoted in future years, on 24 February 1922. He argued that the naval limitation agreement rendered the USN incapable of operations in the western Pacific; Britain was the only power capable of countering Japan. This, in turn, depended on the completion of the Singapore base and the fuel oil reserves, and the mobility of the fleet. He recommended that a large part of the fleet should be stationed in the Mediterranean 'well on the route to the East'. Beatty agreed, but felt the time was not ripe for putting the idea to the Cabinet.[41]

During the period while these momentous matters of high strategy were being determined in Washington, the Admiralty's sites committee was at work in Singapore. A conference was held at Fort Canning on 30 January 1922, chaired by Sir Alexander Duff, C-in-C China, and attended by the sites committee, with the local navy, army and colonial officials. They considered four sites and the dockyard layouts possible at each, and they selected the mouth of the Sungei Sembawang, even though the river would have to be diverted (see Map 3). The proposed lay-out included an enclosed basin 1600 feet by 2000 feet, entered by two locks which could do duty as double-ended graving docks (see Map 4). A seaplane base was proposed at Seletar, three miles to the east of the dockyard.[42] A note sent to naval intelligence by one of the officers who had reconnoitred the hills overlooking the site on the Johore side, reminded them that most of this land had been purchased by Japanese. This was filed, but made no difference.[43]

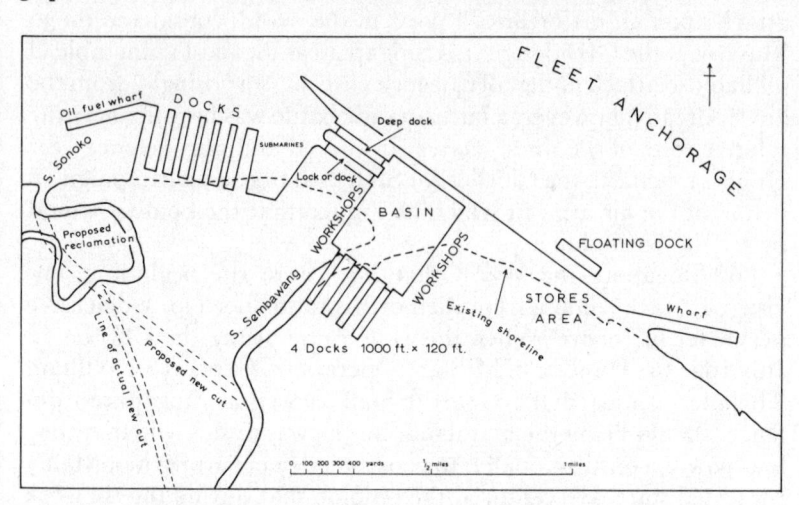

MAP 4. The first proposals (1922) including an enclosed dock basin

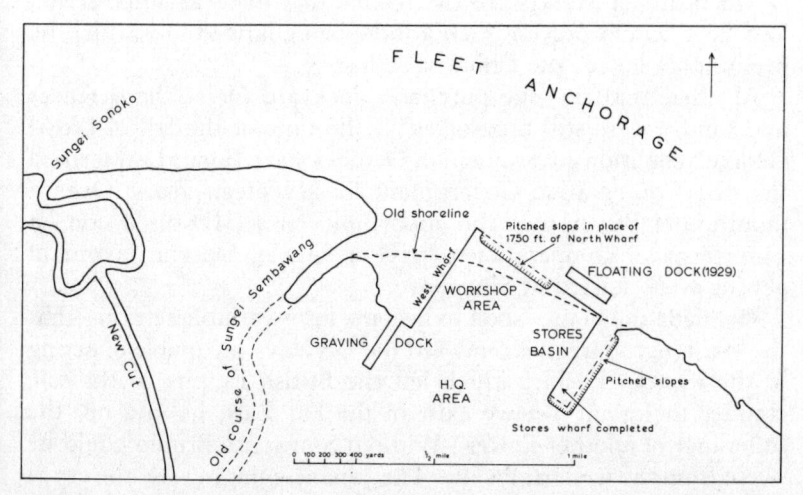

MAP 5. The truncated scheme (1926), which was completed with half the walls unbuilt at first

VII

With the site selection and outline engineering plans under way, there remained the matter of defences. The decision to build the base had, of course, suddenly produced the prospect of Singapore becoming a major target. In fact, in their study of the likely scales of attack upon all major British ports in the world, considered on 30 May 1922, the CID designated Singapore as the most vulnerable of all liable to attack under all categories except (surprisingly) from the air.[44] Already, however, a bureaucratic battle was brewing over the relative roles of the three services in coastal and port defences. Sir Hugh Trenchard, the Chief of Air Staff, had begun his campaign on behalf of the air arm, in which he argued that the bomber would better the battleship.

For Singapore the War Office had, from the beginning, envisaged attack coming from the north and the need for a defensive perimeter in Johore. When this issue came before the CID on 12 July 1922 the Director of Military Operations, General Sir William Thwaites, repeated the General Staff view that Singapore's defences should be on the mainland, but he was unsure whether they had power, constitutionally, to construct defence works in a Malay protected state. He ventured the opinion that during the six week period before relief the Japanese could land ten to twelve divisions on the coasts of Malaya. Beatty scoffed that this was 'impossible'; 'our fleet' would prevent such a force being landed – by which he presumably meant the China squadron.[45]

All these matters – site purchase, dockyard plans, the defences and funds – were still unresolved at the time of the fall of Lloyd George's coalition government in October 1922. Bonar Law formed the first Conservative Government for seventeen years. Over a month later Beatty took the opportunity at a CID discussion on Empire naval co-operation to give a forceful blast in favour of getting work started at Singapore.

He made the point – soon to become his invariable refrain – that the Washington treaties rendered the US Navy incapable of acting in the western Pacific, which left the British Empire as the sole counter to Japan. Yet we exist in the Far East, he said on 'the sufferance of another Power'. Without Singapore Britain could be swept from the western Pacific. The Japanese might raise the cry of 'Asia for the Asiatics'. Without the base Britain could do nothing.

The Cabinet had made the basic decision; the Dominions should be asked to help. When the CID returned to the subject a fortnight later they had hopeful news from the Treasury representative, Sir George Barstow, who said the Governor of the Straits Settlements (then in England) indicated that the Colony might buy the land for the base. After the deputy Director of Military Operations, Colonel William H. Bartholomew, had repeated the need for a garrison in Johore in case of invasion from the north, the CID approved the Sembawang and Seletar sites.[46]

It remained only to get the money. With the possibility that Straits Settlements would, in fact, make a 'free gift' of the land (saving £125,000), the Admiralty decided to include £160,000 in the 1923/24 Naval Estimates for preliminary site preparations.[47] The estimate for the full scheme was now put at £15½ million: £11,600,000 (plus possibly £1 million more) for Admiralty works, £1,250,000 for the War Office and £400,000 for the Air Ministry. The matter went before the Cabinet on 21 February 1923, when the decision was taken to start work. The Navy Estimates were presented to Parliament by Leopold Amery, the First Lord of the Admiralty, on 12 March (including the £160,000 preliminary vote towards the £11 million Singapore scheme). 'There is in this, of course', declared Amery, 'no suggestion of any differences in our relations with Japan'.[48] The base was described in the committee on supply by Commander Eyres-Monsell (the Parliamentary under-secretary), as 'an insurance, and a small one, for the integrity of our Empire'.[49] A circular despatch was sent to Governors-General on 27 March informing them that the Cabinet's decision had been made without prejudice to the question of contributions from the Dominions, India and the Straits Settlements.

This scarcely veiled appeal was received (as usual) with scepticism in Canada and South Africa, but the naval staff were soon delighted to know of positive responses east of Suez. On 13 June 1923 they heard that the Straits Settlements would meet the cost of land for the naval and air bases. Captain Dudley Pound, the Director of Plans, felt this example might help get money from Australia, New Zealand and India. Beatty agreed and demanded the widest publicity.[50] The Dominions were duly informed and New Zealand offered £100,000 by 3 July.[51] Australia was less publicly eager, but the British request was considered in the Commonwealth Defence Council on 30 August 1923 during the briefing of the Prime Minister for the next Imperial Conference. It was accepted that Australia's strategic position was practically hopeless without the Singapore base. General Monash said it was so vital that the Australian representatives at the Imperial Conference ought to enter into 'contractual obligations' with the British to get it completed. There was also some discussion of the possibility of Australian help with the garrison.[52]

VIII

A start had been made. A name was even decided on. The Hydrographer, in revising the local charts wanted to know what to put in. He thought 'Sembawang' was unsuitable, and 'Singapore Dockyard' was misleading, since it would be at the back of the island; he wanted a distinctive name and plumped for 'Raffles Dockyard'. The Admiralty Board stuck prosaically to 'Singapore Dockyard'.[53] They decided to substitute a large floating dock for one of the graving docks as it could be made available earlier. They also wanted to start an intelligence system to watch Japanese shipping in case a blockship was placed in the Suez Canal as this would be disastrous for the whole eastern strategy.[54]

Compared with these trivialities progress over the planning of Singapore's defences was non-existent because of inter-service disagreements. The army's view was that attack would come from the north, so a perimeter of defence in Johore was required. Thus their proposals for seaward coastal defences to the south were modest. They included two pairs of 15″ guns, but this was a type of gun with which British coastal artillery had no experience.[55] Their plan was discussed at a naval staff conference on 15 May 1923, where it was rejected as completely inadequate. The naval staff saw the main danger as coming from the sea. Since the Japanese fleet could not hope to survive an encounter with the full British fleet, it would take great risks to capture Singapore first by *coup de main*. A naval Staff College exercise had suggested that Japan could spare four to six battleships for such an attack. This called for more 15″ guns.[56] To aid them in their reappraisal of fixed defences against seaborne attack the War Office had detailed reconnaissance reports from Lieutenant-Colonel Henry Russell Brancker, Commander RA in Malaya. Large maps with all the arcs of fire marked in colour were sent back, along with piles of aerial photographs of the entire southern shore line. The Admiralty wanted to double the number of 15″ guns to eight but the War Office suggested six if spotter planes were available.[57]

The air aspects of the defence were, however, the most contentious of all. The air staff argued, in principle, that the air should play a major role in all coastal and port defences. Developments in 1923 led them to plead a larger specific role at Singapore. First, a Combined Staff College exercise at Camberley in March 1923 came up with a proposal for four squadrons at Singapore. Secondly, the Admiralty's decision that the peacetime strength of the naval force at Singapore, once the base was ready, would be 3 battle-cruisers, 1 aircraft carrier, 11 cruisers, 18 destroyers and 21 submarines (a peacetime Pacific fleet after all) suggested the need for a larger air element. Thus in September 1923 the Air Ministry suggested that reconnaissance aircraft, backed by bombers, could prevent any landing within 100 miles of Singapore, during daylight, if local air superiority could be gained.[58] These were only the opening salvoes in the longest battle ever fought over Singapore.

IX

Four years had passed since the first proposals for a base. The defences were quite undecided; the works barely begun. None the less the planners were pursuing their peacetime tasks in their various ways. The Plans Division of the Admiralty, under Dudley Pound, began trying to forecast the probable course of a war with Japan in 1932.[59] But when, at the higher level of the new Chiefs of Staff Committee, the Naval Staff raised the question of procedure for discussing strategic questions, they were rebuffed by the Chief of the Imperial General Staff, General the Earl of Cavan. He said plans in advance of events were pointless. Japan was, in theory, capable of attacking British possessions but only at colossal risk. Plans for a war with Japan rested on the development of Singapore and the passage of the fleet 'and they are all the plans we require at the moment'. In the world as it then was, no campaign plans were needed. Concentrate on imperial defence, he said; we never fought big wars alone, and it was too early to decide which side we would be on in the next one. The problem, for the Earl, was not deciding what operations to plan, but of preventing the numerous operations, certain to be proposed by 'amateur strategists in high places', from being undertaken.[60] Who Cavan's amateur strategists were is not clear. But before the end of the month strategy was certainly in for a new look with the coming to power of the first Labour Government.

2 'Something Less Than the Whole', 1924–26

I

'That infernal place's name will be engraved on my heart'. This comment on Singapore was made by Beatty in a letter to his wife on 23 January 1924.[1] After his four years' struggle to get the naval base started the First Sea Lord feared the bureaucratic battles were about to be repeated 'more bitterly than ever' with the accession of the first Labour Government the previous day. His instinct was correct. Although the Labour Party did not have a parliamentary majority, and was more concerned to demonstrate the continuity of the political system and its own respectability, disarmament was the one area where Ramsay MacDonald, the new Prime Minister, hoped to make a mark. The Singapore Naval Base was a matter in which Labour planned a change of policy. Their general approach was conditioned by their attitude to the Versailles settlement; their desire to reform the League of Nations covenant to create an effective instrument of collective security and by the instinctive pacifism of several leaders, which was expressed in the determination to give a lead in disarmament.[2]

II

Beatty did not intend to let Labour damage the navy. Just over a week after the new government came to power the Chiefs of Staff Committee held its first major discussion on the Singapore base. Beatty took the opportunity to brief Lord Haldane, the veteran Liberal who had been brought in as Lord Chancellor and

Chairman of the CID, and who was attending the COS meeting. Beatty's case was, by now, a well-rehearsed piece. Until there was a proper base, British interests East of Suez existed only by 'sufferance of another Power'. The Washington Treaty made it impossible for the US fleet to operate in the western Pacific. 1931 would be the critical year as the Pacific treaties might then be reconsidered, and if, at that point, there was a fleet base at Singapore, Britain would be in a stronger diplomatic position. So far 'practically nothing' had been done.[3] Four days after this unopposed hearing, the first meeting of the CID under the new regime gave Beatty his first adverse encounter over naval policy. It concerned the fuel oil storage programme. Philip Snowden, the Chancellor of the Exchequer, wanted to reduce by half the one year's supply approved as a goal in 1919. Beatty argued that if trouble arose with Japan the Royal Navy could do nothing to protect the colonies, the Dominions and trade in the Far East. The CID decided to reaffirm the 1919 figure.[4]

The big battle came over the Singapore base. On 18 February 1924 the Government appointed a Cabinet committee under Lord Clynes, the Lord Privy Seal (formerly J. R. Clynes, the trade union leader), to reconsider warship replacements (other than capital ships) and the scheme for the Singapore naval base. The Committee consisted of Snowden, Lord Chelmsford, the First Lord of the Admiralty, Stephen Walsh, Secretary of State for War, Lord Thomson, Secretary of State for Air, J. H. Thomas, Secretary of State for Colonies, and Lord Olivier, Secretary of State for India. The Dominion Governments were informed on 20 February 1924.[5] The committee decided to take Singapore first and held its discussions on 27 February, 3 March and 5 March.

A clear-cut conflict between strategy and foreign policy occurred in the Clynes Committee. Beatty began in an optimistic mood. He told his wife on 22 February that he was preparing his 'dossier' on Singapore. It had been accepted reluctantly by three Coalition Cabinets of Liberals and Conservatives, two Conservative governments and two Imperial Conferences, 'so to reverse the whole decision will not be easy.'[6] But he had not bargained on the tactical skill and tenacity of the new ministers. They allowed him at the first meeting to lecture them on naval policy in the Pacific from 1905 to the Washington treaty, and to make his usual case for Singapore, that Britain existed in the East on the 'sufferance and goodwill' of another power. He presented the project as an insurance policy.

With trade in the Indian Ocean and the Pacific valued at £870 million a year (and involving over 700 ships in any one day) expenditure on the base was like an insurance premium of 2/- per £100 over nine years. Singapore was also well placed to intercept 'raids' by Japan upon Australia or New Zealand; it was the 'finest strategical position in the whole world'. Snowden asked why an Australian base would not do, and the First Lord pointed out that damaged ships would take twenty-four days to get to Sydney and back. Lord Thomson (who had been a Brigadier during the war) wondered if the Sembawang site was open to shellfire from Johore; Beatty dismissed the idea and said the mainland consisted largely of such 'swampy ground' that an advance would be difficult.[7]

When the committee reconvened on 3 March it began with further desultory queries until J. H. Thomas somewhat disarmed the naval barrage by accepting Beatty's case. It was an admirable case for the Singapore base on strategic grounds and Thomas felt 'nothing more need be said in that direction'. Snowden protested that the financial aspect warranted examination, but at that point Ramsay MacDonald came into the meeting and spoke in his capacity as Secretary of State for Foreign Affairs. He summarised the FO case for Singapore, which stressed the diplomatic value of a strong presence in the Far East. MacDonald disagreed with it. The base would prejudice Labour's policy of seeking disarmament. He did not claim that the base should never be built, but not at that moment. 'The scheme should be prepared but pigeon-holed'. Lord Olivier said they should drop all gestures in the direction of armaments and try wholeheartedly to get a disarmament agreement. But what 'if the Millenium did not arrive?' cried Beatty. In case they had to return to conventional methods, could they not at least allow the preliminary work at Singapore to be finished? In the end he pleaded with the Ministers to agree, in principle, that the base was necessary, that Singapore was the right place for it; and to permit the Admiralty to spend £150,000 in 1924–5 for the preliminary works.

The civil servants and service representatives were then sent out of the room and the committee debated what conclusions should be recorded. They readily agreed that, from the naval point of view, Beatty had 'a complete case', but that from the point of view of Government policy 'as a whole', it was impossible to go ahead. Merely to announce that the Singapore project was 'suspended' would not be enough. They should announce that they did not intend to proceed, but would leave it open whether to re-examine the scheme if disarmament failed.[8] Two days later, on 5 March 1924, the committee finalised its recommendation to the Cabinet, that no expenditure should be incurred in the 1924-5 estimates for the development of Singapore but that, if necessary, the Admiralty could spend enough to finish the site preparation. The Cabinet approved this the same day and the Dominions were given an opportunity to comment before the decision was made public. They were asked to reply within a week, if possible, or in any case by 17 March, in time for the presentation of the navy estimates.[9]

The Dominions were sent a draft of the statement MacDonald intended to make in Parliament. 'We stand as we have repeatedly stated for a policy of international cooperation through a strengthened and enlarged League of Nations, the settlement of disputes by judicial arbitration and conciliation, and the creation of conditions which will make possible a comprehensive agreement on the limitation of armaments.' To build the base would undermine confidence in Britain's good intentions on disarmament. In view of the earlier Imperial Conference discussions MacDonald inserted conciliatory phrases about the base having been 'urged only as part of a complete defensive Pacific strategy' and that the decision might have to be reconsidered if it ever became necessary to act upon that strategy. Meanwhile: 'As an earnest of our good faith we have therefore decided not to proceed with the Naval Base at Singapore'.[10]

The Government had not left much time for discussion with Commonwealth partners, but the first reply was brief and promising. Smuts, of South Africa, lent his great prestige as soldier and statesman, by cabling his 'whole-hearted agreement'. He said 'the authority of the British Empire as the protagonist of the great cause of appeasement and conciliation among the nations' would be seriously undermined by the Singapore base, which was also against the spirit of the Washington treaty. 'At a time when we should move forward with clean hands and unchallenged moral authority this would be a step backward.'[11] The Canadian and Irish replies offered no comment. The first adverse response – from William Warren, Prime Minister of Newfoundland – was an 'emphatic' statement that it would be most unwise not to build the base. On 11 March 1924, however, the cables from Australia and New Zealand struck an entirely new note.

Both were long, in the prolix Antipodean manner. Stanley M. Bruce's cable from Australia was in its expression the more diplomatic. It sympathised with the 'great ideals' behind the British move, but disagreed with the methods. 'We believe that the existence and prestige of the British Empire has been and is the greatest factor in the maintenance of the peace of the world . . . . That strength has depended mainly on the British Navy, its power and mobility. We are convinced a base in the Pacific is imperative for that mobility.' It suggested that the greatest landmark in disarmament had been the Washington treaty which had been made with all the signatories knowing about Britain's intentions at Singapore. The Australian Government urged MacDonald to reconsider the decision. Bruce concluded his appeal with a skilfully inserted hint that, while he knew the British decision was based on 'principle and not of expenditure', the Australian Government wished to make it clear that its obligation to contribute towards the cost was recognised and that it intended to ask Parliament, as soon as it met 'for a substantial Australian contribution'.[12]

The New Zealand telegram was more hectoring in tone and raised an interesting constitutional issue. Lord Jellicoe, who no doubt regarded himself as one of the progenitors of the Singapore base, was the Governor-General and had a hand in drafting the protest against the policy of the Government he was supposed to represent! When MacDonald's telegram arrived Jellicoe thought 'it right to offer a few remarks on the subject' for Massey, the Prime Minister. It was 'opposed to common sense', he said, for a nation dependent on sea communications to take a lead in naval disarmament. Without the new base the navy could not dock its latest battleships in the east. Agreement with British policy would 'place a great responsibility upon the Australian and New Zealand Governments'. Jellicoe also suggested some amendments to the draft of the New Zealand cable, which went on 11 March. It was the most forthright of all the Dominion replies.[13]

Massey regretted 'exceedingly' the British decision. It would affect many parts of the Empire, which were 'entitled to protection from the possibility of attack . . . ' He reminded MacDonald of the New Zealand gift of £100,000 and declared: 'we in New Zealand realize what it means to be insufficiently protected'. If the Empire had to rely on the League of Nations 'it may turn out to have been a pity that the League was ever brought into being'. He concluded by protesting 'earnestly on behalf of New Zealand' against the British decision.[14]

These protests fell on deaf ears in London. The exchange with the Dominions was summarised in a new paragraph inserted in MacDonald's policy statement at a Cabinet meeting on 14 March 1924. It suggested (with outrageous blandness) that 'we have a large measure of sympathy in the Dominions with our international policy, even if all parts of the Empire do not feel able to endorse the methods . . .'. The statement was finalised in Cabinet on 17 March. Charles Ammon (the Financial Secretary of the Admiralty) made the announcement in the House of Commons next day in his speech on the navy estimates, and MacDonald read most of the statement by way of explanation.[15]

III

What had the Labour Government really done? Was the Singapore base 'pigeon-holed' as MacDonald had just hinted, or did the decision 'not to proceed' imply the project was abandoned? Was the work stopped? Answers are not as obvious as one might expect because of the momentum of the bureaucracy and the interpretations which its component parts put on the decision.

The Admiralty, as they filed a copy of MacDonald's statement, called it the 'suspension of work' at Singapore.[16] The CID, when it heard that the ODC had nearly finished its studies of the defences, decided with MacDonald's approval that it would be wasteful to break them off.[17] The service departments simply went on with their planning. The air staff felt the decision might be reconsidered later and welcomed the chance for time to prepare the case for air defences.[18] In the War Office work continued on the gun defences. Colonel Archibald Wavell (GSO 1 in the strategic branch of the Military Operations Directorate) informed his opposite number in Malaya that, in spite of the Government's decision 'we propose to carry on with all our defence investigations', so that if the project was revived they would have all the data available. Colonel Brancker's reconnaissances continued in Malaya.[19] The naval staff continued along the same lines. Captain Pound, the Director of Plans, gave yet another semantic label to the decision when he suggested that, as the 'decision to postpone' the base deprived the

Navy of the power to deter Japan from attacking Singapore, the defences became all the more important.[20]

Service planning for the Singapore base clearly *never* stopped. Nor, as it happened, did the site preparations. Even as it made the vital decision on 5 March the Cabinet agreed that, although the navy estimates could show nothing for the development of Singapore the Admiralty could spend £12,500 to finish the site drainage works to prevent it becoming a mosquito swamp and to recover stores. Sir Lawrence Guillemard, the Governor of the Straits Settlements (who was something of a wag), romanticised this in his memoirs by writing that, as the work 'was desirable on its merits and not strictly work on the base, I felt justified in going on with it, and by the time it was finished the Labour Government had gone out of office'.[21] If the last part of the sentence was true, the hint of a daring gubernatorial defiance was not. The Government knew what was going on.

IV

The Labour Government had cancelled the project publicly but privately allowed the planning to go on. This meant that when Stanley Baldwin returned to power at the head of a Conservative Government on 7 November 1924, nearly everyone was ready to revive the scheme.

The naval staff, as usual, was quick off the mark. The new First Lord of the Admiralty, W. C. Bridgeman, sent a memorandum to the Cabinet on 20 November 1924 in which he suggested that Ramsay MacDonald had said the scheme was only in 'abeyance' until he had attempted a disarmament agreement. At the same time Hankey discussed it in the context of war planning with Austen Chamberlain, the Secretary of State for Foreign Affairs, and Lord Curzon, the new Chairman of the CID.[22] There was now also the prospect of help from another Colony. A telegram from the Governor of Hong Kong on 25 November 1924 held out the possibility of a contribution. His timing could hardly have been better. The Government decided, in principle, to revive the scheme the next day,[23] but the old proposals were by no means a foregone conclusion.

With Winston Churchill at the Treasury a long battle for the money was in store. Every aspect of the scheme was about to be reviewed and, in all this, the Colonies and Dominions found themselves playing an increasingly significant role. Revival, in principle, was included in the Speech from the Throne at the opening of Parliament on 9 December 1924. Before this public announcement the Dominion Governments had been told, and asked if they could help, as some indication of their support would be 'helpful in disarming the opposition'. A Hong Kong offer of £250,000 was made on 16 December.[24] There was, however, to be a long delay before the project really got going again.

There were several reasons for this delay. First, there was the debate about the relative roles of air and artillery defences. This had been going on since the start of the scheme, but was given a new twist by Churchill, who had earlier been Secretary of State for Air, and expected 'a large economy in using air power . . .'.[25] Secondly, there was debate as to the urgency or otherwise of the scheme. This issue was the subject of a very important CID meeting on 5 January 1925, when members endeavoured to envisage the future in the East.

Austen Chamberlain said he regarded war in the Far East as a remote prospect. He could not conceive of Japan single-handedly taking on the British Empire unless Japan was aided by some new European grouping. And in that case the prospect of the British fleet being allowed to leave European waters was 'quite another question'. He deprecated any policy of competitive naval building against Japan; Singapore was just 'a necessary link in Imperial communications.' Churchill took the same view. He had always supported the Singapore base, but saw it as a guarantee to Australia and New Zealand that they would not be cut off. He thought the 'moral aspect' was the key part of the argument, as he did not think that in 'our lifetime or in that of our children' Japan would attempt to invade Australia or the colonies. He then came up with the idea that, if the base at Hong Kong could be downgraded as a gesture to Japan, the decision to revive Singapore could be represented as a British 'withdrawal' in the East.

At this point Beatty, who rather enjoyed sparring with Churchill (under whom he had served as Naval Secretary before the war), interjected a more urgent note. He insisted Britain was defenceless in the East. The situation *vis-à-vis* Japan in 1925 was worse than that *vis-à-vis* Germany in 1914. Japan could, in fact, deal a naval blow which they were 'absolutely powerless to prevent' and from which they would 'never recover'. Chamberlain, however, reminded him of Japanese resentment over the ending of the Anglo-Japanese Alliance and put the Foreign Office view that the Singapore base should proceed at a normal rate and not be unduly hastened, to avoid causing anxieties for Japan. Churchill went further and demanded a subcommittee to study the rate of construction; to review the methods of defence, including the roles of artillery and air; and even to review the choice of site. Beatty said he was anxious to get some facilities to service a battle-cruiser squadron at Singapore by 1928–9, but he had to accept the committee, which meant going over all the old ground again. Lord Curzon was chosen as chairman; the other members were the service Ministers, the Chiefs of Staff and Churchill.[26]

The Curzon Committee lost no time in getting down to business and decided, first, on 16 January 1925, to tackle the question of the site. Beatty came in a surprisingly conciliatory mood. He was willing to discuss reductions in the size of the base, but pointed out that even if fully built it would not 'by itself' be capable of docking the entire main fleet. They would still need Keppel, Penang, Trincomalee and Colombo.

The question of the site's vulnerability to an attack from Johore was raised again, this time by Churchill, but the CIGS, the Earl of Cavan, now assured him that two different G.O.Cs in Malaya had reported that an attack in strength from the mainland was 'impossible'.[27] This represented a major change of direction for the defence scheme. Its effects, however, were in part mitigated by the decision to place some of the 15" and 9.2" guns on mountings giving an all-round traverse. If supplied with shrapnel and high-explosive ammunition, these guns could be used against hostile landings in Johore or against a force already landed.[28]

On 5 February the Curzon Committee interviewed some officers with local experience and suffered a long diversion (which infuriated Beatty) from Admiral Leveson, Commander-in-Chief, China, who preferred Keppel Harbour as a site, partly for economy, but partly because the Sembawang site would make an easy target for bombers, which could fly along the Johore Strait.[29] However, the Governor of the Straits Settlements confirmed the choice of Sembawang in a telegram and, on 17 February, similar support was given by Sir Lawrence Power and Admiral Learmouth.

Curzon accepted the case for the Sembawang site, but asked if the proposed *scale* was not too large. Nobody in the room, he declared, really contemplated that in their lifetime there would ever be a gathering of one hundred warships at Singapore! Beatty admitted that the Admiralty case might be regarded as 'a policy of perfection', but his immediate concern was the next three years. If they could only get out the floating dock, they could use Keppel in the meantime, and possibly adjust their long-term plans. Churchill agreed to this as the 'first echelon in the Old Strait'.[30] Thus an interim report of the Curzon committee recommended the installation of the floating dock, and expenditure of £787,000 on site borings, anti-malarial work, and the provision of a water supply. It was approved in Cabinet on 2 March 1925.[31]

Just a year after Labour's decision 'not to proceed', Beatty had one small tangible piece of progress to show – the agreement to install the floating dock. This was to enable the navy to station a battle-cruiser squadron in the Far East by the time the Pacific treaty was liable for review.

V

No sooner was this minor step forward achieved than Winston Churchill challenged the strategic concept behind the intention to send a fleet to the Far East. To mount this assault the Chancellor first used the Cabinet's Committee on the Naval Construction programme chaired by Lord Birkenhead. On the very day of the Cabinet's approval of the floating dock Churchill turned a discussion of the Admiralty's cruiser replacement programme into an excuse for a review of the entire Singapore strategy.

The Admiralty wanted 70 cruisers. That compared with 100 in the decade up to 1914. The 48 available in 1925 was the smallest number in over sixty years. For a war with Japan the whole fleet would not be sent to the East, so some cruisers would have to remain in European waters with the home battleships. The 5:3 ratio with Japan allowed for equality in the East, with some units at home. If Japan would have 25 heavy cruisers (8″ guns) by 1928/29 Beatty wanted the same: 25 in the East, with 6 at home and 39 for trade protection added up to 70. Even then this 'bare equality' gave the Japanese the advantage because they could choose their own moment to strike. But if that happened, put in Churchill, the navy might not be 'anywhere near them', so they were setting themselves an impossible task. He warned Beatty to expect a challenge to every particular.[32] Beatty had to leave the meetings because of other business at this point, but when the Committee reconvened later in the day Churchill mounted a formidable attack on the cruiser programme and the Singapore strategy. He started by making his own comparisons. Britain had 49 cruisers, the rest of the world other than Japan had 39; if the older types were left out, the figures were 38:14. Japan would have 29 by 1928. Britain would have 56 (plus 2 possible Australian cruisers and 16 flotilla leaders). That made the comparison 74:29. It was 'ample superiority'. From numbers Churchill turned to strategy. Beatty had given them the plans for war with Japan in the Pacific. It required a battle fleet, superior to Japan's, to go to eastern waters, with all its supplies, reinforcements and fuel. Yet even then (on Beatty's own admission) the danger was not eliminated, because Japan could choose its moment. So why send out the fleet at all? If the Government decided that, for the next ten years, no preparations were to be made for sending a battle fleet to Singapore to fight with Japan, things would be greatly simplified. Japan could only attack the fleet if it was sent east: if it was not, there would be nothing to attack. The 25 best cruisers could be used for trade protection. He proposed two things: that the cruiser total should be reduced from 70 to 50; and that the CID should be asked to rule that no preparations should be made for ten years (other than the work already sanctioned at Singapore) to send the fleet to the Far East. The present strategy involved attempting a physical impossibility therefore they might as well make a virtue out of necessity.[33] Churchill did not try to stop the modest work authorised for Singapore, but he saw the chance of delaying expenditure on warship construction and, presumably, the new dockyard.

The Cabinet referred his proposals to the CID. It met (with Beatty back) on 30 March and 2 April. The CNS simply pleaded for adequate fuel storage, a safe anchorage at Singapore and the ability to 'hold on' in the Far East. This was the intention of the battle-cruiser squadron, for which the floating dock was planned. But Churchill won his strategic point. The CID agreed that it would not be necessary to incur additional expenditure in the next ten years for placing a battle fleet at Singapore, superior or at least equal to that of Japan, to fight a decisive battle in the Pacific.[34] Beatty, however, won on the cruiser programme. Churchill continued to bray about 'unwarrantable and improper' demands on the taxpayer, but Beatty, who was prepared to resign, dug in his heels and Baldwin insisted on compromise. Seven new cruisers were approved for the years 1925–8.[35]

VI

After all the battles over finance and strategy in 1925 (not forgetting the unresolved controversy over artillery and air power) the naval staff were left without any further progress towards the Singapore dockyard. But the imminence of another Imperial Conference towards the end of 1926 gave them the chance of getting a decision since the Government would soon have curious Dominion Prime Ministers to contend with. As they prepared to use this increasingly useful tactical lever the naval staff also agreed to modify their scheme.

On 16 April 1926 Captain Wilfred A. Egerton, the Director of Plans, suggested that if they were to press for the £11 million scheme Labour had suspended (which with the defences, would cost even more) they could still expect Cabinet opposition. Should they, then, not try to get 'something less than the whole'?[36] They could add to it later. The 'ultimate objective', of a first-class fully-fortified naval base capable of maintaining a fleet in every particular, had already been given away. The 1923 scheme was less than that. Could they now accept a 'much modified scheme'? The essential needs were fuel oil reserves, a defended anchorage, floating dock and navigational aids. Part of this was in train. Next in priority were a graving dock, wharves, repair workshops and stores. They could postpone a supply base and cooled ammunition depot until after 1936. If they did not give up something they might never get the base.

Beatty was attracted by this idea and called a conference of the Sea Lords on 26 April 1926. They all agreed that they must get 'a definite, if limited, policy' decided on about Singapore before the Imperial Conference in October. The First Lord of the Admiralty hesitated briefly about the idea of a reduced scheme because he knew there was the prospect of another large contribution, this time from the Federated Malay States. But in June 1926 the Civil Lords were asked to try and fit the scheme to a £7¾ million ceiling.

Leopold Savile, the Civil Engineer-in-Chief, conferred with the heads of the Admiralty divisions, who found, at first, that they could not make a base 'workable' in peacetime and 'adequate' in wartime for £7¾ million. Savile then considered what could be cut out. The stores depot and the ammunition supply depot – yes. The graving dock – this would be a good 'climb down' politically but might mean damaged ships having to crawl back to Malta. The 'least unsatisfactory' way of saving would be to omit 1750 feet of the north wharf walls and over half the stores basin walls, leaving pitched slopes in their places. These omissions were 'drastic' and should only be made if it were a choice between them or nothing. The view of the Controller, Rear-Admiral Ernle Chatfield, was that the reduced wharfage was 'totally inadequate for war requirements', but sufficient for peacetime purposes.[37] This 'truncated scheme' (as it came to be called) would cost £7¾ million (see Map 5, page 33)

VII

The naval staff pressed for this scheme with growing confidence after they learnt, on 23 June 1926, that the Federated Malay States gift was to be £2 million. They used this to get a decision from the Admiralty Board on 15 July and next day passed the matter to the CID to get a decision before the Imperial Conference.[38] The matter was looked at by the Curzon Committee, (still deeply enmeshed in squabbles over artillery and air defences) but, here again, the two Malay millions worked their magic. On the day of the Cabinet, which accepted the Malay States gift, Hankey told Trenchard he had had a 'brain wave'. Could not the CAS make a 'graceful' concession to the CNS and CIGS by saying that, although he stuck to his views about the superiority of torpedo bombers over 15" guns, 'this windfall' would permit some 'over-insurance' in Singapore's defences?[39] This paved the way for a compromise on 20 July over Stage I of the defences (including three 15" guns) without prejudice to a re-examination of the air role before further decisions were made.[40]

Both matters went to the CID two days later, where Churchill had a final grouse. He had always supported the Singapore base but never imagined it would be used as a peg for alarmist armaments policies. He supported the one power standard of comparison with the USA but felt the recent emphasis on the Japanese danger was giving a 'wrong direction and an unwise distortion' to British strategic thought. On this, as with the cruisers, he lost. The truncated scheme and Stage I of the defences were approved and endorsed by the Cabinet on 3 August 1926.[41]

The need for something to tell an Imperial Conference had been the spur to making the decision in principle in 1921, and over the first appropriations in 1923. The decision over the truncated scheme in 1926 was made in the same way. It meant that Baldwin could refer to the FMS £2 million in his opening speech at the Conference on 19 October. As to whether this 'bait' would catch further financial fishes remained to be seen. As it turned out, however, the role of the Commonwealth in the financing of the Singapore base was a remarkably large, interesting, and in the long run influential, one.

3 'A Bait to Catch Some Money', 1923–28

I

The Singapore strategy was born out of economy and nurtured on parsimony. Having decided that it could not afford a fleet to match that of Japan, the British Government planned the base so that it could fit a single fleet into a two-ocean strategy. Construction was delayed for financial rather than ideological reasons. From the start, however, a Commonwealth share in the costs was expected.

The base was intended, primarily, as an 'insurance' in imperial defence, therefore the idea of sharing the premium was not unreasonable. The security of Australia, New Zealand, India, the Malaysian dependencies, even the Pacific Islands, was seen to focus on Singapore and the arrival of the main fleet. Precedents for sharing already existed in the naval subsidies formerly paid by the Dominions, India and Malaya and the 'defence contributions' (usually about 20 per cent of their revenues) which the Crown colonies paid toward the costs of their garrisons. The interesting new element, which crept into the Commonwealth's sharing in the Singapore project, was that it was used by the British service departments to commit their own Government to the scheme.

This 'imperial lever' was employed from the very start of the scheme. In the preparations for the 1921 Imperial Conference, which led to the decision to build the base, the Admiralty suggested that portions of the Empire should be invited to share the costs as Britain could hardly be expected to bear the full burden.[1] Similarly, when the CID recommended that a decision should be made, on 31 June 1921, it added the recommendation that, as large expenditure could not be incurred in the near future, the greater the assistance which could be given by overseas governments, the sooner the base could be completed.[2]

After the Dominion leaders had been told at the Imperial Conference, the question of financial contributions was brought up at a meeting in Winston Churchill's room in the Colonial Office on 19 July 1921. The Admiralty's recommendation was that

> Australia, New Zealand and India should be asked to contribute a considerable portion of the expenditure necessary to develop Singapore as a fleet base, since they are intimately concerned therein. Great Britain is already involved in considerable expenditure in modernizing Malta as a naval base and thus enabling the fleet to be sent there, which is all a part of the general strategic plan for the safety of the Empire in the East, as the fleet at Malta is considerably nearer Singapore than when in Home waters.[3]

Lord Lee, the First Lord of the Admiralty, put it more generally. The size and cost of the naval requirements of the Empire, he said, made it 'impossible that the mother country can continue to bear the whole burden itself'. Massey, of New Zealand, responded straightaway. His Dominion was quite prepared to take on whatever additional burdens might be necessary. India, on the other hand, could not. Edwin Montagu, the Secretary of State for India, declared that the country was too poor. More than half the Government of India's revenue went on military expenditure ($62\frac{1}{2}$ crores of rupees out of 100 crores) mainly on the Northwest Frontier. The per capita income of the people was only 60 rupees. India was interested in the Singapore scheme, but if it had any surplus revenue it would give priority to forming a Royal Indian Navy and developing a base at Bombay.[4]

These discussions were confined to generalities. A further eighteen months elapsed before the British Cabinet authorised the first appropriations, which were included in the naval estimates on 12 March 1923. At this point Pound suggested that Colonies, Dependencies and India should also be told as well as the Dominions.[5] A circular despatch went out on 27 March 1923 indicating that £160,000 would be spent in 1923-4 towards the £11 million scheme. This was 'without prejudice to any conclusions which the Dominion Governments may reach on the question of contributions towards the Naval development of Singapore'.[6]

II

Assistance was obtained first from the Straits Settlements. Sir Lawrence Guillemard, the Governor, had visited England in 1922, and Sir George Barstow of the Treasury suggested to him that the Straits Settlements Government might buy the land needed for the naval base and airfields.[7] On the very day of the Cabinet's decision, 21 February 1923, the Admiralty took this matter up with the Colonial Office. The Governor was then consulted by telegram, and Sir Gilbert Grindle, the Assistant Under-Secretary for the Colonies and Protectorates Division, noted: 'the Straits are very generous and will probably do what is wanted.'[8] But Guillemard's reply indicated that he had not expected the Straits Government would have to *pay* for the land. What he had offered 'free of charge' were the services and help of his Government in securing the site. But when asked specifically if the Colony would provide the land 'as a free gift', Guillemard consulted the unofficials on his Executive Council and replied in the affirmative. Thus by 3 May 1923 Britain had secured the first Commonwealth contribution. 'This is exceedingly generous', wrote Edward Gent, Assistant Principal in the Far Eastern Department.[9] Fulsome thanks were forthcoming from the Secretary of State for Colonies and John F. N. Green, senior principal in the Dominions Division, suggested that the information should be passed on to Australia and New Zealand.[10] The Dominions were informed on 13 June that the Straits Settlements had made a free gift of 2845 acres valued at approximately £200,000. (Actually it came to 1¼ million Straits dollars—£145,833.)[11] Pound, in the Admiralty, felt that this would help in getting contributions from Australia, New Zealand and India. Beatty thought it was most satisfactory and demanded that 'the widest publicity should be given to this contribution'.[12] The details were duly given to Parliament on 11 July, when Lord Linlithgow, Civil Lord of the Admiralty, announced the Singapore gift in the House of Lords. Unfortunately he made a slip of the tongue and said the gift was from the Federated Malay States, not the Straits Settlements, and subsequently had to apologise in a letter to *The Times*.[13]

III

These attempts to use the news of the British navy estimates and the Straits Settlements gift as bait for further Commonwealth offers were not entirely successful. The Australian Government's response to the despatch of 27 March 1923 took the form of a request that the general post-Washington naval situation be discussed at the 1923 Imperial Conference.[14] Smuts reacted most unfavourably: 'A great fortified base at Singapore may in its effects on Japanese opinion produce far-reaching reactions for the foreign policy as well as the Naval policy of the Empire'.[15] In the case of New Zealand prodding was hardly necessary. Massey had already indicated his eagerness to help, and he fulfilled his promise in 1923 quite independently of the Straits Settlements gift.

As we might expect, Jellicoe, the Governor-General, could not resist a gentle hint on his own part. When he passed on the despatch announcing the British naval estimates, he added: 'a generous contribution from NZ would set a fine example to other parts of the Empire'.[16] Only a week later the Navy Office in Wellington had word that Massey was thinking of a contribution of £100,000. Massey spoke strongly for Empire naval preparedness in a speech to a Civic Luncheon in Christchurch on 5 June and finally announced the £100,000 gift in his Budget speech to Parliament on 3 July 1923.[17] At the Imperial Conference in London, in October 1923, he called this 'a preliminary vote – it can be multiplied several times over as the work goes on'. He told Leopold Amery, the First Lord, before leaving for New Zealand, that he did not object if the Dominion's contribution to Singapore exceeded the United Kingdom's in the coming year, and Amery assured him the money would be used on things not yet provided for in the British estimates.[18] But it was never used. With Labour's suspension of work in 1924 the New Zealand gift lapsed. And after such fulsome support, it was hardly surprising that New Zealand's protest was the most forthright during the time of the Labour Government.

More serious than the lapse of the New Zealand gift in 1924 was the loss of a contribution from Australia. Stanley Bruce's protest to Ramsay MacDonald mentioned that 'a substantial Australian contribution' was contemplated. The sum was not disclosed, but a Member of Parliament, Walter M. Marks, suggested that Australia should give £1 million over 10 years.[19] During the period of Labour's suspension, however, Australia put its money into warships. Bruce told the House of Representatives that nothing could be offered for Singapore at that time. Instead £6½ million was voted to for two 10,000 ton, 8" gun cruisers, two submarines and a seaplane tender.[20] Of course, any Australian naval expansion represented a contribution to imperial defence, but it meant that when Baldwin's Government revived the Singapore scheme in November 1924, Bruce could not offer a contribution. Instead of the anticipated aid from the second largest Dominion, the next contribution came from the tiny Colony of Hong Kong.

IV

Hong Kong provided a fascinating case of a Crown Colony virtually blackmailing the imperial power. Just at the moment when the First Lord of the Admiralty was urging the Baldwin Government to proceed with Singapore, the Governor of Hong Kong, Sir Edward Stubbs, revealed that the Colony had lying unused, in a suspense account, a sum of £250,000, the 'profits' accumulated as a result of shipping control operations towards the end of the 1914-18 war. Stubbs suggested that he could induce the unofficial members of the Legislative Council to donate the money for the Singapore base – with a condition. There was 'no chance of their agreeing', unless the Admiralty dropped its opposition to a local reclamation scheme in Kowloon (on the mainland opposite Hong Kong Island) where the Colony wanted to build a ferry terminal. This would deprive the Admiralty of certain water frontage reserved for possible extensions to the Kowloon naval depot.[21] The prospect of another colonial quarter-million naturally delighted Leopold Amery, who wrote to 'Willie' Bridgeman hoping that the Admiralty would 'see its way to humouring local feeling' by waiving objections to the reclamation scheme. Bridgeman happily played along: 'we need have no scruples over waiving our objection'. But he felt it undesirable that 'there should be any overt indications of this quid pro quo having accompanied the gift, as it would thereby be the less inspiring as an example "pour encourager les autres"'.[22] The formal offer of £250,000 was made by the Governor in a telegram on 16 December 1924.

Then something cropped up which nearly spoiled it. Hong Kong, like most of the Crown Colonies, had to make a contribution towards the cost of its garrison. This could not exceed 20 per cent of the Colony's revenue, and in some years the actual costs fell short of this. Stubbs followed up his telegram with a request that the £250,000 gift should not pass through the books in any way which would make it liable for the 20 per cent military contribution. The Colony was not going to contribute to imperial defence twice with the same money, but as Sir Gilbert Grindle knew, the Treasury were 'quite capable of claiming it'.[23] This time the Treasury did not, but the War Office did. The Secretary of State for War, Sir Laming Worthington-Evans, asked what his department's 'rights in the matter' were, and they then demanded that they should be told about suspense accounts. Grindle rebuffed them. He said the sum was 'a pure windfall' and, after accepting it, the British Government could not claim a percentage. This little episode of bureaucratic pettiness meant that a public reply for Hong Kong was not possible for some months. It also revealed that the Colony's gift alone would exceed the United Kingdom's appropriation for 1925–6, which was only £204,000 for preparations for the floating dock.[24]

V

Although the Admiralty had a brief taste of optimism, it soon became apparent that the Hong Kong quarter-million was, indeed, a pure 'windfall'. Even New Zealand now had other priorities. Amery's cable announcing the revival of the scheme indicated that the British Government would like to be able to announce some Commonwealth contributions when they made the decision public. It would be 'helpful in disarming the opposition'. But New Zealand was planning to add a second light cruiser to the New Zealand Division of the Royal Navy. The Dominion's deputy Prime Minister, Sir Francis Dillon Bell, was all for contributing £250,000 for Singapore as well as taking on the cruiser and wrote: 'I should like to see Mr Massey's name behind a real lead to the Empire'.[25] Massey preferred to stick to one thing at a time. He would ask Parliament for a Singapore contribution in due course, but in 1925 he died. It was also election year. More than two years were to elapse before New Zealand fulfilled its earlier promises.

Bruce of Australia could only say that Australia would, in future, be influenced by what other parts of the Empire contributed. And while imperial sources seemed to be drying up, in 1925 Winston Churchill was mounting his assaults on naval expenditure. Beatty found the Baldwin Government 'actually behaving far worse to us at the Admiralty than the Labour Party'.[26]

'A Bait to Catch Some Money', 1923-28

As if to rub in the disappointments of 1925 a negative was also confirmed from India. Montagu had offered no hopes of an Indian contribution in 1921, but the idea did not die. When a tentative enquiry about a contribution to Singapore came in July 1922, the Government of India held out no prospect of help.[27] Rumours persisted and questions were asked in the central Indian Legislative Assembly by M. Ramachandra Rao in January and August 1925 and again by Runglal Jaiodia in January 1926. The official answer by Sir Ernest Burdon, Secretary of the Army Department, was always that, while it was interested in Singapore the Government of India was 'not committed to any action or liability' in connexion with the building of the base.[28]

VI

Disappointment from India had the unexpected effect of prompting the biggest Empire gift of all. It happened that Lord Lee of Fareham (who had been First Lord of the Admiralty at the time of the decision to create the Singapore base in 1921) was staying in Kuala Lumpur with Sir George Maxwell, the Chief Secretary of the Federated Malay States (FMS) when, in February 1926, Lord Winterton, parliamentary Under-Secretary for India, told the House of Commons that India had neither been asked for, nor had offered a contribution for Singapore.[29] After reading this in the *Malay Mail* on 23 February Lee asked Maxwell if the FMS (which had paid for the battleship HMS *Malaya* in 1912) had considered a contribution to the naval base. Maxwell, who had assumed that the naval base was assured, said he felt the Malay States should contribute to something extra and had been thinking of two European regiments for the garrison. Lee replied that the base was by no means secured, but a substantial Malay contribution might 'turn the scale and make it a certainty'.

This seed soon germinated in the tropical atmosphere of Kuala Lumpur. Maxwell called over the editor of the *Malay Mail* and Lee provided copy for a feature on 'Naval Policy in the East' which appeared on 25 February 1926, along with an editorial calling for a 'really determined speed up' of the Singapore base. Maxwell consulted Arthur M. Pountney, the Financial Adviser of the FMS, who suggested that a contribution of £2 million spread over five years would be feasible. Lee spoke with Sir Lawrence Guillemard, the High Commissioner. Maxwell put up the idea formally saying he could drop a hint in the ear of the Sultan of Perak 'in such a way that the suggestion might seem to His Highness to originate with himself'.[30]

Guillemard had been thinking on similar lines. He wrote a frank private letter to Lord Lee on 9 March.

> Great minds jump together. I had already in my own mind turned down the British Regiment idea, which was Maxwell's idea.
>
> The Rulers had never heard of it and it would be a grievous mistake politically. R.I.P.
>
> What is more interesting is that I had already, after you left but before getting your letter (?telepathy) conceived the same idea as you.
>
> I think it will come off and that I shall perhaps bring Johore in as well as the FMS and be able to offer something well over 2 millions.
>
> To save time pending negotiations I will send a secret telegram to Amery asking whether, if an offer materialises, it would ensure the preliminary equipment.
>
> Meanwhile MUM in capital letters is essential.
>
> If any rumour leaks out some damned fool at home will suggest it as something that we *ought* to do.
>
> That would take all the grace out of the offer, and might at worst even put our fish down for good.
>
> The Malay, like all really sporting fish, is very shy.[31]

Guillemard cabled the Colonial Office on 21 March 1926 to enquire whether a £2 million gift would help the 'rapid completion' of the works associated with the first stage of the dockyard, involving the floating dock.

Amery naturally was thrilled. He immediately got in touch with Bridgeman and they saw the prospect of using the 'imperial lever' again. Amery wanted to use the FMS gift 'as a bait to catch some money' from Australia and New Zealand. Bridgeman agreed that, if the offer could be timed to arrive just before the 1926 Imperial Conference, it would be useful in encouraging the Dominions to put down some more money.

If we could get Dominions and Colonies to carry half the total cost we ought to be able to find the rest

	£
Hong Kong	250,000
Singapore land	150,000
" new proposal	2,000,000*
Australia and NZ, between them say	2,600,000
	5,000,000

this comes to nearly half.[32]

*Another mistake! It was the FMS.

In the Colonial Office the civil servants viewed it all more soberly, but even they saw the possibilities for a little bureaucratic point-scoring. Alexander Clutterbuck (of the Eastern Department) wrote of the proposed offer: 'This is generous, perhaps too generous, but it is doubtless good policy'. Sir Gilbert Grindle saw it as a chance to force the Treasury to allow FMS loans as trustee securities. Sir Samuel Wilson, the Permanent Under-Secretary, hoped the Admiralty would accelerate the scheme, as the opportunity was 'one which must not be missed'. Guillemard was told by cable that the offer would be 'a splendid lead' for the coming Imperial Conference, and that, if possible, the Admiralty would like to use the money not just for the preparations for the floating dock, but to further the 'larger scheme' for which no appropriations had yet been made.[33]

Meanwhile Amery and Bridgeman were eagerly fingering the 'imperial lever'. On 29 April 1926 they lunched with Lord Lee and the imperialist trio agreed that nothing should be allowed to risk the offer falling through; Guillemard should be left to fix the timing and the conditions. They now thought it best to spend some of the money on the floating dock preparations and hoped the Treasury would agree that the sums 'saved' thereby should be applied afterwards for the main scheme. They also talked about the prospect of another Labour Government and agreed that the more they could do towards pressing on at Singapore and accepting contributions from Commonwealth Governments 'the more difficult it would be for them to close it down again'.[34]

Everything went according to plan. On 23 June 1926 the Sultan of Selangor rose in the Federal Council in Kuala Lumpur to move that £2 million be offered to the imperial Government. Maxwell seconded; the Sultan of Perak, who followed, recalled that his father had moved the gift of HMS *Malaya* in 1912, and said he liked the idea of a contribution to the Singapore base.[35] Guillemard rushed off the prearranged, coded cable, 'Passed'. Amery was able to break the news to the British Cabinet the same day. The gift was to be spread over five years, and, as Guillemard emphasised (no doubt to Amery's delight), payment was 'conditional upon the decision to proceed with work on the Base remaining unaltered'.[36]

VII

The Federated Malay States' two millions – the largest single contribution from an overseas Commonwealth Government – was, in its timing, a most significant landmark. It came at a time when the naval staff were trying hard to press acceptance of the 'truncated scheme' and when the air staff were holding up decisions about the defences by their stance in the dispute over 'Guns v Air'. The Malayan gift broke the hold-up. As soon as Amery told the Cabinet Hankey persuaded Trenchard that he might compromise over the first stage of the defences. The Admiralty used the £2 million windfall to get a decision on the 'truncated scheme' in time for the Imperial Conference in October. A clear policy could be put to the Dominions and on this depended 'the best hope of obtaining further financial assistance'.[37] The proposal was acceptable to the COS and the CID and was approved in Cabinet on 3 August 1926. Sir George Maxwell, who retired later in the year after twenty years in Malaya, had crowned his career with a worthy imperial service.

However, as 'bait' to catch more money, the Malay millions proved disappointing. Guillemard expected a contribution from Johore. The First Lord talked about £2½ million from Australia and New Zealand. Baldwin duly threw out the baited hook in his opening speech to the 1926 Imperial Conference on 19 October 1926 by announcing the 'generous, patriotic, and far-sighted action of Their Highnesses, the Rulers of the four Federated Malay States'.[38] In his statement about defence a week later he appealed to the Dominions in the East 'to consider most carefully whether there is any way in which they can cooperate in the development of Singapore, either now or in the next few years. There could be no more valuable contribution to the defence of the Empire as a whole'.[39] But there were no further offers at this stage. Instead, in the second half of 1926 a bitter struggle began about a further contribution from the Straits Settlements.

While the Admiralty had been able to float their 'truncated scheme' for the dockyard with the help of the Malayan millions, the War Office was getting anxious about lack of progress on the defences. The Straits Settlements had already paid for nearly 3000 acres of land (costing roughly £146,000) for the naval base and air fields. But in view of the 'splendid example' of the FMS the Secretary of State for War asked Amery if it would be possible for the Colony to help with the fixed defences. Amery refused. He felt it would not be 'exactly dignified' for the British Government to ask for more.[40] The War Office then tried different tactics. Having failed to get the land free (like the Admiralty and Air Ministry) it accepted that it would have to pay so the sum would be added to the annual cost of the garrison, which could be recovered under the statutory military contribution of up to 20 per cent of the Colony's revenue.

The Colonial Office was infuriated. 'This is very insidious', wrote Harold Beckett, Principal in the Far East Department, ' . . . in justice to the Colony we must resist this attempt to steal at the back door'.[41] Sir Gilbert Grindle replied to the War Office, drawing the important distinction that the free gift of land for the naval base and airfield had been for 'Imperial military purposes', whereas the statutory military contribution of up to 20 per cent of the revenue was for the 'garrison' – meaning troops employed for the defence of the colony in normal circumstances.[42] Worthington-Evans, who was a solicitor by profession and an experienced minister, took the matter back to Amery. He was alarmed, he said, at the idea of drawing distinctions between expenses for the defence of the Colony and other costs of the garrison. He hoped the Singapore base would not be used to raise 'insoluble questions' as to how much of the garrison was there for the defence of the Colony and how much for the defence of anything else. But Amery would not give way. He knew that the 20 per cent military contribution was unpopular at the best of times. Governor Guillemard wanted the matter resolved by the Cabinet. The Malay States had been liberal, the Straits Settlements had paid for land, and he still thought Johore would join in. 'I don't think Malaya ought to pay any more.'[43] Amery told Worthington-Evans that the two departments' viewpoints were 'irreconcilable'; the British Government had gone quite far enough in the direction of 'taxation without representation'.[44] In this deadlock the Treasury were brought in; an inter departmental Committee was appointed. At the other end the Legislative Council of the Straits Settlements started to attack the 20 per cent system. In the event, it was seven years before the Colony made a further contribution. The War Office having stirred up a hornet's nest, it took years of negotiation, and a new situation in the Far East, to settle it down.

VIII

While the Colonial Office and the War Office were squabbling about the garrison costs the New Zealand Government was again considering how it might fulfil the promises made so eagerly four years before. By 1926, when the Dominion was expected to take the Malayan 'bait', the New Zealand Division of the Royal Navy consisted of two light cruisers (on loan from Britain), two imperial sloops for Pacific Island service, two training ships and an oiler. Any increased expenditure was to be earmarked for a third cruiser. During the Imperial Conference Gordon Coates, the Prime Minister, began to weigh up the relative costs of taking on the new cruiser and contributing to Singapore. The Admiralty got wind of the possibility that New Zealand might increase its annual naval expenditure by about £250,000. The Plans Division hoped that some of the increase might be devoted to Singapore. They suggested that the Dominion could earmark it specifically for part of the work and there would be no difficulty in naming, say, a 'New Zealand Dock'.[45]

After studying the views of the British Chiefs of Staff, Vice-Admiral Alan Hotham (former Commodore of the New Zealand Station and now acting as Coates's adviser) suggested that the defence of the Singapore base should have first priority, adding a personal view that air superiority was also involved. He recommended that instead of taking on a third cruiser the Dominion should contribute £225,000 a year for five years to the Singapore base. Coates was more cautious. He would not agree to £225,000. He favoured £100,000 or £150,000 a year, 'or say £125,000 for 8 years, = £1 million', on the condition it was used for specific purposes and there would be a firm completion date.[46] Hotham and Frank D. Thomson, head of the New Zealand Prime Minister's department, met Admiral Field, the deputy Chief of Naval Staff, on 29 October 1926. They accepted the Admiralty view that priority should be given to Singapore, but explained that £225,000 a year was too much to expect. The sum would be decided 'in NZ'. Before leaving London Coates talked with Churchill who outlined ways in which New Zealand might borrow £1½ million to contribute towards Singapore with repayments until 1947. He warned Churchill that such a sum was 'somewhat larger than our tentative proposal' and added that New Zealand did not want its money to pay for extras; its object was to relieve Britain of some portion of its burden 'as well as to assist in our own defence'.[47]

The Dominion Government finally decided on a £1 million gift spread over eight years. The announcement on Saturday 23 April 1927 – the weekend before ANZAC Day – prompted Harry Holland, the militant socialist leader of the Labour Party, to declare: 'while the church bells were calling the people together to honour the memory of the dead, the propaganda was being made for a project that would arouse the fiercest antagonisms between the East and the West, and furnish the guarantee of future warfare...'[48]

Unlike the other Commonwealth gifts the New Zealand million was not 'taxation without representation' and was subject to debate in Parliament. The Labour members (often echoing the political debate in Britain) denounced the contribution and one outspoken member cried 'Government by Downing Street'.[49] Harry Holland, who was a longstanding pacifist, reminded the House of Representatives of Ramsay MacDonald's cancellation and claimed that in the 1924 general election the British people had voted against the Singapore base, because 8 million Conservative votes, compared with 5½ million for Labour, 3 million Liberal and 107,000 Independent, meant a Conservative minority. Compared with the British and other Commonwealth contributions New Zealand's £1 million was out of all proportion to the size of its population. He also said it violated the spirit of the Washington Treaties. But Labour had only 10 seats. Sir Joseph Ward, the leader of the old Liberals, congratulated Coates. £125,000 a year was a small price to pay 'to get the whole power and prestige of the British Navy'. There was no other power in the world, he said, to equal the British Empire. New Zealand was 'one of six virile nations all attached to the heart of our

Empire – a galaxy of wonderful young nations'. One member, David Jones, put the businessman's point of view, which was that New Zealand was 'getting out very cheaply by paying over £1,000,000 to obtain security'. Henry Holland (not related to Harry) said that the vote of money would show that 'no one can step on the tail of the lion but the cubs overseas will be ready to fly to his assistance .... I love the Old Country with all my heart, and there is no sacrifice too great for me or for my family to make to help the Mother-country in the hour of her need'.[50] In the Treasury, in London, the atmosphere was less euphoric: They had hoped, from Coates' conversation in London, that New Zealand would contribute 'rather more than this'.[51]

IX

New Zealand's gift, added to those of the Straits Settlements, Hong Kong and the Federated Malay States, meant that the combined Commonwealth contributions exceeded the sums spent by Britain by 1927, when the major civil engineering works were put out to tender.[52] This meant that the 'imperial lever' could be brought into play again. When, for example, there was renewed talk of reducing naval expenditure, Sir James Parr, the New Zealand High Commissioner in London, cabled Coates suggesting that the occasional 'tactful statement' in favour of a strong navy and the need for the Singapore base would greatly help the Admiralty.[53] Parr protested at a CID meeting on 5 July 1928 when Churchill called for cuts in expenditure in view of social conditions in Britain and an impending general election. Churchill also wanted the Ten Year Rule to be extended on a day-to-day basis, which Amery called a 'revolving credit of peace', and the British Cabinet accepted the principle.[54] Parr told the Committee that naval reductions would alarm Australia and New Zealand and said that Japan was a threat to the western Pacific. But the Australian representative, Sir Granville Ryrie, doubted this and said that in view of American investments in Australia, the United States would never countenance Japanese aggression. Parr alerted Coates to the possibility of cuts in the Singapore base, and added: 'Of course I made a vigorous protest – but Australia gave me no help!'[55]

The imperial lever gave Amery and Bridgeman an additional clout when Churchill tried to put off the main contract for the wharves and graving dock in 1928. The British ministers admittedly faced a dilemma. A general election was likely in 1929 and increased defence expenditure would not be popular. On the other hand Labour might get back and try to stop the Singapore base, so even Churchill agreed the contract should be signed *before* the election. His idea was that a decision on the contract should be postponed 'as unostentatiously as possible' until just before the election. But the First Lord reminded him of the FMS £2 million, the New Zealand £1 million and the recent Imperial Conference's priorities. If they delayed now it might cost more later and lead to trouble with the Commonwealth contributors.

Churchill was used to this type of scrap and merely changed tactics. He doubted the ability of the contractors to fulfil their tenders, which in some cases varied considerably from the Admiralty estimate of £3,900,000. The lowest bid, by Sir John Jackson Ltd (builders of the Simonstown base in South Africa) for £3,737,214 was £162,786 less than the estimate. The others came to more. Norton Griffiths bid £660,000 more than Jackson's; Lindsay, Parkinson and Co. £764,800 more, and Topham, Jones, Railton exceeded Jackson's by £1,159,000. If a solid firm like the last, said Churchill, bid a million more he wondered how Jackson's could do it. But his colleagues pointed out that Jackson's tender was close to the Admiralty estimate, they had done good work on the Hammadi Barrage on the Nile and they were prepared to enter a bond for £200,000 to guarantee satisfactory completion. Baldwin wanted to hold defence expenditure for a year, but Lord Stanhope, the Civil Lord of the Admiralty, pointed out they would have to give six months after calling for tenders again. Finally the First Lord applied the 'imperial lever' by expressing his fear that there would be 'an outcry in New Zealand' if work was postponed. Although he agreed to see if Jackson's could retard early work, the firm was awarded the contract on 27 September 1928.[56]

In the development of the naval base the 'Jackson contract' was the big landmark. The remaining unsolved matters concerned the defences. The War Office made no headway in its attempt to squeeze more money out of the Straits Settlements. In fact there were protest meetings in Singapore in 1928 demanding that the 20 per cent military contribution, which had been levied since 1899, should be reduced. As if to compound their difficulties the War Office also suffered a serious set-back in the debate over air or artillery defences. Gunnery trials, which followed the 1926 compromise over the first stage of the defences, indicated serious deficiencies in the heavy coastal defence guns. On 13 December 1928 Worthington-Evans had to ask the CID to defer further expenditure on the defences for a year. The Cabinet agreed on 19 December. Churchill got his economies in unexpected fashion. For Trenchard, the Chief of Air Staff, it seemed the moment of opportunity. He told the CID he had been waiting for five years for this situation. In the Air Ministry, it seemed as if the controversy over Guns v Air had finally come to a head.[57]

4 'Guns v Air', 1921–28

I

The controversy over 'Guns v Air' was, in the long run, the most damaging debate in the entire Singapore story. Air power was neglected (though not ignored) in the early planning. Lack of air superiority was to be decisive in 1941. But, just as the whole development of the base did not occur in isolation from naval strategy and the deterrent role of the fleet, so its air defences could not be divorced from the tensions which surrounded the infant Royal Air Force.

Sir Hugh Trenchard, the Chief of Air Staff, said at the height of the controversy: 'I feel that the defence of Singapore is a vital stage in the development of the Air'.[1] But Beatty chided him for producing merely a 'somewhat nebulous scheme', and later reached the point of declaring that their differences appeared to be so fundamental that it was 'hardly worth continuing the discussion'.[2] For more than a decade Singapore's defences showed up the bitter antagonisms aroused in the British armed services by changing technology.

II

The planning of the naval base coincided with the opening rounds of the struggle over the future of the RAF, which came into being in 1918 by the fusing of the Royal Flying Corps and the Royal Naval Air Service. When Churchill, Secretary of State for Air, presented the white paper on the permanent organisation of the air force in 1919 he said the first duty of the RAF was 'to garrison the British Empire'.[3] On the other side of the globe, Colonel Vere Bettington, who went out to advise the New Zealand Government on air policy (like Jellicoe on the Navy), wrote: 'A Nation thinking in three dimensions will lead and defeat a Nation thinking in two . . . . New

Zealand should consider the Imperial as well as her domestic aspect of the future Aerial policy'.[4] But not everyone was so confident about air power. Already Beatty and Sir Henry Wilson, the CIGS, were regretting the establishment of the independent air force. In the early 1920s the future of the RAF was by no means secure, and this was part of the background to the discussions on Singapore's defence.

Yet, in spite of the basic uncertainty, Trenchard and the air staff continued their advocacy and had some successes. They tentatively asserted the role of aircraft in Indian frontier defence in the 1919 paper, by suggesting that it was not too much to hope that before long the RAF would have a role, not as additional to the garrison, but as 'a substitute for part of it'.[5] In 1920 a squadron of 12 planes had quick success against the 'Mad Mullah' in Somaliland. Next year it was agreed that the RAF rather than the army should police the Iraq mandate. By the 1921 Imperial Conference, when each service produced papers on imperial defence, the Air Staff spoke with more confidence.

Each department gave particular attention to the eastern empire. The Admiralty brought together its recent studies on Empire naval co-operation and the possibility of sharing the costs of the Singapore base. The War Office also stressed the importance of seapower, but because of increasing difficulties it wanted self-sufficiency in the East and was looking not to the air, but to new rail communications – a Cape to Cairo railway; a line from Egypt to India, and a link to Australia by a railway through Burma and Malaya to Singapore.[6] The air staff now asserted that more use should be made of the air force 'as an independent arm used not as an auxiliary but as a substitute for naval and military forces'. Large areas of sea could be covered better by land-based squadrons than from expensive aircraft carriers. Air power made fleets vulnerable, even in defended harbours, therefore a chain of air bases might be more economical than naval bases.[7] A paper for the Dominions suggested that 'Aerial supremacy' was likely to become the 'dominating factor in all war' and, on coastal defence, it pointed out that heavy coastal artillery was expensive, of limited range and comparatively immobile. The torpedo bomber should provide sufficient deterrent and the Dominions might prefer to spend their money on aircraft rather than coast defence guns.[8] Little of this was written specifically for the Singapore base project, and most of the arguments were hotly denied by the Admiralty and the War Office.

But the air staff doctrine was clearly relevant to Singapore and around the relative merits of torpedo bombers and coastal defence guns controversy was to rage for more than a decade.

III

The air arm was given a very modest role in the early plans for Singapore. The ODC's main paper, prepared for the 1921 Imperial Conference, had only general comments on the defences, and noted that the existing batteries covering Singapore Harbour were designed to deter a squadron of light cruisers and a raiding party of up to 2000 men. The new naval base would also need an air base for aircraft assisting 'in the defence of the island and fleet anchorage' and for servicing planes of the Fleet Air Arm.[9] The Air Ministry envisaged a two-squadron contribution. The first stage would involve a flight of Bristol fighters, a flight of seaplane spotters and a repair unit; each of these would later be doubled to squadron strength. Accommodation for them would cost £337,000. This compared with the War Office estimates of £1¼ million for defences and the Admiralty's absurdly optimistic first estimate of £2,057,000 for the docks. When it came to site selection, the War Office suggested that an air officer should join the Committee so that 'aerial considerations of all kinds' could be given 'due weight *ab initio*'.[10] The RAF representative on the sites committee was Wing Commander F. E. T. Hewlett, who suggested Sarangong Harbour for a seaplane base and Jurong (in the west of the island) for the aerodrome. Neither was chosen and the first air base was at Seletar, three miles southeast of the dockyard site[11] (see Map 3, page 26).

If the air force was accorded a modest role, the question of the main deterrent led to controversy between the War Office and Admiralty. Cavan, the CIGS, wanted Singapore to have the heaviest type of gun available.[12] The Military Operations Directorate also insisted that troops would be needed to garrison the southern part of Johore,[13] but this view later got discarded in the debate about the guns.

Coast artillery was conceived in three dimensions. Heavy guns, 12" or 15" with a range of 40,000 yards, were intended to deter battleships. Medium guns, 7.5" or 9.2", could deal with light cruisers and other vessels, and light guns, 4.7" or 6", were for closer combat, especially in case of night raids. Beach defences would also require two-pounder pom poms to counter coastal motor launches. The War Office's first proposals for Singapore in June 1923 were for two pairs of 15" guns (at the eastern point of the island and to the west of the town), four pairs of medium guns, and five pairs of 6" guns, plus searchlights, anti-aircraft guns and beach batteries (see Map 6).[14] The naval staff rejected this as totally inadequate. The Director of the Gunnery Division of the Admiralty argued that if ten Japanese battleships were to attack Singapore, each firing one round per minute from their ten 15" or 16" guns, the defences would undergo a bombardment of 100 rounds per minute. A pair of 15" guns could return fire at the rate of two rounds per minute and, in face of a smokescreen, they could not spot their targets without local air superiority. The Director of Artillery had asserted that shore batteries had 'no chance whatever' against a moving fleet. The 15" guns must be numerous enough to keep a hostile fleet out of range. Four 15" were not enough.[15] The Admiralty had plenty of surplus 1914–18 vintage guns of this calibre available for adaptation.

By 1923, when the Cabinet authorised money for preparatory work on the dockyard, the defences were only at the study stage. The air force was given the minor role of reconnaissance and artillery spotting; the army and navy agreed on the nature but not the size of the main deterrent; the army was unsure, as yet, whether to face south or north. The approximate estimate of capital costs, at the time of the Cabinet's decision, well illustrates this situation: Admiralty £12,600,000, War Office £1¼ million (irrespective of the costs of the garrison), and Air Ministry £300,000–£400,000.[16] Before trying to resolve its difficulties the War Office awaited the results of the reconnaissances in Singapore and Malaya undertaken in the second half of 1923.

IV

In the interval before the reconnaissance reports were available, and during the hiatus caused by the Labour Government's cancellation in 1924, the air staff began to feel that time was on their side. Planning for the defences depended on the estimated scale of attack. In 1922 Singapore had been rated the most vulnerable port in the Commonwealth, liable to attack by long-range bombardment, to other attacks by warships or block ships, to attacks from submarines, and by landing parties, but not by aircraft.[17] Over the

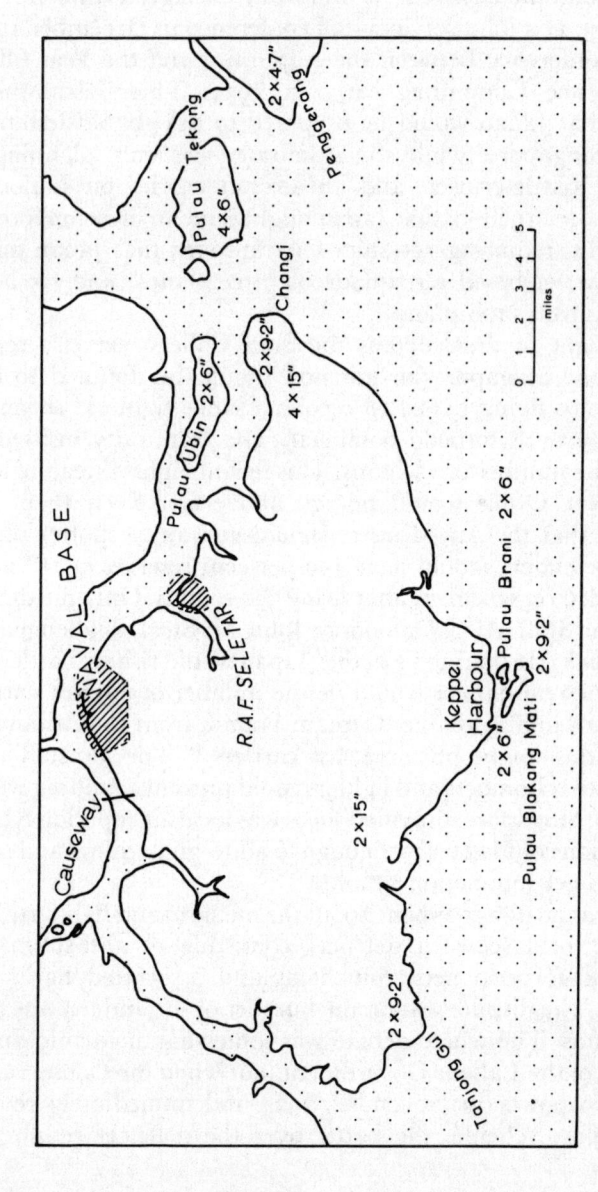

MAP 6. The first coastal artillery proposals (1923). In 1926 the central battery of 15" guns was changed to Blakang Mati; three were authorised in 1926, only to be suspended in 1928

next year detailed aspects of the likely scale of attack emerged during a combined exercise at the Staff College, Camberley, in March 1923; at a joint services staff conference in December 1923; and at a conference between the Admiralty and the War Office Coast Defence Committee early in 1924. These assumptions emerged: that Japan would be prepared to risk six battleships to bombard Singapore, while the Admiralty was only planning to have three battle-cruisers and an aircraft carrier on station at Singapore after 1928–9; that Japan might send an invasion force of two divisions, requiring 100 ships for transport; that Japan might use nine carrier-based air squadrons (162 planes) and six land-based squadrons (108 planes).

In the light of these details the Staff College exercise report suggested the Singapore air garrison should be doubled to four squadrons (10 flying boats, 18 reconnaissance fighters, 18 single-seater fighters, 18 torpedo bombers). The Admiralty insisted on doubling the number of 15″ guns. This meant eight instead of four, but the War Office would not go above six. Even then they demanded that the Air Ministry should guarantee spotter planes and that defenders should have 100 per cent reserves of 15″ guns, which needed replacement after firing 300 rounds. Only the deputy Chief of Air Staff, Air Commodore John M. Steel, challenged the scale of attack. He doubted whether Japan would risk six battleships and said the real danger would be the number of aircraft carriers which Japan had available. Captain Pound, from the Admiralty, suggested this might be three fast carriers.[18] The air staff were convinced that bombers and fighters could prevent a landing within 100 miles of Singapore, provided there was local air superiority; that no expedition could get close enough to allow guns, mines and other defences to get into action at all.[19]

There was no disagreement about the medium and light artillery, nor about local seaward defences consisting of anti-submarine booms, anti-torpedo nets, minefields and associated lights and indicators. The dispute was on the number of (or, indeed, the need for) 15″ guns. The whole debate was somewhat academic during the tenure of the Labour Government, but when the Conservatives returned to power in November 1924 and immediately revived the Singapore scheme, the battle over the defences resumed in earnest.

V

The doctrine of 'substitution' now found a powerful ally in Winston Churchill, who saw it as a means of economising. Writing about Singapore to Sir Samuel Hoare, the new Secretary of State for Air, on 12 December 1924, he suggested

> the best defence even now – and how much more in ten years time – against a landing would be by aeroplanes. Surely the aeroplane side of this problem requires re-examination.... Further, I am by no means sure that heavy bombing machines might not be a substitute for the two great batteries of guns it is proposed to mount. If so, how much better to have this cost represented in mobile air squadrons rather than tied up forever to one spot in two heavy batteries.[20]

Trenchard was delighted. He told Hoare that the Singapore question reacted on all air policy throughout the Empire and that Churchill's letter embraced things he had had in mind for six years.[21] Squadron-Leader Peter Drummond, of the Plans Division, drew up three possible configurations for the defences. If the garrison and beach defences were so strong that a surprise landing was impossible, torpedo bombers would not be necessary; if there were sufficient bombers and submarines available, they could reduce the garrison; if the heavy guns were sufficient to deter bombardment, there was no need for bombers; if there were sufficient bombers, there was no need for 15″ guns. Scheme C was virtually the current proposal. Scheme A, which dispensed with 15″ guns, would give the greatest security for the money, but presupposed the existence of squadrons not available in 1925.[22] (See table, p. 76.)

The debate revolved around the relative merits of 15″ guns and torpedo bombers. It moved up from the service staffs to the COS Committee and eventually needed the intervention of the politicians in the CID and Cabinet. This meant that at the same time as Churchill was using the CID and the Curzon Committee to challenge the basic assumptions of naval strategy as well as the details of the warship construction programme, Trenchard sought, through the COS Committee, to delay a decision about expenditure

	Scheme A	Scheme B	Scheme C
Navy:	Submarines and light craft	Subs and light craft	Subs and light craft
Army:	Medium guns Garrison	6 × 15″ guns Medium guns Larger garrison Mobile armament	8 × 15″ guns Greatly increased garrison Mobile armament
Air Force:	10 flying boats (for long-range reconnaissance in 200 m. semi-circle) 30 torpedo bombers 18 fighters 18 spotters	10 flying boats 20 torpedo bombers 18 fighters 18 spotters	18 fighters 18 spotters
	76 aircraft	66 aircraft	36 aircraft

on 15″ guns. This debate lasted from February to July 1925. It became bitter and repetitive and a clear alignment emerged, with Trenchard opposed by Beatty and Cavan.

Trenchard argued that air power was cheaper, more mobile, had longer range than guns and that the Japanese fleet would make a good target. Four RAF units (a squadron of fighters, two squadrons of torpedo bombers and a flight of spotters) would be much cheaper than the 15″ guns. These aircraft would fly out to Singapore from Iraq or India in the case of an emergency. Cavan's case was that Singapore needed as 'complete protection' as possible. Spotter planes were certainly needed for the guns, and fighters to protect them, but bombers would be a 'luxury'. He also eliminated the need for a garrison in Johore as the GOC in Malaya had reported that attack from this direction was unlikely because of the terrain. Army reinforcements of two Brigades could reach Singapore from India in 12½ days, and would now only be needed to quell 'internal disorders' and deter hostile landings. Beatty stuck out forcefully for the 15″ guns. They would provide a 'complete deterrent', make Singapore 'absolutely safe'. Beside this Trenchard's scheme was quite untried. His squadrons would not be stationed permanently in Singapore, so would provide no deterrent. If Japan attacked using four carrier-based squadrons the RAF would not even have air superiority. Trenchard obstinately maintained that they could save a lot of money, at 'slight risk' by adopting his scheme, but he could not say definitely where his bombers would be stationed. Trenchard was inarticulate, ungrammatical and vaguely visionary at the best of times. Now his rather feeble defence of this evasiveness was that naval strategy had had centuries to evolve; the air force was only in its formative phase. Beatty said he should produce a 'concrete plan'; Cavan felt the CID should settle the matter – on the basis of principle, not costs.[23]

Trenchard appealed to the Prime Minister in a long memorandum on 15 July 1925. The air force, he wrote, was still regarded as a counter to air attack – something *in addition* to conventional defences. He argued that air power should be employed to relieve the other services of some of their responsibilities and so save money. The navy had traditionally stressed its universal mobility. Aircraft could operate, from a chain of bases, in the same way, but against armies too. 'Should we . . . not . . . adopt the Naval policy for the Air rather than the Army policy?' Singapore was a vital stage in the development of air power and, as the Foreign Office did not envisage a war with Japan for ten years, the problem was not urgent. If the defences had to be ready in three years, he could not guarantee the right aircraft. But they could await new developments. Aircraft were cheaper than guns, which represented 'capital locked up'. His plea was that they should spend no money on 15" guns, and await developments.[24]

The question came before the Cabinet's Committee on Singapore on 27 July 1925 when it was agreed that Hankey should set out comparative tables of costs. Then on 15 October, with Baldwin, the Prime Minister, in the Chair, the Committee lent political weight to Trenchard's side. Churchill spoke for the advantages of substituting air for guns, with which Cavan completely disagreed. Hoare accepted the Foreign Office assessment that war was unlikely and felt they could be taking little risk if they experimented at Singapore. If, in four or five years, bombing aircraft did not improve, they could then instal the guns. Amery reminded the committee that it had always been British policy to favour mobile forces, so he inclined to favour aircraft. Beatty seemed to be cornered. He protested that Trenchard never produced any concrete plans: 'He had merely presented a somewhat nebulous scheme'. Finally, a compromise was made. The local seaward defences (booms, nets and mines) and the medium, light and anti-aircraft artillery defences were approved. Expenditure on 15″ guns was postponed until the following summer to give the Air Ministry an opportunity to produce an alternative.[25]

Thus in 1926, as the Admiralty tried to get its 'truncated scheme' for the dockyard accepted before the Imperial Conference, the Air Ministry was given its chance. It was particularly concerned with time factors; the problem of getting air reinforcements out to Singapore, and finding suitable aircraft. The Admiralty had specified a period before relief of 42 days. This meant that as a Japanese invasion fleet could arrive after 10 days, Singapore would have to hold out for 32 days. But Beatty had now to admit that a warning of Japanese preparations might take 8 days rather than a previously anticipated 24 hours. The air staff found this 'ridiculous' and also wondered why the 'Japanese armada' could cover 2600 miles in 10 days while the British fleet (unhindered by transports) wanted 42 days to cover 6000 miles from Malta.[26] As regards aircraft a 'new type of torpedo bomber' would possibly be ready by 1929. This was the Hawker *Horsley* bi-plane, which could fly for 4 hours with a 2000 lb torpedo at 110 m.p.h., or for 5 hours, carrying 900 lb bombs at 120 m.p.h., and could cover 700–800 miles with reserve fuel in place of bombs in transit.[27]

In spite of all its studies, however, the air staff fluffed its opportunity. When Trenchard sent his proposals to Hankey on 19 May 1926, he admitted that it was impossible to produce 'a concrete scheme' at that time. Unforseen modifications in aircraft and control systems were likely and he thought it better to wait and reconsider Singapore's defences in two or three years' time. All he could suggest was the four-squadron force and the development of an air reinforcement route from Iraq and India to Singapore. This meant building new airfields at Akyab, Rangoon, Mergui and Victoria Point (in Burma) and Alor Star and Kuala Lumpur (in Malaya) at the cost of £200,000. Reinforcement times would be Basra to Karachi four days, Karachi to Agra two days, Agra to Calcutta two days, and Calcutta to Singapore six days[28] (see Map 7).

Beatty jumped on this weakness. This was no alternative scheme of defence, he declared, but merely 'a scheme for air reinforcements'. He did not think any Admiralty in the world would be deterred from attacking Singapore by the knowledge that bombers were stationed there. Under Trenchard's scheme they would not

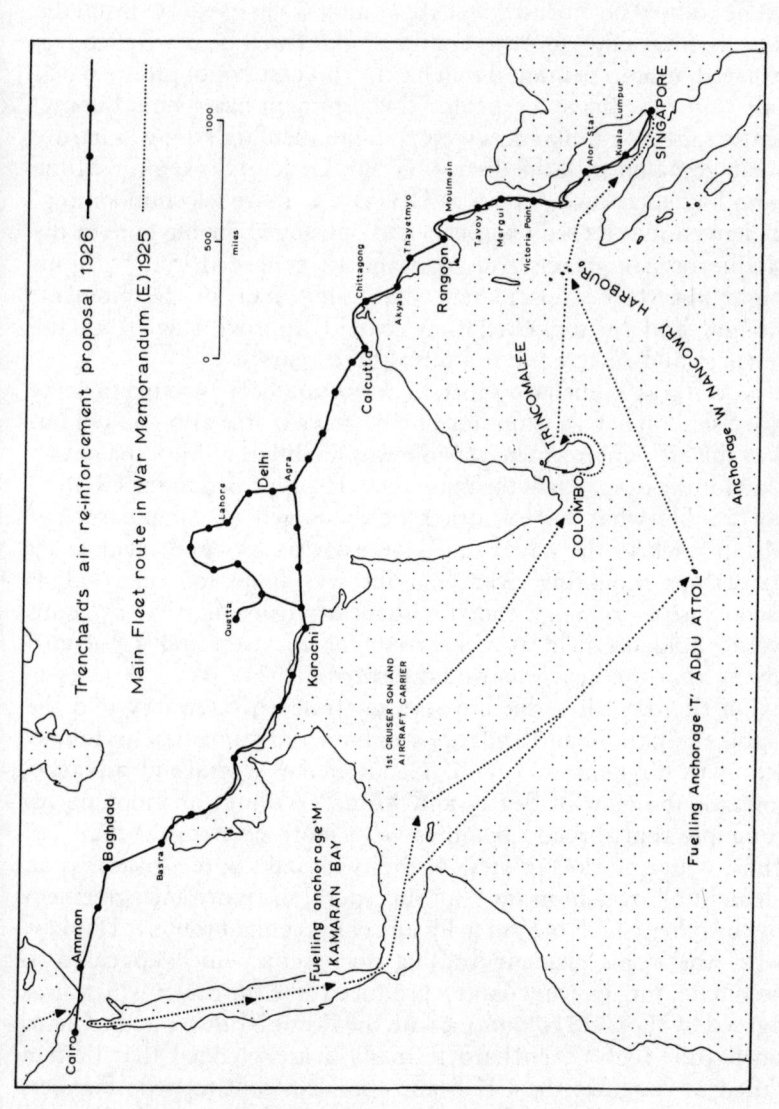

MAP 7. The main fleet and air force routes

even be there, whereas no Admiralty would contemplate attacking in the face of 15″ guns. Air defences might be feasible in the future, but he wanted no more delays as it would take five years to instal the guns. By that time, torpedo bombers might well be more effective, declared an unrepentant Trenchard, who cast doubt on the naval staff's time factors and repeated the argument based on economy. Beatty said their differences were so fundamental that it was hardly worth going on with the discussion. But General Sir George Milne (who had succeeded Cavan as CIGS) was more accommodating. He agreed that torpedo bombers had outranged the big guns in the Mediterranean exercises in 1924 and he conceded that 15″ guns might lose their value in ten years' time. Not for the moment, though, and he suggested they should approve stage I of the defences and review the rest after three years.

Now it was Trenchard's turn to be obstinate. He wanted to delay a decision on *any* 15″ guns for one more year. He also pointed out that the air reinforcement scheme was no different from the navy's plan for the despatch of the main fleet. He appealed to the CIGS to say frankly what sort of attack he envisaged on Singapore, but Milne stuck to the naval staff view that six 15″ guns against six battleships mounting over 60 guns was none too many. This inconclusive exchange ended with Beatty asserting that 15″ guns would hold the field as a deterrent for 20 years and Trenchard saying that the next war would disprove it.[29]

On the day after this impasse, 23 June 1926, Amery told the Cabinet about the FMS gift of £2 million and immediately Hankey wrote to Trenchard. Could he not make 'a graceful advance' towards the view of Beatty and Milne? Without abandoning his principle that torpedo bombers were more economical than 15″ guns, could he not, in view of the 'windfall', agree to accept an element of 'over-insurance' at Singapore, in return for agreement by the other Chiefs of Staff to his air reinforcement route?[30] Hankey, who was in his element drafting documents which appeared to reconcile the irreconcilable, produced the formula which was agreed by the COS committee with the Prime Minister in the Chair, on 6 July 1926. Trenchard formally acknowledged that he had failed to convince the CIGS and the CNS that torpedo bombers were better than 15″ guns. He would not oppose a decision on Stage I of the defences (including three 15″ guns), provided there was a 'fresh and unprejudiced investigation' before a decision on Stage II. Meanwhile, the air staff would regroup its squadrons, to make air reinforcement feasible, and the chain of airfields between Calcutta and Singapore was authorised. Beatty was ill at the time of this compromise, but had appealed to Trenchard from his sick bed. Admiral Field, who deputised at the COS committee, spoke appreciatively at the meeting about Trenchard's attitude.[31] The compromise was accepted by the Cabinet on 3 August 1926.

VI

Trenchard told his biographer that the 1926 compromise was the 'worst blunder' of his career: 'I was too trusting'.[32] Yet, in an unexpected fashion, he *did* see a delay in expenditure on the guns. It came about, not because of his advocacy, but from second thoughts in the War Office. Even before the compromise over Stage I the new CIGS, had had his misgivings about the estimated scale of attack and the standard of defences planned.[33] In March 1927 the Army Council commissioned Lieutenant-General Sir Webb Gillman, Inspector-General of Artillery, to visit Singapore, inspect the proposed gun and searchlight sites, consider the layout of barrack accommodation, and study plans for magazines and ordnance depots.

Gillman had to spend over three months in Singapore before returning in July 1927, because of the controversy over the Straits Settlements' 20 per cent military contribution, and the Governors' refusal to release any more land to the War Office. Gillman was assisted by Colonel L. N. Malan, Chief Engineer, Malaya, and Lieutenant-Colonel R. F. Lock, Secretary of the Ordnance Committee. Their main technical recommendations concerned the resiting of certain guns protecting the eastern approaches of the naval base. They also suggested that, in view of local conditions such as the enervating climate, endemic malaria and venereal diseases among the local population and a high level of 'murders, robberies and strikes', the garrison should not be scattered in isolated detachments but concentrated in high-standard barracks, with good amusement facilities. More significantly, however, Gillman raised the question of whether the artillery proposals were not too lavish. He considered that guns would be sufficient to deter a hostile Asian power and that once the air squadrons and the fleet arrived Singapore would be extremely difficult to capture. Meanwhile there was a probability that the defences already authorised might be found 'unnecessarily strong'; he suggested that before any money was spent the 'future potentialities of the sister Services' should be carefully reviewed.[34]

The CIGS took the matter to the COS Committee on 24 November 1927. With Gillman in attendance, he admitted that the defences had been planned in watertight compartments, that the War Office plans were 'perhaps almost super-perfect', and he sought a re-examination of the scheme. By now Beatty had retired and his successor, Admiral Sir Charles Madden, who had recently delayed the dockyard completion date by one year, did not object. Gillman said a more mobile form of defence would be more economical, thinking, specifically, of submarines. Madden, however, could not guarantee more than six to eight submarines at sea at any one time and they would work out of Hong Kong. The CIGS suggested that a subcommittee, chaired by Sir Webb Gillman, should reconsider the defence plans in the light of the availability of submarines and the speed with which aircraft could be got to Singapore.

Trenchard was persuaded by Hankey not to reopen the old controversy, and he was conciliatory. He said he had never looked at the matter simply as 'one of Guns v Air', but of co-operation between the air force, the land defences and the Fleet Air Arm. He agreed that in the heat of the old controversy they had 'rather wandered off the right track'. He would not go back on his promise over Stage I, but he would welcome further investigations, including the general issue of defences.[35] Madden made a brief attempt to restrict the re-examination to the question of whether the existing plans were adequate or excessive, but Trenchard and the CIGS now got together, and Gillman was tactful enough to avoid the old controversy.

The Webb Gillman Committee was appointed at a deliberately high level. Gillman was now Master-General of Ordnance, Rear-Admiral Pound was assistant-CNS and Air Vice-Marshal Cyril Newall was deputy-CAS. They were specifically enjoined to consider the role of all three services. It proved a salutary exercise as many of the assumptions of the past five years had to be abandoned. The naval staff indicated that plans for the stationing of a battle-cruiser squadron at Singapore, which Beatty had mooted since 1923, would be dropped. One flight of flying boats had recently reached Singapore; more were to follow to make up a squadron. Overland attack from Malaya was now definitely ruled out: the main dangers were seen as bombardment from the sea and landings by raiding parties on Singapore Island. But the main army reinforcements were still to come from India and the political situation there, during the visits of the Simon Commission, raised doubts about their availability. Apart from this, the committee suggested that Stage I (three 15" guns) should be spread over five years to 1932-3, and that advantage should be taken of any redistribution of the fleet or the air force to save expenditure.[36]

Webb Gillman's Committee (and, it might be said, the retirement of Cavan and Beatty) briefly restored harmony to the COS Committee and it seemed that inter-service co-operation in the defences was assured. But Trenchard (also about to retire) had never abandoned the principles he had compromised on in 1926. That meant a full reconsideration of the air role at Stage II in five years' time. But in 1928 a completely unexpected hitch appeared.

The War Office conducted a series of coastal defence artillery trials at Malta and Portsmouth, which revealed serious technical and operational deficiencies in the type of guns they wished to instal at Singapore. The trials were the first attempt to gather up-to-date material as a basis for planning coastal defence policy, but the 9.2" guns used in the trials dated from before the 1914-18 war. At Portsmouth they had two series of shoots. In the first, 42 rounds were fired in 30 minutes, the nearest falling within 10 yards of the target; in the second series, 30 rounds in 39 minutes, none fell within 50 yards of a ship at 18,000 yards range. A battleship could have fired over 100 rounds from a pair of 15" guns in the time and from a battleship with eight 15" guns, the actual rate of fire would have been four times as great. There clearly had to be technical improvements. Gillman, who later reported on the dismal showing, suggested that improvements such as mechanical loading and elevating of the guns would eliminate crew fatigue. Shells with better ballistic and armour-piercing properties were needed. The attempt to achieve bull's-eye shooting was 'obviously quite unreliable' and the army would have to adopt the naval system of surrounding the target by concentrated salvoes from several guns. All this would take time and money.[37]

Meanwhile the situation was so serious that the Secretary of State for War took the matter to the CID before Gillman's full analysis was ready. There was obviously reason to doubt the capability of the guns, so Sir Laming Worthington-Evans asked that all expenditure on 9.2" and 15" guns for Singapore should be deferred until further trials had been made. Trenchard jumped at this. He said he had been waiting for this situation for five years and asked to see the report. The CIGS said it was not yet fit to be circulated and the War Office did not know what was wrong with the guns. Churchill, who had in his career headed each service department, could not resist twitting them for having secrets from each other. The CID had no alternative but to suspend expenditure on the guns until 1929–30, to which the Cabinet agreed on 19 December 1928.[38] Trenchard's blood was up, and another round in the contest 'Guns v Air' seemed likely. Moreover, before the details of the report of the 1928 gun trials became available the 1929 general election led to the second Labour Government. In fact Sir Webb Gillman's report was discussed at the very meeting when Ramsay MacDonald had his first brief introduction to the COS subcommittee on 11 June 1929.[39]

Trenchard (possibly hopeful of the new regime) tried to reopen the question. Under the compromise of 1926, of course, the 'unprejudiced re-examination' was due to take place before Stage II of the defences, *after* the installation of the first three 15″ guns. But Trenchard now gave a long restatement of his views, claiming that the Air Ministry had made a lot of progress since 1926. The air reinforcement route was nearing completion, a squadron of reconnaissance flying-boats was already stationed at Singapore and a squadron of *Horsley* torpedo bombers was forming. He claimed that recent trials indicated that bombers were ten times more effective than guns. He did not want to provoke controversy, but he wanted the question reopened. Milne, who had already proved himself less dogmatic than Cavan, admitted that the Army Council did not relish its coast defence responsibilities; if the navy were prepared to accept Trenchard's scheme, the army would happily bow out. Singapore was going to be costly and it was an unhealthy spot for the garrison. Trenchard called this a most important statement but the meeting was inconclusive and the COS adjourned to await the results of further gun and bombing trials.

Before this frustrating meeting (and again in writing afterwards) Sir Maurice Hankey put another possibility for compromise to Trenchard. Pending the resolution of the long-standing dispute, why not offer to take responsibility for the defences temporarily? The CNS, now faced with the prospect of an undefended floating dock, would hardly turn the offer down. Squadron-Leader Slessor, of the Plans Division, was immediately attracted to the idea. Once a bomber squadron was established in Singapore the Air Ministry could 'present a *fait accompli*' in two or three years time when Stage II was examined. Trenchard agreed, and arrangements were made to despatch 36 squadron in 1930.[40] This minor compromise quietened the controversy for a time, but it flared up again, when Trenchard prepared his 'swan song' before retiring, which again made large claims for the general superiority of aircraft over artillery in coast defence.[41]

By this time, however, the Singapore base itself was under review. The Labour Government was planning major moves in naval disarmament and therefore the fate of the whole scheme once again hung in the balance.

5 'Slowed Down as Much as Possible', 1929–32

I

Soon after the accession of the second Labour Government in June 1929 the long-term significance of the Commonwealth stake in the Singapore base became evident. In 1924 the Dominions had been informed about Labour's suspension of the scheme, but Australian and New Zealand protests had made no difference. The Baldwin Government accepted money from Hong Kong, the Federated Malay States and New Zealand; approved the truncated scheme, and signed the Jackson contract. In all this there was the deliberate intention of incurring obligations which it would be hard to go back on. The Admiralty and the Colonial Office had eagerly encouraged the Empire gifts and pressed ahead, knowing that a general election was coming. Even if Labour won, there was now a good chance that the Singapore decision would be irreversible. Therefore, in spite of the tedious battle over Guns v Air and the subsequent suspension of expenditure on the big guns, construction of the dockyard had commenced and, by the end of 1928, the large floating dock, constructed at Wallsend-on-Tyne, arrived in the Johore Strait. (See Plates 19, 23, 27 and 32.)

II

In the general election of May 1929 Singapore was not a specific issue, but disarmament was. Baldwin and MacDonald both pledged themselves to the principle of disarmament and promised to respond to President Hoover's overtures for an Anglo-American naval agreement.[1] While the British voters went to the polls on 30 May, the American President, making a Memorial Day address at Arlington National Cemetery, called for warship reductions by the application of a 'rational yardstick with which to make reasonable comparisons'.[2] When he took office for a second time on 5 June 1929, Ramsay MacDonald immediately responded to the American initiative.

During the second half of 1929 he paid close attention to negotiations with General Dawes, the American envoy; he visited President Hoover in Washington in October, and invited the Washington treaty powers to attend a naval conference in London in January 1930.[3] It was in this context that doubts were again thrown on the wisdom of continuing at Singapore. Irrespective of finance or the guns, the Labour Government was expected to reconsider the Singapore base as part of their renewed bid for a disarmament treaty.

In anticipation of the new onslaught the Admiralty Board decided (on 3 June 1929 - the day Baldwin made up his mind to resign) to place on record its policy over the last four years. This was based on a 'one power standard'. Capital ships and aircraft carriers were governed by the Washington Treaty ratios, the number of other vessels by the need to protect the British Empire and secure a free passage for trade. All war preparations were based on the requirements for a war in the Far East. For this the Singapore base would be ready by 1937, and the main fleet was based in the Mediterranean for ease of passage to the Atlantic or the Far East. Warship construction not governed by the Washington ratios was directed towards achieving a strength of 70 cruisers, 144 destroyers, 72 submarines and 53 sloops. On disarmament policy the Admiralty stood by three principles: a preference for light 6″ gun cruisers as against heavy 8″ gun cruisers; a reduction in battleship size to 25,000 tons and 12″ guns, and the abolition of submarines. It also preferred a slow replacement programme to a building 'holiday', as it wanted to ensure the retention of industrial skills.[4]

The Labour Cabinet began its review of naval policy on 21 June 1929. MacDonald had already met General Dawes and started discussions about a possible agreement to extend the Washington treaty ratios to cruisers and other vessels. The Cabinet received a paper from the Admiralty giving current expenditure on warship construction and the Singapore base and the consequences likely from reductions in both. Of the £7¾ million 'truncated scheme', £700,000 had been spent by 31 March 1929 plus £930,000 on the construction and installation of the floating dock. Most of this money had come from the FMS. Even if the Government stopped the scheme, new expenditure was unavoidable. They would have to meet about £800,000 of contractor's commitments already made; £350,000 compensation to Jackson's for loss of contract, and £1,588,000 in repayments to the FMS, Hong Kong and New Zealand.[5] The Cabinet decided, immediately, that no outstanding tenders for the 1928/29 programme and none for 1929/30 would be let while naval policy was reviewed by a Fighting Services subcommittee, made up of the Prime Minister, the Chancellor of the Exchequer, Philip Snowden, the Foreign Secretary, Arthur Henderson, and the service ministers, Alexander (First Lord), Tom Shaw (War) and Lord Thomson (Air).

This committee met with the naval staff on 25 June and heard Admiral Madden explain the warship programme. When they next convened on 28 June, Hankey, the secretary, was excluded from the meeting, and no minutes were kept.[6] But the Committee worked fast, producing its first report on 6 July 1929. By suspending work on two cruisers, and cancelling two submarines and a submarine depot ship it suggested that the Government could save £1 million and also make a 'gesture of good faith' in international affairs.[7] Singapore needed further study, but MacDonald decided to inform the Dominions that the base was under review.[8]

A cautious explanation of what was happening was supplied to Stanley Bruce, the Australian Prime Minister, by his friend Richard G. Casey, the Australian External Affairs Liaison Officer, who had access to Cabinet papers in Hankey's office. He suggested that Bruce should request that changes affecting Australia should be discussed in the CID with an Australian representative present. Casey was not pessimistic. The Labour Government, was 'committed to doing something about Singapore, but there is reason to think they will not completely hamstring the Base but will be satisfied with face saving'.[9]

A possible formula was suggested to MacDonald the same day by Hankey, who, with his Royal Marines background, his Australian family connexions, and enthusiastic imperialism, had always strongly supported the Singapore strategy. He performed another masterly exercise in reconciling opposing views. These were, as he put it: the new Government's deep commitment to stopping the base for political and financial reasons; the Admiralty's desire for completion; Australia's and New Zealand's full acceptance of the scheme; the Hong Kong, New Zealand and Malay States contributions; War Office and Air Ministry interest in the defences;

Foreign Office concern about good relations with Japan, and the Colonial Office's concern for Malaya.

> What is desired is a scheme which, in the first place will fulfill the Government's promises; in the second place will achieve big economies, and in the third place will not outrage either Naval, Australian, New Zealand or Malay States opinion – bearing also in mind that on grounds of general policy – e.g. from the point of view of Unemployment especially – it is desirable to keep on the best possible terms with the Dominions in the South Pacific.

To make a clean sweep at Singapore would be difficult, as the floating dock was already there and to move it would be costly. But they could reduce Singapore to the status of a floating base by dropping the graving dock. This would require compensation to the contractors, but as a floating base would require some shore works, a contract for these might be acceptable as compensation. The Government could then announce the reduction of Singapore to a 'nucleus, a mere floating base'; the navy could then be sure at least of a floating dock; money would be saved; Japan satisfied. The COS would have to reconsider the defences and Trenchard's air scheme might be adopted provisionally, but the future of the defences would depend on the size of battleships determined in the disarmament negotiations.[10] This proposal was a radical one from the naval staff point of view but MacDonald appears to have considered it seriously. 'Put in a Singapore Jacket', he wrote,[11] and it seems he took it to the Fighting Services Committee meeting on 11 July. Again no minutes were taken, but on the same day the Prime Minister asked the COS how the defences would be affected if Singapore became a floating base.[12] Not at all – came the candid answer of the COS – the defences depended on the estimated scale of attack, which did not change, even if Singapore was reduced from a refit base to a rest and refuel base.

The service chiefs remained divided. Madden wanted to press on with preparing the gun sites while the War Office tried to solve its technical problems with the guns. Though he welcomed the impending arrival of a torpedo bomber squadron, he did not think it would add materially to the deterrent. Milne went as far as to say he would welcome the whole question of the defences being 'reconsidered afresh', possibly with a new CIGS with an open mind on the subject.[13] The basic decision, however, was out of their hands. The

Cabinet Committee, not the COS committee, would recommend the Singapore policy.

III

As was only to be expected, the Australian and New Zealand Governments began to express concern and wanted discussions in the CID. They also tried to concert their efforts by exchanging protest cables. Australia was well served by Casey, in London, who urged Bruce to take a 'conciliatory attitude'. Knowing, no doubt, about Hankey's proposed compromise, he hinted that 'total abandonment' was unlikely and that the Government wanted to do enough to make a gesture for Parliament.[14] MacDonald had immediately informed the Australian and New Zealand Prime Ministers about the cancellation of the two cruisers and his talks with the American Ambassador but he said the review of the Singapore base would not be finished before Parliament adjourned for the summer recess. The matter was to come before the CID on 25 July, when the Australian and New Zealand High Commissioners would be present.[15] Casey, sending his own gloss to Canberra, said it was practically certain that both the floating dock and the graving dock would be retained, and added that the Dominions were 'largely responsible', though the question of compensation to the contractor had played its part. He hoped Bruce would make an 'appreciative reference' to the British Government's attitude.[16] Not having Casey's entrée to the Cabinet secretariat, Parr, the New Zealand High Commissioner, took a more alarmist view, and went to see MacDonald, who promised the 'fullest consultation' with New Zealand.[17]

The manner in which MacDonald fulfilled his assurance became controversial. To start with he announced the Government's firm intention of achieving a naval accord with the United States, as a preliminary to a wider naval treaty, on 24 July 1929 – *before* the crucial CID meeting. But, when asked in the House of Commons whether a decision had been made about Singapore MacDonald replied vaguely that in the 'large survey, that has been included'. He read this statement to the CID next day and gave the provisional conclusions of the Fighting Services Committee about Singapore. These were that the financial savings from a complete stoppage would be comparatively small so the Jackson contract would continue; that while the services disagreed over the defences, the original scheme would stand, but that, for a period of at least two years, a bomber squadron from Britain should be based at Singapore.

During the discussion Parr of New Zealand expressed the greatest concern about the cut in cruiser strength in view of the size of Japan's fleet. He was glad the graving dock would continue. Sir Granville Ryrie, the Australian High Commissioner, reminded the committee that while Australia had not contributed to the base, its 1924 naval programme was 'regarded definitely as a complement of the Singapore scheme'. MacDonald assured them that the Dominions would not be 'left in the dark' about Singapore.[18] This assurance did not convince the Prime Minister of New Zealand, Sir Joseph Ward, who soon protested about the short time often given for consultation and reminded MacDonald that in defence and foreign affairs the United Kingdom Government was in a real sense 'the agent or trustee of His Majesty's other Governments'.[19]

Although the Labour Government had found that it could not stop the main dockyard construction, it had not yet determined on a clear policy for Singapore. In answer to the query as to whether the new dockyard could be converted to commercial use, the Admiralty produced a paper on 16 September 1929 giving details of essential expenditure necessary to make the graving dock usable, such as a caisson gate and cranes, and an indication of where savings of about £300,000 could be made. Conversion to a commercial port would, however, require expenditure of an equivalent amount. This was referred by the Cabinet, on 25 September, to the Fighting Services Committee, which also received reports from the War Office and Air Ministry.[20] On 22 October, while MacDonald was in the United States visiting President Hoover, the Committee finally formulated a policy on the Singapore base. Although the graving dock would have to be completed, the committee felt that, in view of the forthcoming naval conference in London in 1930, it would be 'indefensible' to go ahead in complete disregard of possible changes in the size of capital ships. It recommended, therefore, that the work at Singapore should be 'slowed down as much as possible'; that all work which could be suspended should be suspended, and that no new work should be begun. This was agreed by the Cabinet on 6 November, after MacDonald had returned from the United States, and was announced in Parliament on 13 November.[21]

Behind the scenes there was a rather angry exchange with New

Zealand. The Dominion Government was only 'consulted' by telegram on the day before MacDonald's statement to Parliament, and the acting Prime Minister, Sir Thomas Wilford, protested that what seemed to be 'a distinct change of policy' over Singapore had been made without consulting the Dominion. This was a serious charge and was actually discussed by the British Cabinet, which made a slight rewording of MacDonald's statement to Parliament to the effect that the work would be slowed down – pending the results of the five-power naval conference.[22] But the Dominion Government was not appeased since Alexander then told Parliament that the Dominions had been consulted. If *notification* was regarded as the equivalent of *consultation*, cabled Wilford, he could only dissent; his Government could be 'seriously embarrassed' by questions in the Dominion Parliament if they were left ignorant of British policy changes.[23]

In Australia, as usual, there was less alarm, mainly because of Casey's behind-the-scenes knowledge. He assured his Prime Minister that, while Singapore might be discussed informally at the London Naval Conference, it was improbable that the scale of construction would be modified. He considered that the whole question was 'politically awkward' for the British Government; that a possible agreed reduction in the size of battleships was being used as a peg with which to impress Labour party supporters and foreign nations of the Government's sincerity about disarmament. He did not believe they had any hopes of avoiding the completion of the naval base.[24]

While MacDonald concentrated on the preparations for the London Naval Conference the rather vague decision that the work at Singapore should be 'slowed down as much as possible' had to be absorbed by the interested parties. A conference held in the Admiralty on 18 November 1929 considered what actual works they could 'slow down' or 'suspend', but ended up by deciding to prepare the 1930 estimates as if the base was continuing and amend later as necessary. In practice, completion of the Jackson contract meant finishing the graving dock and part of the wharves. But it did not include a caisson to close its entrance, nor an electrical generating station, workshops, roads, railways, capstans and crane tracks.[25] In other words it would not be usable.

Questions continued to be asked in Parliament about whether the Dominions had really been consulted. The New Zealand High Commissioner felt his government should capitalise on the disquiet in Britain and keep up its protests. A British civil servant from the Foreign Office, Philip Nicols, who was working on exchange in the Prime Minister's department in Wellington, was sufficiently alarmed to send a confidential summary to the Dominions Office of local press opinion, which, he said, emphasised the Singapore question from a purely New Zealand point of view, which was 'unusual'. He might have been surprised to know that his letter went up to Cabinet.[26] In Australia, however, Casey's careful prompting of the Government's response was reinforced after the October general election by the return of a Labor Government. This meant that the British Government's actions were even more sympathetically received. The new Prime Minister, James Scullin, told the House of Representatives on 21 November 1929 that he was assured that no drastic policy changes would be made without proper consultation.[27] Back in London, Ramsay MacDonald told the House of Commons, somewhat speciously, that the 'slowing down' announcement was not a *change of policy*; it was something done pending the naval conference. Therefore it had not been necessary to consult the Dominions, who would, of course, be fully consulted before 'any decisions were taken affecting the scheme as a whole'.[28]

IV

Although the decision to slow down work at Singapore caused some anxiety in the Pacific Dominions and exercised the attention of the relevant British departments, MacDonald's main preoccupation was Anglo-American relations and naval disarmament. An attempt to extend Anglo-American parity to auxiliary vessels had floundered at Geneva in 1927 upon the British insistence on 70 cruisers, 25 for the fleet and 45 for trade protection. This, combined with the Anglo-French 'compromise' of 1928, when the British conceded parity in 8" cruisers, led to growing Anglo-American ill-will. In February 1929 the United States naval bill, authorising fifteen 8" cruisers and an aircraft carrier in three years, seemed to presage a new naval race. It was a race Britain could not afford, hence the willingness of Conservative and Labour leaders to respond favourably to Hoover's overtures. Before invitations were issued to the Washington treaty powers to attend the London naval conference MacDonald accepted the principle of overall Anglo-American 'parity'. He reduced the British cruiser requirement from 70 to 50, and traded United States superiority in 8" gun cruisers for a large British superiority in 6" gun cruisers.[29]

The Naval Conference met between 21 January and 22 April 1930. During this period the British, American and Japanese politicians achieved, against the wishes of their professional advisers, a considerable measure of disarmament, which was embodied in the London Naval Treaty. The three powers agreed to scrap within the next 18 months sufficient battleships to reach the Washington treaty targets of 15:15:9 which had originally been timed for 1942. By a building 'holiday' they would delay replacements until after 1936. Britain and the USA agreed to a total of 15 and 18 heavy cruisers respectively. Japan would only adhere to the treaty in return for an improvement in the Washington ratio to 5:5:3½ (or 10:10:7 as they put it – that is 70 per cent of the largest rival) and equality in submarines. The US agreed to delay the construction of three heavy cruisers until 1935 if Japan would accept a total of twelve. This meant that during the currency of the treaty the Japanese would in fact have 70 per cent of the American heavy cruiser strength. They also received 70 per cent in light cruisers and parity in submarines.[30]

	British Commonwealth	*USA*	*Japan*
Capital ships (WNT targets after 18 months)	15 525,000 tons	15 525,000 tons	9 315,000 tons
Heavy cruisers – guns over 6.1"	15 146,800 tons	18 180,000 tons	12 108,400 tons
Light cruisers – guns less than 6.1"	192,200 tons	143,500 tons	100,450 tons
Destroyers	150,000 tons	150,000 tons	105,800 tons
Submarines	52,700 tons	52,700 tons	52,700 tons

The effect on the British total (which included the Dominions' vessels) was a major diminution of superiority over Japan. As the New Zealand Naval Staff's summary clearly noted, the British margin over Japan was reduced as shown below.[31]

	Before 1930 Treaty	After Treaty
Battleships	10	6
Cruisers	26	17 (3 heavy, 14 light)
Destroyers	53	39

A naval race with the United States had been avoided and some additional economies had been achieved, at the cost of a considerable weakening *vis-à-vis* the one naval power against which active preparations for war were made.

V

Once the naval treaty had been signed, preparations began for the Imperial Conference planned for October 1930. Lord Parmoor, the Lord President of the Council and one of the leading pacifists in the Cabinet, felt that the naval treaty gave an opportunity for reconsidering Singapore. In view of the reduction of British battleship strength from 20 to 15 and the battleship building 'holiday' until 1936, he wondered if they could not stop developing Singapore as a base for battleships.[32] Passfield, the Dominions Secretary, insisted, however, that the Dominions must be properly consulted this time.[33] And when the Cabinet's Fighting Services Committee considered Singapore on 22 May they had to admit that the Dominions' stake in the base could not be ignored. If the Government had been 'quite free' they believed the right policy was 'to abandon the base forthwith'. But the committee could not get away from the fact that one of the Dominions (New Zealand) was strongly against abandonment, and it realised that any decision could be reversed by a later British government (as in 1924), which would only add to the cost. The 'slowed down' programme would have to continue until arrangements could be made at the Imperial Conference to get a 'definite and permanent settlement'. The Cabinet approved this policy at the end of May 1930.[34]

Casey wrote to Scullin in Canberra that it was a matter of 'marking time' until a full and final discussion at the Imperial Conference. He added that he had learnt, privately, that of the £2,230,000 spent on the Singapore base to 1930, no less than £2,100,000 had come from the Empire gifts, leaving only £200,000 paid by Britain.[35] This Commonwealth stake in the base – so important four years earlier in getting things moving again – was clearly becoming a critical counter in the balance in favour of retention. The MacDonald Government looked to the Imperial Conference to reach an agreed policy.

The preparations for the 1930 Conference again highlighted the differences between the British defence planners and the Labour ministers. A rather trivial example of this occurred over an historical survey of the naval base scheme produced by the ODC on 4 June 1930. Ramsay MacDonald's private secretary, Patrick Duff, thought the paper was biased in favour of the scheme – that the many quotations from previous CID memoranda tended to 'load the dice' against the Labour Party's policy. MacDonald agreed that Hankey should be approached about getting a 'more colourless' resume. Hankey was indignant; the paper had been through the CID procedure; no Cabinet minister had raised queries, it did not make a case for or against, and had already been sent to the Dominion representatives. MacDonald agreed that 'it must stand'.[36]

Another sign of the British schism about Singapore can be seen in the discussions of civil servants charged with preparing a financial history of the scheme. The Treasury representative in these discussions was Assistant Under-Secretary Percival Waterfield, who up-dated Casey's figures about the respective Commonwealth and United Kingdom payments. Of £3,145,000 spent by 30 September 1930, £2,279,000 (plus the land) would have been provided by the Straits Settlements, Hong Kong, the FMS and New Zealand. Of the overall scheme – dockyard, defences and air bases – which was now estimated at £18,760,580, Britain's contribution would eventually reach £15,346,580 compared with £3,396,000 from Commonwealth contributors. If it was stopped at the end of September, £13½ million could be saved.[37] The trouble was that the civil servants did not know what the Cabinet meant by getting a 'permanent settlement' from the Imperial Conference. As Waterfield put it: Dominions' agreement to abandoning the scheme was unlikely; equally unlikely was the chance of further financial help. The Treasury officials toyed with the idea of stopping work after the graving dock and telling Dominion leaders that, in view of the international situation and the depression, they should now complete now only what could not be interrupted and decide later whether to go on or not.[38] But service departments were eager to get ahead and the Dominions also had other ideas.

Australia, under a Labour Government, was not expected to make much trouble. What was probably not known in London was that the Australian Chiefs of Staff were also divided on defence policy and some were doubtful about the basic imperial strategy. If the CNS, Rear-Admiral William Munro Kerr, (a Royal Navy Officer) insisted that the British navy was sufficient insurance against the invasion of Australia, the CGS, General Sir Harry Chauvel, and the CAS, Air Commodore Richard Williams, believed land forces and shore-based aircraft were also required because of doubts as to whether the British fleet would be sent to the Pacific and doubts about the 'inviolability' of the Singapore base.[39] However, this lack of confidence in imperial strategy (which would later become a fairly strong stream of criticism in Australia and New Zealand) was not allowed to detract from the basic Australian position in 1930, which was that:

> The greatest contribution to a feeling of security in Australia would be the knowledge that Singapore is regarded by other countries as an unassailable base.... It is strongly recommended that Australia uses her influence to secure the completion and fortification of the base. In no other way can the security of Australia be so greatly enhanced for so small an expenditure.[40]

In New Zealand support was always strongest for the base, but not unanimous. The New Zealand Labour Party had sent a telegram to the British Labour Party during the naval conference cordially supporting the decision to review the Singapore base.[41] But the naval staff took the opposite view. Commodore Geoffrey Blake, commanding the New Zealand Station, argued that the London Naval Treaty, which reduced Britain's measure of superiority over Japan, made the Singapore base 'even more necessary' than before. Without it the mobility of the fleet was reduced with 'consequent increased risk to the security of the sea communications of New Zealand'. Once the CID's historical survey of the Singapore project reached them the Dominion Navy Board was even more adamant. They presumed that the 'slowed down' policy of 1929 had been made with Dominions' approval (which, of course, was not so). They suggested that the money New Zealand had spent on Singapore could be regarded 'as an insurance premium against the disturbance of the status quo in the Far East'. They recommended that at the Imperial Conference the Dominion representatives should press for completion, possibly with Australian and Indian help; that if the scheme was modified the Government should press for the return of some or all of the £375,000 New Zealand contribution.[42] They were not interested in Singapore as a commercial port because so little of New Zealand's trade went in that direction. With this advice George Forbes, the Prime Minister, went to London determined to do his best to secure the completion of the base. He also held a card up his sleeve, as New Zealand had not yet ratified the London Naval Treaty.

VI

The Imperial Conference opened on 1 October 1930 with most of the delegates concerned about trading and constitutional matters rather than the Singapore base. However, the British Government wanted a settlement on the question, so the conference immediately created a subcommittee of United Kingdom, Australian and New Zealand representatives. The chairman was Philip Snowden, the Chancellor of the Exchequer. The other British members were Arthur Henderson and the three service ministers; Scullin of Australia was accompanied by Frank Brennan, the Attorney-General, and R. G. Casey; the New Zealanders were Forbes and Sir Thomas Sidey, the Attorney-General.

On 15 October – the day before the subcommittee met – the British Cabinet decided on a policy to put to the Australians and New Zealanders. After considering telegrams from the Governor of the Straits Settlements, who said a fully protected base would be an asset to Malaya, but an undefended one would invite attack, and from the Governor of Hong Kong, who said the Singapore base was vital to the defences of Hong Kong, they slightly reformulated their 'slowed down' policy. There would be no change in the intention of 'ultimately establishing a defended naval base at Singapore'; the Jackson contract and the air base would be completed; the remaining expenditure on dockyard equipment and defences would be suspended for five years, when the precise scale of the defences would be reviewed in the light of the next naval conference.[43] When he put this to the Australians and New Zealanders next day, Snowden naturally emphasised the financial aspect, though he also said that a military threat in the near future was regarded as unlikely. After Scullin had asked a few questions, Forbes argued obstinately for the original scheme. He said 'the whole Pacific Ocean would be practically defenceless without such a Base'. He was unimpressed by talk about Japanese goodwill, the Kellogg Pact, or the League of Nations. He said 'there was a strong feeling in New Zealand that they were defenceless without a Base at Singapore'. Scullin supported the British view. It was a matter of weighing the costs against the risks, he said. The London Naval Treaty, which Japan had signed, was the only real piece of progress in disarmament, and he had 'never been greatly impressed by the suggestion that Japan might invade Australia'. If there was a flare-up, it wouldn't come in the Pacific, said Scullin, war would not come as a 'bolt from the blue'. Forbes admitted that he could not 'demand' the completion of the base but he emphasised forcefully that New Zealanders regarded 'the fleet and Singapore as their main defence'. The experts had endorsed it; the slowing down had disappointed New Zealanders. 'When they had given their contribution towards the Base they had regarded it as an insurance in defence and as long as there was no defence they had no insurance.' Snowden agreed that when the New Zealand money was given it was given on the understanding that the base would be completed, but he pleaded with Forbes that the situation had changed, that the United Kingdom had come to New Zealand and asked them to agree to a postponement. Forbes said if the position was put in that way 'he could say nothing' but New Zealand would feel more secure if the base was finished without delay. Snowden thanked him, and left Hankey and Frank Thomson, head of the New Zealand Prime Minister's department, to draft a report endorsing the British policy, but noting New Zealand's reluctance.[44]

VII

As the decision about Singapore represented something of a capitulation by the New Zealand delegation and would obviously cause anxiety in the Dominion's defence establishment, Hankey sought ways of restoring Forbes' *amour propre* and ensuring continued co-operation in imperial defence. Therefore, during the period when they were drafting the report, he invited Thomson to his house in Surrey for the weekend of 25/26 October. In the course of their conversations he gathered that Forbes was considering creating a defence council or 'replica' of the CID in New Zealand, and wanted the best professional advice as a basis for defence planning, especially as to which roles the armed forces should be trained for. This hint was more than enough. Hankey, together with Thomson, drafted a possible letter from Forbes to MacDonald requesting such advice.[45] Forbes raised the matter at a meeting of the CID on 28 November, and he sent the letter to Ramsay MacDonald next day.[46] During the following week a member of the New Zealand Staff Corps, Lieutenant-Colonel Nathaniel W. B. B. Thoms, DSO, was invited to a meeting of the COS committee to explain Forbes' wishes.

Certainly, here, among the senior service staff, the atmosphere was more cordial than among the politicians of the Singapore Committee. In fact the British COS were eager to extend the Dominion involvement in imperial defence from the well-tried naval sphere into that of overseas garrisons. Field Marshal Milne thought it was 'rather ridiculous' to reinforce Singapore from Britain when it could be done more quickly from Australia. Canada might agree to take responsibility for Bermuda and Australia and New Zealand for some role at Singapore or Hong Kong.[47] This was something in which the British could hardly take the initiative, but Forbes' request (albeit orchestrated by Hankey) was just what they wanted. They listened to Colonel Thoms explaining New Zealand's needs on 4 December 1930. He pointed out that defence expenditure was not large in New Zealand. Forbes' Government (the United Party) depended for its parliamentary majority on the support of the Labour members, who, he said with slight exaggeration, 'were chiefly Pacifists', and any government had to heed the opinion of farmers who did not like public expenditure. The general view was that there was little risk of invasion, so the armed forces, such as they were, could be used somewhere else for imperial defence. How and where? What the Government wanted was not political, but 'technical' advice – an appreciation of the world situation, especially as it affected the Pacific and Indian oceans and trade routes, with some suggestion as to where New Zealand might contribute. They already regarded themselves as partly responsible for the defence of Singapore and would, he said, also like to contribute in India. In the event of war a Division would be available.

The British Chiefs of Staff willingly undertook to provide an appreciation. When Thoms left the meeting the CIGS suggested that in ten years' time he could envisage New Zealand and Australia assuming responsibility for defence in the Pacific, since the United Kingdom could not continue to be responsible for the security of all the trade routes of the Commonwealth.[48]

The appreciation was completed in March 1931. Entitled *Imperial Defence as Affecting New Zealand*, it ran to over thirty pages, and after a summary of the principles and development of imperial defence, it listed all Britain's commitments, region by region, along with the present forces available to meet them. New Zealand's chief interests were seen as the defence of sea communications, the Suez Canal, the Persian Gulf oilfield, the air reinforcement route through India and the Singapore base. The paper dealt, in some detail, with matters much broader than the scope of this book, but Singapore was given a central place.

All discussion of the 'Far East' had been based on the threefold assumption that the Singapore base would exist; that a battlecruiser squadron would be stationed there, and that the main fleet could arrive in 42 days. As the 'pivot' of imperial defence in the East Singapore was also the focus of New Zealand's defence.

> The security of the territory, communications, and trade of New Zealand against attack depends ultimately on the success in the Pacific of the general scheme of Imperial defence . . . Provided that the British fleet arrives on time, and finds a properly equipped base at Singapore, New Zealand has nothing to fear beyond sporadic attack.

Thus the main recommendation of the COS was the entirely predictable declaration: 'There is . . . no more effective manner in which New Zealand can contribute to its own defence than by assisting towards the completion of the base and its defence'. As well as cash, the Dominion might agree to send reinforcements to the garrison in time of war, possibly to Egypt, Aden, Trincomalee, or Hong Kong as well. They might even consider contributing artillery units to the peacetime garrisons of Singapore or Hong Kong and send air force elements to serve with the RAF in the Far East.[49] This paper was an important document for New Zealand. Oddly enough the COS forgot to mention the one commitment New Zealand had recently made. In August 1930 the Cabinet had agreed to send two platoons, in the event of war, to Fanning Island, the British cable-station site between Hawaii and Samoa.[50] But the

1931 paper was something of a theoretical exercise, written for long-term guidance, not in response to a crisis or a specific threat.

The real crises of 1931 were political and economic. Governments were trying to grapple with the depression; defence expenditure throughout the Commonwealth was reaching its inter-war nadir. The international horizon had apparently been brightened by the London Naval Treaty, so that in the Pacific section of the New Zealand paper, the COS quoted the view of the 1930 Singapore Committee that 'Japan was unlikely to disturb the peace'. In fact the British Cabinet reaffirmed the Ten Year Rule in 1931 and began to make preparations for the long-awaited Geneva disarmament conference in 1932.

In such an atmosphere, when the problem was depression and the policy was disarmament, defence preparedness was unpopular. But the British COS, each in turn, did sound notes of warning. The CIGS declared that the regular forces, in relation to commitments, had 'reached an irreducible minimum'. The CNS said the fleet was so diminished by the naval treaty, the Ten Year Rule and years of economy that it was 'incapable' of ensuring efficiently the protection of trade. The CAS placed Britain fifth among the air powers.[51] It was hardly surprising that, when on the night of 18/19 September 1931, the Japanese army used the Muckden railway incident as the pretext for beginning the occupation of Manchuria, Britain had no inclination to interfere. It was in no position to do so. At Singapore, by this date, Jackson's, the construction company, were pressing ahead with the dockyard. But in 1931 it consisted of three vast holes in the ground with the beginnings of some massive concrete walls (see Plates 23, 25, 27, 29, 31).

6 'The Writing on the Wall', 1932-35

I

Work on the naval base and its defences was accelerated, not as a direct result of the Manchurian War, but because of the shock of the 'Shanghai incident' of January 1932. The outbreak in Manchuria came at the time of Britain's worst domestic crisis. The Labour Government, which had recently renewed the Ten Year Rule and was preparing hopefully for the world disarmament conference, was overtaken by the financial crisis. The National Government, formed on 24 August 1931, sought overseas credits and massive expenditure cuts followed, including pay reductions which led to mutiny in the Home Fleet. Britain went off the gold standard. The 'doctor's mandate' election was held in October.[1] This was hardly a time for defence decisions. In December 1931 the truce in the Guns v Air controversy was prolonged in the usual way; by reference to a Cabinet Committee.[2] The Admiralty also reduced the number of ships in commission to a minimum: of the ten battleships at home, three were put in reserve and seven on four-fifths complement.[3]

With such crises and preoccupations at home the Government was unwilling and unable to exert its influence over Manchuria, where British territory, lives or property were not threatened. The Government followed the Foreign Office's somewhat contradictory advice and endeavoured to avoid antagonising Japan, preserve China's integrity and uphold the prestige of the League of Nations. Some people, indeed, were rather sympathetic to Japan, and anyway, preferred them to expand northwards rather than towards Malaya or Australia.[4] Singapore was hardly mentioned in this crisis, although the Governor of the Straits Settlements used the situation as an argument for requesting a second British regular battalion for the garrison in Malaya. The Dominions Office suggested getting a New Zealand battalion – an idea which was to crop up several times over the next few years.[5]

II

The response to Japan's action in Shanghai, however, was quite different. With nearly £150 millions worth of investment, 6000 British residents and two infantry battalions as garrison, Shanghai held the biggest concentration of British interests in China. In 1927 the Government had been prepared to send a Division to protect the British settlement against the Chinese nationalists. Early in 1932 it faced the problem of a sudden Japanese incursion. On 18 January five Japanese were set upon (at the secret instigation of Japanese officers) by Chinese factory workers. A mob of Japanese residents fired the factory and forced their Consul-General to demand reparation. When the ultimatum expired on 28 January the Japanese commander summoned reinforcements and an air and land assault was mounted on the suburb of Chapei. By February 50,000 Japanese troops were engaged with a Chinese army on the northern outskirts of Shanghai.

News of the outbreak reached London on 20 January 1932, and although reinforcements were sent from Hong Kong, it was clear that Britain could not contemplate intervention. Policy centred on the League and close accord with the United States, but in the event the British ambassador proved a useful mediator.[6] The Japanese withdrew in May, but not before this crisis (unlike the Manchurian incident) had induced a careful review of Britain's situation in the Far East and the entire defence position in case of further unexpected Japanese moves.

Singapore figured largely in this review. When the COS committee met to make emergency plans on 4 February 1932 Admiral Field, the CNS, admitted that Singapore was at the mercy of 'anyone who wished to attack it', but he assumed Britain would never go to war with Japan unless 'absolutely dragged into it'. Field Marshal Milne said they ought to do what they could for Hong Kong and Singapore, and again mooted the possibility of help from Australia or New Zealand, but Sir John Salmon, the new CAS (who had recently visited both Dominions) felt Australia would always put local before imperial defence. On the suggestion of the CIGS the committee decided to accelerate their Annual Review for 1932 with the object of ending the Ten Year Rule. Meanwhile they appointed a deputy Chiefs of Staff subcommittee to consider short-term measures in the Far East, including the idea of securing some Australian and New Zealand assistance.[7]

The naval staff followed up with a warning as to its inability to safeguard British interests in the Far East. The effect of the Ten Year Rule had been to leave the navy deficient in almost all kinds of *matériel* so that it would be impossible to hold on to Hong Kong, Singapore and Trincomalee until the fleet arrived. It would probably have to withdraw 'so far to the west as to leave India uncovered'.[8] When the Cabinet received this bleak assessment on 10 February 1932, Baldwin (who deputised in the chair for MacDonald who was in hospital for an eye operation) noted blandly that the efficiency of the Services would have to be considered as soon as the results of the disarmament conference, which, ironically, had just opened at Geneva, were known.[9]

The deputy COS subcommittee, made up of Rear-Admiral Dreyer, Major-General Bartholomew and Air Vice-Marshal Burnett, was equally pessimistic in its report on 22 February. It emphasised the 'suddenness' of Japan's action at Shanghai and took as its basic assumption that the British Government would 'in no circumstances themselves' resort to war. After surveying the small scattered forces available in the Far East, and the fact that the battle-cruisers *Hood* and *Repulse* were in the West Indies, 2000 miles behind the 'starting point' from which the fleet would sail East, the Committee's conclusions were devastating. At Shanghai the British forces had no hope of maintaining themselves: the ships ought to sail immediately if hostilities were likely and the troops should withdraw to Canton by rail. Defence of Hong Kong would be a 'forlorn hope', but it would have to hold out as long as possible to gain time for Singapore where the defences were 'totally inadequate'. It would take four months to install local seaward defences consisting of minefields and anti-submarine booms; four months to install three more pairs of 6" guns; six weeks for an army division to come from India; two weeks for three air squadrons to arrive from India and Iraq, four months to bring seven more squadrons, which would also need more airfields. As for Australia and New Zealand, their naval forces would be available on the outbreak of war, but their armies were doubtful and air forces almost non-existent. The Dominions might 'at the best' be seen as a source of later reinforcements. The Ten Year Rule and the Guns v Air controversy were blamed for this situation, which led to the emphatic conclusion: 'that our present political difficulties in dealing with the Sino-Japanese problem at the present juncture arise very largely from the insecurity of our naval bases at Hong Kong and Singapore'.[10]

The Annual Review of the COS, completed on the following day, concentrated on the same point. It argued that all the assumptions behind the Ten Year Rule had been invalidated. It noted that the Manchurian crisis of 1931 had come 'out of a relatively clear sky', that at Shanghai there had been the 'shortest notice'. These events prompted inquiry into Britain's readiness to face sudden aggression by Japan. 'The position is about as bad as it could be.' So weak were Hong Kong and Singapore that they presented tempting opportunities. 'The whole of our territory in the Far East, as well as the coastline of India and the Dominions and our vast trade and shipping, lies open to attack.' It would be the height of folly to allow this defenceless situation to go on, and there were 'terrible deficiencies' in all the armed services. The COS made three recommendations: that the Ten Year Rule be cancelled; that a start be made in meeting commitments, with 'First priority . . . given to requirements in the Far East'; and that this should *not* be delayed until after the disarmament conference, 'We cannot ignore the Writing on the Wall.'[11]

When the CID considered these recommendations on 22 March 1932 it also received a warning from the Treasury, where Neville Chamberlain was beginning to make his mark as Chancellor of the Exchequer. What was the alternative? Britain was no more in a position financially and economically to engage in a major war in the Far East than it was militarily. 'What has to be considered therefore is one set of risks balanced against another.' The Treasury put the financial risk higher than any other.[12] The Cabinet (with Ramsay MacDonald back in harness) accepted the COS recommendations on 23 March, but decided to await the outcome of the Geneva disarmament conference.[13] The National Government, still dominated by the economic crisis, was unwilling to give up its hope for disarmament. It did not *act* on the cry of the COS at this stage, although it did *accept* that 'first priority' should be given to the defence of bases in the Far East.

Over the next three years the Singapore base (the main priority) was given due attention from three different directions: from the Admiralty, which got the full dockyard scheme restarted; the China Fleet, where the practical problems of preparedness were studied, and from some of the leading civil servants and politicians in Whitehall, who, because of the rise of the Nazis in Germany, challenged the Far East priority and began, in fact, to challenge the whole basis of the imperial strategy.

III

While the COS were endeavouring to end the Ten Year Rule and alert the government to Britain's weakness in the East, the Admiralty Staff were assessing the state of the Singapore dockyard. At a meeting on 11 February 1932 one of the deputy Civil Engineers-in-Chief, T. B. Hunter, made it clear that since the 1930 decision to 'slow down' the scheme they would have the graving dock and certain wharves completed by 1935, but these would not be 'available for any practical use'. The full truncated scheme of 1926 (originally scheduled for completion by 1937) included a caisson, pumping equipment, capstans, roads, railways and crane tracks, an electrical generating station and workshops. Just to make the dry dock usable would require a further £380,000, and no sums had yet been voted for the naval armament and mining depots or the anti-submarine booms. Of the £7¾ million truncated scheme only £5,145,916 had been authorised; a further £407,500 was needed to get the dockyard working, and the subsidiary works would use up the balance of £2,196,584. Next, the Admiralty Staff turned to the defences. Captain J. H. D. Cunningham, the Director of Plans, explained that the only existing defences were five pre-war 9.2" guns and six 6" guns on Blakang Mati covering Keppel Harbour. These were out of range of the Johore Strait, which was covered by only two 6" guns at Changi. The anti-submarine booms and minefield equipment were not yet available, and there had of course been no decision over the air and artillery roles. Vice-Admiral Addison, the Director of Dockyards, insisted that unless the full truncated scheme was finished the base would be useless. He was told by the engineers that the present intention was to retain the coffer dam in front of the dockyard works to keep them dry. Five years would be needed for completion of the full scheme once it was restarted.[14]

The naval staff decided to seek authority to reactivate the project. The First Lord of the Admiralty was informed, on 22 February, that as soon as the Cabinet Committee on the Guns v Air issue had reported, the scheme ought to be resumed in full. If the graving dock could be used for docking, Keppel commercial yards could be used for repairs. The First Lord agreed to this on 4 March 1932 and, ten days later, the Admiralty Board formally recommended the appropriation of £380,000 to finish the graving dock, and the reconsideration of the defences, once the Guns v Air matter was resolved.[15] They were also kept alive to the Commonwealth stake in Singapore, as Savile, the Civil Engineer-in-Chief, who visited Singapore, encountered anxiety in Malaya about the delays, in view of the FMS gift. The Director of Plans also warned that New Zealand might reconsider its gift.[16]

The Cabinet Committee on the Guns v Air issue (the Coastal Defence Committee) had been at work over the same period. Under Stanley Baldwin's chairmanship this small group (which did not include any service ministers) made an impartial study and reported on 24 May 1932. The members (a somewhat unlikely combination) were Sir Philip Cunliffe-Lister, Secretary of State for Colonies, Sir Donald MacLean, President of the Board of Education, and Sir John Gilmour, the Minister of Agriculture and Fisheries. After getting the inevitable historical background paper from Hankey and papers from the three COS, the committee interviewed the latter in turn. It met six times between 18 February and 25 April and Cunliffe-Lister suggested that they keep Singapore in mind as the concrete case.

Sir John Salmond, Trenchard's successor as CAS, was heard twice. He stressed the inaccuracy of guns, the mobility of aircraft and the results of recent successful bombing trials. 'Are we going to take a leaf out of the future', he asked, and prepare the defences for new conditions? For Singapore he advocated one army division, six air squadrons (double the existing strength) and *no* 15" guns: 'the big gun has had its day'![17] Admiral Field, the CNS, stressed difficulties of visibility and air navigation over the sea and the fact that aircraft had often, on exercises, failed to find the ships. 15" guns provided the best deterrent, he said, and multiple quick-firing pom poms would successfully defend ships from aircraft.[18] For the War Office Field Marshal Milne and Lieutenant-General Sir Ronald Charles (the Master-General of Ordnance) did not try to gloss over the dismal 1928 gun trials. But the 1930 trials had been so successful that the navy would not risk its radio-controlled target ship again, and in the 1931 trials, using dual observation posts, 20 per cent accuracy had been achieved. They contrasted the hitting power of a flight of six aeroplanes (each carrying four 450 lb bombs), which would be 24 per hour, with that of a 9.2" gun (firing 2½ rounds per minute), which meant 150 per hour.[19]

After hearing the COS's arguments Cunliffe-Lister said the only thing against installing 15" guns was the possibility that aircraft *might* prove better in the future. On the evidence before them they could not recommend the air scheme. Maclean felt they could say that air power was a valuable addition, and in some places essential. Gilmour wanted to stress the co-operation of all services.

In their report of 24 May 1932 the committee pictured the choice as between substitution or co-operation and it plumped for the latter. It could not recommend the air scheme because of the inherent uncertainties. Co-operation of all three services should be the keynote, 'the gun retaining its place as the main deterrent' to naval attack. Aircraft would increase security and add to the deterrent. The committee recommended that Stage I should now proceed at Singapore and Stage II be considered by the CID later. The RAF should continue to co-operate in reconnaissance, artillery spotting, fighter defence, and all forms of attack.[20]

Hankey passed these findings on to the Prime Minister on 27 May, but found MacDonald most unhappy about a reversal of the Labour Government's Singapore policy. 'The fuss that can be made of it is considerable.' With unrest over wage reductions and cuts in the dole, rising defence expenditure would be resented. He had no information to make him believe it was urgently necessary.[21]

Just before the matter went to the CID and Cabinet there was some renewed Australian interest. Sir John Latham (the Commonwealth Attorney-General) was visiting London and Baldwin agreed that he could see the Coast Defence report. Latham also met the COS committee on 2 June 1932 to request advice about how to divide Australia's modest defence budget between the three services. This was not unlike the New Zealand request in 1930 and the COS readily agreed to supply a paper along the lines of New Zealand's. When he was asked, categorically, by the CIGS, how a request to send troops or air squadrons to Singapore would be received in Australia, Latham replied 'most sympathetically' – but not at present. The CNS reiterated the orthodox doctrine of imperial defence, that the one thing which would save Australia from attack was the presence of the main fleet, which would depend on the existence of an adequately defended Singapore base.[22] Latham also attended the CID meeting when the Coastal Defence

Report was discussed a week later. Ramsay MacDonald felt that to proceed with Stage I of the Singapore defences would amount to altering a 1930 Imperial Conference decision, but Baldwin said that that decision had been based on the Ten Year assumption, and after Shanghai it was clear that if Japan 'ran amok' in the East Britain would be helpless. The First Lord of the Admiralty supported this and Latham said he would be glad, from an Australian point of view, if Singapore went ahead.[23]

The CID approved Stage I of the defences, including some RAF co-operation. The defences were now 'overtaking' the construction of the dockyard. Although the First Lord of the Admiralty had gained the impression that the CID had meant to approve *both*, and pointed out that as yet the dockyard represented 'little more than a hole in the earth', Hankey confirmed that the CID's decision was limited to the defences. It was meaningless unless the base was completed, and he suggested the matter should go to the Cabinet.[24] Thus the Admiralty prepared a paper for the Cabinet suggesting that to finish the defences before the base was 'somewhat illogical'. It also stressed the importance of the project for the Commonwealth, citing recent suggestions from the FMS that it might press for the return of its £2 million, and the fact that New Zealand had scaled down its annual contribution from £125,000 to £100,000. The immediate need was the £380,000 to make the graving dock usable. The Admiralty's view, that the CID decision on Stage I of the defences carried the corollary that 'sufficient work should be done on the Base to make it usable' was accepted by the Treasury.

The Prime Minister was the last to hold out. 'This is a serious step to take and must be done open-eyed.' It meant restoring the Singapore project and he did not like going to Geneva 'with this up our sleeves'. When the matter came to the Cabinet on 11 October 1932, approval in principle only was given, with the proviso that no new expenditure could be incurred during the armaments truce of the Geneva Disarmament Conference.[25]

It took a further six months and the drive of a new CNS, Admiral Sir Ernle Chatfield ('the finest officer the Royal Navy produced between the wars'),[26] to get a decision. At his first COS meeting on 28 February 1933 Chatfield discussed rumours that at the time of Shanghai Japan had had a plan to attack Singapore with a Division in 8–10 days. With Singapore undefended, the whole basis of British policy was 'built upon sand', so Chatfield announced that he had decided to change the China Fleet's war orders (discussed below) accordingly. Meanwhile, the COS looked into what immediate improvements could be made.[27] Chatfield declared that they should go to the CID 'with a bold face' and say that if they were not given the troops and the armament depot they would 'wash their hands' of the responsibility for defending Singapore. Meanwhile the Admiralty were sending a mine layer, HMS *Adventure*, and recommissioning HMS *Terror*, a First World War monitor mounting two 15″ guns. The Air Ministry would send out another squadron immediately, and more later when airfields were available. The CIGS suggested cutting the completion time for Stage I from 5 to 3½ years.[28] In their recommendation, dated 31 March 1933, the COS appealed to the authority of their warrant and formally warned the Government of the inadequacy of Singapore's defences.[29]

If the COS were in a blunt-speaking mood, Hankey was not averse to putting the hard word on MacDonald: 'Is it not time that the National Government took the question of the defence of Singapore more seriously?' Any of the recent Far Eastern crises might have led to a disaster: 'If the unexpected did occur, as well it might, and we lost Singapore – the pivot of our strategical position in the Far East – there would be a calamity of the first magnitude. We might well lose India, and the faith in us in Australia and New Zealand would be shattered. The disaster to our trade would be overwhelming.' Recent arguments in favour of not proceeding had lost their force. The desire for a 'policy of pacification' was weakened by Japan's defiance of the League. The dispute over Guns v Air had been settled a year before. The financial argument was hardly tenable beside expenditure on 'such objects as roads used mainly for joy-riding, swimming baths, recreation grounds, town halls, and artificially anticipated works of various kinds (such as the sewage works in my own Parish) . . .'

> Whatever the case in the past it is hard to find a decent excuse today for further delay. If disaster occurred, it would seem incredible to posterity, especially in the face of the warnings of the last two years, that we could have jeopardised the British Empire for the sake of a few hundred thousand pounds in a Budget of nearly £800,000,000.[30]

When the CID met on 6 April 1933 the former Prime Minister of

Australia, now High Commissioner in London, Stanley Bruce (who was to have a significant role over the coming decade) reminded the members of Australia's interest in Singapore. The CID endorsed the COS proposal and on 12 April the Cabinet finally agreed to the resumption of the full 'truncated scheme' for Singapore. Stage I of the defences was to be speeded up for completion in 1936; a second airfield would be built; an additional RAF squadron sent out; the Admiralty's emergency measures would go ahead, and the battalion still at Shanghai could be moved to Hong Kong at the War Office's discretion.[31] At last, fifteen months after Shanghai, a firm decision to strengthen Singapore had been made.

IV

The Chiefs of Staff having established some priorities and persuaded the National Government to accelerate work at Singapore, it was for the naval commanders in the East to achieve some state of preparedness in the region. In this they had a simple strategic plan to implement – the safe arrival of the main fleet at Singapore. Their guide was the *War Memorandum (Eastern)* prepared in the Admiralty and subjected to periodic revision and study by staff conferences. The original version of 1920 was expanded by the Penang Conference in 1921; the 1924 revisions went to a conference at Singapore in 1925; a major change was made in 1928; a further revision of 1931 (before Shanghai) was available for an emergency conference early in 1932, and a post-Shanghai revision of 1933 (reversing the 1928 change) was taken by a staff conference at Singapore in 1934 as the starting point for putting local forces in a state of readiness.[32]

The *War Memorandum* envisaged three phases in a war with Japan: I, the *Period before Relief*, during which the fleet would move east and Singapore and Hong Kong had to be defended; II, the *Period of Consolidation*, after the arrival of the fleet, when it would move north to Hong Kong; III, the *Period of Advance*, when 'pressure' would be exerted upon Japan. Phase I of this scheme was carefully worked out in the mid-1920s when the fleet movements were perfectly practicable, but there was, of course, no base to go to. Phase III was spelt out in some detail in 1931, but even before the Manchurian and Shanghai crises it bore the mark of unreality. From the very beginning, moreover, there was always the proviso that part of the fleet would have to remain in European waters.

Phase I, the period before relief, had been put at 3 months in 1920, but was reduced to 42 days and then to 28 days, if 7 to 10 days were allowed for preparations. This meant arrival at Singapore on the 28th day after zero – departure from home waters – or 22 days from the Mediterranean. During this period the Commander-in-Chief of the China Station would co-ordinate units from the East Indies, China and New Zealand Squadrons, the Royal Australian Navy (if committed by the Australian Government), and possibly reinforcements from Africa and South America. Their task was to safeguard Singapore and Hong Kong and ensure the safe arrival of an army brigade from India. These 4000 troops would take seven days from Madras and nine days from Calcutta to reach Penang, whence they would go by train to Singapore. Two bomber squadrons would fly from India and Iraq in two weeks. It was estimated that Japan would be able to attack with one Division after nine days and bring up two more Divisions in twenty-three days. The most favourable weather for such operations would be between November and May.

By 1925 detailed timetables, arrival graphs, and fuelling berths had been prepared for the transit of 10 battleships, 4 battle-cruisers, 2 aircraft carriers, 11 cruisers and 48 destroyers. The capital ships would refuel at the south end of the Red Sea, pass both sides of Socotra Island, refuel again at Addu Atoll in the Maldives. One carrier and a cruiser squadron would refuel in Colombo and the destroyers at Trincomalee and Nancowry Harbour in the Nicobars, which was the final assembly point. The fleet would then pass between Nicobar Island and Atjeh Head into the Straits of Malacca by night, to reach Singapore at first light (see Map 7). Formidable supply arrangements would be needed, including 240 oilers (of which only 31 would be available on the outbreak of war). The victualling requirements for 60,000 men over 90 days included 6½ million lbs of potatoes and 400,000 sheets of greaseproof paper.

During the later 1920s certain modifications were made to Phase I. Beatty's plan for stationing a battle-cruiser squadron at Singapore once the floating dock was ready was changed in 1927 because the maintenance facilities would be so limited. Only adverse political circumstances would justify sending the battle-cruisers.[33] All major British ships, however, were given a war disposition: EI meant 'Singapore immediately': E, 'Singapore as soon as possible' (if the European situation permitted), and U signified 'Europe'.

In Phase II the fleet, having arrived successfully, would steam on to Hong Kong, arriving 38 days after leaving Home waters. Although it was vital to the strategy, Hong Kong could not be developed as a base under the terms of the Washington Treaty. Thus in 1928 Vice-Admiral Tyrwhitt, commanding the China Squadron, suggested a major modification in the plan. Hong Kong's strategic position suggested that Japan would have to seize or neutralise it before attacking Singapore. As Stage I of Singapore's defences had been approved, the Admiralty agreed that some risk could be accepted there and that the China Squadron (with the Australian and New Zealand cruisers) should concentrate for the defence of Hong Kong.[34]

Phase III, the advance north from Hong Kong, would see the climax of the Anglo-Japanese War. The fleet would either destroy the Japanese fleet in a great battle or exert 'pressure' in other ways. The 1931 revision outlined some of the possibilities. An invasion of Japan was ruled out; direct attack upon a Japanese expeditionary force in a foreign country was not recommended, although raids in harbours might be undertaken. Attacks on the lines of communication to her overseas forces might be sufficient to force Japan to desist in her objectives; otherwise there was economic blockade. The best prospect for success, in the view of the naval staff, would come from operations against Formosa or the Pescadores, to draw out the Japanese fleet – presumably to its demise. Such, in brief, was the shape of the paper planning which went ahead in the days when the 'Singapore base' consisted of a floating dock, Keppel commercial dockyard and a 'hole in the ground'.

V

Scepticism about the whole scheme was not confined to socialists, pacifists and Australians. Several senior naval commanders expressed themseves in unambiguous terms. Vice-Admiral Richmond, one of the Navy's leading 'intellectuals', was in command of the East Indies Station at the time of the 1925 conference and wrote a severe critique of the *War Memorandum*. It was not a war plan, he said, but a plan of naval movements, unrelated to the actions of the sister services. The proviso that some part of the fleet would remain in Europe gave the whole idea an air of 'unreality'. Britain was not strong enough to deal with two enemies at once and Richmond said it was better to acknowledge this than to live in a 'fool's paradise'.[35] Admiral Kelly, who commanded the China Squadron at the time of the Shanghai crisis, held an emergency staff conference in January 1932 and reported that if the *War Memorandum* represented the Government's policy, he could only describe the defences of Singapore as 'deplorable'.[36]

Admiral Chatfield took the same view, when he took over as CNS in February 1933. He found that the 1928 revision, giving the China Squadron and local reinforcements the role of safeguarding Hong Kong in the period before relief (which was based on the assumption that Stage I of the defences would be ready by 1931), had not been revised when Labour 'slowed down' the project. Therefore, when the Cabinet's decision on the emergency measures was passed on to the Commander-in-Chief, China, Chatfield also reversed the 1928 decision about the role of local naval forces during the period before relief. Safeguarding Singapore now came first.[37]

These interim arrangements and the 1933 version of *War Memorandum (E)* were the subject of a staff conference early in 1934 conducted by Vice-Admiral Dreyer. Although he had only recently been involved at the London end, as deputy CNS, Dreyer (who had been Jellicoe's chief of staff in 1920) was shocked at the state of unreadiness he found in 1933. He affected surprise at finding no 'war plan' other than the plan for 'the trek out of the Fleet'. He determined to turn the China Squadron from being a 'police force' under three weeks notice, to a 'war force' under four hours notice.[38]

The staff conference in January 1934 was attended by Vice-Admiral Dunbar-Nasmith, commanding the East Indies Squadron; Vice-Admiral Hyde, Australian CNS and Rear-Admiral Burges-Watson, of the New Zealand Division. Dreyer announced that from 1 March 1934 a state of readiness would be attempted, and he listed (for the Admiralty) his immediate needs. Singapore, he reported, could hold out against raids, but not against a determined assault in the period before relief. The minelayer had arrived, the monitor *Terror* would be anchored at the corner of Pulau Ubin Island to cover the entrance of the Johore Strait, and the first new coastal artillery unit had come. This represented some progress. But Dreyer wanted reinforcements in all services immediately as a deterrent: a battle-cruiser squadron; 4000 troops; 1000 mines; anti-submarine booms; anti-aircraft guns and searchlights, with crews; two more squadrons of flying boats, and spotter planes for *Terror's* 15" guns. He also raised an important issue of air co-operation. To intercept Japanese aircraft carriers before sunset on the day before they attacked, would require air reconnaissance in an arc of 420 miles radius from Singapore. This was beyond the range of *Southampton* and *Horsley* aircraft. The alternatives were to locate the carriers after daybreak on the day of attack at about 200 miles from Singapore (probably *after* they had flown-off their bombers) or to develop advanced air bases in Sarawak. The other possibility was distant naval surveillance requiring advanced fuelling bases in the South China Sea.[39]

VI

Back in London, the defence planners were faced with the 'writing on the wall' in Europe as well as the Far East. If Manchuria and Shanghai had impelled them to press ahead at Singapore, to revise *War Memorandum (Eastern)* and to put the China Fleet on the alert, the successes of the Nazi Party in Germany induced the first questioning of the Singapore priority. Hitler became Chancellor on 30 January 1933. As the Chiefs of Staff prepared their review of imperial defence for that year they faced what seemed to be a stabilising situation in the Far East but growing uncertainty in Europe. The CIGS, Field Marshal Montgomery-Massingberd (not remembered now as one of the memorable heads of his profession) expected trouble in five to ten years when Germany had rearmed, and he wondered if the Anglo-Japanese Alliance could be resumed.[40] The 1933 review began, in fact, the process whereby the simple strategy of imperial defence – the plan to send the fleet to Singapore – was progressively questioned and qualified.

For ten years preparations for sending the fleet to the East had allowed for only a relatively small force in European waters. The Washington Treaty allowed a sufficient margin to permit sending a fleet superior to Japan's, and to take care, at the same time, of home needs. Gradually over the decade the 'margin of ships sufficient for all circumstances' had been prejudiced. Now, in calculating the margin to be left in Europe, it was necessary to take account of a reborn German navy, with its *Deutschland* class of 11" gun 'pocket battleships'. But matters were only urgent in some types of ship. If the Treaty ratios could be continued in force until 1940, Japan would have 9 battleships, 4 aircraft carriers, and 29 cruisers. Britain should therefore plan to send 12 battleships, 5 carriers and 46 cruisers. This left only 4 cruisers (out of the 50 agreed in 1930) for the rest of the world. This was quite inadequate. The old total of 70 was needed, and the battleships needed modernisation at the rate of at least 3 per year. But if those under refit could be counted; the 20 extra cruisers built; and France become an ally, it would still be possible to meet Germany and Japan at the same time. Thus the Far Eastern priority was retained in the 1933 review.[41] Not everyone agreed, however, and soon the Singapore priority was challenged by those who feared Germany as the real menace.

When the review went to the CID on 9 November 1933 Neville Chamberlain, the Chancellor of the Exchequer, who was to become the leading exponent of concentration on home defence, suggested that the priority recommended by the COS should not be so cut and dried; he, too, regretted the passing of the Anglo-Japanese Alliance. Stanley Bruce, the Australian High Commissioner, thought the big danger was the possibility of Germany and Japan coming together, in about five year's time, after German rearmament.

This meeting was a major landmark in the prolonged transition from the era of disarmament to that of rearmament. While recommending that the COS's order of priority – Far East, Europe, India – should still govern defence expenditure, it accepted that there should be no preparations for war against the United States, France or Italy. It also suggested that the COS subcommittee, with the addition of Treasury and Foreign Office representatives and the Secretary of the CID, should prepare for the Cabinet a programme to meet the 'worst deficiencies' in defence.[42] This was the origin of the celebrated Defence Requirements Committee, chaired by Hankey, in which Admiral Chatfield, Field Marshal Montgomery-Massingberd and Air Marshal Sir Edward Ellington were joined by Sir Robert Vansittart (Permanent Under Secretary for Foreign Affairs) and Sir Warren Fisher (the all-powerful Secretary of the Treasury). The secretary was Major Henry Pownall, RA. This committee sat twelve times between 14 November 1933 and 28 February 1934; indeed, it met to determine its own terms of reference *before* Cabinet approval had been given.[43] During its sessions the challenge to the Singapore priority became more explicit.

During the third meeting, on 4 December 1933, Vansittart

professed disagreement with his department's support of the COS's priority. 'The order of priorities which put Japan first presupposed that Japan would attack us after we got into difficulties elsewhere. "Elsewhere" therefore came first, not second; and elsewhere could only mean Europe, and Europe could only mean Germany.' British resources were not sufficient to match Japan and Germany, and the danger from Germany was greatest. He did not dispute the idea that the Singapore base should be finished; but, after that, they should concentrate on European risks. Hankey put Japan and Germany on the same level of priority and Chatfield took the same view, suggesting that Japan would take advantage of German actions. Montgomery-Massingberd agreed with Chatfield and thought Germany would rearm in about five years. If, in the meantime, Britain strengthened its position in the Far East, Japan might be prevented from attacking during a European war. Concentrate on Singapore first, he said, but begin preparations against Germany. Warren Fisher supported Vansittart's view. Singapore must be finished, but the fundamental danger came from Germany. He felt they should disentangle themselves from the naval treaties (and the United States), and once they had regained Japanese respect they should get back on really good terms with Japan. The two top civil servants challenged the long established central principle of the imperial defence strategy.[44]

The DRC's first report, on 28 February 1934, stressed the importance of good relations with Japan and followed, in general, Vansittart's line. In the Far East the 'ultimate policy' should be one of accommodation and friendship with Japan, after an 'immediate and provisional policy' of showing a tooth. This meant completing the Singapore base. Germany was the 'ultimate potential enemy'. In an outline of the major 'deficiencies' of all services, involving a five to six year programme which would cost £72 millions, Singapore would require £4,435,800 for dockyard works and machinery, £3,605,000 for Stage I of the defences, and £1,430,000 for air defences involving nine squadrons.[45]

As the whole Singapore story had shown, it was always a long haul from paper proposals to government action. The Cabinet sent the DRC report to the Ministerial Committee on the Disarmament Conference, where strategic requirements could be weighed against political and financial considerations. Here, once more, Neville Chamberlain pressed the need to concentrate on home defences (especially the air force) and questioned the navy's eastern priorities. Britain could not afford to prepare for war against both Germany and Japan. He fully agreed with the completion of the Singapore base, but said they should postpone the plan for sending out battleships. Instead, Singapore should become a base for 'submarines and light craft'. This alarmed the First Lord of the Admiralty, Sir Bolton Eyres-Monsell, who said the 'immediate' (indeed 'hourly') threat was from Japan, the 'distant' threat from Germany. The Treasury, he said, was challenging the whole system of imperial strategy; they could hardly tell the Dominions to shift for themselves. Monsell found it 'heartbreaking' that the concept of British seapower should be challenged by the Treasury. It would mean abandoning the one power standard, something no party – not even the Communist Party – advocated. It must surely be wrong, he said, to abandon our seapower in order to create 'what would mainly be a municipal Air Force'. Chamberlain's proposal, with its implications of letting down the Dominions, possibly breaking up the Empire in the east, was not supported by J. H. Thomas (Secretary of State for the Dominions), Sir John Simon (Foreign Secretary), Ramsay MacDonald or Baldwin. The latter thought it would be difficult to get better relations with Japan and that Britain would have to look to the United States. The best the Chancellor could achieve in the seapower part of the argument (but not the air force and army parts) was that new naval building proposals should be postponed until after the 1935 London Naval Conference.[46]

So alarmed was Hankey about what he called Chamberlain's 'rather heretical doctrines' that he considered cancelling a trip to Australia to attend the Melbourne centenary celebrations. As he was also going to alert the Dominion Governments about British strategy and rearmament, he felt he could not face the Australians or New Zealanders if there was a chance that the promise to send the fleet to Singapore might be abandoned. He pleaded with Chamberlain and Baldwin for a Cabinet ruling on the matter. This was not forthcoming, but Hankey did secure an *aide-mémoire* from Baldwin on 31 July 1934 noting that: 'With the object of enabling the Fleet to proceed to Singapore in any major emergency in the Far East' it was the Government's policy to complete the first stage of the Singapore base by 1938; continue with the oil fuelling bases; and make up deficiencies in the navy (although the actual programme could not be made until after the 1935 naval conference.)[47] Thus the Singapore priority still held. Obligations to the Dominions had been a strong argument. The COS were able to reassure Dominion leaders that the Singapore base would be completed when they met during George V's Silver Jubilee in May 1935. But in their annual review for 1935, prepared for this meeting, they included one critical admission:

> That we should be called upon to fight Germany and Japan simultaneously without Allies is a state of affairs to the prevention of which our diplomacy would naturally be directed. With France as our Ally the naval situation in Europe would wear a different complexion, and the main British Fleet would be available to defend our Empire in the East.[48]

VII

There remained only the matter of Stage II of the defences – including two more 15" guns. This also came up in May 1935 and was given an unexpected boost by the Silver Jubilee. On 10 May the Director of Operations at the War Office alerted the Secretary of the CID's Joint Home and Overseas Defence subcommittee that Stage I would be completed sometime in 1936–7; that it was important not to delay Stage II, and he hoped that a recent half-million pound gift from Johore could be used for this purpose.

Yet another imperial windfall had come just at the right time, as had happened at important moments in the past. It was in fact the second gift in two years. In 1934 the Straits Settlements, having just won a six-year battle over its military contribution, had made a modest voluntary gift. The row arose over the War Office's attempt to get land for the permanent defences free. When the Colonial Office resisted the War Office said it would take the money from the military contribution amounting to 20 per cent of the Colony's revenue. A long inter-department battle then began in London. The Treasury suggested 17½ per cent. The Colonial Government finally opted for a fixed sum annually. This was agreed in 1932 as 4 million Straits dollars (£467,000) for five years. Each year (from 1934) the Legislative Council also voted an additional voluntary gift of half-a-million dollars (£58,000).[49]

The gift from Johore was of a different order. Sultan Ibrahim inquired on 27 April 1935 as to whether £500,000 would be acceptable as a Silver Jubilee gift.[50] The Sultan had on several

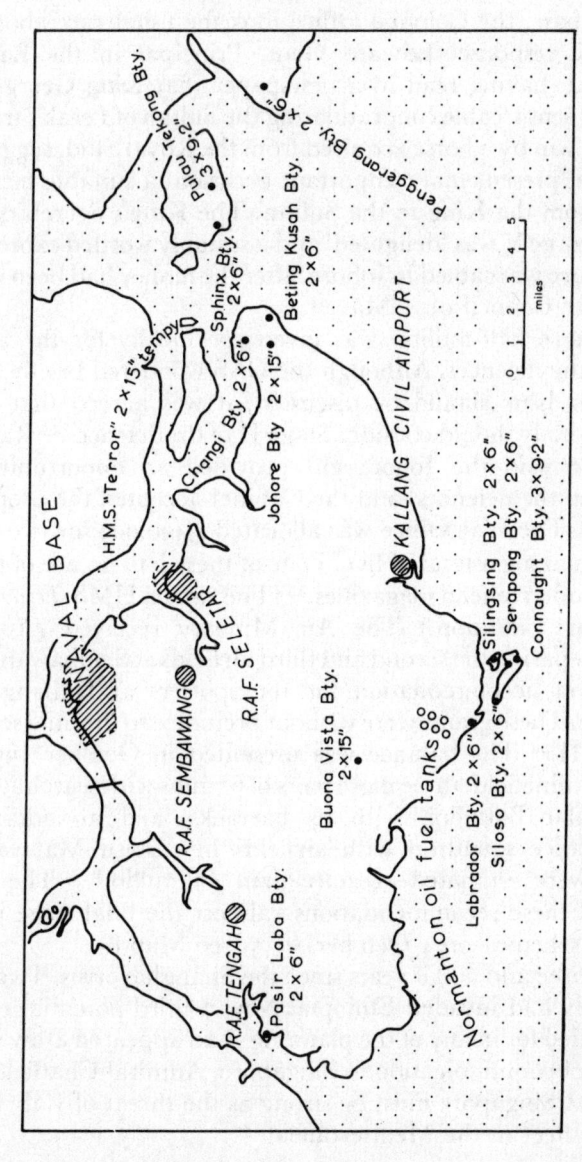

MAP 8. Gun-sites and airfields approved in 1935. The Johore Battery commemorated Sultan Ismail's Jubilee Gift

occasions had strained relations with British officialdom. But as Johore was clearly the most important Malay state in relation to the Singapore base, the Colonial Office took the usual care about an appropriate response. Edward Gent, Principal in the Eastern Department, having read in a newspaper that King George V's trainer had sent a cable congratulating the Sultan of Perak's trainer on a recent win by a horse acquired from the Royal Stud, suggested that on the 'present more important occasion' a suitable message could go from the King to the Sultan. The King's Secretary was alerted. George V was 'delighted' and a suitably worded expression of his pleasure was cabled to Johore, after the money had been voted by the State Council on 2 May.[51]

The Johore half-million was given specifically for the acceleration of the defences. Although the CAS wondered briefly if the Guns v Air issue should be discussed, it was agreed that some ministerial body should consider Stage II of the defences.[52] Ramsay MacDonald said the Johore gift provided an opportunity for speeding up the defences, and the Cabinet accepted the proposals on 24 July. The War Office was allocated £400,000 for two more 15″ guns, making a total of five. Four of these had an arc of fire of 360°, and subterranean magazines.[53] (The two on HMS *Terror* were a temporary addition.) The Air Ministry received £100,000 towards preparing the second and third airfields at Sembawang and Tengah and accommodation for the spotters at Kallang civil aerodrome. These grants were without prejudice to the final scheme for Stage II.[54] The balance was presented in October 1935. A controlled minefield; three more pairs of 6″ guns with searchlights; a third regular Battalion with its barracks, and an additional reconnaissance squadron with airfields in eastern Malaya and Sarawak were estimated at more than £1 million.[55] The COS considered these recommendations – almost the final stage in the truncated scheme – on 4 October 1935 (see Map 8).

It was three and a half years since the Shanghai crisis. Two days earlier Italy had invaded Ethiopia. Now a third potential enemy (not provided for in any of the planning) had appeared athwart the main line of communication to Singapore. Admiral Chatfield now argued that Singapore must be strong as the threat of Italy might detain the fleet in the Mediterranean.[56]

7 'Threats at Both Ends of the Empire', 1935-39

I

Italy was not considered as a potential enemy in the calculation of defence expenditure. Yet the Ethiopian War compromised the eastern strategy. As Admiral Chatfield said: 'the cable of Imperial Defence was stretched bar taut. Italy was the gnat whose weight could snap it'.[1] Since 1932 great efforts had been made to ensure the completion of the Singapore base – the vital precondition for the successful operation of the strategic plan east of Suez. Yet, at the same time, Germany's rearmament began to affect ideas about the disposition of the main fleet, the instrument of that strategy. Increasingly from 1932-3, doubts arose in Britain, Australia, New Zealand and Malaya as to whether the fleet could ever be sent to Singapore. In the second half of the 1930s the basic plan had to be viewed in the light of the debate about a 'new naval standard', the order of priorities if that standard was inadequate for all commitments, and growing uncertainty in the Mediterranean.

II

In Britain the most persistent voice in the attempt to remedy the navy's weakness was Chatfield, CNS from 1933 to 1938.[2] His argument was that the one power standard and the naval treaties had rendered the navy unequal to its responsibilities, and he pressed for a two power standard. He had, at first, to contend with residual hopes for disarmament among the politicians. Ramsay MacDonald tried to salvage something from the Geneva disarmament conference until it collapsed in May 1934. Hope then centred on another London Naval Conference to be held sometime before the Washington and London treaties expired at the end of 1936.

Throughout these multifarious discussions Chatfield stuck patiently to his point – the naval standard must be increased.

The first hint appeared in the 1933 COS annual review, which showed that the margin of British strength had been eroded; that 'we have to take into consideration an increasing German Navy, in calculating the margin of naval power we must leave in Europe if we have to despatch a Fleet to the Far East'.[3] The most positive call for a new standard was made in a naval staff paper of 23 March 1934 prepared for the Naval Conference:

> our naval defence policy should be such as to enable us to provide in the Far East a force of sufficient strength to ensure security for the Empire and its essential interests against Japanese encroachment or attack, to provide also protection for our merchant ships on all sea routes, and at the same time to have sufficient forces in European Waters and the Atlantic to give us security against the strongest European naval Power. This policy has been described as a 'Two-Power Standard'.[4]

Although the Washington ratio gave a virtual two power standard *vis-à-vis* Japan, over the years it had been eroded, especially in cruisers. The question now had to be faced: When a fleet was sent to the east, what was the minimum strength needed at home? If it was impossible, financially, to build naval forces of sufficient strength to match the strongest European power while already engaged with Japan, it had to be accepted that Britain could not 'simultaneously fight Japan and the strongest European naval power'. The 'minimum strategical requirement for security' was stated thus:

> We should be able to send to the Far East a fleet sufficient to provide 'cover' against the Japanese fleet; we should have sufficient additional forces behind this shield for the protection of our territories and mercantile marine against Japanese attack; at the same time, we should be able to retain in European waters a force sufficient to act as a deterrent and to prevent the strongest European naval Power from obtaining control of our vital home terminal areas while we can make the necessary redispositions.[5]

This formula, which shortly began to reappear as a sacred verse in strategic scripture, has been dubbed a 'somewhat optimistic adaptation of the One-Power Standard'.[6] It also became customary to date the doctrine from 1932.[7] It is clear from the context, however, that it was intended as an *increase* on the one power standard and was later treated as a step along the road to the 'new naval standard' of the later 1930s. Possibly the dating from 1932 was an example of the 'cheating' perpetrated in the CID secretariat when Hankey's assistants were unable to supply the precise documentation for a statement.[8]

Chatfield ensured that this minimum requirement was presented in all the discussions on defence deficiencies, the naval disarmament conference, the 1935 COS review,[9] and also explained at the Silver Jubilee Prime Ministers' meetings of May 1935. These meetings were soon followed by the Anglo-German naval agreement of 18 June 1935, which permitted Germany to build up to 35 per cent of Britain's strength. On the face of it a surprising concession, this agreement was made because Germany was expected to reach such a strength anyway, and a fixed ratio with Germany would simplify calculations about naval dispositions in the Atlantic and Pacific.[10] The picture was further complicated by the Ethiopian crisis.

Preparations against Italy did not feature in the CID's defence planning. Yet the sudden possibility, in 1935-6, of a conflict in the Mediterranean over the League of Nations sanctions seriously affected the Far Eastern strategy. 'We have relied on practically abandoning the Mediterranean if we send the Fleet east', wrote Chatfield.[11] He told the COS committee on 6 September 1935, while hasty moves were being made to reinforce the Mediterranean Fleet, that during a war with Italy there could be no question of defending British interests in the Far East.[12] In fact, reinforcements sent to Gibraltar and Aden during the crisis included cruisers from Australia, New Zealand and the China Squadron. One of the main reasons why the COS urged the Government to avoid war with Italy was their fear that the fleet would sustain damage which would prejudice its ability to fight Japan.[13] This lesson was not lost on the Defence Requirements Committee which was considering the naval building programme at the same time. Even a two power standard was insufficient if Italy had to be considered. Hankey wondered whether if, in a Far Eastern war, Italy were hostile, Britain should prepare to abandon the central and eastern Mediterranean, even Egypt, for a time. The CIGS said this would have serious repercussions in the Middle East, but to Hankey a collapse in the Far East would lead to the break-up of the Empire. He felt the navy should be strong enough to maintain its position at Singapore in addition to holding the Germans and keeping Italy neutral. This meant, for Chatfield, the two power standard or a French alliance.[14]

Hankey, who realised a major principle of imperial defence was at stake, felt the DRC should say 'boldly' that the navy should be strong enough to provide a safe defensive in the Far East and maintain Britain's position *vis-à-vis* Germany. Chatfield agreed, but it would need the building (as soon as the Washington treaty ended) of seven new battleships, four aircraft carriers, and an annual addition of five cruisers. With a total of twenty battleships, eleven could be sent to the Far East to meet Japan's nine, and nine remain at home against Germany's likely seven. As they drafted the DRC report Hankey wanted a naval standard which would provide 'a reliable deterrent at Singapore and at the same time dealt satisfactorily with Germany'.[15] This implied:

> a *new* standard of naval strength defined as follows: (i) To enable us to place a Fleet in the Far East fully adequate to act on the defensive and to serve as a strong deterrent against any threat to our interest in that part of the globe. (ii) To maintain in all circumstances in Home Waters a force able to meet the requirements of a war with Germany at the same time.[16]

Before this *new naval standard* (a semantically camouflaged two power standard, with a shift in emphasis towards Germany) went to the Cabinet, the chance of extending the Washington Treaty system was lost.

Japan had announced its intention of denouncing the treaties in 1934, and when Britain and the United States refused to concede parity, under the guise of a 'common upper limit', Japan left the London Naval Conference in January 1936. This meant that Britain's new programme could commence. A new urgency arose in March 1936 after Germany's reoccupation of the Rhineland. The COS now insisted on disengagement from the Mediterranean since preparations for war with Germany and Japan required a peaceful Mediterranean. This was the constant refrain in 1936 and bore fruit, in January 1937, in the rather vague Anglo-Italian agreement recognising freedom of transit. In fact Chatfield took the opportunity of a discussion on the strategic importance of Cyprus to rub in the message: 'The contingency of our becoming involved, simultaneously, in a war with Japan, Germany and Italy was one which should not be allowed to eventuate as it would involve the maintenance of a Three Power Naval Standard'.[17]

Although the two power standard was not authorised by the Cabinet, the 1936 rearmament budget and the supplementary estimates permitted work to begin on the shipbuilding programme, including the *King George V* and the *Prince of Wales*, the first of the new 36,750-ton battleships mounting ten 14" guns. By 1937 the naval staff took the view that the question of the new standard was of somewhat 'academic interest'. But the goal was now 20 capital ships, 15 aircraft carriers, 100 cruisers, 198 destroyers and 82 submarines. The capital ship requirement (never to be met) was calculated at one and a half times Japan's strength, plus 6:

Japan	Britain	Germany
9	20	7

With this total Germany and Japan could still be matched if Italy were neutral. In 1936, however, Chatfield had admitted that, if there had been a real crisis, only seven battleships would have been available for the Far East.[18]

III

The main concern of the naval staff, once rearmament was under way, was in restoring the credibility of the scheme of imperial defence. Clearly there were doubts as to whether under existing conditions in Europe and with the rise of the German Navy, Britain would be able to send an adequate fleet to the Far East.[19]

In Australia those doubts had been all too evident to Hankey during his visit in 1934. Although he insisted that, if the fleet arrived on time and found a properly equipped base at Singapore, Australia had nothing to fear but raids, Hankey found the Australians divided. Sir George Pearce (Defence Minister 1932–4) was an imperialist, who had private dreams of Australia, New Zealand and South Africa combining to pay for a battleship to be stationed in the Pacific, and for each of the Dominions to provide a regular battalion for a Dominions' Brigade of Guards, which might be posted to Singapore in an emergency.[20] But Pearce gave up the Defence portfolio. Hankey also met the exponents of the 'invasionist' school of thought, who rejected the assumptions of the scheme of imperial defence. In 1935 the retiring Chief of the General Staff, Major-General Julius Henry Bruche, and his successor designate, Colonel J. D. Laverack, both wrote comments on Hankey's report. They doubted Britain's ability to send the fleet because of events in Europe. They saw invasion as a real threat and suggested Australia should adopt 'self-reliance', with increased spending on the air force and the army. Australia should not rely on the promise to send the fleet without an 'absolute guarantee' from Britain. These points were also made by Colonel H. D. Wynter, in a lecture to the United Services Institution, which included one passage which was identical to Bruche's memorandum.[21] While the United Australia Party Government under Joseph A. Lyons continued to support the imperial strategy, the opposition Labor Party was now led by John Curtin, who took an interest in defence policy. He declared that mere reliance on Singapore might be 'hopelessly inefficient'.[22]

In New Zealand, the Chief of the General Staff, Major-General Sinclair-Burgess, was keen to raise a regular battalion for service in Singapore or India.[23] But before anything had been done the NZ Labour Party came to power at the end of 1935 and the CGS feared that the new ministry had little concept of 'imperial cohesion'. As it turned out he was wrong. The new government appointed a strong Cabinet committee to review defence organisation and spending. It determined to assist with defence in the Pacific region, but it rather shook the British defence establishment for a couple of years by making known it was thinking of giving up its two cruisers in favour of a stronger air force.[24] The new government was also advised by Sinclair-Burgess that, in spite of the British rearmament programme, he doubted whether the main fleet would be sent to the Pacific until the situation in Europe was safe, which might leave 'two or three years' in which a hostile Asian power could consolidate its control of the Pacific Ocean.[25]

Such doubts were not confined to the two loyal, but independent minded, southern Dominions. In the last months of 1936 Squadron Leader Lawrence Darvall, of the Operations and Intelligence Division of the Air Ministry, toured the air establishments in the Far East. At Singapore he found that the army and naval commanders and the Governor, Sir Shenton Thomas, were coming round to the opinion that, for some time to come, it was probable that the main British fleet could not in fact be sent to Singapore in an emergency, and that the fundamental basis upon which the existing defence schemes rested, which was the arrival of the main fleet at Singapore within between 30 and 40 days, was 'at present false'.[26] He claimed they were all placing their hopes in the RAF and were anxious that the air reinforcement route should be tried out. Such an exercise was conducted by the AOC Far East, Air Vice-Marshal Arthur Tedder, in 1937.[27]

Even if the special pleading in favour of army and air expenditure evident in all these expressions of doubt about the naval strategy are discounted, they revealed a significant loss of confidence. For this reason the British Government had to think carefully how it would reassure the Dominions during the Imperial Conference following George VI's coronation in 1937.

IV

In their preparations for the 1937 Imperial Conference the British COS produced two major documents, *The Review of Imperial Defence* and the *Far East Appreciation*. Both had important material on the Singapore strategy. The Review was a long and very 'political' document. When the COS committee considered an early draft on 5 February 1937, Hankey again referred to the Italian threat to Mediterranean communications. Chatfield reminded him of the ruling that preparations should not be made for wars with France, the USA or Italy, but he did suggest the insertion of the following significant paragraph:

> The chief danger which Imperial Defence has to face at the moment is that we are in the position of having threats at both ends of the Empire from strong military Powers, *i.e.* Germany and Japan, while in the centre we have lost our traditional security in the Mediterranean owing to the rise of an aggressive spirit in Italy . . . .[28]

Chatfield also knew that the Australians and New Zealanders would want to know whether the fleet would go to Singapore immediately on the outbreak of war in the Pacific. Hankey thought it was 'undesirable that they should press us for definite commitments, in the same manner as we have no intention of asking for definite reciprocal commitments from them'. However, certain 'broad statements' about the situation in a world war were included in the review.

> The security of the United Kingdom and the security of Singapore would be the keystones on which the survival of the British Commonwealth of Nations would depend. . . . A British fleet would have to proceed to the Far East leaving sufficient strength in home waters to neutralise the German fleet. . . . We could rely on France to neutralise the Italian fleet in the Mediterranean to some extent . . . [but] weakness in the Mediterranean would not be nearly so serious as the surrender of our sea power in the Far East. . . . This situation demands recognition of the principle that no anxieties or risks connected with our interests in the Mediterranean can be allowed to interfere with the despatch of a fleet to the Far East.[29]

This statement of priorities would, for the next few years, join the 'new standard of naval strength' as a sacred text in the strategic canon.

Before the Imperial Conference opened on 14 May 1937 the British COS had some preliminary meetings with Australian and New Zealand ministers and gained some idea of the issues these Dominions would raise. The meeting with Walter Nash, the New Zealand Finance Minister, who came ahead of his delegation, was rather awkward. Included in the Dominion's recent defence review was a report on the air force by Wing-Commander the Hon. Ralph Cochrane, RAF, and the New Zealand Government, inclining towards an air defence policy, was thinking of giving up the cruisers *Leander* and *Achilles*. Nash spoke obstinately and rather repetitively in favour of two medium bomber squadrons, which would be only 36 flying hours away from Singapore, while Chatfield pleaded patiently for the retention of the cruisers. Hankey outlined the 'great concerted scheme of Imperial Defence' into which the cruisers fitted, and said if New Zealand withdrew them 'she would be pulling out bits of the whole structure'.[30] This argument went on and on, but a decision could not be made in London. The meeting with Sir Archdale Parkhill, the Australian Defence Minister, was more cordial. Parkhill supported the concept of imperial defence. He quickly grasped the key points in COS papers, and noted the proposed 'new' naval standard, but he was concerned about time factors. Australia was still undecided on the relative weight to be given to the three services, and doubts about the fleet would lead to calls for a larger army and air force. Hankey reminded the COS that Australia was the one Dominion willing to spend largish sums on defence and he suggested showing the delegates the *Far East Appreciation*.[31]

The British ministers now had to decide how honest they could be with the Dominions. When the Cabinet's new Defence Policy (Plans) Subcommittee met, in May 1937, to consider the line they would adopt at the conference, it was agreed that the First Lord would have to say that the fleet 'as it is to-day' could not fight simultaneously in the east and the west– hence the plans for the new naval standard, which had yet to be finalised. They could not take a negative line and imply it was impossible to implement naval policy in the Far East for fear the Dominions would abandon imperial defence. Yet it would be equally wrong to let the Dominions think that there was no question of our ability to defend our interests in the Far East 'irrespective of their cooperation'. It was decided to 'leave them guessing', even that it would be a good idea to 'give the Australians a fright'. Sir Thomas Inskip said it was only necessary to tell them the truth.[32] The COS were not anxious to do this. If the Dominions were to see the *Far East Appreciation*, the CIGS suggested certain phrases implying that Singapore might fall during the period before relief should be cut out.[33]

V

The Imperial Conference was, of course, not primarily concerned with Far East strategy. Like its predecessors, it was a great Commonwealth occasion, with the added interest of the coronation, and the change-over from Baldwin to Neville Chamberlain as premier actually during the conference. The plenary sessions concentrated on international affairs, the Ethiopian crisis, the League of Nations, imperial preferences, shipping and communications.[34] A committee was set up to examine an Australian proposal for a Regional Pact in the Pacific to include the USA and Japan. Nevertheless some important questions emerged in the two sessions on defence which led to a series of smaller meetings between the Australian and New Zealand delegates and the British COS. In these the New Zealand Labour Prime Minister, Michael Joseph Savage (who was also an outspoken critic of appeasement and Britain's failure to strengthen the League) professed himself very anxious about Pacific security.

On 24 May, Sir Thomas Inskip, the Minister for Defence Co-ordination, presented the *Review of Imperial Defence* and outlined Britain's rearmament plans. Parkhill indicated that Australia's policy was based upon imperial defence as the deterrent to potential invaders of his country. He noted that Britain's preparations against Germany would be ready by 1934, but those against Japan not until 1942. Savage, who began by saying that the 'Commonwealth must stand or fall together', said New Zealand doubted whether the fleet would be sent to Singapore if Britain was engaged in Europe when Japan attacked. This elicited from Inskip the specific reply that the Royal Navy did not look after the UK alone, but the COS always considered strategy as covering 'all parts of the Commonwealth equally'.[35]

The Tasman neighbours gave a similar response to Sir Samuel Hoare's rather vague exposition of naval strategy on 26 May. The 'very existence of the British Commonwealth of Nations' rested on the ability to send the fleet to Singapore and, at present, Britain could do this and have sufficient for home security, but he admitted in 1938-9 they would have to rely on France v Germany and could only send a fleet to the Far East 'slightly inferior' to Japan's. Parkhill unfailingly put his finger on the key paragraphs in the *Review* about Singapore being one of the 'keystones' of Commonwealth security and noted that the Far East was given priority over the Mediterranean. Savage, however, read out a carefully worded statement of New Zealand's concern. Was it possible to maintain a battleship force permanently in the Far East? If not, could the Dominion have a 'positive statement' that a fleet in sufficient strength would be sent even if Britain was embarrassed in Europe? What strength would be available? He also asked something of particular interest to the Dominion: What was the strategic importance of the Pacific Islands? He wanted answers in writing and a meeting with the COS. From the chair, Baldwin (on his last working day as Prime Minister), closed with the laconic prediction that Japan would not 'run amok' unless there was a war in Europe; as long as they kept the peace in Europe, all would be well.[36]

Inskip, Savage and Parkhill arranged a special meeting with the COS about Pacific security questions and the COS now decided that the 'co-operating delegations' – Australia, New Zealand and India – should definitely see the revised *Far East Appreciation*.[37] This long paper, which was an appreciation of how a war in the Far East would have to be fought, provided answers to some of the Dominion questions. It was based on the assumption of no simultaneous war in

Europe, but contained some very specific detail about the disposition of the fleet. The plan envisaged sending twelve battleships to meet Japan's nine. It recited the 'new naval standard' and gave details of the expected distribution of all existing capital ships between 1937 and 1940. Numbers available for the Far East would be:

   Summer 1937–Spring 1938 10
   Spring 1938–Summer 1939   8
   Summer 1939–Spring 1940 10

This meant that only in 1938–9 would Britain have less than Japan's nine. The appreciation did, however, include the usual proviso that if war broke out in the Far East while Britain was at war with Germany the timing and size of the fleet sent to Singapore would 'depend upon the conditions which have actually arisen.'[38]

Chatfield introduced the *Appreciation* at the meeting chaired by Inskip on 1 June, and attended by the British COS, Malcolm MacDonald (Secretary of State for Dominions), Parkhill (for Australia), General Bartholomew (Chief of Staff, India), Savage, Nash and Carl Berendsen (head of the New Zealand Prime Minister's Department), and Captain Tom Phillips (Director of Plans at the Admiralty). The answer to Savage's questions about stationing a fleet at Singapore permanently (the Jellicoe solution) was that it would be too 'challenging' an act diplomatically; it would also require two-thirds of the fleet to be credible, which in turn would need a vastly enlarged Singapore base, and anyhow the fleet might be needed in Europe.[39] The ironies contained in these points may have been missed. To meet New Zealand's concern about the Pacific Islands the COS produced a detailed paper, which was discussed at another meeting on 7 June. It listed all the islands, noting their political attachments and physical capabilities and suggested their main significance was as possible fuelling anchorages. The Australian and New Zealand air forces might assist in reconnaissance in the Pacific, but landing grounds would have to be developed.[40] Chatfield tried to get an answer about the New Zealand cruisers at this meeting, but Savage, who agreed that New Zealand would 'sink or swim' with Britain, said the decision would be made in Wellington.

If the New Zealand questions focused on the doubts about the despatch of the fleet to Singapore, the Australian questions were more searching and political. The British answers, in all cases, were vague. Would Britain go to war to defend Hong Kong? It was impossible to say beforehand. Were the Netherlands East Indies vital to Singapore and imperial defence? Yes, but it was 'inadvisable to announce this'. What degree of harmony was there with the USA in Asia? General harmony, but no specific agreement. How far could the USA be relied upon? 'Nothing specific' could be relied upon from the USA. At the special meeting with Australian delegates on 21 June Parkhill wanted to know how long Singapore could hold out. Chatfield (a patient if humourless soul), said it would be 'a reasonably safe assumption' to say that Singapore would not fall before the arrival of the fleet, but he would not say it was 100 per cent secure, not even 99.1 per cent secure. Seventy-five per cent? asked Parkhill, but the CIGS suggested 'a very much higher percentage'.[41]

The Imperial Conference formally ended on 15 June 1937. It had exposed most of the fundamental questions about Singapore and strategy, but it had not provided many 'positive statements'. On the one hand, Britain had promised that Singapore was one of the twin 'keystones' of Commonwealth security; that it had actual plans to send eight to ten capital ships, that the Far East had priority over the Mediterranean. On the other hand, the Government refused to give specific undertakings as to the timing and size of the fleet which would be sent if war broke out in Europe first.

One wonders how far the British planners believed in their own priorities. Chatfield had been anxious about the Mediterranean ever since the Ethiopian War. Shortly after the Imperial Conference the CID discussed the Mediterranean and Chatfield admitted that, in spite of the accepted ruling that no risks there were to be allowed to delay the fleet for Singapore, Britain could not afford to abandon Egypt, Palestine and the Red Sea.[42] Two days later, on the night of 7/8 July 1937 fighting broke out between Chinese and Japanese troops near Peking. The Undeclared War began. By September Japan was blockading the China coast and China appealed to the League. Chatfield's attitude was the same as in the Ethiopian crisis. He could only hope that Britain would not be dragged by the 'sentimentals' to apply sanctions against Japan. 'We have got quite enough troubles on our hands in Europe to make it most undesirable to send the Fleet out to the Far East.'[43]

Moreover, throughout the 1937 conference period, discussions had been going on behind the scenes about extending the period before relief. The matter had been raised in 1936 by the Government of the Straits Settlements as part of the plans for provisioning. The Overseas Defence Subcommittee wanted to revert to a 42-day period (28 days from zero, plus 14 for bad weather). Chatfield felt this was too short. Up to 10 days were needed for preparations, and 17 more if the fleet had to go round the Cape. Thus 10 plus 42 plus 17 meant 69, which could be expressed as 70. So long as Singapore held out the situation in the Far East could always be retrieved once the fleet had arrived. The COS discovered that they also had to contend with a period before reprovisioning, and the army was already working on holding supplies for 60 days. The ODC were asked to cost the provisioning needs for 50, 70 and 90 days, and on 4 March 1938 the CID formally recommended a 70-day period before relief. Bruce thereupon began his customary recitation of Australia's interest in Singapore but was deflected on this occasion by the Secretary of State for War, Hore-Belisha, who referred to the longstanding, but as yet fruitless, effort to get some Australian help with the garrison.[44]

VI

Amid all these uncertainties there was one visible advance. On 14 February 1938 a ceremony was held at Singapore to mark the opening of 'KG6', the King George VI dry dock. Plans for this event had slowly matured since early 1937, when it became known that the dock would be finished on time by Jackson's in July, and that Stage I of the defences were also nearing completion. The full dockyard was not expected to be completed until 1941. But it was felt that something impressive had to be laid on for the Malay Sultans after all their generosity, which included another contribution of 2½ million dollars (over £200,000), given in November 1937 towards the cost of two air squadrons. It had to be a 'minor ceremony' of a 'local character' to avoid diplomatic complications or publicity for the base's shortcomings. Admiral Chatfield felt that, with the war in China, it was hardly the time for ceremonial in Singapore, but advantage was taken of the presence of a large number of vessels for a combined exercise planned for the first week in February 1938.

It was hoped that the King might open the dock by wireless, but the navy's transmitters were not up to it. Instead the Governor of the Straits Settlements sailed round from Singapore in his official yacht, which cut the tape as it entered the dock. Two squadrons of the Fleet Air Arm provided a fly-past, the Straits Settlements RNVR two escort launches. Among the 42 vessels in attendance were the aircraft carrier *Eagle*, the 8″ cruisers *Norfolk* and *Dorsetshire* and three ships of the Royal Indian Navy. Most significant of all were the American cruisers *Trenton*, *Memphis* and *Milwaukee*, sent as a 'demonstration' by President Roosevelt following secret staff talks in London.[45] They naturally excited comment from French, German and Japanese sources in London, but the visit was passed off as 'fortuitous'. The Civil Lord of the Admiralty, Colonel J. T. Llewellan, who was travelling to Australia, thanked the Governor in a speech. All the Malay rulers attended, with their Residents, as did the leading civil servants, service commanders, foreign consuls, the British Minister from Thailand and Australia's Chief of Air Staff. New Zealand did not send a representative as the Government was preoccupied with its social security bill. The Japanese Consul-General attended the opening but not the reception. British newspapers featured pictures of the colourful Malay rulers, the Governor's yacht and illuminated warships, but not the RAF aerial photos which showed the unfinished wharves and the absence of cranes. The press did, however, give convenient publicity to the rumour that 18″ guns were being installed, thus contributing to the illusion that an 'impregnable fortress' had been finished.[46]

Such an illusion offered no comfort to the local commanders, who must have been pondering, amid the bands and bunting and silk-clad Sultans, on the lessons of the combined exercises held in the previous week. They continued to absorb them for the rest of 1938. From 2 to 5 February the aircraft carrier *Eagle*, two 8″ cruisers, one 6″ cruiser, six destroyers, and a company of regular infantry had fought for 'Blueland', an imaginary Asian state 1200 miles east of Singapore, which had long nursed a grievance about the Colony's high tariffs. Taking advantage of the political situation in Europe it had decided to attack Singapore, 'Redland', by naval bombardment, small-scale landings and carrier-based bombing raids. Singapore's defence organisation, combined operations headquarters, air and submarine reconnaissance system and anti-aircraft defences were to be tested. 'Greenland' (Netherlands East Indies) was neutral.

The exercise was a triumph for the Fleet Air Arm operating from HMS *Eagle*. On two successive nights the carrier sailed undetected to within 135 miles of Singapore. The illuminated hangars at Tengah and Seletar and the shore defence searchlights were visible from 80 miles away. The airfields were 'bombed' at dawn without opposition. The carrier was spotted only after it had flown-off its bombers. It was attacked while landing them, but the Red bombers were attacked, in turn, by the carrier's fighters.

The exercise culminated in a night air raid of which the garrison got no warning. The conclusion of Tedder, the Air OC, was definite. At present they had no way of preventing a surprise air attack at night or at dawn. General Dobbie, the GOC, admitted that the anti-aircraft defences were disappointing and that Combined-Ops HQ was unsatisfactory. By contrast the navy's close submarine reconnaissance patrol was effective and no vessel entered the Singapore Strait undetected. Ships and planes had approached Singapore without warning being given until the planes were heard, or the ships reached the submarine area. Reading these reports in the Admiralty, Captain Victor Danckwerts, the deputy Director of Plans, noted that Singapore needed radar, which already could detect aircraft at 130 miles and ships at 60 miles.[47] Air Ministry scientists did recommend radar for Singapore in 1938, but installation had to wait until 1941.[48]

No real test was made of the heavy artillery or beach defences. The attacking forces were very small, but apparently a night landing-party from HMS *Norfolk* managed to capture the Raffles Hotal unopposed.[49] The army did endeavour to make progress later in the year. They also held their own ceremony later in 1938 to mark the completion of the first 15" gun turret, when Dobbie invited Tedder to fire the first round. If this was intended as a closing gesture in the Guns v Air truce, it misfired. Tedder, seeing the date stamped on the breech of the surplus First World War naval gun, 'rather unkindly asked Dobbie whether 1915 was the best they could do for him'. He doubted the gun would ever fire in anger, as it covered the entrance of the Singapore Strait and he said he would not expect an enemy to 'break in the front door'.[50]

This remark did less than justice to Dobbie, who had already questioned the defence scheme, and who, in 1938, made three prescient recommendations. First, he authorised his chief of staff, Colonel Arthur Percival, to give the War Office a memorandum he had written suggesting that the Japanese might strike at Malaya from southern Thailand. This indicated that the defence of northern Malaya was important and that stronger air forces were needed.[51] Secondly, Dobbie recommended that the beach defences be augmented with anti-tank weapons and he also called for 15 tanks. Thirdly, he conducted an exercise in southern Malaya which proved that country 'formerly regarded as impassable' could be traversed by infantry. He recommended that the defences of Singapore should extend along an arc in Johore of 21 miles radius from the naval base, since the most likely attack would be a landing on the east coast. He estimated that £250,000 was needed for defence works, including a strengthening of the southern beach defences, so that the army could create a reserve for deployment in Johore. Concrete anti-tank obstacles, gun and machine-gun emplacements, cleared fields of fire, mines, barbed wire and improved lateral communications were all called for in Johore.[52] All these suggestions were approved by the War Office, which approached the Treasury for funds, of which only £60,000 was allowed. Tanks, however, were not available; all the War Office could offer was seven armoured cars. The wheel had come full circle. The COS, in London, went back to the policy of 1921 and accepted that the Japanese would probably prefer to carry out an unopposed landing on the east coast and 'advance on the base from the north'.[53] Thus while the world was told, in 1938, that the Singapore base was 'open', the defenders knew that it was still wide open to attack.

VII

In March 1938, less than a month after the opening of the dock at Singapore, Hitler occupied Austria, and then turned his attention to the German-speaking portions of Czechoslovakia. British rearmament was far from complete, so for much of 1938 great pains were taken to appease Italy and Germany. The Anglo-Italian agreement of 16 April 1938, recognising the Italian Empire in Ethiopia in return for Italian withdrawal from the Spanish Civil War, and the September Munich agreement over the Sudetenland both found fervent support in all the Dominions, except Labour-ruled New Zealand.[54] Meanwhile the Australian and New Zealand Governments were both giving a good deal of thought to the problems of imperial defence in the Far East. The Australian Prime Minister, Joseph Lyons, assured Chamberlain in January 1938 that Australia would assist to the full extent of its power, and on 28 April he announced in Canberra a £43 million defence programme, of which £24,800,000 was for new projects over three years. Summing up his Government's defence policy, Lyons declared:

> Australian defence is related to a wider pattern of Empire defence, and its fundamental basis is Empire sea power and the Singapore Naval Base. Nevertheless, complementary to this conception of Empire collective security we should do all that we can to defend ourselves . . . .[55]

New Zealand for its part did not give up the two cruisers, which were part of imperial defence, in favour of the two medium bomber squadrons recommended by Cochrane. It decided to have both and was particularly interested in helping among the Pacific Islands.

In view of this Anzac willingness – the pay-off, perhaps, of the Imperial Conference discussions in 1937 – the British COS agreed to provide another list of possible tasks for these Dominions. At the end of March 1938 the Joint Planning subcommittee (consisting of Captain Tom Phillips, Colonel Edwin Morris and Group Captain John Slessor) summarised these possibilities. In naval defence they referred to an idea, mooted in 1934 and again in 1937, that Australia should acquire a capital ship. At the cost of £8 million, a modern battleship would cost little more that two 8″ cruisers and would provide 'a great deterrent' in Australian waters, as HMAS *Australia* had been in 1914. New Zealand, they suggested, might fulfil its long-postponed aim of taking on a third cruiser. The precedent for Dominion armies was already provided by New Zealand's commitment to send a garrison to Fanning Island. Anzac units might be sent to Hong Kong, Singapore, or Trincomalee, where artillery or anti-aircraft units would be particularly welcome. Similarly, Dominion air squadrons might be sent to Singapore where a ten-squadron force was envisaged, but only four were available in 1938. Until 1940 the only possible reinforcements would be four more squadrons from Iraq and India. Reserves could more easily be sent from Australia. An ultimate goal might be Australian regional responsibility for air defence, with an Australian AOC in the Far East.[56]

In the short term, priority was given to naval and air assistance. There was nothing new in these proposals and some of them were not really welcome to British or Dominion authorities. The British COS decided that the disadvantages of having Anzac troops in the garrisons outweighed the advantages, because of differing pay scales and political complications if the army was called on to aid the civil power.[57]

In the practical response to these proposals the Australian Government was less clear what it should do and was the more cautious of the two Dominions. Sir Earle Page (the Minister of Commerce) and Robert Menzies (the up-and-coming Attorney-General) visited London in May 1938 and had discussions with the COS. Page was shown the 1937 *Review* and the paper answering the Australian delegates' questions including material from the *Far East Appreciation*.[58] They also discussed with Chatfield the idea of Australia buying a battleship. The CNS (who had thought that a new *King George V* class would be a possibility) said one would not be ready before 1943.[59] But the Australian Government had to step warily. During the defence programme debate Curtin, the Labor Party leader, said in Parliament that he was 'very doubtful if Great Britain could come to our aid in sufficient time'.[60]

After Munich, when the Japanese took the opportunity of Europe's preoccupation to advance into southern China, the Australian Government began to panic. Bruce kept telephoning the Admiralty about sending a battleship to Singapore, or Australia buying a battleship in place of one of its cruisers.[61] On 1 November 1938 the First Lord of the Admiralty assured him that seven battleships would be sent to Singapore immediately on the outbreak of war in the East.[62] (This was one short of the *Far East Appreciation* minimum.)

Lyons, the Prime Minister, telephoned Bruce from Canberra and suggested that as an alternative to buying a battleship (which could not be available for five years) Australia should get a private undertaking that a *King George V* class would be allocated to the Far East and spend a reasonable amount of time in Australian waters.[63] It took a month of 'considerable pressure' from Bruce to get an answer to his request – probably because Lord Stanhope (the First Lord) was new to office and Sir Roger Backhouse was taking over from Chatfield as CNS. In Canberra, the British High Commissioner found Lyons had 'worked himself into a kind of desperate anxiety about the defence of Australia against Japan'. Lyons was a sick man; he was worried about his political position, and he gave Sir Geoffrey Whiskard the impression that he had come round to Curtin's viewpoint on defence – that Australia could count on no help from Britain and that it would be Japan's prime target.[64]

This news from Canberra, combined with Bruce's importunities, led to a review of the Admiralty's role in Australia's defence. The First Lord informed Bruce that although a definite assurance could not be given, a battle-cruiser (not a *King George V*) might become the flagship of the East Indies Squadron in 1942.[65] Admiral Backhouse suggested the preparation of a new paper on Australian Naval Co-operation. It put formally (on 20 December 1938) the substance of the conversations with Bruce since Munich. It reiterated the doctrine that the ultimate security of Australia depended on the main fleet, but it included a few changes of emphasis. First, the cost of maintaining in full commission the fleet required in the Far East, as well as a force necessary for security in Europe, was now admitted to be beyond Britain's resources. The timing of the fleet for Singapore would be affected because of the recent expansion of the German navy. Secondly, it left it open for Australia to acquire a battleship by paying for one of the 1938–9 building programme. Thirdly, it gave the current capital ship strength as fifteen (of which three were under reconstruction). Thus the average availability in 1939 would be twelve. The five new *King George V* class would not be ready until 1940–1 to give a total strength of nineteen by 1942.[66] Before this reassessment went to the COS Backhouse admitted to Colonel Ismay (Hankey's successor as secretary) that he felt that the 1937 *Review* and the *Far East Appreciation* were somewhat out of date.

When the COS committee discussed the matter on 13 January 1939 the naval staff's tactics did not meet with approval. Edward Bridges, the Secretary of the Cabinet, felt that a simple addition to the 1937 *Review* would suffice. The paper for the Australians was left to hang fire and was overtaken by new considerations in February 1939.

By contrast, New Zealand showed a more positive mood in 1938 and received (unexpectedly) a more fulsome guarantee than was accorded the Australians. The Dominion's particular concern was the South Pacific and possible threats to its Island Territories (Western Samoa, the Cook Islands and Niue). It also realised that the British Colony of Fiji would, in hostile hands, pose a threat to New Zealand. Therefore, on the basis of the 1937 Imperial Conference paper on the strategic importance of the islands, the Dominion Government offered to survey possible landing grounds for an air reconnaissance network between the Dominion and Fiji, and along four routes radiating from Fiji. These went north to the Gilbert Islands; northeast to Fanning and Christmas Island;

northeast to Samoa, the northern Cooks and the Line Islands, and eastwards to Tonga and the Cook Islands. It also suggested a conference in Wellington to settle the details. The British COS naturally welcomed this initiative.[67] (See Map 9.)

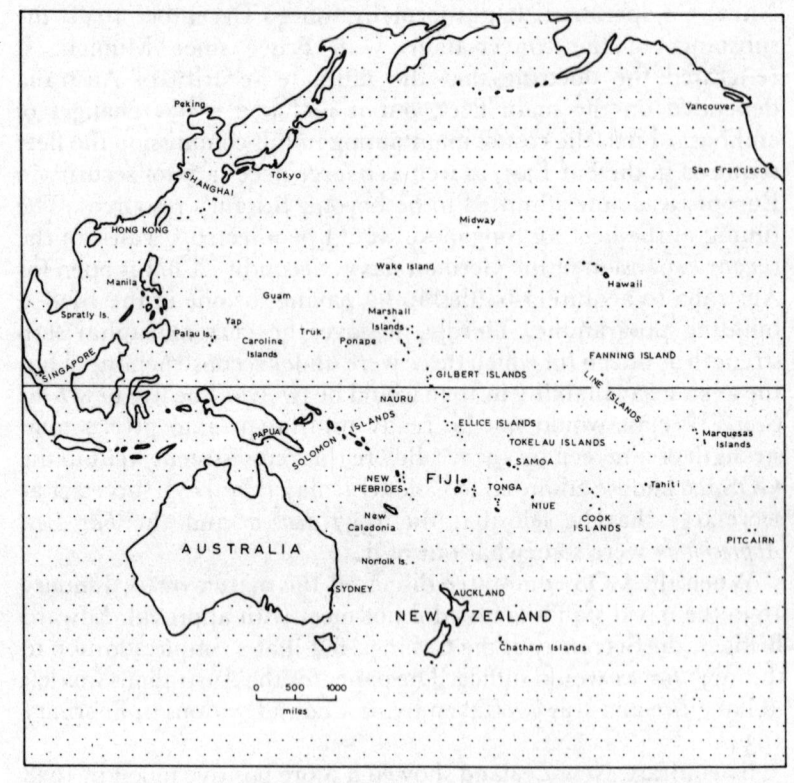

MAP 9. Australia, New Zealand, Fiji and the Pacific Islands

By the end of 1938 these proposals, combined with the earlier ideas about Dominion contributions in the Far East, prompted the New Zealand Government to suggest a widening of the scope of the proposed Wellington conference to a consideration of Pacific security generally (land, sea and air), the timing of the naval reinforcement of Singapore, and possible New Zealand garrisons in islands such as Fiji and Tonga.[68]

The COS subcommittee discussed this wider proposal on 27 January 1939, with Sir Charles Dixon of the Dominions Office and

Sir Harry Batterbee (who was about to become Britain's first High Commissioner in Wellington). Sir Arthur Newall, the CAS, wondered if the Dominion Government was not trying to arrange a 'miniature Imperial Conference' and was very sceptical. But Batterbee said they should not 'pour cold water' on the idea. The COS decided they could provide a United Kingdom delegation from senior officers on loan to Australia.[69] Moreover, as New Zealand was about to spend money, in spite of its own severe financial difficulties, the British COS decided they ought to provide another up-to-date strategic review to give a sound basis for the Dominion to make its choices.[70] The paper, *New Zealand Cooperation in Imperial Defence* (1 February 1939) was a conflation of the 1937 Review and the *Far East Appreciation* with certain modifications. Thus it was now admitted that, if Japan struck while Germany and Italy were attacking Britain's trade in the Atlantic and the Mediterranean, naval forces would be dispersed and 'it could not be guaranteed that the whole of the Fleet destined for the Far East could be despatched immediately'. However, it confirmed the 1937 priority with the words: 'in the event of war with Japan, we should send a Fleet to Eastern waters *irrespective* of the situation elsewhere'.[71]

This was the most categorial promise the British Chiefs of Staff had yet made. Before it reached Wellington in April 1939, Japan had occupied the Spratly Islands, Hitler occupied Bohemia, and the British Government had begun to have misgivings about the promise.

8 'So Many Variable Factors', 1939-40

I

The naval staff predicted that 1939 would be the 'worst year' because of the time-lag in the shipbuilding programme. The promise to send the fleet to Singapore 'irrespective' of the situation elsewhere had also to be viewed against a deteriorating political background. Japan occupied Hainan on 3 February and annexed the Spratly Islands on 30 March, thus pre-empting or screening the British fleet's intended fuelling anchorages at Yu Lin Bay and Cam Ranh Bay[1] (see Map 10). Germany entered Prague on 15 March and Italy invaded Albania on 7 April. As a result of the war-scares of early 1939 the Government arranged staff talks with the French and sought alliances in eastern Europe. Yet the Admiralty insisted that, until the *King George V* class of battleships was completed in 1940-1, the capital ship strength would be nearly as bad as at the time of the Manchurian crisis. It was true that the first two of four new *Lion* class battleships had been ordered, but neither had been laid down. These 40,000 ton ships, armed with nine 16" guns, would be the first British battleships comparable with the latest American, Japanese or German ship. But none would be ready before 1944. The total available strength in mid-1939 was reduced to ten by the refit programme. The 1937 promise, which placed the Far East before the Mediterranean, assumed that between eight and ten battleships would go to Singapore if Italy was neutral. In 1939 this promise became the subject of debate among the COS and the Cabinet, and it was slightly modified. In 1940, when Italy entered the war, the 1937 priority had to be reversed.

II

Doubts about the 1937 promise arose *before* the Japanese, German and Italian moves of early 1939. They began, for the naval staff, in

MAP 10. Japan moves south

the aftermath of Munich, when Bruce, the Australian High Commissioner, had sought new assurances about battleships for the East, and the Australian Prime Minister, Lyons, admitted his own fears that they would never come. As the COS began to consider how to word a new assurance to Australia, in December 1938 Admiral Backhouse, the CNS, had to admit that the promises in the 1937 *Review* and the answers to the Australian questions based on the *Far East Appreciation* ought to be revised. If the worst came to the worst he still hoped that the navy could send some battleships to the Far East, but he was concerned that the timing would be affected by the mobilisation of a sufficient force, since this could not be maintained permanently in commission.[2] In the face of this admission, Gort, the CIGS, drew attention to the 1937 priority, which put the Far East before the Mediterranean, and the deputy-CAS, Air Vice-Marshal Peirse, said that he would be sorry to see the COS repudiate what amounted to an 'absolute promise' to send an adequate fleet to the Far East.[3] Thus the COS treated the Australian question with circumspection and they quietly delayed. On 13 January 1939 they suggested drafting a qualification about the timing of the fleet, to be added to the naval appendix of the 1937 *Review*. When they considered this draft a month later they realised that the period before relief would need lengthening and, as the Australian Government would have to be told, they again postponed a decision.[4] However, on 24 February 1939 the matter came up in the more urgent context of a CID discussion of the *European Appreciation 1939–40* as part of the preparations for the Anglo-French staff talks planned for the following month.[5]

At this meeting Chamberlain, the Prime Minister, noted that the promise to the Dominions about the fleet for Singapore had been 'categorical and unqualified'. Yet, he said, the implication of the statement that the strength of the fleet would depend on the war in the European theatre, was that the fleet sent to the Far East might be inadequate. He wondered if the Dominions should be informed of this. Sir Kingsley Wood said it would be a great shock to the Dominions. Lord Chatfield (who was now in the Government as Minister for Defence Co-ordination) defended the 1937 priority. He calculated that with France as an ally Britain would still be able to send nine capital ships to the Far East, leaving four British and five French to match the six of Germany and Italy. Even a smaller number sent to Singapore would prevail because of the 'greater efficiency' of the British fleet.[6] The CID decided to refer the *European Appreciation* to a new Strategic Appreciations Sub-committee. As Backhouse claimed he did not have a chance in the CID meeting to express a view on the Far East strategy, he sent a paper to the SAC on 28 February giving up-to-date figures on the availability of battleships. Until September 1939 the total would be only twelve, of which two would be under refit, leaving ten. Germany had two battle-cruisers and the three 'pocket battleships', therefore Britain needed to keep six in home waters. If Germany sent one or two to attack Atlantic shipping Britain would need three or four to pursue them. The number which could then be spared for the Far East could not exceed four or five, which would be inadequate, and this took no account of a Mediterranean war.

Admiral Backhouse's pessimistic analysis was considered by the

BEGINNINGS

1. *Admiral of the Fleet Lord Jellicoe at work in Christchurch, New Zealand, September 1919, during the Empire Naval Mission (*The Press, Christchurch*)*

2. *Normanton Oil Fuel Depot, west of Singapore in 1924. (Part of the year's supply approved by the Cabinet in 1919) (War Office Records, Public Record Office)*

GUNS V. AIR

3. *A 15" naval gun, adapted for coastal defence (Imperial War Museum)*

4. *David, Lord Beatty (Chief of Naval Staff, 1919-27) (From A. Marder, From Dreadnought to Scapa Flow, Oxford University Press)*

5. *The Earl of Cavan (Chief of the Imperial General Staff 1922-26) (Illustrated London News)*

THE PLANNERS

6. *Hawker* Horsley *proposed as a torpedo bomber in 1929 (Imperial War Museum)*

7. *Sir Hugh Trenchard (Chief of Air Staff 1919-29) (From Montgomery Hyde,* Air Policy Between the Wars, *Heinemann)*

8. Left *Air Vice-Marshal Arthur Tedder (Air Officer Commanding, RAF Far East)* and right *Air Vice-Marshal Richard Williams (Chief of Air Staff of Australia) at the dockyard opening ceremonies, 1938 (Admiralty Records, Public Record Office)*

GUNS V. AIR

9. *The boom of the big guns practising gave comfort to the inhabitants of Singapore (Imperial War Museum)*

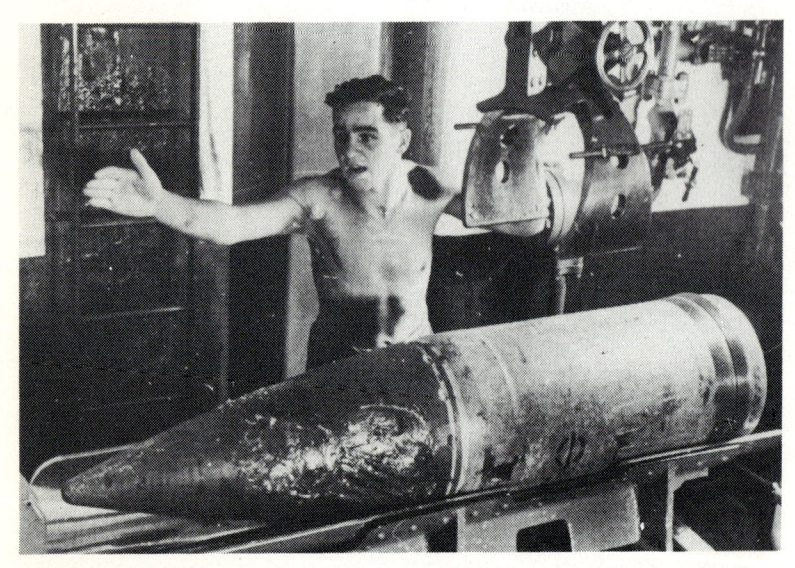

10. *One of the 15" guns was mounted in an above-ground turret with magazines alongside and only a 35° arc of fire. The other four were in naval-type turret mountings, with magazines below and a 360° arc of fire (Imperial War Museum)*

THE EQUIPMENT

11. *Vickers* Vildebeeste *torpedo bomber. The small island (appearing left of the tail) is Pulau Brani and the long island (behind) is Pulau Blakang Mati (Ministry of Defence, Crown copyright)*

12. *Bristol* Blenheim *fighter-bomber (Imperial War Museum)*

INFLUENTIAL PERSONALITIES

13. *Sir Maurice Hankey (Secretary of the Cabinet and of the CID to 1938) (Reproduced by permission of Lord Hankey)*

14. *Sir Leopold Savile (Civil Engineer-in-Chief at the Admiralty 1919-32) (Institution of Civil Engineers)*

15. *Stanley M. Bruce, Prime Minister of Australia (1923-29), Minister in London 1932-33 and High Commissioner in London 1933-45 (From C. Edwards,* Bruce of Melbourne, *Heinemann)*

16. Left *Richard G. Casey (Australian External Affairs Liaison Officer 1923-32 and subsequently a Cabinet Minister)*
Right *Robert Menzies (Attorney-General 1932-39, Prime Minister 1939-40) (Argus Collection, State Library of Victoria)*

17. Lieutenant-General Sir Webb Gillman (Master-General of Ordnance 1927-31) who chaired the defences committee (Royal Artillery Institution)

18. Sir Arthur Jackson (Managing Director of Sir John Jackson (Singapore) Ltd), knighted in 1938 for his work on the dockyard (B. Sunley and Sons Ltd)

19. The floating dock under construction in Swan Hunter's yard at Wallsend (Imperial War Museum)

MEN WHO ENSURED COMPLETION

20. *Admiral Sir Ernle Chatfield (Chief of Naval Staff, 1933-38) (From A. Marder,* From the Dardanelles to Oban, *Oxford University Press)*

21. *Sultan Ibrahim of Johore, whose Jubilee gift of £500,000 in 1935 was commemorated by the 15" gun Johore Battery (from G. Bennett,* Why Singapore Fell, *Angus and Robertson)*

"COUNSEL FOR DEFENCE."

22. *Sir Thomas Inskip, appointed Minister for the Co-ordination of Defence in 1936* (Punch)

23. *Contractor's photograph, 1 July 1931, showing the floating dock, coffer dam, and early stage of the west wharf wall (G. Maunsell and Sons)*

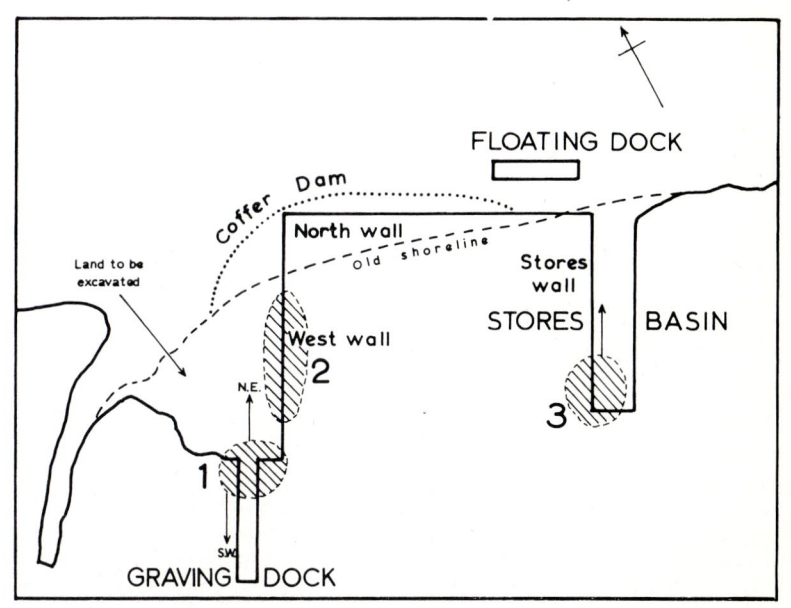

24. *Guide to dockyard photographs.*
   Excavation began well inland at 1 the graving dock entrance and caisson gate chamber, 2 the West Wharf Wall and 3 the Stores Basin. Walls were constructed in these 'holes in the ground' and then excavation and filling followed before flooding (Author)

'K.G. VI'

25. Looking south-west *through the dock entrance, September 1932 (G. Maunsell and Sons)*

26. *The Governor's yacht,* Seabelle II, *cuts the tape at the opening ceremony, 14 February 1938. To its right the aircraft carrier,* HMS Eagle *(Admiralty Records, Public Record Office)*

THE KING GEORGE VI GRAVING DOCK

27. Looking north-east *to dock entrance, where land has yet to be excavated, November 1932 (G. Maunsell and Sons)*

28. *The completed dock in 1940 when the* Queen Mary *(a troopship which brought part of 8 Australian Division) was docked (Imperial War Museum)*

THE WEST WHARF WALL

29. *Progress on the wall by December 1931 (G. Maunsell and Sons)*

30. *The 8" gun heavy cruiser,* HMS Norfolk *and (left) the 15" gun monitor* HMS Terror *dressed for the opening in 1938. The pitched slope was left in place of the north wharf wall (Admiralty Records, Public Record Office)*

THE STORES BASIN

31. *Progress by November 1932. Large-scale excavations will follow on the right (G. Maunsell and Sons)*

32. *The half-finished Basin in 1938. Pitched slopes, in place of the south and east walls (Admiralty Records, Public Record Office)*

'FORCE Z'

33. *HMS* Prince of Wales *after arrival at the Naval Base, 2 December 1941 (Imperial War Museum)*

34. *HMS* Repulse *leaves the Johore Strait at sundown 8 December (Imperial War Museum)*

SERVICE LEADERS

35. *Air Chief Marshal Sir Robert Brooke-Popham, C-in-C Far East 1940-41 (From G. Bennett,* Why Singapore Fell, *(Angus and Robertson)*

36. *Admiral Sir Tom Phillips C-in-C Eastern Fleet (Imperial War Museum)*

37. *General Sir Archibald Wavell Supreme Commander ABDACOM, Jan-Feb 1942 (Imperial War Museum)*

38. *Lieutenant-General Arthur Percival, GOC Malaya, (Imperial War Museum)*

39. *Major-General Gordon Bennett, GOC 8th Division, Australian Imperial Force (From G. Bennett,* Why Singapore Fell, *Angus and Robertson)*

SURRENDER, 15 FEB 1942

40. *Percival signs the surrender document in the Ford Motor Factory (Australian War Memorial)*

41. *Victor and vanquished – well turned-out to the end (From M. Tsuji, Singapore: the Japanese Version, Ure Smith)*

SAC on 1 March 1939, when Chatfield reminded the members that a hostile Italy on top of Germany and Japan had not been considered when the new naval standard was planned, and so he suggested that the United States should be informed that if Britain had to face Germany, Japan *and* Italy simultaneously it might not be able to hold on to its position in the Pacific without American aid. Backhouse insisted they could not ignore Italy and wanted to revise the promise to the Dominions accordingly. Chatfield preferred to stick to the promise. Even if Germany, Japan and Italy were enemies simultaneously Britain would have to send the fleet east 'or risk the Empire'. They agreed that it was undesirable (if it could be avoided) to say anything more to the Dominions about the limitations of the fleet.[7] It was not avoidable, however, because of cables from Canberra and a blunder in the bureaucracy.

By the time the SAC met again on 13 March, Chatfield had to report that Australia House had got 'an inkling' that Britain was weakening on the idea of sending the fleet to Singapore. He therefore became much firmer in his adherence to the 1937 priority. The COS had always maintained Britain could not fight Germany, Japan and Italy but he now insisted, quixotically (and prophetically) that 'if we were faced with such a war he felt it would be better to lose the Eastern Empire by fighting than by default'. It was agreed, however, that a new appreciation should be furnished for the southern Dominions, including the implications of having to face Germany, Japan and Italy simultaneously. During these discussions both Backhouse and Gort mooted the idea of sending two of the older battleships to the Indian Ocean as a deterrent.[8]

Before the new appreciation could be drafted the source of the Australian 'inkling' became evident, and yet another suggestion for sending capital ships to the East arrived. Bruce, who was then visiting Australia, told his Government that he did not think Britain would be able to send capital ships to Singapore if Japan attacked during a European war. Admiral Colvin (the Australian CNS) had thought of another way out. Still hoping that Australia would buy a capital ship in 1943 he wondered if, in the meantime, Britain would lend an existing ship. He also hoped he might persuade the Australian Government to pay for the maintenance of a second capital ship in eastern waters and he even proposed that a third might be purchased jointly by other Dominions and Colonies. Backhouse replied, on 17 March, that it was not only a matter of money, but of productive capacity. He assured Colvin that there had 'never been doubt' about sending a capital ship force to Singapore. The only uncertainty related to its strength.[9] On the same day as this reply there were more Australian alarms from a quite unexpected quarter. An anxious John S. Duncan (the acting Australian High Commissioner) went to the CID Office and showed Ismay, the Secretary, a copy of the minutes of the CID meeting of 24 February when Chamberlain had questioned the promise to send the fleet to Singapore irrespective of the situation elsewhere. Did this mean, he asked, that the British promise was being revised? The real answer, of course, was yes. But it was still in the early stages. No *decision* had yet been taken, and the document had been sent to Alfred Stirling, the Australian External Affairs Liaison Officer, through someone's 'gross stupidity'. Ismay did his best to fudge the issue, by quoting previous papers, including the promise to New Zealand to send a fleet to the East 'irrespective of the situation elsewhere'.

Duncan said he would not pass the matter on to his Government.[10] However, Lyons, the Australian Prime Minister, was soon on the phone to Neville Chamberlain, probably because of the German occupation of Prague on 15 March. In return he was given an assurance about the fleet, on 20 March, which was by no means as categorical as that sent to New Zealand on 1 February.

> In the event of war with Germany and Italy, should Japan join in against us it would still be His Majesty's Government's full intention to despatch a fleet to Singapore. If we were fighting against such a combination never envisaged in our earlier plans, the size of that fleet would necessarily be dependent on (a) the moment when Japan entered the war and (b) what losses if any our opponents or ourselves had previously sustained.
>
> It would, however, be our intention to achieve three main objects
> (i) the prevention of any major operation against Australia, New Zealand or India,
> (ii) to keep open our sea communications,
> (iii) to prevent the fall of Singapore.[11]

There were follow-up meetings with Duncan and Stirling to clarify this statement, but Bruce later claimed that it arrived in Canberra with the force of a 'bombshell'.[12]

By now, however, Backhouse (who was a sick man) professed

himself 'somewhat tired of this particular question about Australian defences,'[13] and the naval staff pressed ahead with their revised appreciation. After studying the naval situation in a war against Germany and Italy with Japan a threat, and with Germany, Italy and Japan simultaneously, the deputy CNS, Vice-Admiral Andrew Cunningham, reported on 5 April that with the battleship strength at its lowest (only ten out of fifteen being available) there were six in home waters and four in the Mediterranean. It was not open to question that battleships would have to be sent to Singapore if Japan attacked, but whether this could be done to the exclusion of British interests in the Mediterranean would have to be decided at the time. It might be necessary to eliminate Germany or Italy first.

> The conclusion which emerges from the foregoing considerations is that there are so many variable factors which cannot at present be assessed, that it is not possible to state definitely how soon after Japanese intervention a Fleet could be despatched to the Far East. Neither is it possible to enumerate precisely the size of the Fleet that we could afford to send.[14]

After approving this formula on 17 April, the SAC sent it to the CID and also suggested alerting the French as to Britain's need to send the Fleet to the east.[15] Thus the French were given the substance of the new formula before it had been formally approved by the CID and long before the Australians and New Zealanders were told.

III

While the British were revising their policy in the first half of 1939 two very different sets of staff conferences were being held in London and Wellington. The Anglo-French staff talks, spread over the period 29 March–3 May, were concerned with the overall picture of a European war, especially the impact on the Mediterranean. Far East strategy occupied only one session. In the Pacific Defence Conference, held in Wellington from 14–26 April, the main subject, naturally, was Pacific security, and the Singapore strategy had a central place. It is therefore highly ironical that the Anglo-French talks, while based on up-to-date material, could not record agreement, while the Wellington conference, based on the British promise which was already under revision, produced some useful agreements.

The Anglo-French talks dealt with the Far East on 25 April. The British memorandum, which included the new 'so many variable factors' formula, accepted that an immediate despatch of the fleet to the East might play into Japan's hands and invite Italian attacks upon the eastern Mediterranean. The worst situation would be if Britain had to choose between abandoning the Far East or the eastern Mediterranean. The accepted priority, of course, was that the Far East came first, but the paper prepared for the Anglo-French talks followed Cunningham's suggestion that the Government of the day would have to decide on the naval dispositions.[16] The French paper was more categorical and concluded that it was 'better to adopt the defensive for the moment in the Far East than to lose the command of the Eastern Mediterranean'.[17] The staff talks failed to reconcile these differing approaches. Captain Danckwerts, for the Admiralty, emphasised that sending the fleet to Singapore was central to British policy and all Australian and New Zealand defence arrangements were 'based on that theory'. He admitted that the possibility of war with Italy somewhat changed the situation and Britain had insufficient naval forces for all three theatres. He asked whether, if France was reinforced in the western Mediterranean, it would take measures to secure the Mediterranean 'as a whole'.

Vice-Admiral Jean Odend'hal, leader of the French delegation, said he would need to refer to Paris before answering. Danckwerts said that, when the US fleet was sent to the Pacific, Britain would be obliged to send a force to the Far East, and the decision might have to be faced as to whether the Far East or the eastern Mediterranean should be abandoned temporarily. Odend'hal stuck to the French paper – that it was better to give up in the east – but Danckwerts reminded him of Britain's commitments to Australia, New Zealand, India and other eastern territories. Odend'hal agreed the loss of Singapore would be a severe blow, but the loss of the war in Europe would be 'infinitely more disastrous'. The discussion was inconclusive. However the agreed paper at the conclusion of the talks lent slightly towards the French view: 'It is thus a question of balancing risks, and the issue cannot be decided in advance; but the weakening of the British Eastern Mediterranean Fleet should not lightly be undertaken'.[18]

IV

On the day after the Anglo-French talks touched on the Singapore strategy, the Pacific Defence Conference finished its work in Wellington. But, while the London talks were based upon an awareness of Britain's weakness in capital ships in 1939–40, the British delegation in Wellington were not aware of recent thinking in London. They knew that the New Zealand Government was anxious to receive assurances about the timing and strength of the fleet to be sent to Singapore, since until command of the seas was established the Dominion felt it could not send forces overseas. It was, however, eager to assist in imperial defence, especially in the Pacific Islands.[19]

Before the conference the New Zealand COS received the already outdated guarantee contained in *New Zealand Co-operation in Imperial Defence* (1 February 1939). They felt that the British paper went 'farther than any previous statement' and 'clears up any doubts' as to whether the British would reinforce the naval forces in the Far East immediately if Japan attacked. They noted, however, that '*No indication* is given as to the time which may elapse before the Fleet reaches Singapore'. In their advice to the Dominion Government they accepted that Britain was bearing the main burden of preparations against Germany, Italy and Japan and that in a major war 'the defence of New Zealand's interests ultimately lies outside New Zealand altogether'. Thus the Dominion's ability to assist on land and in the air in the defence of the empire might prove the most effective contribution to the country's security 'since the fall of Singapore might expose New Zealand to invasion, and the defeat of the United Kingdom would mean the break-up of the British Empire'.[20] They then listed the possible New Zealand contributions: navy – a third cruiser, two escort vessels, asdics, and the stiffening of merchant ships for armament; army – a battalion could be sent to Singapore a month after enlistment; air force – a general reconnaissance squadron could, if available, be sent to Singapore after July 1941.

The Dominion Government did not act on these suggestions. Before making up its mind it wanted further details of the British strategy. Thus the main interest of the Pacific Defence Conference centred in its strategical committee. Other committees discussed supply problems and trans-Pacific air routes. The last was a particular concern of the New Zealand Government, since there had been disputes over the sovereignty of a number of islands in the central Pacific connected with Pan American Airways' pioneer route. Pan-Am was also trying to play-off Australia and New Zealand and the Dominion Government was eager for a united Commonwealth approach to Pacific aviation. The chief concern of the strategical committee was possible action by Japan in the southwest Pacific during the period before relief, and action which could be taken to safeguard the Pacific Islands, shipping and New Zealand's territory.

Most of the answering, on behalf of the United Kingdom, fell to the services representatives, Air Vice-Marshal Sir Arthur Longmore (an ex-naval officer with a taste for nautical metaphor), who had recently completed a mission advising on aircraft manufacture, Vice-Admiral Sir Ragnar Colvin, who was CNS Australia (and doubled-up as leader of the Australian delegation) and Major-General Pierse Mackesy. Also representing the UK were Sir Harry Batterbee, the new High Commissioner in Wellington and Sir Harry Luke, Governor of Fiji and High Commissioner for the Western Pacific. The Australian Government had been reluctant to participate and since Lyons died a week before the conference the future of the Ministry was uncertain. It sent a somewhat lower-level delegation; Admiral Colvin, Colonel Vernon Sturdee (Director of Staff Duties, Army HQ) and Wing Commander George Jones (Director of Recruiting, RAAF). For the hosts, the representatives were Peter Fraser, the Deputy Prime Minister, Walter Nash, the Minister of Finance, Frederick Jones, the Minister of Defence, and the senior civil servants Carl Berendsen (head of the Prime Minister's Department) and Bernard Ashwin (Secretary of the Treasury).

The Conference was opened on 14 April 1939 by Michael Savage, the Prime Minister, whose homely metaphor was perhaps one of the more memorable statements of the conference. What was going to happen when war broke out? 'It was like starting to play a football match; the captain could not say where he was going to have his men definitely until certain things happened . . .' He was followed, in the first planning session, by Carl Berendsen, who said he would not touch on anything strategical, or tactical, or technical. He was going to confine himself to the one subject fundamental to all their discussions: 'the question of knowing the strength of the reinforcements and the time in which they can be expected to be available in the Pacific'. He took as basic assumption the worst case (a war with Germany, Italy and Japan simultaneously) and accepted that 'Singapore, distant and western though it is, is . . . the basis of naval defence [of] British trade routes in the Pacific'. He then summarised all the British papers from the 1937 *Review* to Chamberlain's telegram to Lyons of 20 March 1939. Although he did not question the basic fact that a decision would be reached in the European theatre of a war and that the fleet could not go to Singapore if it would prejudice such a decision, he wanted to isolate the question of the arrival time of the fleet. The conclusion he drew from British promises over the last two years was that a fleet would be despatched as soon as possible, in as great a strength as possible, but circumstances might arise in which it would be impossible to send a fleet in sufficient strength. The period before relief would be 70 days, or more than 70 days. During that period a hostile Asian power would have unquestioned naval supremacy in the Pacific limited only by 'the strength of the Japanese forces, their choice of objectives and the dictates of prudence'. This was a devastatingly frank appraisal.

It was 'very refreshing to get a real broadside like that', said Air Marshal Longmore, 'It shattered us somewhat, of course.' But he reminded the New Zealanders about the uncertainty as to Japan's movements; this might give Britain time to neutralise the German navy first. Japan was bogged down in China and he hoped they would stay 'stuck in that mud'. But he could only reiterate the British promise. His government, he said, 'do definitely propose to send a force of capital ships, perhaps in two batches, which will be able to act on the defensive'. Longmore did not know this was being reviewed in London and his statement was quite consistent with the latest version of *War Memorandum (Eastern)* which listed an 'Eastern Fleet' of 8 battleships, 3 aircraft carriers, 16 cruisers and 7 flotillas of destroyers, the capital ships being organised in two battle squadrons and a carrier squadron.[21] Colvin, who was well aware of Australian scepticism about the fleet, said if he was asked whether Britain could afford to send the fleet to the East, his reply was always; could she afford not to? Australia and New Zealand simply did not have the vessels to protect their shipping.

From the extremely frank discussions which followed, five important questions asked by New Zealanders deserve comment. First, Nash, revealing the major local fear, wanted to know if Japan could make direct raids upon Australia and New Zealand from bases in the Japanese mandated islands, before the fleet reached Singapore. Colvin agreed that 'tip and run raids' were possible, but would be limited by the need for fuel and supplies, and by Japan's major uncertainty about the arrival of the British fleet. The New Zealand Defence Minister said the main worry was that Japan might establish a base in Fiji.

Secondly, Ashwin asked how long Singapore could hold out for, in view of suggestions that Australia or New Zealand help man the garrison. General Mackesy said the British army reinforcement scheme was ready; it had been on the point of implementation at the time of Munich. The plan was to put a 'full battalion [a misprint for Brigade?] straight into Singapore the moment things look ugly'. He admitted that although the present period before relief was 70 days, it might be extended to 90 days, which was the period before provisioning. Although it seemed like a gamble, he said, besieged fortresses could always hold out for longer than expected – witness, Mafeking, Ladysmith, Kut and Ypres! Thirdly, Dan Sullivan, Minister of Industries and Commerce, asked about the chance of a direct air attack on Singapore. In reply, Longmore did not rule this out, because Japan might gain bases in Borneo or Thailand. To the fourth and fifth questions put by Walter Nash, the British really had no answer. What if Germany, Italy and Japan synchronised their attack? 'Another broadside!', said Longmore, 'It is really guess work, isn't it.' But he felt Japan would wait and see what happened in Europe. The general strategic discussion concluded with this famous exchange:

> *Nash*: ... assume that all those things we have provided for with regard to Singapore do not work out in the way we have provided for them ... what do we do then to defend Australia and New Zealand when Singapore is gone and the fleet that comes after is smashed up?
> *Longmore*: I think the answer to that is to take to the Waitomo caves.
> *Nash*: The only place where we can see anything that is glowing.[22]

It was clear that the British delegates could give no more categorical promise than had already been given, so the conference turned to the details of possible Dominions' contributions in the Pacific. The conference report took note of the Singapore strategy, recorded the estimated scales of attack on Australia, New Zealand

and the Islands, and certain measures necessary to meet them. It was agreed that an air reconnaissance line from New Guinea to Tonga would be operated by Australia and New Zealand, the dividing point being at the New Hebrides. It was recommended that 6" guns be installed in Fiji and that its defences be reinforced to two battalions. New Zealand would consider sending a brigade to the islands. New Zealand (which had already accepted responsibility for Fanning) also agreed to send companies to Western Samoa and Tonga; Australia would give some assistance in Nauru, the New Hebrides, the Solomon Islands and Norfolk Island.[23]

Although the general atmosphere in Wellington was cordial[24] the British delegation had had a rather rough time in the conference and Longmore admitted (when he reported in person to the COS in London on 25 May 1939) that they had found themselves 'in rather a difficult position'. The most serious aspect of the Wellington Conference was pointed out by Phillips, the Vice-CNS. The two Dominion Governments obviously did not have an 'up-to-date expression' of British policy on the despatch of the fleet to Singapore. As the Admiralty was again revising *War Memorandum (Eastern)*, which would go to the Australian and New Zealand Naval Boards as a matter of routine, he said the CID should consider telling the Dominion Governments first.[25]

The revision of the British policy had, of course, originated with Backhouse's anxieties at the end of 1938 and Neville Chamberlain's query in February 1939 about the categorical promise to send the fleet. The new formula, drafted by Cunningham for the SAC on 5 April, was approved by the CID on 2 May. At this meeting the First Lord of the Admiralty, Lord Stanhope, stressed the recent assurances given to Greece, Rumania and Turkey and the effect that the withdrawal of the fleet from the eastern Mediterranean would have on the French. Inskip, now Secretary of State for the Dominions, pointed out that there had been 'a considerable scaling down of our undertaking to the Dominions' to send a fleet in all circumstances, and told the Committee that Bruce and Nash were due in London and would seek definite assurances. Chamberlain felt his cable to Lyons of 20 March was quite clear. If Britain were defeated, the fate of the Dominions would be sealed. Britain would do all it could to protect the Dominions, but the important thing was to defeat the enemy. This would have to be put frankly to the Dominion representatives. Halifax, the Foreign Secretary, suggested that the United States should also be informed of this situation.[26]

The American Naval Staff were told of the revised formula during secret staff talks in Washington on 12 and 14 June 1939. Commander T. C. Hampton RN travelled discreetly as a civilian, and spoke with Admiral Leahy, the American Chief of Naval Operations, and Admiral Ghormley, the Director of Plans. There was no attempt to secure an agreement, but the talks may, in the long run, have had a dangerously misleading affect. Admiral Leahy (expressing a purely personal view) envisaged the US fleet sailing to Singapore from Hawaii with 10 battleships taking (with the period of assembly) about 60 days. This would depend on Britain sending an 'adequate token force' to co-operate. He also thought that the 90-day period before relief was a bit tight and suggested it should be at least 120 days. He asked about the docking and repair facilities at Singapore and it was agreed that about 2,500 skilled and semi-skilled personnel from the United States would be needed at Singapore if the US fleet were to go.[27] This discussion probably excited British hopes, which were later to be disappointed.

The Dominions were not told about the Washington talks, which were even kept secret from the US Navy Department. Whether Chamberlain really meant to inform the Dominions of the 'variable factors' formula is not clear. But as the Director of Plans at the Admiralty worked on the revisions to *War Memorandum (Eastern)* he realised that the question of telling the Dominions could not be shelved. The revised totals of capital ships for Singapore were now as follows: if Italy were neutral or eliminated from a war, seven capital ships would go east; in a war against Germany, Japan and Italy simultaneously (and with the USA neutral) four would be sent, but if the USA were an ally, the figure would be two. Danckwerts realised this 'was a new departure in policy' and he omitted Australia and New Zealand from the circulation.[28] Phillips insisted that the Dominions be told. Before this was done the Tientsin silver crisis occurred in the Far East. The COS's recent assumption that war would start in Europe was suddenly shaken. The moment for telling the Dominions about the new policy was singularly unpropitious, so the telling was blurred.

V

In June 1939 the Japanese blockaded the British Concession in Tientsin, where there had been longstanding controversy about

Chinese guerillas taking refuge. The Japanese also demanded that silver bullion held in Tientsin as backing for the Chinese currency should be surrendered and a new Japanese-backed currency be recognised in China. Because of the blockade Chamberlain had to divulge two unpalatable things to Australia and New Zealand at the same time. First, Britain could not, alone, contemplate force to raise the blockade. The COS did their usual sums. To face Japan's nine battleships, a fleet of nine battleships would have to be sent to Singapore. With only ten available for operations anywhere in mid-1939 the best that could be done in the Far East would be two battleships, one carrier and two cruisers. It was quite inadequate. Therefore it would not be a proper strategic measure to send a fleet, unless American help could be assured. The Cabinet accepted this on 21 June 1939.[29] Secondly, to make matters worse, on 24 June Robert Menzies, Prime Minister of Australia since 26 April, cabled to ask whether the assurance about the fleet still stood.

The CID considered both these issues on 26 June. Chamberlain declared that sooner or later, if war broke out, Germany, Italy and Japan would be ranged against Britain. The attitude of the United States was still uncertain, France the only sure ally. He accepted that the fleet could not be used in the present crisis; that they could not stop Japan from freezing the British out of China. He assumed that his colleagues did not want retaliation over Tientsin which might lead to war. Although Malcolm MacDonald, the Colonial Secretary, hoped something could be done because of the effect on Britain's prestige in India and the Colonies, Halifax insisted that no help could be given to Tientsin.[30] It was agreed that Chamberlain would have to tell the Australian and New Zealand representatives and also inform them of the latest policy with regard to the fleet for the East.

This was done at a meeting with Bruce and William Jordan, the New Zealand High Commissioner, held in Chamberlain's room at the House of Commons on 28 June 1939. Chatfield and Halifax were also present. Chamberlain explained that in his reply to Menzies' cable he had reaffirmed his cable to Lyons of 20 March. Bruce (who had only just returned from Australia) said that that telegram had given a shock to his government. Chamberlain pleaded new circumstances since then. 'In the past, it had been thought that the possibility was that we should find ourselves involved in a war with the Axis Powers, and that subsequently Japan might intervene on their side. Now it looked as though it might be the other way round: for, if we sent our Fleet to Singapore to deal with Japan, the temptation to the Axis Powers to take advantage of the situation would be almost irresistible.' The number of battleships was limited. It was useless to send an inadequate fleet to Singapore, therefore Britain would keep in close touch with the Americans.

Bruce said he thought the Australians would take a different view of the Tientsin crisis, and would probably support certain sanctions against Japan. But if a war was likely, they would want 'specific information' about the size and timing of the British fleet. He also volunteered the information that on his way back from Australia he had visited President Roosevelt, who, when asked the American attitude to a possible Japanese naval move south of the equator, had replied: 'You need not worry'.[31]

Possibly because of the immediate concern with the China crisis Bruce missed (or did not comment on) the main implication of Chamberlain's somewhat hazy reference to the fleet. A fortnight later he had another meeting, at the Dominions Office, with MacDonald, Chatfield and Lord Stanhope, in which he tried (like the New Zealanders at the Wellington conference) to get the question of the size and timing of the fleet cleared up. He referred to the assurances he had been given after Munich that seven battleships would be sent. (At this time, of course, Backhouse was already having his doubts.) Compared with those assurances Chamberlain's cable of 20 March, with its reference to 'a combination never envisaged in our earlier plans', had come as a 'bombshell' to the Australian Government. Chatfield was used to the Australians. He explained the way that recent circumstances affected policy. Italy's invasion of Albania and the German-Italian alliance had suggested that war would start in the west. If Japan did not intervene for a time, there was a chance that Italy could be knocked out first, and then the bulk of the fleet could be sent to the East. Now, with the Tientsin crisis, war might start first in the East. Then what, burst out Bruce, did His Majesty's Government propose to do about it? Did they, or did they not, intend to send a fleet to the Far East, and if so of what size? The same old question! And Bruce added: What secrets were being kept from Australia? Chatfield patiently explained as best he could. The French might be upset if the fleet was withdrawn from the eastern Mediterranean. He also admitted that the period before relief had been recently extended to 90 days (which was back to the three months estimated in 1920).

The plan now was to keep the fleet in the eastern Mediterranean until the last moment. 'This would keep our enemies guessing . . .' He agreed it might seem rather indeterminate, but there was no question of Britain abdicating its position in the Far East without a fight. It was hardly the assurance Bruce wanted. He thought he understood what would happen if war broke out in Europe first. As to what would happen if the war started in the East, he professed himself to be 'still in the dark'.[32]

War was avoided over Tientsin. The British did not give up the silver, but they compromised with Japan. The Craigie-Arita formula of 25 July recognised that Japan had to maintain order in the parts of China it occupied. By the summer of 1939 the British defence planners had all but revised the 1937 priority which put the Far East before the Mediterranean. Not formally – for the Singapore commitment remained. As Chatfield put it, they were keeping their enemies guessing. Perhaps he should have said: 'Our enemies are keeping us guessing'.

One who had stopped guessing was the Air OC in the Far East, Air-Vice Marshal Philip Babington. In mid-August 1939 he was writing to Group Captain Slessor (Director of Plans at the Air Ministry) about improving the air defences at Singapore. Anglo-French staff talks had been held in Singapore in June, and it was suggested that the existing eight squadrons should be doubled to sixteen (250 aircraft).[33] For Babington (as for the Australians and New Zealanders) the basic question was, whether the fleet would arrive. 'From what we understand, there is no prospect whatever of anything more than the Mediterranean Fleet arriving in the Far East. There is no certainty as to if and when it will in fact arrive . . .' He knew the intention was to send the fleet as 'cover' for Australia and New Zealand, but he felt they could not base plans on its arrival. Reliance on this doubtful contingency had always 'messed up' defence measures in the Far East.[34] Three weeks later war with Germany began. Within a few days plans were being made for doubling the period before relief of Singapore from three to six months.[35]

VI

Looking back on the statements about the Singapore strategy made in the summer of 1939, one might conclude that the British planners were more confused than was really the case. They realised, quite clearly, that they could not fight Germany, Italy and Japan simultaneously. Put in the simplest terms it would require a three power standard and the rearmament programme did not fully accept the two power standard. In the 'worst contingency' the role of France and the United States would be crucial. It is also worth remembering that expressions of the Eastern strategy were usually made for specific circumstances – the Anglo-French talks, the Pacific Defence Conference, and, most frequently, to meet the incessant queries of the rather superior High Commissioner for Australia. Yet the events of 1939 – Prague, Albania, Tientsin – led to moments of urgent preoccupation which hamstrung the consistency of the strategical scripture. Exegesis became all-important, and, surprisingly, the German war in September 1939 served to simplify things, bolster faith, and led to a reaffirmation of the 1937 priority.

As soon as war was declared Australia and New Zealand associated themselves with Britain and provided useful naval assistance. The two Australian 8″ cruisers and five destroyers came under Admiralty command. HMAS *Perth*, which was in the West Indies on its delivery voyage, went to join the South Atlantic Squadron. The New Zealand 6″ cruiser *Achilles* set off for the West Indies station, via the Horn. HMS *Leander* took an infantry company from Auckland to Fanning Island as planned. The New Zealand Government offered an army division for overseas service in eight months time. Australia mobilised a division and corps troops. It did not offer the army for overseas service at once but quickly offered six air squadrons. The British War Cabinet suggested that the two Dominions should retain the bulk of their forces until Japan's response to the German War could be assessed. Winston Churchill (who had joined the Cabinet as First Lord of the Admiralty, the office he had vacated 24 years before) argued that Dominion forces should be seen beside the BEF in France.[36]

VII

Before decisions were made about the deployment of Dominion armies a Commonwealth Conference was called in London in November 1939 to discuss the general strategic situation, and problems of finance, supply and co-operation. At this conference (known as the Dominions' Ministerial Visit) the British were eager to secure Dominion troops to demonstrate the solidarity of the Empire.[37] But before they committed themselves the Australians wanted to be sure about the fleet for Singapore, just as the New Zealanders had at the Wellington Defence Conference in April.

The chief Australian representative was Richard Casey (the Minister of Supply), who as external affairs liaison officer had played a significant behind-the-scenes role in the Singapore controversy of ten years before. Anticipating his questions Churchill produced a paper, *Australian Naval Defence (Winter 1939)*, which reiterated the 1937 promise that the Far East came before the Mediterranean. He began by picturing Singapore as a 'fortress armed with five 15-inch guns' and a garrison of 20,000 men. It could only be taken after a seige by an army of at least 50,000, which could last for four or five months, during which it could be interrupted at any time by the arrival of the fleet. It was not considered that the Japanese, 'a prudent people', would embark upon 'such a mad enterprise'. Invasion of Australia was even less likely. Italy was neutral. The German Navy was small. The Admiralty accepted the responsibility for the defence of Australia and (after containing the German heavy ships) had forces at its disposal for this purpose. The Admiralty was grateful for the use of Australian cruisers and destroyers and the 'loyal and clairvoyant strategy' which appeared to have denuded Australia of its defences. 'But we wish to make it plain that we regard the defence of Australia, and of Singapore, as a stepping-stone to Australia, as ranking next to the mastery of the principal fleet to which we are opposed, and that if the choice were presented of defending Australia against a serious attack, or sacrificing British interests in the Mediterranean, our duty to Australia would take precedence'.[38] This was intended as a private communication to Casey.

Before the matter was discussed, however, Ismay alerted Chamberlain to the fact that Churchill's paper made certain 'far-reaching strategic statements' which went somewhat further than the Government 'were prepared to go before the war broke out'. He suggested that Australians and New Zealanders could interpret this as meaning that if Japan entered the war Britain would abandon the Mediterranean to reinforce Singapore.[39] Therefore, just before the Dominions meeting on 20 November 1939, the War Cabinet discussed Churchill's paper. Chamberlain said the Government had not been prepared, in advance of the event, to decide whether the Mediterranean should be abandoned. Churchill did not think his paper went further than Chamberlain's telegram to Lyons of 20 March. He was convinced, in any case, that if Australia were invaded Britain would have to 'seal the ends of the Mediterranean' and go to their aid. Chatfield supported Churchill. He found the naval situation in November 1939 'almost identical' to that in mid-1937 when the *Far Eastern Appreciation* was prepared. He said (as he had in 1937) that he could not give a 100 per cent guarantee and it was impossible to state in advance the size of the fleet and the time of its movement. Chamberlain quoted the 'so many variable factors', but Inskip insisted that the defence of Australia against a real attack must come before the Mediterranean.[40]

During the meeting with the Dominions' representatives later that day Casey made the same points as Savage had made in 1937. He was worried that no battleships would be at Singapore until after Japan made a move. Here Churchill took a firm line. The Navy could not keep battleships 'tethered' at Singapore against a mere threat. Jordan, the New Zealand High Commissioner, pointed out that the present situation was more favourable than the worst contingency envisaged at the Wellington conference. And in the light of Churchill's paper for Casey, New Zealand was prepared to send the first echelon of its division overseas in January 1940. Bruce referred again to the promise of seven battleships which he had received after Munich. Chatfield reminded him of the modification in the 20 March telegram and of Singapore's ability to hold out for up to six months. This alarmed Casey, who had been reassured by Churchill's paper, but was disturbed by the drift of the discussion. For years, he said, Australia had believed that if Japan went to war an adequate fleet would go immediately to Singapore. If Australians were to put their full effort into the war they needed a 'most comprehensive undertaking' about Singapore. Churchill stuck to his guns. It was a 'false strategy' to keep a fleet at Singapore without regard to the wider situation; it might immobilise half the fleet. Casey said he wanted to get the completest assurance he could for the Australian Government, but Jordan said it was impossible for the United Kingdom to make a more complete assurance than it had.

Churchill agreed to reword his paper and make it available to both the Dominion Governments.[41] The War Cabinet approved this on 21 November when Churchill mentioned the Australian fears and said the New Zealand delegate had taken a 'much more realistic view of the situation'. Chamberlain agreed to have a word with Casey. Churchill revised his paper, inserting 'and New Zealand' throughout after 'Australia'. He also added a characteristic phrase to the passage about a choice between defending the Dominions or the Mediterranean to the effect that 'our duty to our kith and kin would take precedence'. In the context of the sentence, which referred to Singapore as the 'stepping stone' to the Dominions, it was really a reaffirmation of the 1937 priority. Moreover, it appears to have done the trick.[42] Casey announced that Australia would begin sending the AIF overseas in the next month.

VIII

It was ironical that Churchill, who had had no part in the 1937 promises or the 1939 qualifications, should word the fulsome assurance of November 1939. For in one of his first acts as Prime Minister six months later, he reversed the priority. He also suggested that the Dominions would have to look to the United States for protection. In part this was simply a restatement of the view Churchill had held since the early 1920s that Britain would never have to face Japan alone. But he and the naval staff may have been lulled into false expectations by a recent visit to the Admiralty of the American naval attaché in London. On 16 April 1940 Captain Alan Kirk, USN, called on Admiral Phillips, the VCNS, to express his fear that Japan might strike at the Netherlands East Indies if Germany overran Holland. Kirk's idea was that the US fleet should move west from Hawaii to the Philippines to deter a hostile move against the Dutch East Indies. Realising that docking facilities at Manila would be inadequate he wondered whether the Singapore base would be available. Phillips naturally promised full assistance.[43] Next day the War Cabinet also discussed the Dutch Indies and instructed the Foreign Secretary to inquire as to the American Government's attitude. However, in view of the naval attaché's approach the Cabinet subsequently decided, instead, to assure President Roosevelt that the docking and repair facilities of Singapore would be available for the US fleet.[44]

Fears about the Netherlands came true on 10 May when the German drive to the Channel began. On the same day Chamberlain resigned and Churchill became Prime Minister. He failed to prevent the opening of the Mediterranean War. Mussolini would not be persuaded to stay neutral and Italy declared war on 10 June. On 13 June Churchill had to tell the War Cabinet of his meeting with the French premier, who pleaded release from the pledge not to make a separate peace. The Dominions had to be told of the new situation. If France collapsed Britain would fight on, but she could no longer think of guaranteeing the security of the Pacific Dominions.[45]

> In the unlikely event of Japan, in spite of the restraining influence of the United States of America, taking the opportunity to alter the *status quo* in the Far East, we should be faced with a naval situation in which, without the assistance of France, we should not have sufficient forces to meet the combined German and Italian navies in European waters and the Japanese fleet in the Far East. In the circumstances envisaged, it is most improbable that we could send adequate reinforcements to the Far East. We should therefore have to rely on the United States of America to safeguard our interests there.[46]

One of the 'variable factors' in Admiral Cunningham's formula had come into play. Or, to go back to the imagery of Michael Savage of New Zealand, 'certain things' had happened. It is important to remember, however, that the *priority* had been reversed: the *strategy* was not abandoned. Churchill and the Admiralty hoped the Americans would send their fleet, but they still clung to the policy of sending a British battle fleet to Singapore.

9 'Kith and Kin', 1940–41

I

In June 1940 the 'worst situation' previously envisaged in Europe was exceeded. Not only was Italy added to Germany as an enemy, but France was lost as an ally. For the Commonwealth east of Suez the Singapore priority was reversed. The British Government admitted that, if Japan chose to strike in the Pacific, Britain could not, alone at that moment, defend all its interests. Yet it is important to remember that the eastern strategy was *not scrapped*.

Churchill had always assumed that in a war with Japan the United States would be an ally. The plan to send a fleet to Singapore still existed. If Italy could be defeated in the Mediterranean the plan would again become feasible. In the meantime, by patience in its relations with Japan, and careful cultivation of potential allies, Britain sought to stave off war in the Pacific, while endeavouring to build a defensive net to secure the eastern Commonwealth.

Japan's encroachment upon Southeast Asia was generally predictable in a way that the Pearl Harbor attack was not. Faced with steadily increasing American trade restrictions Japanese Governments used each reverse of the western European powers to move a step further south towards their colonial empires. Italy's entry and the fall of France were followed by Japan's demand that the Burma Road and Hong Kong supply routes to China be closed and that the British garrisons and gunboats be withdrawn from China. Pressure was exerted on the Vichy Government for facilities in French Indo-China, and the Netherlands East Indies was pressed for trade guarantees. The Battle of Britain was followed by the German-Italian-Japanese Pact, the proclamation of the New Order in Greater East Asia and Japanese occupation of northern Indo-China. Germany's invasion of Russia in June 1941 was followed by Japan's move into southern Indo-China and growing pressure on Thailand.[1]

II

In the creation of the defensive net to contain Japan Singapore remained the focus of British thinking. In its relations with Australia, New Zealand, the Netherlands and the United States the British Government sought to create a system which would save the Singapore Naval Base until the time when the fleet could come.

The first task was to explain the *volte face* of mid-June to the Dominions and seek their help during the period of Britain's discomfiture in Europe and the Mediterranean. In this, the now familiar contrast between Australia and New Zealand was again evident. Reacting in a calm way to the cable of 13 June announcing that Britain could not send a fleet to the Pacific, the New Zealand Government said it did 'not in any way demur to this decision (which they have always regarded as a possibility)'. But the British were reminded that the promise to send a fleet to Singapore was the basis of all New Zealand's defence preparations and the Dominion Government assumed 'this undertaking will again be made operative as soon as circumstances may allow'.[2] Meanwhile, it earnestly requested a full review of the Far East situation.

This review was undertaken by the COS in London in June–July 1940 and it soon provoked the anger of the Australian High Commissioner. In a preliminary paper on 25 June the COS argued that the strategic and economic importance of Malaya remained high. British policy should be to induce the United States to declare its interest in the *status quo* in the Pacific. As the fleet could not be spared at that time it was all the more important that land and air defences in Malaya should be strengthened. But troops could not be spared from Britain or the Middle East. The only sources were India or Australia. The COS suggested that Australia be asked to send one army division and two air squadrons to Malaya as soon as possible. In their draft of a cable explaining the situation to the Australian and New Zealand Governments the COS indicated that Dominions' anxieties about the fleet were appreciated, but since the fall of France the British navy was not strong enough to meet the German and Italian navies as well.[3]

When the War Cabinet discussed this proposal on 26 June Halifax reported that the United States Government had declined to commit itself on the Far East. The Secretary of State for Colonies, Lord Lloyd, said Sir Shenton Thomas (Governor of the Straits

Settlements, who was then in London) was calling for the development of Malaya's air defences. The Secretary of State for the Dominions, Lord Caldecote (Inskip), felt the proposed cable was inconsistent with the promise about the fleet used as arguments, during the DMV Conference in 1939, to persuade Australia and New Zealand to send their troops to Europe and the Middle East.[4] Nevertheless the cable of explanations and the request to Australia for a division (or a brigade group) and two squadrons was sent on 28 June.

It was to be expected that Stanley Bruce would be unhappy. Colonel Leslie Hollis (an assistant secretary to the Cabinet) reported that the Australian High Commissioner had 'flown off the handle'. General Ismay, the Cabinet Secretary, had a talk with Bruce. He admitted the frequent promises that in a choice between the Far East and the Middle East the Far East came first in priority. But that choice was not presented. Japan was not in the war. Germany and Italy threatened Britain and its communications. The COS had always held that Australia was safe from invasion if (a) the British fleet was 'in being' and (b) Singapore was secure. The first 'still holds good' and to ensure the second, Britain was asking for Australia's help.[5]

While reinforcements were sought from Australia, diplomatic support was expected from the United States, where Australia had appointed Richard Casey as Minister. This added a useful voice alongside that of the British Ambassador, Lord Lothian. In fact President Roosevelt has assured Casey privately that, if the Netherlands East Indies were attacked by Japan, the USA would not be indifferent. In the meantime, however, the official American policy was to continue with economic pressure through control over trade in strategic materials. British hopes that an American fleet might be sent to Singapore were disappointed.

As no firm commitment about American action in the event of Japanese advances was forthcoming, the British sought US approval for their efforts to appease Japan. On 17 July 1940 the British Government agreed to close the Burma Road for three months, and on 6 August to withdraw her garrisons from northern China. But members of the Government felt somewhat aggrieved when Cordell Hull, the US Secretary of State, announced publicly that the Burma Road closure was an unwarrantable interference with world trade. The British could not afford to risk war with Japan on their own. And they feared that the American trade embargoes would focus

Japan's attention on the highly vulnerable Netherlands East Indies.[6]

It had long been recognised that the Netherlands East Indies were vital for the security of the Singapore base and of Australia and New Zealand. In 1937 the CIGS called them the 'Achilles Heel' of Britain's defences in the East,[7] and Casey had raised the matter at the DMV meetings in 1939, as he did in Washington in 1940. But the British naval staff always maintained that no commitment should be incurred for the defence of the Netherlands East Indies without American backing. When the fears occasioned by the American trade embargoes caused the COS to study the question, a deadlock occurred. Sir Cyril Newall, the CAS, General Dill, the CIGS, and Ismay, the Secretary, insisted that the Dutch (whose government-in-exile was in London) were allies, that an enemy in the Dutch Indies would threaten Singapore and the Dominions. They wanted a commitment. Admiral Pound, the CNS, insisted Britain could not defend the Netherlands East Indies, and that a Japanese attack on them need not necessarily involve the British Commonwealth. Unable to agree, the COS had to seek a Cabinet ruling.

The War Cabinet discussed the problem on 29th July 1940. Churchill began by reading a prepared minute containing his views. Personally he rated an attack on the Netherlands East Indies as a greater menace than an attack on Hong Kong. Australia and New Zealand could be 'cut off' and, if Britain acquiesced, the Dominions would feel 'deserted'. But he was sure the USA would not be indifferent if Japan attacked the Dutch, and he did not consider the matter urgent. Pound stated the naval views bluntly. He said they could not base their strategy on 'sentiment'. Attlee felt it would be a great blow to Britain's prestige if the Dutch Indies were allowed to go without a finger raised in their aid. A final decision was postponed. Churchill wanted to play for time. The debate was resumed several times over the next sixteen months. As Japanese negotiators pressed their trade demands in Batavia, the Dutch Government in London sought a guarantee of help. But the naval staff succeeded in preventing a unilateral commitment.[8] In the immediate aftermath of the fall of France, then, the prospects for a defensive net in South-east Asia were uncertain. This was the background to the new *Far East Appreciation* completed on 31 July 1940.

III

The new appreciation superseded that prepared for the Imperial Conference of 1937. The assumptions then had been that an attack would be seaborne and that within three months the fleet would be at Singapore. Now, with Japan established in Hainan and southern China, and French Indo-China and Thailand vulnerable to pressure, an overland threat to Malaya was possible, while, for the time being, the fleet could not be sent. British strategy was still based on the plan to send the fleet to Singapore. But until Germany and Italy were defeated this could not be done. The 'best hope' would be an early success against Italy in the Mediterranean. Meanwhile, new tactics were required in the period before relief. It became necessary to hold the 'whole of Malaya' rather than just Singapore Island. In this the policy would be to 'rely primarily on air power in conjunction with such naval forces as can be made available'. Increased land forces were also necessary to defend the air bases, as well as the naval base.

At that time the RAF and the RAAF had 8 squadrons (88 first line planes) in Malaya – with the possibility of help from 13 Dutch squadrons (144 planes). The air strength in Malaya needed to be more than doubled. The COS suggested for northern Malaya 4 bomber and 2 fighter squadrons (96 first-line planes), for Singapore 2 torpedo bomber and 2 fighter squadrons (64 planes) and for reconnaissance east of Malaya, 3 squadrons (48 planes). The total recommended for Malaya was 208 first-line planes. A further 5 squadrons were recommended for reconnaissance in the northeast Indian Ocean and 4 for Borneo, making 336 planes in the area as a whole. Much of the army reinforcement would be needed to defend the air bases. At the time there were 9 infantry battalions and ancillary units and the COS proposed a minimum of 6 brigades (2 divisions) provided the recommended air strength could be achieved.

As immediate reinforcement the COS recommended that one Australian and one other division, and two fighter and two reconnaissance squadrons be sent to Malaya; that the last garrisons be withdrawn from North China as part of a general settlement with Japan; and that New Zealand prepare to send a brigade to Fiji. They also suggested that staff conversations with Dutch, Australian and New Zealand representatives be allowed at

Singapore.⁹ Explaining this last proposal the COS accepted that commitment to the Dutch Indies would be a matter for a future government decision in the light of circumstances. Australia and New Zealand were 'becoming somewhat restive' and reluctant to send further forces overseas until the new appreciation was completed.¹⁰

There was a separate paper on naval forces and help for the Dutch Indies. The China, Australian and New Zealand stations could produce 1 heavy cruiser, 6 light cruisers, 5 old destroyers, 6 armed merchant cruisers, 3 escorts and 8 MTBs. The Dutch had 2 cruisers, 7 destroyers and 16 submarines. As for reinforcements, the Naval Staff had its simple arithmetic to explain. To match Japan, 9 capital ships and an equivalent strength of carriers were necessary. Britain had 13 capital ships available – 5 at Home, 4 in the eastern Mediterranean, 2 at Gibraltar and 2 covering Atlantic Convoys. To send 9 to Singapore would mean abandoning the Mediterranean, and taking 2 from the Atlantic and 1 from Home. The situation was worse than in 'any previous appreciation' and the Mediterranean could not be abandoned. The best that could be done was to base 1 battle-cruiser and 1 aircraft carrier at Ceylon to cover Indian Ocean convoys.¹¹

The War Cabinet discussed the new appreciation on 8 August 1940 at the height of the Battle for Britain. Churchill said it was premature to discuss helping the Dutch East Indies, but the Cabinet must decide what to tell the Dominions. His view was that they should announce a policy of first beating Italy in the Mediterranean, which required the presence of a strong fleet there. He hoped to avoid war with Japan by careful diplomacy. If Japan struck it was unlikely that the first moves would be against Australia or New Zealand, but against Hong Kong, Singapore or the Netherlands East Indies. If that happened Britain could, in the first instance, send 1 battle-cruiser and 1 aircraft carrier to Ceylon. He assumed Australia and New Zealand would not want Britain to alter its policy merely because of the possibility of raids. If the Dominions were threatened US intervention was likely. But, if the worst came to the worst, 'We could never stand by and see a British Dominion overwhelmed by a yellow race' even if it meant abandoning the Mediterranean. Churchill wanted to send a personal message to the Australian and New Zealand premiers along these lines. Caldecote felt this would make a 'tremendous difference' to the southern Dominions.¹²

Here were the origins of the famous telegrams which Churchill sent the Australian and New Zealand premiers as a 'foreword' to the *Far East Appreciation*, on 11 August 1940. He said he did not think Japan would declare war unless Germany invaded Britain. But if it did, Singapore ought to stand a long siege. The battle-cruiser and aircraft carrier would be sent to Ceylon, and the Australian and New Zealand cruisers sent home. If need be, the Mediterranean fleet could be sent through the Suez Canal.

If however contrary to prudence and self-interest, Japan set about invading Australia or New Zealand on a large scale, I have the explicit authority of the Cabinet to assure you that we should then cut our losses in the Mediterranean and proceed to your aid, sacrificing every interest except only the defence and feeding of this Island on which all depends'.[13]

At first glance it would seem that Churchill was revising the reversal of priorities made in June; that he was repeating his assurance made at the DMV Conference in 1939, returning, indeed, to the priority of 1937. This was certainly the effect his cable had in Australia and New Zealand. The Australian COS in a report of 23 August accepted that the defence of Singapore was still the dominant factor in the defence of Australia.[14] The New Zealand COS found Churchill's cable 'most heartening' and said it 'relieves our fear that in the present circumstances it would be impossible to release a British fleet for service in the Pacific which would be adequate to deal with the Japanese Fleet'.[15] Churchill was, however, referring to the unlikely contingency of an actual *invasion* of Australia or New Zealand. There was no promise that the fleet would be withdrawn from the Mediterranean immediately Japan made a move in the Pacific. But nor was it an idle promise. The ultimate commitment to Australia and New Zealand was clearly meant. And it was to be maintained, even at the cost of serious disagreement with the United States.

Churchill continued to declare that the Japanese threat was 'overrated', and he still held that the primary defence of Singapore was the fleet. As against the new COS appreciation he insisted that 'holding the whole of Malaya . . . cannot be entertained'.[16] But in September 1940 a new anxiety arose. While London suffered from German air offensive, the Japanese were seeking from the Vichy regime in France the right to use airfields and ports in northern

Indo-China (Tonkin) and were casting their eyes on Thailand. The British COS reported that even if the Japanese subdued all southern China and French Indo-China they would have forces available to attack Singapore.[17] These fears became more real on 22 September when the Japanese entered Tonkin (the present North Vietnam) and less than a week later, on 27 September, the Axis Pact was signed, which recognised Japan's predominance in 'Greater East Asia'. Soon there were fears that the Japanese would move into the airfields at Saigon and into Cam Ranh Bay – the best harbour on the Indo-China coast.

At this point United States concern for Southeast Asia was aroused to the point that force as well as trade restrictions were considered. The US naval staff even made enquiries about the Singapore Naval Base, where furious efforts were being made to complete the wharf walls omitted in the truncated scheme and to bring the workshops and equipment into operation. This excited hopes in Churchill and the British naval staff, in October 1940, that an American cruiser squadron might visit Singapore. Roosevelt told Lord Lothian, the British Ambassador, that he was contemplating sending a fast cruiser force to Samoa, Australia, the Netherlands East Indies and Singapore. Such a move was urged by Stanley Hornbeck, Political Adviser in the State Department, but opposed by Admiral Stark, the new Chief of Naval Operations, who knew that the United States was unprepared for war, but felt that the US fleet would be needed in the Atlantic.[18]

It was to be several months, however, before any firm move could be taken towards the achievement of a defensive net around Singapore. Roosevelt was preoccupied with the presidential elections until November 1940. The Australian Government now had three air squadrons at Singapore, but hesitated about the request for an army division. It wanted a full air appreciation of the Far East situation. In London, meanwhile, Churchill created an interdepartmental committee under the chairmanship of R. A. Butler, Parliamentary Under-Secretary for Foreign Affairs, to seek ways of causing 'inconvenience' to the Japanese 'without ceasing to act politely', and review problems of co-operation between Britain, the Dominions, India and the United States. This committee immediately raised the question of Japanese pressure on southern Indo-China and Thailand and a need for staff talks with the Dutch.[19]

IV

Over the next six months the possibility of British Commonwealth-Dutch-American co-operation in Southeast Asia was the subject of no less than six sets of staff conferences. Although some practical agreements were made, the general effect of the discussions was to highlight differences of approach and expose deficiencies of preparation.

The series began with the Singapore Defence Conference, 22–31 October 1940. Here the local British Commanders, Vice-Admiral Layton (C-in-C China Fleet), Lieutenant-General Bond (GOC, Malaya) and Air Vice-Marshal Babington (AOC Far East) were joined by the deputy Chiefs of Staff of Australia (Captain J. Burnett, RAN, Air Commodore W. D. Bostock, and Major-General Northcott), the CGS of New Zealand, Major-General Sir John Duigan, and the CAS, Group-Captain Saunders, the GOC Burma, the Director of Military operations, India, and the COS of the East Indies Station. Towards the end they were joined by an American observer, Commander A. C. Thomas, naval attaché at the US embassy in Bangkok.

The purpose of the conference was to discuss a tactical appreciation based on the British COS *Far East Appreciation* completed in July. The conference worked on the assumption that the US would be neutral; that Australian and New Zealand cruisers would be available and that one battle-cruiser and one aircraft carrier would be based in the Indian Ocean. Invasion of Australia and New Zealand was ruled out, but Japanese occupation of some Pacific islands, in order to threaten sea convoys, was envisaged. Attacks were deemed likely on Hong Kong, Malaya, Borneo, Burma, the Netherlands East Indies and Timor. Raids on Darwin, and other parts of Australia or New Zealand, were a possibility.

First priority was given to the defence of Malaya and the conference produced a formidable list of deficiencies. Aircraft and advance airfields were the prime need to prevent Japan getting within striking distance of Singapore. For Burma and Malaya 582 aircraft were called for (compared with the 208 of the British appreciation for Malaya). This was 449 more than the 88 actually available. For the whole region from Burma and the Indian Ocean in the west, to Fiji and Tonga in the east 1404 planes were needed (the deficiency being 1055). At sea, with the Australian and New

Zealand cruisers involved on the Indian Ocean and home waters convoy escorts, this left one 6″ cruiser and three armed merchant cruisers only for convoy duty further afield. Thus the conference envisaged all the Dominion cruisers returning to their home waters leaving the Indian Ocean dependent on reinforcements from 'elsewhere'. The army deficiencies in Malaya were put at 12 infantry battalions, 6 artillery regiments, 8 anti-tank batteries, 3 companies of field engineers, 3 tank companies and over 200 anti-aircraft guns and searchlights. The only possible sources for reinforcements were India and Australia; nothing was immediately available from New Zealand. The conference called for further staff discussions with the Dutch over naval co-operation and convoy routing, and with the United States about army and naval reinforcements. The 'principal question' was how far the United States would be willing to make up naval deficiencies and from which port they would operate. Singapore, Hong Kong, Manila, Guam or Honolulu were mentioned, Manila being considered the most suitable.[20]

This conference was shortly followed, during 26–29 November 1940, by Anglo-Dutch conversations in Singapore, when Captain William Purnell, COS of the American Asiatic Fleet, appears to have attended as observer.[21] Here mutual air reinforcement arrangements and reconnaissance responsibilities were outlined. The British agreed to cover the Indian Ocean and the South China Sea north of the Equator and the Timor and Arafura Seas (north of Australia). The Dutch would cover the South China Sea south of the Equator and south of a line from northeast Borneo to New Guinea (apart from the Timor and Arafura Seas). The question was raised as to what would constitute a hostile Japanese act, and the conference proposed a Japanese crossing of the line 6°N between northern Malaya and Borneo.[22]

Long before they received the full report of the Singapore Conference the British COS realised that the presence of the American observers would probably jeopardise their hopes of getting an American fleet at Singapore. Once a report of the inadequacy of Singapore's defences reached Washington the Americans would be unlikely to risk their ships. Moreover, at the very time of the first Singapore Conference, the British naval attaché in Washington, Captain A. W. Clarke, RN, had been permitted by Admiral Stark to have an unprecedented look at United States war plans. On 29 October 1940 Stark showed him a preliminary draft of 'Plan Dog', which indicated a gloomy view of British prospects in the Mediterranean. The United States Navy could not contemplate simultaneous offensives in the Atlantic and the Pacific. If it came into the war, the Atlantic would come first and the Far East would be given the second place.[23] Stark had come to the conclusion that sending the US fleet to Singapore had to be ruled out. Churchill and the British Chiefs of Staff accepted this. The naval staff did for the time being, but they did not abandon the idea of a US fleet at Singapore. Meanwhile they had to fall back on the original British plan. In November 1940 suggestions for sending British battleships were revived from two quite different quarters.

In Australia, as a new Advisory War Council, created on 28 October, absorbed the implications of the Singapore Conference, John Curtin, the Labor leader, suggested on several occasions that a British battleship should go to Singapore so that the Australian cruisers could be concentrated nearer home. Menzies, the Prime Minister, cabled to London for three or four battleships to be despatched.[24] In London, R. A. Butler, Chairman of the Far East Committee, revived the idea of sending a battle-cruiser and an aircraft carrier to Ceylon to stimulate morale in Indo-China, Thailand and the Dutch Indies, and to hearten Australia and New Zealand.[25] But, in the view of A. V. Alexander, the First Lord of the Admiralty, the 'only *real* deterrent' to Japan was the American fleet and that depended on American willingness to co-operate.[26]

All lines of argument led back to the attitude of the United States. When the Dutch Foreign Minister professed himself 'mystified' at Britain's reluctance to enter a commitment over the Netherlands East Indies, the naval staff insisted that a commitment was not possible until the American attitude was known. For this reason great importance was attached to three major staff conferences early in 1941. The American-British-Canadian (A-B-C) talks were held in Washington from 29 January to 27 March. The Anglo-Dutch-Australian (A-D-A) talks were in Singapore on 22–25 February and the American-Dutch-British (A-D-B) talks followed in Singapore 20–27 April. Of these, the A-B-C talks were the most significant for the 1939–45 war as they covered the basic strategy for an Anglo-American war effort and the basic decision was taken to give the Pacific the secondary place after the defeat of Germany.

V

By the beginning of 1941 and the period of intensive staff consultations, the possibility of a defensive net around Singapore was at last becoming discernible. Australia announced it would send a brigade of its 8th Division on 1 December 1940. The New Zealand COS recommended that a battalion and an airfield construction unit should be sent, although the Dominion Government did not act at this stage.[27] The British had appointed a Commander-in-Chief in the Far East, and, in keeping with the new role accorded to the air arm, the appointment went to Air Chief Marshal Sir Robert Brooke-Popham, who had been Governor of Kenya since 1937. He reached Singapore on 18 November 1940 and went to Australia in February 1941 to consult the Commonwealth COS. They agreed that Singapore remained vital to Australia's security, but they wanted Malaya, the Netherlands East Indies, Australia and New Zealand to be treated as a strategic whole and were especially concerned that a complete plan of naval dispositions should be drawn up. Brooke-Popham's command did not, however, include the naval forces.[28]

At the A-D-A Conference in Singapore on 22–25 February 1941 agreements were made between the British Commonwealth and Dutch representatives in the presence of a team of American observers. Brooke-Popham and his staff, and the local services' commanders (Layton, Bond and Babington) were joined by Major-General H. ter Poorten, from the Netherlands Indies, Rear-Admiral Grace, Major-General Northcott, and Air Commodore Bostock (from Australia, who also represented New Zealand) and the American observers, Captain Purnell, COS, the Asiatic Fleet, Captain Archer Allen and Lieutenant-Colonel F. G. Brink (naval and military observers in Singapore) and Commander A. C. Thomas, naval attaché from Bangkok. The A-D-A parties agreed that an attack on each would endanger the others. They accepted that an attack on Australia or New Zealand would be hazardous while the Singapore base was still available; it would also require a Japanese base in the Netherlands East Indies, which would be precarious if Malaya remained in British hands. Therefore the first attack would probably be on Malaya, where the basic need was the security of Singapore.

The governing factor would, again, be the United States. Its active support could not be taken for granted, but the Japanese could not be sure that the United States would not intervene. The Dutch agreed to release three bomber squadrons, one fighter squadron and six to eight submarines for service in the South China Sea. Australia agreed to take responsibility for the reinforcement of Koepang (in Dutch Timor) and Amboina, which stood almost as 'gate posts' to Australia and its territory in New Guinea. Two bomber squadrons and two brigade groups were earmarked for this task. Arrangements were made for rerouting convoys. On the assumption that a British battle-cruiser and an aircraft carrier would be transferred to the Indian Ocean, it was agreed that the Australian and New Zealand cruisers should return to their home waters on the outbreak of hostilities. Boundaries of the respective reconnaissance areas were drawn. Finally, the conference considered what Japanese moves might constitute a *casus belli*: incursions into Thailand west of 100°E or south of 10°N; large ship movements towards the Isthmus of Kra; a crossing of 6°N, or attacks on Timor, New Caledonia or the Philippines. But this was a matter for Governments to decide.[29] These arrangements were subject to ratification by the respective governments. The Australian COS (who immediately consulted with their New Zealand opposite numbers) were most dissatisfied that a full plan of naval dispositions was again omitted. Menzies was so alarmed about the weakness of Singapore that he decided to visit London in person.[30] The Dutch Government-in-exile, however, was eager to ratify.

VI

The American representatives at Singapore were only there as observers. In Washington, however, the US attitude to Singapore was being made clear at the A-B-C talks, which began at the end of January 1941. During the first plenary session there was one major point of agreement and one serious difference. The latter was over Singapore and Slessor recalled it was 'the only serious divergence'. It was quickly agreed that Germany should be defeated first. The Atlantic and European area was considered 'the decisive theatre' and US operations elsewhere were to be such as to 'facilitate that effort'. In the Pacific the British still maintained that the security of Singapore was the key to their position in the Far East. It was essential for the 'cohesion of the British Commonwealth' and the continuance of its war effort. The Americans understood the argument, but did not think the Japanese would penetrate the Indian Ocean even if Singapore fell. However if the Japanese established bases in the Netherlands East Indies, Thailand and Indo-China it would be doubtful if Singapore could remain tenable as a base. Its defences were known to be weak. The fundamental tenet of the US Naval Staff was that the American Pacific fleet should not be dispersed and should also be available for quick redeployment in the Atlantic.[31]

A general review of naval dispositions in the Pacific was made on 3 February 1941. Rear-Admiral Richard Kelly Turner, the fire-eating War Plans Officer for the Chief of Naval Operations, said the United States would probably assume full responsibility east of 180° (roughly a line from Midway to Fiji), and would also support the Dominion navies up to 155° (Bougainville) and would endeavour to deny use of the Marshall Islands to the Japanese. It would also assist the 'associated forces' and in holding the Japanese north of the 'Malay barrier'. But it would not reinforce its Asiatic fleet at Manila because of the over-long lines of communication. Instead, it envisaged sending reinforcements to the Atlantic and Mediterranean in order to release British battleships (with safer lines of communication via Suez and the Cape) for the Far East. In other words, the Americans were supporting the British Singapore strategy they had first encountered in the 1938 talks. However, Rear-Admiral Danckwerts RN suggested that the crux of the matter was the extent to which the US fleet would restrain Japan. If the US fleet was 'comparatively inactive' the British COS feared they might have to despatch the British fleet in fulfilment of the promise to the Dominions. This would be a wasteful distribution in the immediate future. The British felt the American Pacific and Asiatic Fleets should be co-ordinated, but the Americans said the distances were too great. The British made another attempt to secure some reinforcement on 10 February, when Rear-Admiral Bellairs suggested tentatively that the Asiatic Fleet should be augmented by an aircraft carrier, four heavy cruisers and submarines. The Americans countered by asking for data on how long Singapore could hold out.[32]

Churchill was infuriated by the British delegates' obstinate adherence to the Singapore strategy and their continuing attempt to involve the Americans. On 17 February 1941 he sent a testy memorandum to the CNS.

What has been the use of all this battling? Anyone could have seen that the United States would not base a battle-fleet on Singapore and divide their naval forces . . . The first thing is to get the United States into the war. We can then settle how to fight it afterwards. . . .
I do not see why, even if Singapore were captured, we could not protect Australia by basing a fleet on Australian ports.[33]

However, the divergence over the significance of Singapore continued at Washington. It appeared again during a survey of the strategic situation in the Pacific on 26 February 1941. The British delegation represented the long-established position of Singapore as one of the two keystones of Commonwealth defence.

> This has been based, not only upon purely strategic foundations, but on political, economic and sentimental considerations which, even if not literally valid on a strictly academic view, are of such fundamental importance to the British Commonwealth that they must always be taken into serious account. Just as United States strategy has to take account of the political factor and the element of public opinion in relation to the integrity of their Western seaboard, so British strategy must always be influenced by similar factors in the Dominions of Australia and New Zealand, to whom we are bound not only by the bond of kinship and a common citizenship, but by specific undertakings to defend them.[34]

Although they admitted that the British fleet could not be sent at present, the British delegates said that if Singapore were ever in serious danger, and the United States withheld its support, Britain would sacrifice its position in the Mediterranean. Singapore was second only in importance to the British Isles.

The British also wanted to know what was meant by holding the 'Malay barrier' as they could not hold Hong Kong, the Philippines, and Borneo as well as Singapore. Singapore was their card of re-entry for the fleet and the real solution was the placing of battleships there. They again appealed for an American aircraft carrier and cruiser squadron.

The American delegates were, however, emphatic that it would be a mistake for the British to plan the defence of Malaya on the possibility of American support. US strategy was based on the maintenance of sea communications and holding Japan north of a line drawn roughly from Singapore to Fiji, and west of 180°. In the view of the American COS Singapore had been built up 'as a symbol of the power of the British Empire'. Its value as a symbol was so great that its collapse would be a serious blow. But serious blows could be absorbed without leading to final disaster. They thought the retention of Singapore 'very desirable' but not if it jeopardised the major effort of the allies. This difference was so fundamental that it was included in the final report. Admiral Turner felt that, with nine American and six British battleships, Japan's ten would be satisfactorily contained. But the British said they would only send six to the Pacific if they knew the American fleet was at Hawaii, otherwise at least nine would be necessary to meet Japan.

The A-B-C 1 Report, completed on 27 March 1941, is remembered primarily for the Europe-first strategy. But it was relevant for Singapore for two reasons. First, because of the basic disagreement about Singapore's importance. Here the extent of the disagreement may have been due to a misunderstanding. Admiral Stark informed his fleet commanders (a few days after the agreement) that the British wanted the whole US fleet at Singapore. But the A-B-C record indicates that the British delegates asked specifically for certain reinforcements to the US Asiatic Fleet and for co-ordinated actions. (Maybe, off the record, they again sang the virtues of Singapore as a base for the Pacific Fleet, but this was certainly no longer Churchill's policy.) Secondly, the Americans agreed to transfer three battleships and one aircraft carrier to the Atlantic, so that the British could transfer three battleships and an aircraft carrier to the Indian Ocean.[35] Indirectly, then, the Americans were supporting the old British plan. The eastern strategy had not been abandoned. Maybe A-B-C 1 would make it practicable after all. This question remained a live issue because of Australian and New Zealand dissatisfaction with the A-D-A Conference's failure to make a detailed plan of naval movements and because of the presence in London during February–May 1941 of Robert Menzies, the Australian Prime Minister.

The Australians, as usual, wanted to see in detail how and when naval reinforcements would be sent. And the British, as ever, refused to commit themselves to such detail. Therefore, when the Defence Committee of the British Cabinet met on 9 April 1941 to discuss Menzies' request (but in his absence) for reinforcements to Singapore, on the A-D-A hypothesis that the United States would be neutral, Churchill was in an intransigent mood. He thought war unlikely in the Far East in the next three or four months. The Secretary of State for Air, Sir Archibald Sinclair, was reluctant to comply with Menzies' idea of sending *Hurricane* fighters to Singapore and suggested aircraft should be sought from the USA. Admiral Pound said that, apart from holding to the assurance that Britain would cut its losses in the Mediterranean if required, it would be wrong to abandon the Middle East until it was absolutely necessary to do so. Attlee was against making promises which they might not be able to fulfil. Churchill also thought the hypothesis of American neutrality unlikely and declared it was 'wrong to give up sound strategical ideas in order to satisfy the ignorance of the Australian Opposition'. As to the thorny question of whether to make a commitment about going to war if the Netherlands East Indies were attacked, Amery, Cranborne and Sinclair wanted to do so, but the view of Churchill and the naval staff prevailed: Wait and see what the Americans would do.

Menzies attended the Defence Committee on 29 April 1941 and was given the substance of these decisions.[36] The same line emerged from the Joint Planning Staff in answer to the Dominion queries arising from the A-D-A Conference. The London staff were hampered because, unlike the Australian and New Zealand COS, they had to rely on a telegraphic survey rather than a full conference report. Faced with the Dominion demands for details about reinforcements they resorted to a familiar phrase: there were 'too many variable factors' to allow a firm forecast of forces which could be sent to Singapore.[37] Nevertheless, as preparation for the next round of staff conferences, Brooke-Popham, the C-in-C, was assured that, once the US navy relieved the British at Gibraltar, in accordance with the A-B-C 1 agreement, British battleships would proceed to Singapore via the Cape.[38]

Further staff conversations in Singapore failed to resolve these uncertainties. From 21–27 April 1941 the American-Dutch-British (A-D-B) Conference involved the same representation as the A-D-A meeting. The Australians were led by Admiral Colvin, the CNS, the New Zealanders by Air Commodore Saunders. This time the Americans, led by Captain Purnell, came as delegates to implement the A-B-C 1 agreement. They had to make it clear that their Asiatic Fleet would *not* be reinforced, but they would give some assistance west of 180°. The conference drew lines of responsibility for local defence and recommended a single command for the region.[39] But the Americans were nonplussed to find an elderly RAF officer as

C-in-C and to find the British clinging to their Singapore strategy. The American COS in Washington refused to ratify the arrangements. The only positive result came from British-Dutch conversations held at the same time which produced a plan for naval and air deployment, which would apply only to Commonwealth and Dutch units if the US were neutral.[40] The Dutch were willing to provide one crusier, two destroyers and two submarines under British control.[41]

By the middle of 1941, then, the defensive net of British Commonwealth, Dutch and American forces remained extremely loose. A pattern had been woven at the staff conferences, but there was a great reluctance to make firm commitments. When the British COS reviewed future strategy in mid-June 1941, they assumed that if Japan entered the war the United States would too. As no US fleet could be expected at Singapore, there would be a delay of about two months before a British fleet arrived. If Singapore held out, Australia would be safe. If not, the strategic consequences would be 'disastrous'.[42]

VII

A week later Germany invaded Russia. Early in July the Japanese Government decided to make preparations for a southward advance. These included seeking the use of eight airfields around Saigon in southern Indo-China and collaboration with Thailand, where Japan had built up influence by mediating in the Franco-Thai War of November 1940–March 1941. Japanese warships appeared at Cam Ranh Bay on 24 July and by the end of July the Vichy Government had acquiesced in the occupation of southern airfields. These moves were immediately followed by the American freezing of Japanese assets (a plan which had been under discussion since the end of 1940), and similar moves by the British, the Dominions and the Netherlands East Indies. Although an actual oil embargo was not explicit in the US freezing order, it did lead to an effectual end of oil exports to Japan.[43] On 17 August 1941, following the meeting of Roosevelt and Churchill in Placentia Bay, Newfoundland, Roosevelt warned the Japanese that the United States would be compelled to 'take all steps it may deem necessary' to safeguard its interests if Japan stepped further south. Churchill broadcast that Britain would range itself 'unhesitatingly' on the side of the Americans.[44] In this new situation, which brought the Japanese to within 700 miles of Singapore, the plan to send a British fleet was revived.

Early in 1941 Menzies was told that only one battleship and one aircraft carrier were available for the Indian Ocean. But after the A-B-C 1 Report the plan in *War Memorandum (Eastern)* was revised to take account of expected American help in the Atlantic. And once the *Bismarck* had been sunk in May 1941 the naval staff began planning to send a fleet of 7 capital ships (3 modern battle-cruisers and 4 unmodernised battleships), 1 aircraft carrier, 10 cruisers and 24 destroyers to the Indian Ocean, for movement to Singapore not before March 1942. This was almost the fleet envisaged in the 1937 appreciation. In August 1941, when Churchill cabled from Newfoundland that the United States would take a firm line over southern Indo-China, the naval staff began to consider how they would implement the plan. At that point it was possible to send one modernised battle-cruiser, HMS *Repulse*, and four unmodernised battleships, *Royal Sovereign*, *Revenge*, *Ramilles* and *Resolution*. But during an Admiralty meeting on 20 August Sir Dudley Pound, the CNS, said that if the US sent sufficient modern battleships to the Atlantic capable of facing the German *Tirpitz* (completed in 1941), Britain might be able to send one of the new *King George V* class to the east, along with *Nelson, Rodney* and *Renown*, as well as the four 'R' battleships and, possibly, three fast aircraft carriers.[45]

At this point Churchill, recently back from Newfoundland, brought a different approach. On 25 August he wrote to Pound suggesting that a small 'determined squadron' of the best capital ships should be sent to the Aden-Singapore-Simonstown triangle. He had in mind the *Duke of York*, the *Repulse* or the *Renown* and a fast aircraft carrier, which would have a paralysing affect on the Japanese. Pound replied that the *Duke of York* was not 'worked up' and that he did not like Churchill's idea.[46] Back came Churchill, in forceful style, on 29 August. It was 'faulty disposition' to send slow, old battleships to the Indian Ocean. They would become 'floating coffins'. It might please the Australians to count numbers of battleships in 'their neighbourhood', but, on the analogy of the *Tirpitz*, he was impressed by the value of a small, fast force. He thought a *King George V* might 'indeed be a decisive deterrent'. Nothing was decided. This did not stop Churchill from letting the Australian and New Zealand Prime Ministers know by cable on 31 August 1941 that Britain was considering a force of first-class units in the Aden-Singapore-Simonstown triangle by the end of 1941.

Before the matter went further there were new demands for battleships from Australia. At the time of the Japanese move into southern Indo-China Menzies, disappointed at the mildness of the American warnings, proposed returning to London as he had been invited to join the British War Cabinet. This idea was rejected by the Australian Advisory War Council and in August Menzies resigned as Prime Minister in favour of the Country Party leader, Arthur Fadden. It was agreed that the Australian special representative in London should be Sir Earle Page (who had briefly been Prime Minister in April 1939) and that he should visit Batavia, Singapore, Manila and Washington en route. Thus Page attended a conference in Singapore on 29 September 1941, chaired by Duff Cooper (the British Minister of State in the Far East) which included Brooke-Popham, the C-in-C, the Governor, and the British Ambassadors to Thailand and China. Here it was agreed that the 'only real deterrent' to Japan would be a British fleet at Singapore and they stressed the propaganda value of one or two battleships.[47]

A few days after the Singapore conference the Australian Government resigned and John Curtin took office at the head of a Labor ministry on 7 October. His first Cabinet meeting considered Churchill's cable about sending capital ships to the Indian Ocean. It is highly ironical that Curtin (who as one of the 'ignorant' Australian Opposition had long been something of a bane of Churchill's) should use an almost identical phrase to Churchill's in favour of a small battleship force. On 17 October he urged the despatch of the new force as soon as possible and hoped for modern capital ships in view of their 'deterrent effort' and possible 'decisive influence'. On the following day Page telephoned Curtin from Washington and was told about the British plan. Curtin told him to demand four battleships and, if he got them, he could sail home in one.[48]

The question of the Far Eastern Fleet came before the Defence Committee of the Cabinet on 17 October, when Churchill revived his idea of a small, fast squadron. If the *Tirpitz* could tie down three times as many battleships, a small British force would have the same effect on the Japanese. He wanted the *Prince of Wales* to join the *Repulse* (which had just arrived at Durban on convoy duty) and a fast aircraft carrier. He was supported by Eden, who felt a *Prince of Wales*-type ship would have a much greater political impact than some 1914–18 war battleships. He was opposed by A. V. Alexander, the First Lord, who pointed out that the *Tirpitz* analogy was false. The German ship was a threat to British convoys, whereas the proposed Eastern Fleet was for convoy protection, not convoy raiding. Sir Tom Phillips, the Vice-CNS, said that the Japanese fleet had a mix of old and new capital ships and that three modern battle-cruisers and four old battleships operating close to British territories and shore-based aircraft would be the match of any Japanese force. Churchill did not impose a decision. He invited the CNS to study his proposal for reconsideration by the Defence Committee in three days time.[49]

At the meeting on 20 October Sir Dudley Pound was back to plead for a balanced eastern fleet. Churchill accepted that if *Tirpitz* broke out the War Cabinet would have to accept responsibility for shipping losses, but Pound made two points. First, *Tirpitz* was not the only problem, there were also *Scharnhorst* and *Gneisenau* and he wanted three *King George V*'s to contain *Tirpitz*. 'If we detached the "Prince of Wales" to the Far East, we should lay ourselves open to incurring additional losses as a result of unsound dispositions.' Secondly, the Japanese would not be deterred merely by one fast battleship. They could easily afford to put four of their old battleships to escort any southern invasion convoys. 'What would deter them, however, would be the presence at Singapore of a force (such as the "Nelson", the "Rodney" and the R. Class battleships) of such strength that to overcome it they would have to detach the greater part of their Fleet and thus uncover Japan.' He said if the USA would base its fleet at Singapore the situation would be different, but the Americans had been 'quite adamant' about keeping it at Hawaii. Eden again supported Churchill because of the political value of a 'really modern ship'. In this Pound saw the chance of compromise. He agreed about the political value of the *Prince of Wales* arriving at Cape Town, and suggested it should sail there forthwith and 'a decision as to her onward journey' be taken in the light of the situation when she arrived.[50] So the *Prince of Wales* sailed on 25 October. Churchill cabled the good news to Roosevelt, Stalin and Curtin. The version that went to Peter Fraser, Prime Minister of New Zealand, ran: 'Nothing is so good as having something that can catch and kill anything. It keeps them bunched'.[51]

Churchill had made a political decision. He no doubt believed in the 'deterrent' effect of his advance squadron. The idea had, of course, in one form or another, often been suggested since Beatty's day, when the plan was for a battle-cruiser squadron at Singapore in peacetime. Now, the *Prince of Wales* and the *Repulse* were gestures towards allies, especially the Australians. And Churchill knew that Sir Earle Page was on the doorstep. The Australian envoy was welcomed to the War Cabinet less than a week after the *Prince of Wales* sailed. In a meeting devoted to the Far East and Australia's role in the war Page made a statement of Australian views on 5 November 1941, and pleaded for deterrent forces in Singapore by December 1941/January 1942 at the latest. Churchill could reply with news of the *Prince of Wales* as the beginning of a major fleet.[52] A week later Admiral Pound expounded the naval staff plan, which was for seven capital ships by January/February 1942. (*Prince of Wales, Repulse* and *Renown* and four *Royal Sovereigns*.) The CAS said the air force was working towards the goal of 336 aircraft and the CIGS said the garrison was 63,000 strong plus 14,000 volunteers; it had 200 AA guns. Churchill insisted that Britain was 'resolute to help Australia' if it were menaced by invasion. But he hoped Page would agree that they could not send to Singapore forces which could be better employed against Germany and Italy.[53]

The *Prince of Wales* reached Cape Town on 16 November. The aircraft carrier *Indomitable* which should have joined it ran aground in Jamaica. The review of policy agreed on 20 October appears not to have taken place, and Admiralty orders already indicated Singapore as its destination.[54] Phillips, the former Vice-CNS, had been appointed Commander-in-Chief of the Eastern Fleet. When asked by the Admiralty if his two capital ships would await the *Revenge* before proceeding, he preferred not. He said that if *Prince of Wales* and *Repulse* went ahead to Singapore the Japanese would assume they were a 'striking force'. If they arrived with one old battleship it might suggest Britain was forming a 'line of battle' but could only spare three, and this would encourage the Japanese. The capital ships came together at Colombo on 28 November. In view of the deadlock in the US–Japanese talks in Washington, the pressure of the Japanese upon Thailand and other evident military preparations, Phillips was ordered to fly ahead to Singapore, and to Manila to consult the American Asiatic Fleet Commander, Admiral Hart.

On 2 December 1941 the two capital ships escorted by four destroyers, sailed up the Johore Strait and anchored at the naval base. The BBC announced that the *Prince of Wales* and 'other heavy units' had reached Singapore. This was designed to mystify the world, but it infuriated the ship's company of *Repulse*, who resented being treated as HMS *Anonymous*.[55] For twenty years the Admiralty had nurtured plans for sending the 'main fleet' to Singapore. This small force was something of an anti-climax. It had no carrier. But it *was* an advance squadron of a large fleet. Another battle-cruiser and the older battleships were to follow. The planning of twenty years was about to be fulfilled. Ironically, however, Phillips agreed with Hart that Singapore was not a suitable base, and that the Eastern Fleet should soon move on to Manila.[56]

10 'A Close Run Thing', 1941–42

I

Four days after Admiral Phillips' striking force anchored beside the wharves at Sembawang, Australian air force reconnaissance planes from Kota Bahru, on the northeast coast of Malaya, spotted two Japanese convoys in the Gulf of Siam. Next day, 7 December 1941, an RAF *Catalina* flying-boat was shot down and an Australian *Hudson* fired upon. These were the opening shots of the Pacific War. By the end of the night of 7/8 December the full scope of the Japanese moves were evident. Churchill's 'decisive deterrent' having failed, the long-established plan for holding the 'fortress' until the main fleet arrived had, now, to be put to the test.

Yet, as Admiral Richmond had written sixteen years earlier, the eastern strategy was not so much a war plan as a scheme for naval reinforcements – a timetable for the 'fleet in being' to come and provide 'cover' for the Commonwealth east of Suez. Not only was it a scheme of naval reinforcement. The air and army elements also needed additions. Trenchard's basic argument had been the 'flexibility' of air power. Unlike the big guns, anchored in concrete, his squadrons could come from the Middle East and India. The same with the army. For years the garrison had been minimal: two regular battalions and the local volunteers. Thus, to hold the 'fortress' until the fleet arrived, the air force would speed its squadrons along the line of prepared airfields; the army would move units from India by sea.

Apart from the seaward defences of Singapore Island little in the way of siege defences had been prepared.[1] The need to defend 'Malaya as a whole' was not formally accepted until the 1940 *Far East Appreciation*. Even then, Churchill had not approved. The larger role accepted for the air force came at a time when the squadrons to implement it could not be spared, because of the needs of the war in the Mediterranean. Moreover there was no prior commitment to help in Singapore by Australia or New Zealand in spite of numerous hints for more than a decade. Nor was there any certainty of American help. Only the Dutch seemed willing, yet the British refused to commit themselves to the defence of the Netherlands East Indies until the last moment. Above all, it must be remembered that in 1941 the main crisis for the Commonwealth was in the Mediterranean. Churchill seemed to be convinced that war could be avoided in the East. This meant that in December 1941, when the Japanese landed in Malaya, Britain's eastern strategy became a race to provide reinforcements before the invaders could reach Singapore.

II

For the attackers, of course, Singapore was only one target. On the wider stage Japan was embarked upon its race with destiny. In 1942 the navy would reach the peak of its power. Thereafter the American warship construction programme would give supremacy to the US navy. The Japanese had to reach their objectives fast. Recognition by the world of the new order in Asia would have to be secured before their oil tanks ran dry and their relative strength declined. As to how exactly they would end the war, they were by no means certain.[2]

The goal of a new order in Asia had long been clear enough. Japan, Korea and Manchukuo would constitute the centre of expertise, industry and finance. China, India, Siberia, Southeast Asia, Australia and New Zealand would provide raw materials. Moral justification would stem from Japan's 'stabilising' influence and leadership in saving Asia from communism and liberating it from western imperialism. As to the fulfilment there had been agonising disputes over directions, methods and timing.

After quitting the League of Nations and the Naval Treaty system Japan found itself in the paradoxical position of being free at last to build a navy to match the Americans, but of feeling 'encircled' by the great powers. When the decision to adopt a 'positive' policy of expansion was made back in 1936 it was hoped that relations with the powers could be improved by diplomacy; that trade and influence in Southeast Asia could be peaceably achieved. But the armed services made contingency plans. The navy envisaged a fleet of 12 battleships, 12 aircraft carriers, 28 cruisers, 96 destroyers and 70 submarines.³ It was to be ready by the end of 1941 and include two 18″gun *Yamato* class ships, greater than any British or American battleship. At the same time the General Staff feared a war with Russia on the borders of Manchukuo; they also believed that British power would have to be eliminated before the southern regions were occupied and that, eventually, Japan would have to face the USA.

The basic dilemma was always one of direction – north or south? The army, well established in Manchukuo, in the main looked north to the Russian menace though part thought China must be dealt with first. The navy looked south to the oilfields of the Netherlands East Indies. The war in China from 1937 gave priority to the south. It led to the increasing disapproval of the United States and Britain. Then, before the problems of China and the north had been brought to a conclusion, the European War, the German occupation of Holland and France, and the possible invasion of Britain in 1940 promised a moment of opportunity in the south. When the colonial powers were prostrate, rich tropical fruits would be ripe for the picking. And, as the American trade restrictions (partly caused by President Roosevelt's preparations for an Atlantic War, and partly designed to restrain Japan) bit closer on supplies of strategic resources, the products of Southeast Asia became imperative necessities.

Thus in June 1940 the 'Greater East Asian Co-prosperity Sphere' was announced. Pressure was exerted on the British to stop supplies to China, on the Dutch to supply more oil and on the French to grant facilities in Indo-China. The friendship of Thailand was cultivated. The army and the navy at last agreed on objectives. The war in China was to be brought to a conclusion, then Japan would move south. Force might become necessary, so, from the latter months of 1940, active planning for war began.

In the first half of 1941 the possibilities of diplomacy had still not been exhausted. Negotiations began in Washington in March. Japan was eager for the American trade restrictions to be relaxed; the United States wanted to ensure the recognition of the territorial integrity of China and the countries of Southeast Asia. Japan made a neutrality pact with Russia in April 1941. When Germany invaded Russia two months later the problem of the north was stabilised for the time being. By mediating between French Indo-China and Thailand, Japan increased its influence over the latter.

It was accepted that force would probably be necessary to achieve the new order in the south. At the same time the freezing of Japanese assets by the USA, the British Commonwealth and the Netherlands East Indies and the cutting off of oil supplies gave a new desperation to Japanese actions.

Oil became the urgent need. To get the oil, which had been refused in negotiations, the Netherlands East Indies would have to be occupied. First, however, Singapore must be captured before an Anglo-American fleet could be assembled to strike back. To capture Singapore the Chiefs of Staff insisted on bases in southern Indo-China and Thailand. But it was this very move into Saigon and Cam Ranh Bay in July 1941 which finally roused the United States. Withdrawal of the Japanese forces became the condition for a resumption of American trade.

The moment of decision came in August 1941. The navy was reaching the limit of its projected strength. The American fleet was divided, by the diversion of a third of its strength to the Atlantic. The British Eastern Fleet was not yet formed. At the end of 1941 Japan approached its moment of naval supremacy in the Pacific. Moreover, the British carrier-borne aerial torpedo attack on the Italian fleet in Taranto harbour on 11 November 1940 had demonstrated a way by which the American fleet could be immobilised in Hawaii.[4] But if sea-borne landings were to be accomplished in Southeast Asia, weather conditions would be best in late November, or early December at the latest. After that beach landings could be ruled out until March or April 1942. Similarly, aircraft carriers could not operate from the stormy, unfrequented seas north of Hawaii in the depth of winter. By 1942 it would be too late. Japan's oil stocks would be lower, the US navy stronger. In December 1941 the Japanese navy would achieve 70 per cent of the American naval strength; in 1942 it would fall to 65 per cent, 1943 to 50 per cent and 1944 to 30 per cent.[5] The opportunity, it seemed, had to be grasped or lost. On 6 September 1941, before a sceptical Emperor, who had privately reminded them of their four years of costly frustration in China, the Japanese service leaders demanded a decision by the first week of October.[6] The navy was using oil at the rate of 400 tons an hour. The supplies of the Netherlands East Indies would be wanted.

It was decided that if the negotiations in Washington showed no prospect of success by early October Japan would move south and fight the British, the Dutch and the Americans. There were many in

Japan who wanted to avoid the decision. October passed with the dilemma unresolved. A new deadline was set on 5 November. If the Washington talks did not succeed by the end of the month, the war would begin. It was not a joyous decision. The army and navy planners could not promise success. They were unsure how the war would conclude.[7] But they were caught in the web of their own strategic planning, rather as the British had been trapped in their own project for building the Singapore naval base.

As a last diplomatic gesture the Japanese offered a 'modus vivendi' which would have put the clock back to before the move into southern Indo-China and the freezing order. Japan would withdraw its units from southern Indo-China to northern Indo-China. Japan and the USA were to agree not to make military reinforcements in Southeast Asia and to co-operate to develop the Netherlands East Indies. The USA was to undertake to meet Japan's oil needs and to abide by non-discriminations in trade. The Americans replied, on 26 November 1941, by demanding that Japan withdraw all forces from Indo-China *and* China. This was received in Tokyo as a 'humiliating ultimatum'. On 30 November it was decided that the negotiations would continue until 1330 on 7 December (Washington time, that is 0230 on 8 December Tokyo time). Half an hour later, the carefully planned opening moves would begin.[8]

III

If the main objective was the oil of the Netherlands East Indies, the preliminary moves were the destruction of the US fleet in Pearl Harbor and the air force in the Philippines (to hold off the one power capable of stopping the occupation of the Dutch Indies), and the capture of Singapore (to prevent the British from exerting any power in the region). As it turned out the landings in Malaya preceded the Pearl Harbor attack by just over an hour. But the international date-line sometimes misleads people into forgetting that the Mayalan invasion of 8 December started before Pearl Harbor on 7 December, and the fact that the dispersed scenes of action as well as the various metropolitan capitals were all in different time zones, further confuses the picture.

The order of action on 8 December 1941, by Tokyo time, would appear to be: 0030 hrs, occupation of the International Settlement in Shanghai, where one British gunboat was subsequently sunk; 0215 hrs, landings at Kota Bahru, Malaya; 0325 hrs, first bombs on Pearl Harbor; 0600 hrs landings at Singora and Patani in southern Thailand; 0630 hrs air raid on Singapore and the northern airfields of the Philippines; 0900 hrs, air raid on Hong Kong; 0930 hrs, air raid on Guam; 1100 hrs, air raid on Wake Island and 1330 hrs, air raid on Clark Field, the main air base close to Manila. Only twelve hours, and the staggering extent of the challenge to Anglo-American power was revealed.

In England, Winston Churchill's first information was from the 9 o'clock news on Sunday evening 7 December at Chequers, where he was dining with the US Ambassador. He immediately rang President Roosevelt who said: 'We are all in the same boat now'. The Prime Minister felt 'the greatest joy', and (as he later wrote) 'went to bed and slept the sleep of the saved and thankful'.[9] Long-term prospects for winning the war were now assured. So far as Singapore was concerned, his immediate thoughts were on the seapower situation.

Japan had, in a day, seized a clear position of supremacy in the Pacific. Australia, New Zealand and the Pacific Islands were all open to attack. What should become of Britain's sole mobile force, the *Prince of Wales* and the *Repulse*? At an inconclusive meeting on 9 December the view was expressed that they should 'go to sea and vanish among the innumerable islands'. Churchill's instinct was that they should cross the Pacific and join the remnant of the US fleet, so that soon there would be a 'fleet in being' which could provide a shield for Australia and New Zealand.[10] A sound enough idea in the context of traditional blue-water strategy, it was not much help to the Singapore base.

IV

For the British Commonwealth defenders of Malaya the first week of the Pacific War involved three disasters, which nullified the tortuous defence preparations of 1941. These were the failure to prevent or disrupt the Japanese landings; the loss of the *Prince of Wales* and *Repulse*; and the collapse of the air force in Kelantan and Kedah.

In the eighteen months before December 1941 thousands of reinforcements from various parts of the Commonwealth had been assembled in Malaya. They fell short of the requirements accepted in the *Far East Appreciation* of 1940. However, priority had, in theory, been given to the air defences of Malaya, especially surveillance in the Gulf of Siam and an ability to attack a seaborne invasion fleet. Of the 336-plane, 22-squadron force promised as a target for the region, less than half had been provided. These included the obsolete 140-mph Vickers *Vildebeeste* torpedo-bomber in the role of main strike plane, and the inadequate 295-mph Brewster *Buffalo* as the chief fighter.

Of first importance for the air defences were the 'forward' squadrons on the airfields in northern Malaya and the east coast. These bases (which had been sited without army consultation) also dictated the shape of the army's defence plan. On the northeast coast of Kelantan, just south of the Thai border, were the three airfields at Kota Bahru, Gong Kedah and Machang. Here there was an Australian squadron of twelve Lockheed *Hudson* reconnaissance planes, two RAF half-squadrons, each with six *Vildebeeste* torpedo-bombers, and there were two *Buffalo* fighters and a *Beaufort* photo-reconnaissance plane. Halfway down the east coast at Kuantan, in Pahang, stood another Australian squadron of eight *Hudsons*, an RAF squadron of eight *Blenheim* bombers and another half-squadron of six *Vildebeestes*. In the northwest, in Kedah, covering the Isthmus of Kra and the main road and rail routes from Thailand, the RAF had a squadron of eleven *Blenheim* bombers at Alor Star, and at Sungei Patani there was a lone squadron of twelve *Blenheim* night-fighters and an Australian fighter squadron with twelve *Buffaloes*. There were some airfields in central Malaya and the New Zealand air force had provided an aerodrome construction unit which was building more in Johore. But at the outset the rest of the air strength was concentrated at Singapore's four airfields. The RAF had a squadron of *Blenheim* bombers, a half-squadron of *Vildebeestes*, a squadron of *Buffaloes* and six *Catalina* flying boats. The RAAF had a *Buffalo* fighter squadron and a *Hudson* reconnaissance squadron, and the RNZAF had sent pilots for a fighter squadron, which was still training on *Buffaloes* and not yet passed for operations.

In all, the Commonwealth air command had not more than 166 first-line aircraft and 86 reserves.[11] They were organised in one night-fighter squadron and four day-fighter squadrons, two light-bomber and two torpedo-bomber squadrons, two reconnaissance squadrons and the small flying-boat unit. Against these forgotten

Far Eastern 'few' the Japanese launched their army's 3rd Air Division and the navy's 22nd Air Flotilla which between them had at least 500 first-line aircraft.[12] The defenders were outnumbered three to one. This difference in air power was to be decisive.

On the ground the army totals favoured the defenders on paper. There were thirty-one battalions made up as follows: fifteen Indian Army, six Australian, four English, two Scottish, three Gurkha and one Malay.[13] The lack of any tanks, until it was too late, was the critical army deficiency. The total manpower of Malaya Command (under Lieutenant-General Arthur Percival, who had been Chief of Staff in Malaya 1936–8) came to about 88,600. They were of very mixed origin and efficiency and included regulars and volunteers. The largest contingent were the 37,000 Indians, who exceed the 19,000 British and 15,200 Australians put together. There were also 16,800 Malaysian volunteers (mainly Chinese, Malays or Eurasians) in four battalions of Straits Settlements Volunteers, four battalions of FMS Volunteers and State Forces from the unfederated states of Kedah, Kelantan and Johore. These local forces, along with five units from the Indian Princely States, were initially used for airfield and static defence. The only regular unit from the country, then, was the Malay Regiment.[14] Many of the Indian units included recent recruits and had been denuded of experienced officers and NCOs because of the rapid expansion of the Indian Army. This large, if motley, army was equivalent to three and a half divisions but was weak in higher formation training.[15]

It was also very thin on the ground and deployed in three isolated groups. The north of Malaya and the forward airfields were guarded by III Indian Corps commanded by Lieutenant-General Sir Lewis Heath, an Indian Army Officer, older and, until recently, senior to the GOC and who had successfully commanded a division in the Ethiopian campaign. His two Indian divisions were deployed separately on either side of the mountainous 'spine' of the Malay Peninsula. On the east coast 9 Division had a brigade at Kota Bahru and another at Kuantan to guard the airfields and adjacent beaches. In the northwest, in Kedah, 11 Division had the dual role of preparing a defensive position at Jitra, north of the Alor Star airfield, to block the main routes in from Thailand, and also making preparations for a pre-emptive strike to the Kra Coast of Thailand. The corps had one brigade in reserve. To the south, in Johore, the 8th Division of the Australian Imperial Force (AIF) had two brigades, one of which had reached Singapore in the *Queen Mary* ten months earlier and had had plenty of training in the country. The Australian Commander, Major-General Gordon Bennett, was a controversial citizen-soldier, who had distinguished himself at a young age in the 1914–18 war, but who had written uncomplimentary things about the regular staff corps.[16] On Singapore Island were the so-called 'Fortress Troops' (equivalent to two brigades) and the heavy artillery units. There was also a brigade in reserve (see Map 11).

In Percival's striking analogy: It was as if Portsmouth Naval Base were on the north shore of the Isle of Wight, defended by a division on the Scottish border, a brigade in Northumberland and another on the Humber, with Corps HQ at Crewe. In southern England there would be a brigade about Oxford and another at the mouth of the Thames. Command HQ would be on the Isle of Wight, which would be strongly defended on its southern coast.[17]

To overwhelm these three and a half divisions the Japanese allocated the 25th Army under Lieutenant-General Yamashita, with four divisions. Of these only three were used. In the first few hours some 12,000 combat troops and some tanks were got ashore.[18] According to Colonel Masanobu Tsuji, who planned the operations, the total Japanese invading army was a little over 60,000 but they had over 100 tanks and armoured cars, and each division had 6000 bicycles.[19] The tanks may have seemed 'amateurish-looking affairs, the metal strung together with no indication of strength or craftsmanship',[20] but they gave the decisive advantage on land.

The force which was supposed to deter or destroy any Japanese invasion convoys was, of course, the British Eastern Fleet. But this would not be fully formed for at least three months. It was without an aircraft carrier or any but the minimum of supporting vessels. When the Pacific War broke out there were also at Singapore three old 6" cruisers from the China Squadron, one Australian and three British destroyers, three local gunboats, and an Australian and a New Zealand armed merchant cruiser. There were also one cruiser and five destroyers under refit or repair. Two more destroyers escaped from Hong Kong and Admiral Hart agreed to detach four destroyers from the US Asiatic Fleet. Further afield, the 8" cruiser *Exeter* was summoned from the Indian Ocean, the Dutch navy had two light cruisers.[21] On 7 December 1941 Admiral Phillips met the New Zealand Chief of Naval Staff (Captain Parry of the *Graf Spee* action), who persuaded his government to send his old ship HMNZS *Achilles*, and Vice-Admiral Sir Guy Royle (the Australian

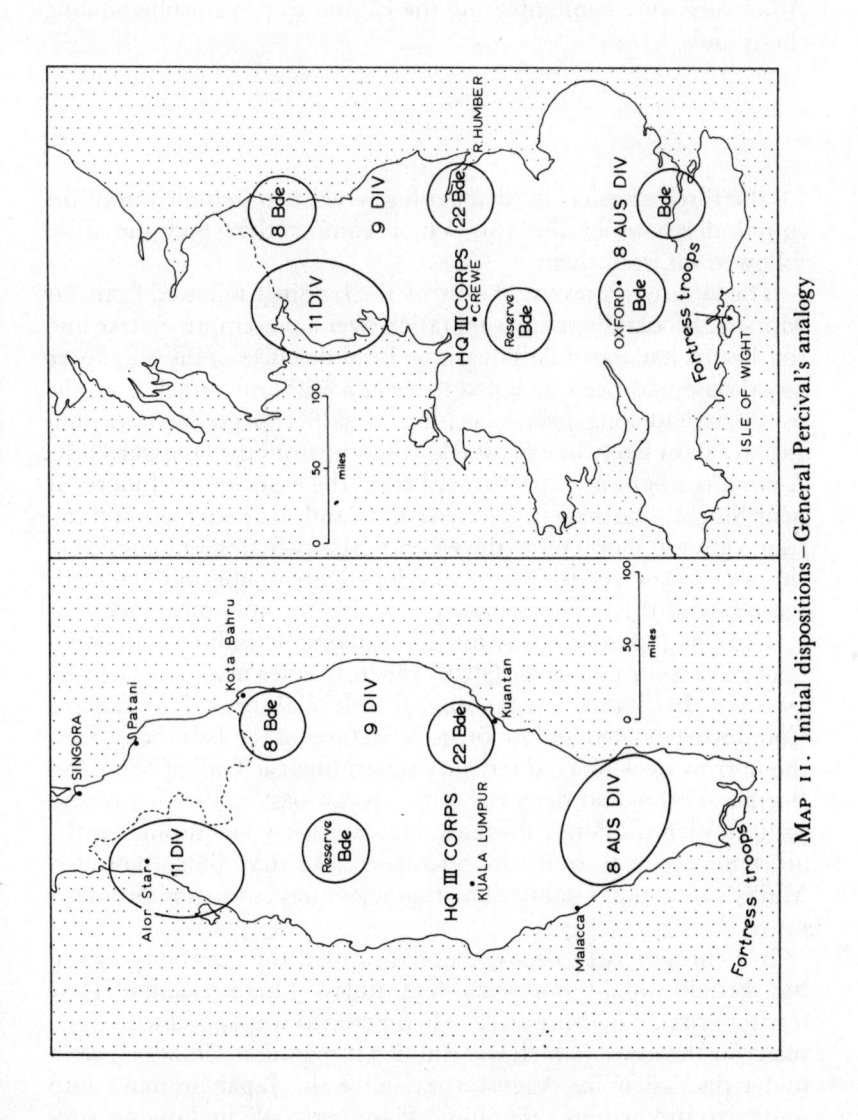

MAP 11. Initial dispositions – General Percival's analogy

CNS), who agreed to release HMAS *Hobart*.[22] This was no 'battle fleet' in the normal sense. Far from providing a deterrent, the Admiralty were contemplating the capital ships vanishing among the islands.

V

Of the three disasters in the opening week, two stemmed from the initial decisions of the two senior commanders and the third followed on from them.

The failure to prevent or destroy the landings followed from Air Marshal Brooke-Popham's hesitation over a pre-emptive strike into southern Thailand.[23] Although the fixed defences of the Singapore naval base had been designed to meet a seaborne attack from the south, it had long been accepted in staff college exercises that Japan's most likely line of attack would be from the landward side. A landing might be expected, either on the east coast of Johore, or near Singora harbour in southern Thailand, whence road and rail routes gave a 'short cut' to the western Malay States. On this side of the mountains lay the more developed areas, the most modern services and the territory most conducive to rapid movement.

Thus, as Japanese economic and diplomatic influence in Thailand grew at the time of the fall of France, the idea of a strategic strike evolved. In January 1941 the British Cabinet's Far Eastern Committee mooted an 'unobtrusive seizure' of the Isthmus of Kra, the narrow neck of Thai territory separating the Gulf of Siam and Burma. This would deny the entire Kra Coast to the enemy and protect Victoria Point, Burma's most southerly aerodrome on the air reinforcement route to Singapore. At that time, however, Malaya Command did not have sufficient forces to attempt such a move.[24]

In February 1941 Brooke-Popham raised the possibility again, but Britain would not seize Kra unless Japan violated Thai territory first.[25] By May 1941, when Percival was appointed GOC, plans for the move (which was dubbed 'Operation Matador') were under discussion. In August 1941, after the Japanese move into southern Indo-China, the Joint Planning Staff in London suggested that 'unobtrusive preparations' commence.[26] The C-in-C was ready by 15 September to order a division forward to Singora, but *not* the further 250 miles to the neck of the Isthmus. The modified plan envisaged reaching Singora at least 24 hours ahead of an invasion force and also blocking the secondary road running south from Patani. But the British Cabinet (in spite of promptings from Australia and New Zealand) would not authorise 'Matador' without the assurance of American support.[27] This was not forthcoming until after the Japanese invasion forces had sailed from Hainan on 4 December. Next day Brooke-Popham was authorised to use his discretion about 'Matador'.

At 1340 hrs (Singapore time) on 6 December 1941 the two Japanese convoys were observed sailing westwards, to the south of Cape Cambodia. Here was a possible moment for launching 'Matador'. III Corps was put on first-degree readiness. Percival assumed that Brooke-Popham would give the order to go. But the Japanese deception plan, of sailing towards Bangkok (before dispersing south to the Kelantan and Kra coasts), led the C-in-C to pause and await further reconnaissance. On 7 December one of the *Catalinas* which went very close to the Japanese dispersal point at about 1000 hrs never returned (it was shot down), and at 1925 hrs another plane, which spotted transports sailing southwards, off Singora, was fired on. This news reached Singapore at 2100 hrs. There could be no doubt about the direction and purpose of the Japanese ships, but now Percival did not advise 'Matador', as the 24-hour margin was already lost. 11 Division could not reach Singora before the Japanese landed. Instead of fighting from prepared positions they would have to go into action after a night drive north.

While 11 Division was still poised at half-an-hour's notice to move, Brooke-Popham ordered a further air reconnaissance at dawn on 8 December. By then it was too late. Soon after midnight 9 Division, manning the beaches at Kota Bahru, was fired on, and Japanese troops from three transports landed in rough surf. The Indian troops and the air force at Kota Bahru put up a stiff fight, but the Japanese got ashore.[28] By 0400 hrs the main landings followed at Singora, Patani and at three points further north, and met only light Thai resistance. The Thai airfields and the railway were seized and Victoria Point, in Burma, threatened. Yet 11 Division, having been on the alert for 'Matador' for 48 hours in pouring rain, did not get their orders until 1330 hrs on 8 December. They were ordered to stop the Japanese at the defensive line at Jitra. After being geared-up for the thrust north they had to turn into unfinished, partly waterlogged, positions, lay barbed wire

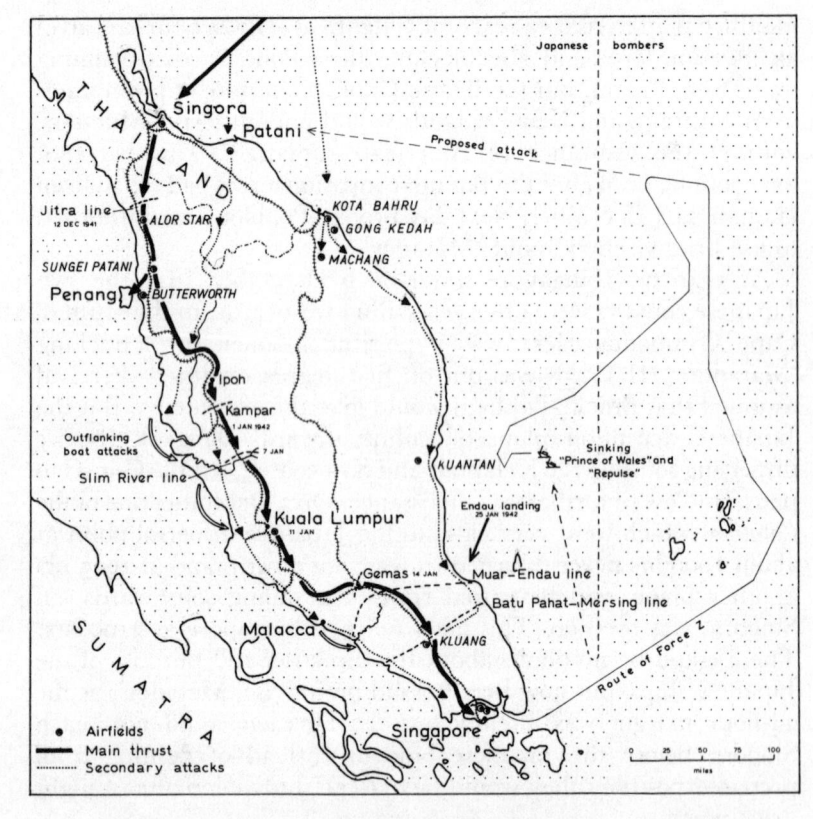

MAP 12. Outline of the campaign

and dig in. In all, the succession of events from the afternoon of 6 December to the afternoon of 8 December must be accounted a disaster (see Map 12).

The second (and more famous) disaster stemmed from an attempt to make up for the first. Given that the Japanese were ashore and the way open for them to enter Kedah and head down the west coast, their build-up of reinforcements, vehicles and supplies must still be continuing. Here, then, was an opportunity for the traditional exercise of seapower. Thus Admiral Phillips, who heard of the initial convoy-sightings on 6 December while in Manila consulting with Admiral Hart, immediately flew back to Singapore. HMS *Repulse*, several hours out on a voyage to Darwin, was recalled and reached Singapore on 7 December. After the events of that night and the evidence of the dawn reconnaissance, Phillips decided to sail with the two capital ships, one Australian and three British destroyers to attack the Japanese invasion convoys off the Thai coast in a surprise raid at dawn on 10 December. If they could reach the objective undetected the two capital ships would be more than a match for the 1914–18 vintage *Kongo* class battleships which Japan had in the vicinity and they would make driftwood of the troop transports and supply ships.

'Force Z' slipped out of Singapore at dusk on 8 December. It was assured of air reconnaissance on the 9th and 10th but *not* fighter cover at Singora because the northern airfields were largely out of action. The ships sped north under cloudy skies on 9 December unaware that they were spotted by a Japanese submarine in the afternoon. Then, just before dusk, the clouds cleared and three Japanese reconnaissance planes appeared. Surprise was lost. After a puzzling delay of two hours Phillips called off the operation on the ground that the target would disperse in the night. But the return to base was to be further delayed. A report (which proved false) of a Japanese landing at Kuantan on the east coast led him to divert 'Force Z' and valuable hours were wasted off Kuantan on the morning of 10 December. The two capital ships were still 220 miles from Singapore when a Japanese reconnaissance plane found them at 1015 hrs. Their end was near. Between 1100 and 1230 hrs, 16 bombers and 50 torpedo-bombers came in three waves and sank the *Prince of Wales* and the *Repulse*. Amazingly, Singapore's headquarters were not aware of the ships' position. Air support was not summoned, even though an Australian-manned *Buffalo* squadron was on stand-by. Not until nearly an hour after the first bombs did the captain of the *Repulse* (not Admiral Phillips) signal that he was being bombed. It took the fighters nearly an hour to arrive and they reached the scene to see the *Prince of Wales* going down. Admiral Phillips, who finally signalled for tugs and destroyers (and sent for his best hat) went down with his flag ship.[29]

The magnitude of the loss, coming two days after Pearl Harbor, probably hid the fact that 'Force Z' could not have succeeded in its objective. The first wave of the Japanese landings had already been accomplished and the second (with the heavy equipment) had not begun. The battleships would have found only empty transports off Singora. To have been effective 'Force Z' (like 'Matador') should have moved on 6 December, but neither the Admiral nor the *Repulse* were in port. A departure in the evening of the 7th would probably have been too tight a timing, but it would have permitted a dawn attack on 9 December and a bombardment of Singora and Patani airfields.

The battleships were sunk by aircraft from bases in Indo-China, but the Japanese rapidly established themselves on the southern Thai airfields. Brooke-Popham's first reaction was that the outcome in northern Malaya would depend on aircraft. With existing reserves he did not think the air defence could hold out in the north for more than two to three weeks.[30] As it was, they did not last more than two or three days. From first light on 8 December the Japanese battered the airfields in Kedah and Kelantan. The Kota Bahru air base was prematurely abandoned by the air force on the afternoon of the first day, and the surviving aircraft were evacuated from Sungei Patani and Alor Star. In this manner, the third, and decisive, disaster of the war became apparent. By the second day the aircraft losses were equal to three bomber squadrons and one fighter squadron – a quarter of the total air strength.

The airfields, which the army had been sent to defend, became virtually unusable. After gallant but costly attempts to bomb Singora, the air force was ordered by GHQ, on 12 December, to concentrate on ground support.[31] But this little availed 11 Division. The Jitra line was breached on 11/12 December by a small Japanese spearhead. A supposed strongpoint, where there were divisional supplies for three months, was broken by two battalions and a company of tanks. On the night of 12/13 December the division withdrew, and when the invaders occupied Alor Star airfield they found hot soup on the mess tables.[32] The port of Penang was abandoned on the night of 15/16 December and 11 Division withdrew south of the Perak River. On the east coast 9 Division moved south to Kuantan. A staff officer with III Corps recalled: 'we were attempting to defend the naval base for which there were no ships ... as we were attempting to defend aerodromes ... for which there were no aircraft'.[33]

With northern Malaya as good as lost General Percival faced the alternatives of withdrawing III Corps to Johore to join the Australians in preparing a strong line in the hinterland of the naval base or of attempting to hold the Japanese as far north as possible so that reinforcements could reach the south. He chose the latter course, and placed his hope on the reinforcements. There could be no help for Hong Kong or the Borneo protectorates. Although a Canadian brigade of two battalions had reached Hong Kong from

Vancouver three weeks before the Japanese attack, the Colony surrendered on Christmas Day 1941. On the same day Kuching, the capital of Sarawak, fell. Labuan fell on New Year's Day, followed in less than three weeks by British North Borneo. These losses had been a foregone conclusion, but in Malaya the defenders did not give up hope.

VI

It took nearly a month before the first convoy (carrying a brigade group from India) arrived on 3 January 1942. But on the first day of the Pacific War the British COS addressed themselves urgently to the problem and the general shape of a reinforcement policy soon emerged. Fighters, bombers, infantry brigades, anti-aircraft and anti-tank guns and tanks were all needed. The most promising possibility was the diversion of 18 East Anglian Territorial Division which was rounding the Cape en route to the Middle East and 51 crated *Hurricanes*, which were at Durban en route to Iraq. Meanwhile, within a few days a brigade of 17 Indian Division was under orders to sail from Bombay, 8 *Hudsons* flew from Australia and 36 set out from Britain, and 18 *Blenheims* went from the Middle East.[34] Churchill, who sailed for Washington, telephoned Ismay before he left with orders to send 'everything that was fit for battle towards the Far East as fast as it could be done'.[35]

Brooke-Popham gave priority to air reinforcements. On 13 December he called for long-range bombers which could strike at the Japanese base in Indo-China. Four days later he said the defenders' ability to hold out would depend on the speed at which air reinforcements reached Malaya.[36] At an inter-allied conference in Singapore, chaired by Duff Cooper (who was appointed Resident Cabinet Minister) it was agreed that the situation 'although serious' need not give rise to 'undue pessimism' provided the necessary reinforcements arrived.[37] The immediate air requirements were stated as four fighter and four bomber squadrons.

The object – never lost sight of – was the retention of the Singapore dockyard as the base of operations for the Eastern Fleet. It is, therefore, highly ironical that after only one week Admiral Layton (who had taken over as Commander of the remnants of the Eastern Fleet) had to report that the naval base was unsafe for ships, and he was sending the remaining vessels to Colombo or Batavia. The

Admiralty agreed that Singapore might not be able to 'remain the strategic centre' as the battle area might shift to the Indian Ocean or Australasia.[38] This change meant that when future Far Eastern strategy was reconsidered by the COS in London on 15 December the naval staff contribution was not ready.

The objective, as outlined by the COS, was to retain such points in the Far East as would prevent Japan from damaging vital interests and would enable British forces to take the offensive. Hong Kong was not such a vital interest (although important for prestige). Australia and New Zealand were certainly 'vital interests' for their manpower and products and contributions to the war in other theatres. Thus sea communication with the Dominions must be maintained. As long as Singapore held and a fleet was 'in being' in any part of the world, Japan's hold on its conquests 'must remain precarious'. But for the naval base to be viable there would have to be 'depth' in the air defence. The possible scale of attack on Malaya was overestimated at 10 divisions, and underestimated at 395 aircraft.[39]

The naval staff appreciation was available on 20 December. The ideal solution, a combined US-British fleet superior to Japan's, was impracticable, so the Indian Ocean and the Pacific were considered separately. There was no question of sending a 'balanced fleet' to Singapore immediately. It would need about three months, and to take the offensive it would require nine battleships and four aircraft carriers. Yet the time-honoured scheme of the *War Memorandum (Eastern)* was only slightly modified. Phase I became the period of land battle in Malaya and assembly of the fleet; in Phase II, when the naval concentration was complete, the fleet would go to the relief of Singapore, repel an attack on Australia, or operate from bases in the Indian Ocean. The VCNS hinted that plans to place three-quarters of Britain's naval strength in the eastern theatre might appear disproportionate. But he added 'the consequences to Imperial unity of a Japanese attack on Australia or New Zealand, unopposed by a strong British Fleet, are incalculable'.[40] The tradition of imperial defence as the *raison d'être* of the fleet was clearly not forgotten.

By the third week of the Malayan campaign, the details of the reinforcement plan had been agreed. The Eastern Fleet would not assemble before April 1942. The army reinforcements would all be landed by mid-February 1942 at the latest. They consisted of two infantry divisions (18 East Anglian Division, diverted at the Cape, and 17 Indian Division, from Bombay), as well as reinforcement troops for III Indian Corps and 8 Australian Division; anti-tank and anti-aircraft regiments; an Australian machine gun battalion and a squadron of seventeen light tanks. It was also suggested by General Bennett in Malaya, by the British COS in London and by Churchill in Washington, that a seasoned AIF division from the Middle East should also be sent to Malaya.[41] The critical element in the air reinforcements (in which great hopes were invested) were 138 *Hurricane* fighters: 51 in crates (diverted from Iraq), 48 to be taken on the aircraft carrier *Indomitable* from Egypt, and 39 from West Africa.[42] There was also the longer-term prospect of 100 American tanks from the Middle East and an armoured brigade of two tank regiments. These arrangements were approved by the British Cabinet on 27 December 1941.[43] Stanley Bruce, the Australian High Commissioner, who attended the Defence Committee meeting, wondered if more should not be done. His own Government, at this time, was alarmed by reports from Malaya, and had cabled Washington to Churchill and Roosevelt demanding greater air support.[44]

In Malaya there was a surge of optimism after the initial disasters. Brooke-Popham cabled on 21 December: 'Confidence increasing as enemy tactics become understood'. His broad plan was to continue operations in Malaya to cover the arrival of reinforcements. Layton reported the situation 'by no means irretrievable' but he was disappointed by the lack of co-operation from the Americans in the Philippines.[45] There were important changes in higher command. A new Commander-in-Chief Far East took over on 27 December. Brooke-Popham, aged 63, had been due for replacement before the war broke out, although it has been suggested that his replacement at such a moment was a mistake.[46] His successor, Lieutenant-General Sir Henry Pownall, did a quick tour of the front, where he found that inexperienced troops had been shaken by the fighting in the north. The Japanese 'undoubtedly threw us off balance; they are well-trained, active and artful as monkeys'.[47] But Pownall felt that, with their present strength, the invaders were unlikely to capture Singapore. The plan was to hold them as far north as possible but not risk the destruction of III Corps. The air force would be used to protect the reinforcement convoys. He, too, suggested the possibility of getting an experienced AIF division from the Middle East.[48] But Pownall's command lasted less than three weeks. The 'Arcadia' conference in Washington created the first Supreme Command of the war. The American-British-Dutch-Australian headquarters (ABDACOM) was to be located in Java and the command was offered to General Archibald Wavell, the Commander-in-Chief of India. Pownall was to be his Chief-of-Staff.

On 5 January 1942 the Australian Government agreed that two AIF divisions should be transferred from the Middle East to the Netherlands East Indies, where they were expected at the end of February or early March.[49] By the first week of 1942 it seemed that what was needed in Malaya was about three months of firm resistance and then the tide would turn. ABDACOM, with its reinforcements, could begin to roll back the Japanese torrent.

At this point, however, there was another disastrous defeat. On the day before Wavell reached Singapore, en route for Java and ABDACOM, the Slim River disaster created what he termed a 'somewhat critical situation'.[50] III Corps had steadily extricated itself from northern Malaya, and was still intact. But it always had to retreat earlier than Percival expected, mainly because it was outflanked by landings in the west coast rivers from portable motor boats which Yamashita had railed across from Singora.[51] Many of the young Indian troops were, said Wavell, 'utterly weary and completely bewildered'. On 4 January they had taken up a position behind the Slim River in southern Perak, which Percival hoped would hold for ten days. But on 7 January 1942 Japanese tanks broke through. An Indian brigade was reduced to half strength overnight. The way was opened to central Malaya and the FMS capital, Kuala Lumpur, and its airfield.

Wavell met with Bennett and Percival and found the latter had decided to cut his losses, withdraw III Corps to Johore and move the Australian division forward to stop the Japanese advance and hold the line Muar-Segamat-Endau across northern Johore. Wavell concurred, but changed the dispositions so that the Australian division was split. He reported to London that it would be a 'time problem between rate of Japanese advance and arrival of our reinforcements'. When next he visited the front, a few days later, he admitted that the battle for Singapore would be a 'close run thing'.[52] His long-term plan was to send the two Australian divisions from the Middle East to Malaya and create an AIF corps to spearhead the counter-offensive. The tired Indian divisions would be withdrawn for garrison duty in the Netherlands East Indies.[53]

Time began to run out in mid-January 1942. Late on 11 January the Japanese entered Kuala Lumpur. On the same day, in Washington, Admiral Stark had asked Field Marshal Sir John Dill, head of the British Military Mission, how long Singapore could hold out. Dill said 'it would be a race between the arrival of reinforcements and the progress of the Japanese'. If the former arrived on time, he saw no reason why Singapore should not hold out 'indefinitely'.[54] Hopes also rose in Singapore. On 13 January the second reinforcement convoy brought an advance brigade of 18 East Anglian Division, an anti-tank regiment, two anti-aircraft regiments and the 51 crated *Hurricanes*. Relief from Japanese air raids was clearly in store. And on 14 January the Australians went into action near Gemas, just north of the Johore border. They successfully ambushed hundreds of bicycle troops and next day knocked out several tanks and counter-attacked.[55] Perhaps the Australians and the air force would save Singapore after all.

The moment of optimism was short-lived. The Australians were outflanked on the west coast at Muar by more Japanese boat landings on the day after the Gemas success. Wavell warned the British Government against false hopes. On 19 December he reported that if Johore fell he doubted Singapore could hold out for long.[56] On the following day, amid great expectations, the *Hurricanes* went into action over Singapore. Among unprotected bombers they took a fair toll, but when the *Zero* fighters came, five *Hurricanes* were shot down. Below 20,000 feet the white hope of the defenders was no match for a Japanese fighter.[57] Meanwhile the army in Johore withdrew to a southern line from Kluang to Ayer Hitam. On 22 January another large reinforcement convoy brought a brigade from India, nearly 2000 Australian reinforcements for 8 Division and (at last) a squadron of light tanks. But they could not save Johore. On 25 January the Japanese made their long-anticipated landing on the east coast at Endau and the decision was made to withdraw to Singapore Island by the end of the month. The New Zealanders, who had just completed three runways in Johore, blew them up and retired.[58] The main body of the British 18 Division landed on 29 January to find themselves on a besieged island. The naval base was closed on 30 January, the floating docks scuttled and equipment and oil tanks demolished. Next day the causeway was blown and there was a 'sensation as after Dunkirk'.[59]

VII

The siege of the 'fortress' – that crisis which had been talked of for over twenty years – began. By now, even the Cabinet in London knew that Singapore was not 'impregnable'. Indeed at his first Defence Committee meeting after getting back from Washington on 21 January, Churchill admitted it was apparent that Singapore could not be considered 'as a fortress'.[60] Percival had made no adequate preparations on the north shore facing Johore on the ground of not disturbing civilian morale.[61] The big guns, on their all-round traverse, could fire on Johore, but armour-piercing shells were of limited value over land. The 9.2″ guns had some high-explosive ammunition. During the later stages of the battle the 15″ guns at Changi and 9.2″ on Blakang Mati were used to bombard Johore Bahru, Tengah airfield and Bukit Timah.[62]

On 5 February one more reinforcement convoy got in, making a total of 7 convoys (44 ships in all) bringing, during the month, no less than 45,000 men.[63] A fight was certainly expected on the island. Indeed, the Australian Prime Minister cabled Churchill that evacuation of Malaya or Singapore would be viewed by his government as an 'inexcusable betrayal'.[64] The Japanese assault began at the northwest of the island on the night of 8/9 February 1942 where the Australians were in position. On the first day the invaders reached Tengah airfield. Churchill capped a series of grandiose cables insisting that every inch of ground should be defended, with an invocation of immortal glory for 18 Division, which, he said, had 'a chance to make its name in history'. This was accompanied by comparisons with the Russians and the Americans, and the declaration that the 'whole reputation of our country and our race is involved'.[65] Wavell, taking the cue, dictated a similar 'wounding exhortation' for Percival.[66] It was certain, he wrote, that the defenders outnumbered the Japanese on the island. He referred to the Americans on Bataan, the Russians turning back the Germans, and the Chinese, who had held out for four and a half years. 'It will be disgraceful if we yield our boasted Fortress of Singapore to inferior enemy forces. . . . I look to you and your men . . . to prove that the fighting spirit that won our Empire still exists to enable us to defend it.'[47]

Singapore could not be saved by imperialist rhetoric. A counter-attack in the west of the island failed to materialise. By the night of

9/10 February the Japanese had penetrated to Bukit Timah, in the centre of the island. On 12 February Percival withdrew to a perimeter around the city. He still had 85,000 men (including 48 battalions) compared with Yamashita's 30,000, and he could not know that the latter were exhausted, short of ammunition and scared of a counter-attack.[68] But Singapore's water supply was running down, with the pipes leaking from the bombing, and the Japanese also controlled the reservoirs. The invaders repaired the causeway on 14 January and made ready for their final assault.

Percival was not prepared to engage in a bloodbath amid the ruins of the city. He had warned Wavell that there must come a time when 'further bloodshed will serve no useful purpose'.[69] And, in contrast to the rhetoric of Churchill and Wavell, the British COS were already calculating Japan's next moves on the assumption that Singapore was lost.[70] Percival said farewell to his air force commander, Air Vice-Marshal Pulford, who remarked that they would both be blamed, but 'God knows we did our best with what we had been given'.[71] The British GOC surrendered in person to General Yamashita at a long-remembered scene on 15 February.

In London, the War Cabinet met (with Sir Earle Page, the Australian representative present) next day. No details about the surrender were available, but there was a general discussion on the situation. The brief record which survives includes the admission that the Japanese 'were formidable alike as fighters and tacticians. Our military performance ... had left much to be desired'. The meeting agreed that, in retrospect, it was a pity that 18 Division had been wasted. But, then, the Australians had cried 'betrayal' if Singapore was not defended to the utmost.[72] In this manner the curtain fell on what Churchill called 'the worst disaster and largest capitulation in British history'.[73] Imperial rhetoric had given way to sour grapes about Commonwealth obligations.

Post-mortem

I

The post-mortem, which began so gloomily on 16 February 1942, has continued from that day to this. Unlike the Americans, who held their great Congressional Investigation on Pearl Harbor, the British did not have a Royal Commission on the fall of Singapore. Many people expected one. When, on 17 February 1942, Churchill asked the House of Commons to avoid 'agitated or excited recriminations', Earl Winterton (a former member of Chamberlain's Cabinet) declared that at some point 'we must have a grand inquest'.[1] A week later there was an opportunity in a debate on the war situation. It followed a Cabinet reshuffle and the humiliating failure to stop two German battle-cruisers dashing up the Channel from Brest to the Elbe. About the fall of Singapore, Churchill said he had no further information than had appeared in the newspapers and gave a remarkably detached summary:

> I will, however, say this: Singapore was, of course, a naval base rather than a fortress. It depended upon the command of the sea, which again depends upon the command of the air. Its permanent fortifications and batteries were constructed from a naval point of view. The various defence lines which had been constructed in Johore were not successfully held. The field works constructed upon the island itself to defend the fortress were not upon a sufficiently large scale.

He again deprecated the possibility of a series of censorious speeches about the details. Members could not indulge themselves too freely, 'having regard to the perils that beset us and to the ears that listen'.[2]

It is certain, however, that Churchill was deeply shocked and scarred by the humiliation of Singapore. He took 'fullest personal responsibility' for giving priority in 1941 to reinforcing the Middle East and Russia.[3] Of the sinking of the *Prince of Wales* and the *Repulse* (which followed one of his rare disagreements with the naval staff) he wrote: 'In all the war I never received a more direct shock'.[4] (He had a bad dream about it twelve years later, while recovering from a stroke, and was so upset that his doctor feared he would have a relapse.) 'I cannot get over Singapore', said Churchill a month after the surrender.[5] In his memoirs he wrote: 'I judged it impossible to hold an inquiry by Royal Commission into the circumstances of the fall of Singapore while the war was raging. . . . but I certainly thought that in justice to the officers and men concerned there should be an inquiry into all the circumstances as soon as the fighting stopped'.[6] He was not alone. The publication of the first volumes of the official history of the Pacific War in 1957 led an Australian-born novelist (who had spent three and a half years in a prisoner-of-war camp) to write:

> During and after the fighting we felt resentful. In the prison camps we swore there would be a big showdown when we came home and told our story. We were not to blame. We blamed those in authority, the British Government, the generals. Some people blamed the Australians, the Chinese, the Malays, the civilians; others blamed the Navy, the Army, the Air Force.[7]

Instead of the 'competent court', mentioned by Churchill, the post-mortem has been conducted by writers of many sorts and interests. Their fascination for the subject shows no signs of ending. Explanations of the disaster have focused upon four aspects in the story: resources, tactics, strategy and race.

II

There is general agreement about the first, the shortage of resources. No one has seriously argued that Malaya Command should have defeated the Japanese with what it had. The critical deficiencies were aircraft (up-to-date types of fighters and bombers), and on the ground, tanks and anti-tank preparations. There is, however, plenty of ground for disagreement over the relative allocation of resources as between the British Isles, Russia, the Middle East and the Far East. Sir Archibald Southby (a retired naval officer) asserted in the House of Commons that: 'One month's supply of the aircraft sent to Russia would have saved Malaya'.[8]

Louis Allen has recently referred to the 200 *Hurricanes* which went to Russia in the second half of 1941: 'they might have made all the difference in Malaya'. He suggests that the damage inflicted on the landing ships at Kota Bahru by the *Hudsons* and antique *Vildebeestes* gave 'a clear indication of what might have happened' if the air strength had been built up to its promised size.[9] Churchill firmly defended his priorities. He told the House of Commons that the decision was 'to make our contribution to Russia, to try to beat Rommel . . . If we have handled our resources wrongly, no one is so much to blame as me'. Raymond Callahan has recently defended Churchill. 'What he did was to see clearly that Britain could fight one war – or lose two'.[10]

There are, however, those who argue that the resources which were available in Malaya were used poorly through faulty decisions and tactics and unnecessary personal disputes. The delay over 'Matador'; the failure of 'Force Z' to summon air support; the hesitation about whether to fight hard in the north or concentrate in strength in Johore; the failure to disrupt the vital west coast boat operations of the Japanese; tardiness in the application of the ambush tactics successfully proven by the Argylls, the Gurkhas and the Australians; the extraordinary lack of defences on the north shore of the island; indecisive deployment on the island, and the inability to counter-attack at the last minute when Yamashita was outnumbered and short of ammunition – all these have been criticised. The official histories, British, Australian and Indian, with their concentration on unit operations provided abundant material for use in this sort of critique. Another set of targets for this school was the problem of communications – the fact that commanders often had to rely on post-office telephone links and civil air services. Similarly, poor relations between the civil authorities and armed services, which themselves were not unified, are blamed. Major-General Kirby, author of the British official history, later criticised the lack of civil planning for war, as did Brigadier Ivan Simson, the Chief Engineer, who found himself Director-General of Civil Defence in Singapore.[11] However, Raymond Callahan has defended Governor Thomas, who gave top priority to increased commodity production, in view of Malaya's role as the leading dollar-earner of the colonial empire.[12]

Critics of the tactics of the campaign subscribe to the 'close run thing' interpretation. Louis Allen, one of the few writers on the fall of Singapore who is familiar with the Japanese accounts, wrote: 'it remains a fascinating imponderable, whether a last-ditch resistance might have had a lasting effect'. He cites a Japanese officer who says the appearance of the white flag on 15 February was greeted with disbelief, then relief, since the attackers were almost on their last wind and felt that 'they might be the ones to surrender'.[13] More dogmatically Allen has asserted: 'the British need never have been defeated'.[14]

III

With the perspective permitted by growing distance in time, and also by the opening of the archives, the third strand of explanation has emerged. Writers have turned from the minutia of decision-making, personality clashes, and operations during the fifty-five fateful days, to concern themselves with strategic explanations. In this strand of criticism there are two distinct dimensions. There have been abandoned – the principle that the navy should be capable priorities – the Middle East and Russia – which were both linked as parts of the effort 'to form a stronger front from the Levant to the Caspian'.[15] There is now, however, a growing school who criticise the long-term eastern strategy, which the Singapore base was built to serve. Taking their cue from Admiral Richmond they suggest that the naval staff was guilty of unreality in its thinking about the Far East and that it had created a dangerous illusion.

Richmond had, of course, been very critical of the details of the plan for sending the fleet to Singapore while he was Commander-in-Chief of the East Indies station in the 1920s. Later he became the first Commandant of the Imperial War College and then Vere Harmsworth Professor of Imperial and Naval History at Cambridge. A fortnight or so after the fall of Singapore he pointed out that 'a base without a fleet is no more use than a sentry box without a sentry'. In his Ford Lectures at Oxford in 1943 he put the disaster in historical perspective. He reminded his listeners of the basic change implied by the policy of naval parity which had been accepted between the wars.

The old principle which had informed the adoption of the Two-Power Standard of the eighteenth and nineteenth centuries had been abandoned – the principle that the navy should be capable of meeting the combined attack of any reasonable coalition, in the several seas in which vital British interests lay. It was the illusion that a Two-Hemisphere Empire can be defended by a One-Hemisphere Navy that sealed the fate of Singapore.[16]

This view was reiterated in 1973 by Ian Hamill, who wrote: 'The Singapore naval base was an imperial symbol designed to give the appearance of reality to a strategic illusion; the illusion that a two-hemisphere Empire could be defended by a one-hemisphere navy'.[17] In 1974 Raymond Callahan said the same, that the Singapore base was 'the symbol of a great illusion – that Britain's Victorian world power remained intact'.[18] In 1975 Stanley Falk wrote: 'Singapore was a symbol: a symbol of imperial might and invincibility, of nineteenth-century colonial prestige . . . .'.[19] Captain Stephen Roskill suggests that, by 1937 at least, 'the concept of the "Main Fleet to Singapore" had, perhaps through constant repetition, assumed something of the inviolability of Holy Writ'.[20] By 1939 it had become 'a strategic principle which had been repeated so often that it had come to assume the authority of a dogma'.[21] An even blunter expression of this trend can be found in the words of John McCarthy, who said that if the defences of Singapore 'proved to be largely an illusion', then the expectation that the British main fleet would be sent there was based on 'little more than fantasy'.[22] A more temperate version appears in Norman Gibb's monumental volume I of the official British *Grand Strategy* series, where he argues that the Admiralty held on too long to the 'dream of a major battle fleet operating 10,000 miles from home' despite the presence of a German fleet and the possibility of losing the Mediterranean lifeline.[23] It would seem that in the 1970s the 'illusionist' interpretation holds the field.

The extreme position verges on the charge of deception of allies. Roskill, for example, found it difficult not to feel, when writing about the 1937 Imperial Conference, that the British Chiefs of Staff and the naval staff in particular 'were less than honest to the Commonwealth delegates', that 'wishful thinking on the part of the COS and Admiralty came near to crossing the border line into outright deception'.[24] Callahan goes further and claims the British 'were never really frank with the Australians'.[25]

Has this strand of criticism gone too far? Are such charges fair? There were, surely, very few illusions about Britain's inability to protect all its interests and fulfil all its obligations in the event of simultaneous challenges on different fronts after 1919. This was the single most important theme in the advice of the COS between the wars. It is now recognised as one of the main sources of appeasement in the 1930s. Possibly Beatty was an exception in the early 1920s, but even he could have had few illusions by 1925 after the parade of Coalition, Labour and Conservative policies.

Even before the acceptance of the Singapore strategy in 1921 it was known that the entire fleet could not go to the East, in case of dangers closer to home.[26] It was also assumed, all along, that it would be most unlikely that Britain would ever have to face Japan alone without American aid. When the CID first discussed the plans for sending the fleet in 1922, Balfour felt that danger to Australia and New Zealand from Japan was 'as nearly illusory as any danger could be', but if Japan did attack he could not conceive that the United States would 'stand by and look on'. Churchill, too, could not imagine Japan adopting a predatory policy in opposition to 'the whole English-speaking world'.[27]

In the 1920s the plan to send the fleet to Singapore was as realistic as possible in the circumstances. The Royal Navy maintained its ratio over Japan. In HMS *Hood*, HMS *Rodney* and HMS *Nelson* it still had the largest and most powerful capital ships afloat. Challenges were not likely in the Atlantic or the Mediterranean. The real weakness in the strategy was slow implementation. The Singapore base was not yet built. This meant that during the Manchuria and Shanghai crises of 1931–2 Britain was simply unable to appeal to force, even if its Government had had the inclination. But there were no illusions about it. The Deputy COS's report on the emergency in February 1932 was an admission of nakedness.

Ironically, the events of 1931–3 led to the ending of the Ten Year Rule and the completion of the Singapore Base at a time when the rise of Hitler cast doubts on the adequacy of the one power standard. On this, too, the naval staff had no illusions. Admiral Chatfield never failed to point out that a two power standard (with a completed Singapore Base) was needed if Britain were to match Germany and Japan simultaneously. If Italy was added to the list, a three power standard would be needed, and this possibility he deplored. Since not even the two power standard was adopted, the naval staff made no bones about the navy's inability to meet two or more enemies *simultaneously*, without allies. The Chiefs of Staff and British ministers resolutely refused to be pinned down by their Australian and New Zealand opposite numbers who repeatedly asked questions about the timing and the size of the fleet for the East during the years 1937 to 1939. Preparations for a war with Italy were not considered until 1939 (except for the Ethiopian emergency in 1935), and although there was serious thought about a Mediterranean strategy in late 1938 and early 1939, the Far Eastern priority was kept for reasons of Commonwealth cohesion. Roskill's view of this period is that: 'To reconcile unquestionable weakness with the need and the desire to uphold Imperial interests was to attempt to square the circle'.[28] Strategic thinking had blurred into wishful thinking. But what were the alternatives?

Hindsight may suggest a number of things: rapid rearmament, including the two power standard; rearmament in the Dominions, with a greater element of self-reliance; a mutual security pact with the United States, the one power with the financial and industrial resources and a really secure location; a British withdrawal from east of Suez to ensure concentration in European waters, and to force Australia, New Zealand and India to fend for themselves – and, perhaps, look after Malaya too.

None of these were viable alternatives at the time. The United States showed no signs of making guarantees, even if President Roosevelt and the Chiefs of Staff were preparing for a leading American role. The Australian and New Zealand Governments, while seeking categorical promises about the timing and size of the fleet for Singapore, showed no signs of any commitment, in advance, to ensure that it would survive the period before relief. British defence planners of the 1930s had to face up to the world as it was, the Commonwealth as it had then evolved, and the fact that they had been unable to persuade their political masters (who had their own good ideological or political reasons) to provide the means to face a threefold threat. They had, indeed, constantly urged the politicians to avoid war by political concession and agreement because of Britain's military weakness.

Singapore as a symbol may have deluded some people – at best the merchants and planters and possibly even the defenders of Malaya. Brooke-Popham is said to have told an American officer that the 'greatest value of Singapore is the illusion of impregnability built up in the Japanese mind'.[29] But it did not delude the Japanese (who made it a prime target), nor the Americans (who resolutely refused to send their own fleet to the dockyard), nor the Australians (who were the most importunate in their demands for the presence of a battle fleet). Above all, the British naval staff realised that

Singapore was only one point in a vast strategic network. 'Backwards' and 'forwards' from Singapore stretched the ramifications of the eastern strategy. Hong Kong was the base for the submarines which provided the forward reconnaissance line. It would also be an advance base for any fleet action in the China Sea, which would also require a mobile base even further north. Singapore's own security could also be threatened from Malaya, Borneo, the Netherlands East Indies and Thailand. The passage of the fleet depended on refuelling bases in the Red Sea, Ceylon, the Maldives and the Nicobars. It also depended on the security of the Suez Canal, where fears of a Japanese blocking attack were entertained as early as 1923.[30] Suez, in turn, depended on the security and friendliness of Egypt and Palestine, which were by no means assured because of their internal problems. Egypt, as the 'Clapham Junction' of the air, was vital to the reinforcement route. An Air Staff paper suggested: 'Egypt must be for the Air Force what Singapore is to be for the Navy – an advanced post on the route to the East'.[31] West of Suez, with Alexandria, Malta and Gibraltar the navy felt secure, until, even here, it found itself embarrassed by Italy in 1935.

It was from this point that crises came thick and fast: the Rhineland and Spain (1936), China (1937), Austria and Czechoslovakia (1938), Prague, Albania, Tientsin (1939). In these four years the inadequacies of the one power standard were starkly revealed. Even though the navy knew it could beat any one rival, battle was not to be contemplated in any of these crises for fear that operations at one place could drain resources from the other two, and invite that simultaneous attack which had become the real nightmare. Although the 'worst possible case' – a threefold threat – did, finally, materialise, it came cumulatively, not simultaneously. Italy delayed for 9 months, and a further 18 months elapsed before the Japanese onslaught. The crisis of the war came in March–May 1942, when the Japanese had the run of the Bay of Bengal, drove the British out of Rangoon and were stretching out towards Australia's territory in New Guinea, while Rommel threatened Egypt. It was the sort of 'worst contingency' that had haunted the COS since 1933. But American involvement fulfilled the twenty-year assumption that Britain would never face Japan alone. And there was the added bonus that Germany was wasting its assets over a thousand-mile front from Leningrad to Rostov in a vain endeavour to grab the oil of the Caucasus.

IV

In discounting the extent of British illusion it is also worth remembering that many of the leading personalities involved in the loss of Singapore, who later wrote the memoirs and the official despatches, had also been connected with the project of building the Singapore base from an early stage in its history. Presumably they were well aware of all its strengths and weaknesses.

Churchill, who was so shaken by the sinking of the *Prince of Wales* and the *Repulse* and coined the label 'worst disaster', claimed that he did not know about the lack of defences on the north shore of the island until he received Wavell's cable on 19 January 1942. He then gave vent to a 'positively spectacular' fit of temper. 'Why didn't they tell me about this? Oh, no; it is my own fault. I ought to have known . . . Did no one realise the position?'[32] And in his memoirs: 'I cannot understand how it was I did not know this'.[33] He contemplated the 'hideous spectre of the almost naked island'. This may be so. Nevertheless, Churchill had, as First Lord in 1939, signed the paper to reassure the Australians and New Zealanders, which described Singapore as a 'fortress armed with five 15 inch guns', which could stand a siege of up to four or five months. Maybe he just simply put his name to the naval staff draft. Yet as Chancellor of the Exchequer in 1924-9 he had taken considerable, and expert, interest in detail in his efforts to cut expenditure. He had backed the idea of air substitution in place of big guns, even tried to take some initiative in this. He had attended, and contributed to, crucial CID meetings when the decisions were taken to delay the defences. It is, therefore, hard to understand how he did not know that the basic defences were designed to ward off a seaward attack. It is also surprising (such was his zest for detail) that he was ignorant of the shape of the defences when he reassured the Australian representatives in 1939. He also must have known that the big guns were not literally 'pointing out to sea' as most of them were on all-round traverse. (Whether they had enough ammunition appropriate for use against land is another question. The 9.2" guns had only thirty rounds of high explosive each.)[34]

Wavell, the supreme commander, had also been connected with the early planning of Singapore's defences. As GSO 1 in the Military Operations and Intelligence Directorate of the War Office in 1924, he had assured his opposite number on the staff at Singapore that

Labour's suspension of the base would not stop the War Office's planning for the defences. Pownall, his chief-of-staff (who was also Commander-in-Chief Far East for three weeks), had been assistant secretary to the CID in 1933–5 and secretary of the DRC, which gave priority to the completion of the base. Percival, the GOC, had had an even closer connexion with Singapore. He was probably the best informed general in the War Office on the subject early in the war and this, no doubt, is why he was appointed to Malaya. As GSO 1 (chief of staff) to Malaya Command between 1936 and 1937 he had played an important part in recommending reversion to the original (pre-1924) defence scheme based on a fortified line in Johore. He had also stressed the point (often made in the staff colleges) that a Japanese invading army would probably make use of the Isthmus of Kra.

In the Admiralty the plan to send the main fleet to Singapore had such a central place in all strategic thinking that hardly any senior naval officer can have escaped involvement. Sir Dudley Pound, the CNS from 1939 to 1943, had been Director of Plans, 1922–5, during the original working out of the details of the Singapore strategy. He had emphasised, particularly, the need to involve the Colonies and Dominions. As assistant CNS, 1927–9, he had seen something of the Guns v Air war. Admiral Chatfield, the most insistent service voice behind the British rearmament programme in the 1930s while he was CNS and chairman of the COS Committee, had been Controller (Third Sea Lord) at the time when the 'truncated scheme' was accepted. As Minister for Defence Co-ordination in 1939 he remained the most consistent defender of the eastern strategy. The Commander-in-Chief of the ill-fated Eastern Fleet, Sir Tom Phillips, had had a similar long connexion with the plan. He was assistant Director of Plans in the Admiralty, 1930–2, when the 'slowed down' programme was speeded up again because of the Shanghai crisis. He then went as Chief of Staff (Flag Captain) to the Commander of the East Indies Station (1932–5) at the time when the *War Memorandum (Eastern)* was revised, and Admiral Dreyer of the China Fleet was trying to awaken the local naval forces. He returned to the Admiralty as Director of Plans in 1935–8 and was Vice-Chief of Naval Staff from 1939 until his appointment as Commander-in-Chief Eastern Fleet. As Percival knew the military strategy, so Phillips knew the naval strategy, from experience on the spot as well as in Whitehall.

The air aspect of Singapore's defence was perhaps less well

represented in high places by men with local experience. Only Air Marshal Tedder, among the senior airmen, had made much mark at Singapore. As AOC Far East 1936–8 he had tried to inject a sense of urgency. By the time of the attack on Malaya he was AOC in the Middle East and had to release the vital *Hurricanes* for Singapore.[35] However, an early interest in the air defences of Singapore had been taken by two of the British representatives at the A-B-C 1 Conference in Washington, Air Commodore John Slessor and Rear-Admiral Victor Danckwerts. Slessor had served in the Plans Branch of the Air Ministry, 1928–30, during the critical phase of the Guns v Air war. As one of Trenchard's 'English merchants', he had drafted some of the papers in the substitution debates. Later, as Director of Plans, he had watched with misgivings as the naval staff wavered between Mediterranean and Far Eastern priorities in 1938–9. At Washington in 1941 he was alarmed about the American attitude to Singapore. He sought comfort from Stanley Hornbeck (Far East adviser in the State Department) who reproved Slessor about the weakness of Singapore's air defences. Hornbeck was one of the few Americans who favoured a determined Anglo-American stance to deter a Japanese move, and would have supported sending part of the American fleet to Singapore. But he warned Slessor that by 1941 the US naval staff 'would not look at it'. In 1956 Slessor wrote:

> I believe an Allied battle fleet at Singapore including aircraft-carriers, and with shore-based fighter cover that could at a pinch have been made available from U.S. naval resources, might well have deterred the Japanese from aggression or, if it had not done so, might have changed the whole course of history in east Asia.[36]

Admiral Danckwerts, as deputy Director of Plans at the Admiralty, had pressed for the installation of radar at Singapore, after the disastrous air exercise in 1938. It was he who told the Americans in Washington that if their Pacific Fleet remained 'comparatively inactive', the British would have to divide their forces; that, in the interests of Commonwealth cohesion, more capital ships would have to be sent to the Indian Ocean than circumstances elsewhere might warrant.

Also present in Washington was another figure with a longstanding interest in Singapore. Richard Casey, the first Australian Minister in Washington from 1940 to 1942, had been Australian

External Affairs Liaison Officer in London during the second half of the 1920s. During the uncertain days of the truncated scheme, the Guns v Air war and Labour's slowing-down policy, Casey had alerted his Government to every move in the Singapore story, and by reminding the British of the Empire (but not an Australian) financial contribution, may have contributed to the continuance of the project. He also attended the Singapore Committee of the 1930 Imperial Conference. Again, in 1939, as leader of the Australian delegation at the DMV talks, he demanded assurances about the British fleet and Singapore. In Washington, he tried, with the British Ambassador, to persuade the Americans to send part of their fleet to Singapore.[37]

In this matter (the one serious difference with the Americans at the A-B-C 1 talks) the British naval staff were being consistent with their policy since 1919. The only real deterrent could be a balanced fleet, equal to Japan's, facing Japan's. If necessary, such a fleet would have to be sent to the east (at the cost of other theatres) if Australia or New Zealand were really threatened. The idea of the fast squadron, of one or two capital ships, so often mooted by politicians and diplomats, so urgently requested by the Australians, and finally forced on the naval staff by Churchill in 1941, had never been part of naval policy since Beatty gave up the idea of sending the battle-cruisers in the mid-1920s.

Nor should it be forgotten that a large fleet *did* go to the Pacific. Admiral Pound was planning, in mid-1941, to send the bulk of the British fleet to the Indian Ocean in 1942. This move was accelerated, as far as possible, during the Singapore reinforcement policy in December 1941. It was, of course, too late. And the new Eastern Fleet retired to the African Coast before Nagumo's five-carrier task force in April 1942. But in 1945 one of the most powerful fleets ever assembled in the history of the Royal Navy steamed north from Australian waters to join in the operations against Japan. It included 4 battleships, 17 aircraft carriers, 10 cruisers and 40 destroyers. There were 6 destroyers of the Royal Australian Navy, the 2 New Zealand cruisers, a cruiser and 2 other vessels of the Royal Canadian Navy; about half the Fleet Air Arm pilots were New Zealanders.[38] Even this impressive display paled in significance beside the US Pacific Fleet with its 12 battleships, 27 aircraft carriers, 21 cruisers and 69 destroyers. But the operations of the British Commonwealth Pacific Fleet and the USN off the coasts of Japan in 1945 suggests that some of those assumptions about Anglo-

American co-operation, which dated from the less friendly days of the 1920s, were not entirely fanciful.

That none of this was in time to save Singapore, brings us back to the vexed matter of strength and timing. Malaya was simply not made strong enough to sustain the 'period before relief'. The Royal Navy was not strong enough to take on the Japanese while it was engaged elsewhere. If the assumption that the Americans would be allies against Japan was realistic, the hope that Japan would be deterred was not. Churchill had staked his hopes on the belief that Japan would not strike unless Britain was defeated in Europe or Africa. For this reason he adopted the traditional doctrine of concentration of force at the critical point. So he cabled Curtin of Australia on 19 January 1942: 'To try to be safe everywhere is to be strong nowhere'.[39] Next month Pownall put it with soldierly bluntness: 'We just hoped it wouldn't happen. And it did'.[40]

V

On the subject of race, writers are more reticent than they are on strategy. However, Sir George Sansom, a distinguished historian of Japan, asserted in 1944 that the fall of Singapore indicated that the whole relationship of eastern and western peoples had entered 'a new phase'. Having retired after 37 years as a diplomat in Tokyo, Sansom worked briefly for the Ministry of Economic Warfare in Singapore in 1941-2 and saw the disaster as a challenge to the prestige of the 'occidental peoples'. This had a far deeper significance than that of 'a retrievable military disaster'. Yet opinion shrank from its implications and sought explanations in local circumstances.[41] By the 1970s, writers were becoming less squeamish about racial issues. Basil Liddell Hart (like the Americans in 1941) said that Singapore's symbolical importance had surpassed even its strategical value, that the 'white man had lost his ascendancy with the disproof of his magic'.[42] Some writers have alluded to racial origins of the Pacific War.[43]

Certainly there were racial undertones to the strategic pronouncements from the Jellicoe reports of 1919 to Churchill's 'kith and kin' telegram in 1940. Many statements were not far removed from 'yellow peril' expressions of the Victorian age. Jellicoe assumed an inevitable clash between Japanese interests and the British Empire. In his private correspondence he suggested that

Japanese activities in India and the Pacific region, on the one hand, and well-known elements like the 'White Australia policy', on the other, could only lead to trouble.[44] In 1940, as the new *Far East Appreciation* was under discussion, Churchill, who now regarded the United States as the real protector of Australia and New Zealand, said that in the last resort Britain could never 'stand by and see a British Dominion overwhelmed by a yellow race, and we should at once come to the assistance of that Dominion with all the forces we could make available'.[45]

Similar feelings were, of course, evident on the Japanese side. In 1920, Major E. L. Piesse, Director of the Pacific Branch of the Australian Prime Minister's department, visited the Japanese Foreign Office. After their conversations on the subject of Japanese expansionism, the Vice-Minister of Foreign Affairs, Hanihara Masanao, put on record this view to the Australian representative:

> Japan has the misfortune of being a non-Christian and non-white Power, and has in consequence to undergo experiences, which are not even dreamt of by an European or American Power. Not the least of such experiences is that Japan cannot share in the mutual tolerance, or at least silence, with which a Power of the west looks on what may be fairly called aggressive or rather self-serving policy . . . toward . . . a weak state by another Power of the same race.[46]

In a book widely publicised in English in 1936, *Japan Must Fight Britain*, a Japanese naval officer argued that either Japan would have to stop expanding, or the British should give up some of what they had. He pointed out in his polemical work, what the British COS had been saying for 15 years, that 'with a one-power standard Navy, it is impossible to carry on a two-power standard war.' His simple conclusion: 'England is already on the down-grade: Japan has started on the up-grade. The two come into collision because England is trying to hold on to what she has, while Japan must perforce expand.'[47] Such mutual feelings of racial superiority led the British to underestimate Japan's capabilities in 1940–2, and contributed to Japanese determination to assert the racial equality denied to them diplomatically at Versailles and socially and commercially all over the colonial world.

There is, however, another dimension to the racial issue which had an even more important effect on the defence of Malaya. Many of the inhabitants appeared to take a virtually neutral stance in 1941, to 'bend to the wind', as it were, before the Japanese onslaught. General Pownall put his finger on the crux of the matter when he wrote: 'The British, Malays, Chinese and Indians are psychologically miles apart'. Malaya, indeed, was not a 'nation', which could respond as such to the crisis. As a former Malayan civil servant wrote, the rubber planters, miners, traders and administrators had devoted themselves to material things; the British impact on Malaya was 'culturally sterile', it had produced a 'plural society with no corporate soul'.[48] The defenders were largely Indian (rather than British or Australian) in origin, and only a very small part of the garrison came from the country.

This stemmed in part from the defensive plan adopted from the mid-1920s to the late 1930s, when the defence of the Singapore naval base was not related to the defence of Malaya as a whole. For example, in 1927, Brigadier-General Casimir Van Straubenzee, the GOC, drew up a memorandum for the local Defence Committee on the possibilities for defending Malaya in the event of a Japanese invasion. It was based on the assumption that population pressure might induce Japan to try to seize part of Australia and that the only possible opportunity would come before the Singapore Base was finished. In this case Malaya could expect fourteen days warning, but in this period the Japanese could achieve local naval superiority, blockade the coast and thus place Malaya's reinforcements from India in jeopardy. If the invasion began before the British fleet arrived the local forces (then very small indeed) would be on their own. The GOC presented the defence of Singapore as the main objective and saw the Malay Peninsula as 'relatively unimportant'. In fact it would suit the Japanese if the defence became dispersed on the Peninsula. Therefore the GOC would concentrate on holding Singapore, and try to deal only with raids and the prevention of civil dissension among the populace in the Peninsula. This meant relying to a considerable extent (in the absence of reinforcements) on the Volunteers. He would be able to muster a mobile field force equivalent to a weak infantry brigade. But from the Volunteer units only Europeans (or 'possibly the best of the Eurasians') could be made into a force fit to face regulars. The field force would consist of the one British regular battalion from Singapore, the Indian Army battalion stationed at Taiping in Perak, the Singapore battalion of the Straits Settlements Volunteers (less its Chinese and Malay companies) and a European battalion from the FMS Volunteers.

The Chinese and Malay Companies would be used for static defence.[49] In all, it was a revealing indication of the racial stereotypes of the age. Many of the plan's assumptions did not even fit War Office policy and the GOC was gently rebuked. More significantly it conflicted with the longstanding wishes of the Sultans of the FMS, supported by the Colonial Office, who desired the creation of a regular Malay Regiment.

Recruiting for the Malay Regiment, which fought very well in the defence of Singapore in 1942, was finally started in 1933.[50] Just before its establishment another revealing glimpse of racial attitudes was provided by a new GOC, Major-General Harry Lionel Pritchard, in a report on the *Fighting Value of the Races of Malaya* in 1930. It was really a report on the Volunteers and began with the assertion that the fighting value of the British 'being well-known' he need not go further. He merely noted a difference between up-country areas where planters volunteered for social reasons and the situation in Singapore, where volunteering was less 'fashionable'. Turning to the Malays Pritchard said they were by nature and temperament not suited to long sustained work. Malays were 'lazy, careless and inattentive to details, very quickly bored'. But they could be relied on to be loyal to their Sultans. Although the Malay Company of the Straits Settlements Volunteers was the worst in Malaya, the Perak Malay Volunteer Infantry was strong because of the interest of the royal family. Of the fighting value of the Chinese, Pritchard had no doubts at all, on the rather novel ground that Chinese burglars and robbers stood up well in their brushes with the police. Chinese were intelligent, had initiative, enterprise, determination and persistence; they had 'a fine fighting value' when it was for personal gain. They made keen Volunteers, but Pritchard did not recommend a Chinese regular unit in case conflicts of loyalties developed as between the British and the Kuomintang. As for the Eurasians, the GOC believed those in Malaya were superior to those in India, and that the 'cross with Chinese' was better than with Malays. The best Eurasians were almost equal to the best British; the worst were 'quite useless for any purpose'. A Singapore Volunteer Company had a magnificent, quite exceptional Eurasian company commander, 'no doubt because he has some Dyak pirate blood in him'. Of the Indians in Malaya, Sikhs were proven fighters, but Sikh policemen had been 'passively disloyal' when a Punjabi Muslim battalion mutinied in Singapore in 1915 (and a Japanese naval landing party helped round them up). Sikhs were well-known intriguers by nature. Tamils from India and Ceylon he ruled out: 'one cannot make Soldiers out of Tamils'. A few did volunteer and were all right as signallers, ambulance drivers and motor cyclists. Sinhalese were satisfactory but too few. The finest fighters of all, in Pritchard's book, were Chins and Kachins from the hill territories of Burma. A battalion of Burma Rifles, paid for by the FMS, was of exceptionally high value, better even than British troops in the jungle.[51]

Pritchard's racial type-casting was almost worthy of Somerset Maugham, whose stories set in Malaya were shortly to be published.[52] The attitudes which both so vividly portray persisted until the outbreak of the Pacific War. The Malay Regiment was created between 1933 and 1935. But it had only one battalion of 793 officers and men until the second battalion was formed in December 1941, bringing a final strength of 1400.[53] The only other opportunities for the peoples of Malaya were in the Volunteer Forces (part-time soldiers) and the Sultan's forces in Kedah, Kelantan and Perak, and those of Johore which had their own small engineer and artillery elements. There was also a Royal Naval Volunteer Reserve, including some Malay seamen, and the Malayan Volunteer Air Force. All these units were largely officered by Europeans.

In 1941 the population of Malaya numbered $5\frac{1}{2}$ million: 43 per cent were Chinese, 41 per cent Malays, 14 per cent Indians and 2 per cent others, including Eurasians, Arabs and Europeans. Yet of the defending army of over 88,000, only 20 per cent came from Malaya itself, and a few thousand of these were European expatriates. The local communities were not recruited into the forces, partly because of the images of 'fighting value' noted by Pritchard, partly because of the needs of commodity production, but also because of political fears, especially over the rivalry between Kuomintang and Communist Chinese. Thus, when a Special Training School in irregular warfare was established in Singapore in July 1941, to train local people in guerrilla activities, the Governor forbade recruiting for economic and political reasons. The ban was rescinded once war broke out. After a meeting with representatives of the Malayan Communist Party, the first intake of young Chinese began training on 20 December 1941.

The idea was to train 'stay-behind' parties of Chinese and Malays with British officers and technicians, who would operate behind the Japanese frontline to disrupt communications and divert Japanese forces. Fifteen such parties were authorised for Perak at the end of

December 1941, and a second STS was opened in Kuala Lumpur a week before the capital was evacuated. In mid-January 1942 a party of Dutch-officered Indonesian armed police, who specialised in jungle guerrilla warfare, arrived and operated behind Japanese lines in northern Johore.[54] Spencer Chapman (whose account *The Jungle is Neutral* is probably the best-known book about the war in Malaya) argued that, if the hundreds of stay-behind parties originally envisaged had been allowed, there would have been enough disruption to give that extra month or so needed for Wavell's long-term plan to have a chance.[55] In the end it was the Malayan Communist Party that went on to create the 5000-strong Malayan Peoples' Anti-Japanese Army, with regiments in each state and an efficient network of communications and civilian supply.[56] It was mainly Chinese in composition, but it did attract some Malays, especially in Pahang. In Kedah a rival Royal Malay Army emerged. A handful of British personnel worked with the MPAJA and later made contact with Southeast Asia Command HQ in Ceylon.

Another small element of local resistance was organised by Lieutenant-Colonel John Dalley, who briefly assisted Chapman in Kuala Lumpur. Dalley was the director of the Intelligence Bureau of the Malay Security Police. In 1942 he was allowed to recruit 2000 Chinese into an irregular unit known as 'Dalforce'. He took care to separate KMT and MCP members into separate companies, and they played a part on the mainland and in the final battle for Singapore. They earned the nickname 'Dalley's Desperadoes', but *The Times* correspondent found this middle-aged police officer 'a crackerjack of a fellow'.[57] The Malay Regiment also had its role. Two companies of the second battalion fought on the west and east coasts, and both battalions fought well on the Pasir Panjang Ridge, west of Singapore, during the last days.[58] These small developments gave a glimpse of what the people of the country might have done if British policy and racial attitudes had been different in the 1930s.

However, there was also evidence to support the British fears about political complications. A small radical movement, of about a hundred writers, journalists and teachers, had formed the Young Malay Union, *Kesatuan Malayu Muda*, in 1937. Some of its leaders were inclined to welcome the chance of liberation by Japan. They were detained by the British in 1941, but released by the Japanese in February 1942 to form a unit known as the 'Avengers of the Country' Army (*Pembela Tanah Ayer*).[59] More significantly, the

Japanese worked on the possibility of anti-British feelings in the Indian Army. An intelligence unit under Colonel Fujiwara, which began work in Bangkok in 1941, made contact with Major Mohan Singh, second-in-command of the 1/14 Punjab Regiment at Alor Star after the first week of the campaign. He then recruited Indian prisoners-of-war to keep order in the early days of the occupation in Kedah. It was the beginning of a major and successful move to appeal to the nationalism of the inexperienced, battle-stunned recruits of III Indian Corps, many of whom lacked the strength of regimental loyalty of older Indian Army veterans. After the surrender of Singapore the Indians were separated from their British officers and about 40,000 out of 65,000 prisoners-of-war followed many of their Indian officers into the Indian National Army, some of whose units entered India, with the Japanese, in the Kohima-Imphal campaign of 1944.[60] Clearly the Japanese invasion was a catalyst for momentous developments among the Malayan communities.

All this underlines a neglected feature of the decision to build the Singapore naval base. The users of any base in Britain or Australia would have felt confident that the local populace, if threatened, would be committed to its defence. Defence of such a naval base would simply be an aspect of the defence of the homeland. At Singapore the populace were not given the opportunity. They built the base with their labour, and provided skilled technicians for the dockyard, but defence was supposed to be provided by other races. Of these, many of the Europeans came too late to get acclimatised, and the majority, the Indians, did not all have their hearts in the fight. So it turned out that the British, like their Japanese adversaries, had set themselves an impossible task.

VI

The civilians in Malaya were said to be living in an unreal world in 1941. Were the decision-makers, on either side, any less dream-like? Fully convinced that they could not face Germany, Italy and Japan simultaneously, the British nevertheless remained committed to the defence of Australia and New Zealand. In Malaya they either hoped that Japan would be deterred by the long-term prospect of American superiority, or that sufficient reinforcements could be found before Singapore fell. Conversely, the Japanese, who were confident of short-term success, had no idea how they would clinch their victories. Why then did these erstwhile allies pursue their fatal courses?

The answer would seem to lie in the irrational, even spiritual, feelings aroused by the love of Empire. 'Imperialism' has been defined in many ways but, in the last resort, it eludes practical description and historians find themselves in fatalistic, mystic or simply fanciful realms. In the first half of the twentieth century Japan's empire was expanding. Britain's could only stay static or decline. But the feelings prompted by both, especially in their naval officers, were not dissimilar. The notes of the discussion during the 17-hour long Liaison Conference in Tokyo on 1-2 November 1941, when the Japanese leaders made their decision for war, show that, when he was asked if the US fleet would attack the Japanese fleet in a few years time, and whether Japan would win, the Navy's Chief of Staff, Admiral Nagano, said 'Nobody knows'. Both the Foreign Minister and the Finance Minister doubted that the American fleet *would* attack Japan and said they did not believe it was necessary to go to war. Nagano replied: 'The future is uncertain; we can't take anything for granted'. He only knew that in three years the US fleet would be stronger and so would the defences of Southeast Asia. 'The time for war will not come later.'[61] And he was supported by the Army's Vice-Chief of Staff, who said:

> In general, the prospects if we go to war are not bright. We all wonder if there isn't some way to proceed peacefully. . . . On the other hand, it is not possible to maintain the status quo. . . . I, Tsukada, believe that war cannot be avoided. Now is the time. . . . The moral spirit of Japan, the Land of the Gods, will shine on this occasion.[62]

General Tojo, the Prime Minister, summed up this feeling later, during the war trials, with the words, 'rather than await extinction it were better to face death by breaking-through the encircling ring to find a way for existence'.[63]

In many ways the fate of the 'main fleet for Singapore' followed similar fatalistic feelings. In 1939, when the new *European Appreciation* raised the need of adding Italy to the list of enemies and the naval staff's anxiety about the commitment to send a fleet to the Far East was put to the Strategic Appreciations Committee, Admiral Chatfield defended the Singapore priority. He admitted that plans against Italy were a new element which the naval standard took no account of. Yet if the worst happened a fleet would *still* have to go to the Far East. Hong Kong would be lost. Only six battleships would be available at home, so Britain would have to rely on the French navy. Yet 'We must do this', he declared, 'or risk the Empire'.[64] When the First Lord and the CNS came back and sought a redefinition of the pledge to the Dominions, Chatfield said that the COS had always maintained that Britain could not fight Germany, Japan and Italy simultaneously. But he now gave his personal affirmation: 'if we were faced with such a war he felt it would be better to lose the Eastern Empire by fighting than by default'.[65]

Who's vision was the clearer? Singapore fell, but a British fleet went to the Pacific. The naval base and associated airfields and army installations had a new lease of life from 1945 to 1968 during the Indian summer of the Commonwealth's strategic forces east of Suez. But on 8 December 1968 (twenty-seventh anniversary of the Japanese landing at Kota Bahru) the dockyard was handed over to the Government of the independent Republic of Singapore. Soon Sembawang Shipyard Limited had won a booming trade in ship repair. Vessels lay, double-banked, awaiting dockyard attention. And alongside the George VI Dock, a new graving dock, four times its deadweight capacity, was opened in 1975. The former was designed to take the largest British battleship, the latter to take the largest Japanese oil tanker.

Bibliography

I. PRIMARY

(a) *Unpublished materials, alphabetically, with locations*

A 981/126 Australian External Affairs Papers relating to 1930 Imperial Conference (Australian Archives, Canberra).
A 981/135 Jubilee Prime Ministers' meetings.
A 981/136-143 1937 Imperial Conference.
A 981/329-331 Defence, Singapore.
A 981/349-350 Imperial Naval Defence.
AD 10–12 New Zealand defences records, Navy (New Zealand, National Archives, Wellington).
ADM 1 and ADM 116 Admiralty records (Public Record Office, London).
ADM 167 Admiralty Board minutes.
AIR 2 Air Ministry, Far East papers (PRO).
AIR 8 Chief of Air Staff.
AIR 9 Director of Plans, Air Staff.
AIR 23 RAF, Far East.
CAB 2 CID Minutes of meetings (PRO).
CAB 4 CID miscellaneous memos.
CAB 5 CID 'C' series memos (Colonial Defence).
CAB 7 and 8 Overseas Defence subcommittee.
CAB 16 Cabinet, ad. hoc. committees.
CAB 21 Cabinet registered files.
CAB 23 Cabinet minutes and conclusions.
CAB 24 Cabinet papers, G, GT and CP series.
CAB 27 Cabinet committees, minutes.
CAB 29 Conferences.
CAB 32 Imperial conferences.
CAB 53 Chiefs of Staff subcommittee, minutes.
CAB 63 Hankey files.
CAB 64 Minister for Defence Co-ordination.

CAB 69 War Cabinet, Defence Committee (Ops).
CAB 79 Chiefs of Staff subcommittee (after 1939).
CAB 96 War Cabinet, Far East subcommittee.
CAB 99 Conferences, wartime.
CAB 105 Telegrams 1941-45
CHT Chatfield papers (National Maritime Museum, Greenwich).
CO 129 Secretary of State for Colonies, correspondence with Governor of Hong Kong (PRO).
CO 273 SS Cols, correspondence with Governor of Straits Settlements.
CO 418 SS Cols, correspondence with Governor-General of Australia.
CO 532 SS Cols, correspondence with Dominions.
CO 717 SS Cols, correspondence with High Commissioner for the Federated Malay States.
DO 35 Dominions Office, correspondence general.
IO Financial Collections 2. Admiralty file 2 (India Office Library London).
LP-IAC Labour Party, Imperial Affairs Committee Papers (Transport House, London).
NZPM 81 New Zealand Chiefs of Staff Papers (National Archives, Wellington. Some of the NZPM files are still housed in the Ministry of Foreign Affairs).
NZPM 86 Pacific Defence.
NZPM 87 New Zealand Forces.
NZPM 153 Prime Minister's Department, Conferences.
NZPM 156 New Zealand, Imperial Defence, General.
NZPM 455 Prime Minister's Department. Countries (including Singapore, Defence).
NA 22 Navy records (National Archives Wellington).
PREM 1, and 3 Prime Ministers papers (PRO).
WO 32 (Malaya and Straits Settlements.) War Office files (PRO).
A. V. Bettington, 'Aerial Defence of New Zealand' (National Archives, Wellington).
H. P. Wynter 'Defence of Australia and its Relation to Imperial Defence', 1935 (National Library of Australia, Canberra).

(b) *Published*

Commonwealth Parliamentary Debates [Australia].
Hansard's Parliamentary Debates (5th series) [United Kingdom].

Bibliography

Indian Legislative Assembly Debates.
New Zealand Parliamentary Debates.
Proceedings of the Federal Council of the Federated Malay States.
Proceedings of the Legislative Council of the Straits Settlements.
Chief of Staff. The Diaries of Lieutenant-General Sir Henry Pownall, Brian Bond (Ed.), 2 vols (London: Leo Cooper, 1972 and 1974).
Documents on Australian Foreign Policy 1937–1949, vol. I, 1937–38, vol. II, 1939, R. G. Neale et al. (Eds.) (Canberra: Australian Government Publishing Service for Department of Foreign Affairs, 1975, 1976).
Documents Relating to New Zealand's Participation in the Second World War 1939–45, vol. III (Wellington: War History Branch, Department of Internal Affairs, 1963).
The Diplomatic Diaries of Oliver Harvey 1937–1940, John Harvey (Ed.) (London: Collins, 1970).
Japan's Decision for War. Records of the 1941 Policy Conferences, Nobutaka Ike (Ed.) (Stanford: University Press, 1967).
The Jellicoe Papers, A. Temple Patterson (Ed.), 2 vols (London: Navy Records Society, 1968).

2. SECONDARY SOURCES

(a) *A chronological list of writings on the Malayan Campaign – annotated*

1942

Gwyn, Sir Charles and Richmond, Admiral Sir Herbert, 'Singapore', *The Fortnightly*, **151**; 237–43. Two authoritative comments written immediately after the surrender.

Miller, Eugene H., *Strategy at Singapore* (New York: Macmillan). For long the best account of the background. Based on published sources.

Brown, Cecil, *Suez to Singapore* (New York: Random House). By the C.B.S. correspondent who was on the *Repulse* when it went down. Banned from broadcasting early in 1942, and so much concerned with complaints about censorship.

Gallagher, O. D., *Retreat in the East* (London: Harrop). By the South African-born *Daily Express* correspondent who also survived the sinking of the *Repulse*, and who was critical of Brooke-Popham.

Lord Strabolgi, *Singapore and After* (London: Hutchinson). Polemic about the rise of Japan by the former Lt-Cdr. J. M. Kenworthy. Good photographs.

McKie, R. C. H., *This was Singapore* (Sydney: Angus and Robertson; London: Robert Hale). A journalist's account of life in Singapore 1937–9. Ch. 22 describes a target practice by one of the 15" guns seen from a tow-ship.

1943

Donahue, Arthur G., *Last Flight from Singapore* (New York: Macmillan). By an American RAF pilot, who gives an account of *Hurricane* operations in Jan–Feb 1942.

Morrison, Ian, *Malayan Postscript* (Sydney: Angus and Robertson). An informative description of the atmosphere by *The Times* correspondent, who had lived in Japan before the war.

Weller, George, *Singapore is Silent* (New York: Harcourt Brace). Memoir by the *Chicago Daily News* correspondent. Also critical about censorship. He was impressed by the general feeling that the USA was expected to save Singapore.

1944

Bennett, H. Gordon, *Why Singapore Fell* (Sydney: Angus and Robertson). A disappointingly bland account by the controversial Australian commander. Includes some excerpts from his diaries and is well illustrated.

Sansom, Sir George, 'The Story of Singapore', *Foreign Affairs*, **22**(2), 279–97. A valuable perspective by a diplomat (and historian) who had served for 37 years in Japan and who worked for the Ministry of Economic Warfare in Singapore before the surrender.

Gilmour, Oswald. W., *Singapore to Freedom* (London: Barrow). An account of the passive civil defence services by the deputy Municipal Engineer of Singapore who was in charge of the Rescue, Demolitions, Debris and Repairs Section, and his escape.

Field, S. E., *Singapore Tragedy* (Auckland: Oswald-Sealey). The personal story of a 37-year-old New Zealander, who worked in the FMS income tax department in 1941, and got away in a Dutch liner.

Playfair, Giles, *Singapore Goes off the Air* (London: Jarrolds). Civilian life in Singapore, 8 Dec 41 to 11 Feb 42, by a someone who came to work for the Malayan Broadcasting Corporation.

1946

Glover, Edwin Maurice, *In 70 Days. The Story of the Japanese Campaign in British Malaya* (London: Muller). Wartime life in Singapore focused around getting out the *Malaya Tribune* by its general manager.

1947

Maxwell, Sir George (compiler), *The Civil Defence of Malaya. A Narrative of the part taken in it by the Civil Population of the Country in the Japanese Invasion* (London: Hutchinson). Useful data about the Volunteer Forces and civil defence organisations.

Stewart, Ian MacA., *History of the Argyll and Sutherland Highlanders. Malayan Campaign 1941–42* (London: Nelson). By the OC, who (from August 1939) took jungle training seriously, and evolved effective tactics and living conditions for British troops in Malaya.

1948

Brooke-Popham, Air Chief Marshal Sir Robert, Despatch, 28 May 1942, Supplement to *London Gazette*, 22 Jan 1948, no. 38183, p. 535. Useful on the setting up of Far East headquarters.

Layton, Vice-Admiral Sir Geoffrey, Despatch, 17 Dec 1941. Supplement to *London Gazette*, 26 Feb 1948, no. 38214, p. 1237. Report on the sinking of the *Prince of Wales* and *Repulse*. Includes the account of Capt. Tennant of the *Repulse*.

Percival, Lieutenant General Arthur E., Despatch 25 Apr 1946. Supplement to *London Gazette*, 26 Feb 1948, no. 38215, p. 1245. By far the fullest of the official despatches. A main source for many later writers.

Maltby, Air Marshal Sir Paul, Despatch, 26 July 1947. Supplement to *London Gazette*, 26 Feb 1948, no. 38216, p. 1347. Full data about the initial air situation, the airfields and aircraft available.

Wavell, Field Marshal, Sir Archibald, *ABDA. Despatch of the Supreme Commander of the ABDA Area to the Combined Chief of Staff on the Operations in the South-West Pacific 15 Jan 1942 to 25 Feb 1942* (London: HMSO). Air was the vital factor on both sides.

Coombes, J. H. H. *Bampong Express. Malaya and After* (Darlington: Dresser & Son). An account of the whole campaign by an officer in 137 Field Regiment RA, which was part of 11 Div. The regiment lost 300 at the Slim River and the author saw the GOC go to surrender under the white flag. Also describes work on the Siam–Burma railway.

1949
Percival, Arthur E., *The War in Malaya*, (London: Eyre and Spottiswoode). Very similar to his official despatch.

Chapman, Frank Spencer, *The Jungle is Neutral* (London: Chatto and Windus). A personal account of activities in Malaya during the Japanese occupation by one of the officers who linked-up with the Communist guerillas. A bestseller in its day, this book is for many people their sole reading on the Malayan campaign.

Penfold, A. W., Bayliss, W. C. and Crispin, K. E., *Calleghan's Greyhounds. The Story of the 2/30th Australian Infantry Battalion 22 November 1940–10 October 1945* (Sydney: 2/30th AIF Association). Includes the fullest account of the Gemas ambush and the history of the battalion involved.

1950
Churchill, Winston S., *The Second World War*, vol. III (London, Cassell). This work and vol. IV (pub. 1951) has been, understandably, very influential and Churchill takes full responsibility for the strategic priorities which denied adequate reinforcements to Malaya. The account gave currency to the well-known idea that the guns were, 'pointing the wrong way' and Churchillian phrases have provided good titles for other writers: 'Naked Island', 'Sinister Twilight', 'Worst Disaster'.

1951
Grenfell, Russell, *Main Fleet to Singapore* (London: Faber and Faber). Polemical but very well informed on naval policy. The author, a former RN captain, spoke to a number of highly placed personalities involved.

Mackenzie, Compton, *Eastern Epic*, vol. I (London: Chatto and Windus). A beautifully-written narrative of the role of the Indian units in the campaign. Part of a general history of the Indian Army in the Second World War.

1952
Dean, H. R., 'The Royal New Zealand Air Force in South-East Asia, 1941–42', in *New Zealand in the Second World War, 1939–1945. Episodes and Studies*, vol. 2 (Wellington: War History Branch, Department of Internal Affairs). One of the serially-published parts of the NZ official history. Describes the (usually overlooked) RNZAF squadron of fighter pilots and the unique aerodrome construction unit.

1954
McCormac, Charles, *You'll Die in Singapore* (London: Robert Hale). Informative memoirs of an RAF Sergeant from Seletar.
Roskill, Stephen W., *The War at Sea 1939–1945*, vol. I. History of the Second World War, United Kingdom Military Series (London: HMSO). Includes the official account of the loss of the *Prince of Wales* and *Repulse*.

1955
Parkinson, C. Northcote, *Britain in the Far East. The Singapore Naval Base* (Singapore: Donald Moore).

1956
Parkinson, C. Northcote, 'The Pre-1942 Singapore Naval Base', *US Naval Institute Proceedings* 1956 (Sept), 939–953. These two works are nearly identical and deal with the background, from published material.

1957
Kirby, S. Woodburn, *The War Against Japan*, vol. I, *The Loss of Singapore*, in History of the Second World War, United Kingdom Military Series (London: HMSO).
Butler, J. R. M., *Grand Strategy*, vol. 2, in UK Military Series (London: HMSO).
Wigmore, Lionel, *The Japanese Thrust*, in Australia in the War of 1939–1945, Series 1 (Army) (Canberra: Australia War Memorial).
Gill G. Hermon, *Royal Australian Navy 1939–42*, in Australian Series 2 (Navy) (Canberra: Australian War Memorial). These UK and Australian official histories, which cover more than the Malayan campaign, provide the most detailed accounts of the fighting – including unit operations. Good maps and photographs. Together they make 1957 the historiographical landmark until 1970 when Brigadier Simson's book came out. In 1971 General Kirby's own unofficial (posthumously published) account also came out. Thereafter the opening of the British archives under the 30-year rule began to make its mark.

1959
Attiwill, Kenneth, *The Singapore Story* (London: Muller). Reminiscences and comment occasioned by the publication of the official histories by an Australian-born writer and playwright who was captured by the Japanese.
Teok Chan Lean 'The Administration of Sir Shenton Thomas, 1934–1946' (Singapore: University of Malaya unpublished

thesis). A survey of the wartime governor based on published material only.

Cain, T. R. and Smallwood, A. V., *H. M. S. Electra* (London: Muller). A popular narrative of one of the destroyers which accompanied the *Prince of Wales* and the *Repulse* and picked-up survivors.

1960

Tsuji, Masonobu, *Singapore: The Japanese Version* (Trans. by M. L. Lake) (Sydney: Ure Smith). A very influential account by the staff officer who planned the Japanese campaign and includes his analysis of the British situation in Malaya. Well illustrated.

Owen, Frank, *The Fall of Singapore* (London: Michael Joseph). A brief narrative.

Bhargava K. D. and Sastri, K. N. V., *Campaigns in South East Asia 1941–42*, in Official History of the Armed Forces in the Second World War. Bisheshwar Prasad, (Ed.) (New Delhi: Combined Inter-Service Historical Section). The Indian official history, which has the fullest account of the opening battles at Kota Bahru.

Ash, Bernard, *Someone had Blundered: the Story of the 'Repulse' and the 'Prince of Wales'* (London: Michael Joseph). The story of the two capital ships from building to the disaster.

1962

Gillson, Douglas, *Royal Australia Air Force, 1939–1942*. Australia in the War of 1939–1945, Series 3 (Air), vol. 1 (Canberra: Australian War Memorial). Includes the best account of the air war in Malaya.

1963

Hough, Richard, *The Hunting of Force Z* (London: Collins). Sets the loss of the two capital ships in the context of the history of the modern battleship.

Beavis, Major-General L. E., 'The Defences of Singapore', *Stand-To* [Canberra RSL journal], **18**(2), 7–9. Technical material about the construction and siting of the big guns by an Australian artillery officer, who was on secondment in the War Office during the speed-up of the defences after Manchuria.

1964

Gwyer, J. M. A. and Butler, J. R. M., *Grand Strategy*, vol. 3, Part I June 1941–Aug 1942. History of the Second World War (London: United Kingdom Military Series). Includes a survey on the strategic reasons for the fall of Singapore.

Robinson, A. O., 'The Malayan Campaign in the light of the principles of War', *Journal of the Royal United Service Institution*, 1964 **109** (635–6), 224–32, 325–37. A critical analysis of the tactics of the campaign by a former GSO 2 in HQ III Corps.

1965

Russell-Roberts, Denis, *Spotlight on Singapore* (Douglas I. O. M.: Times Press). Interesting prisoner-of-war memoirs preceded by an account of the Indian units at the defence of Kuantan and the retreat south.

Ramli, D., 'History of the Malay Regiment, 1933–42', *Journal of Malayan Branch of the Royal Asiatic Society*, **38**(1); 199–243. The story of the only regular Malay unit, including a detailed account of operations west of Singapore just before the end.

1967

Harrison, Kenneth, *The Brave Japanese* (Adelaide: Rigby). A prisoner-of-war book without rancour, by a member of an Australian anti-tank gun crew at Gemas. A vivid account of the tank ambush with good photographs.

Crawford, Hew T. M., *The Long Green Tunnel* (London: Michael Joseph). A captivity book, which includes a brief description of the retreat from Kedah.

Allen, Louis, 'The Surrender of Singapore: The Official Japanese Version', *Durham University Journal*, **29**(1), 1–6. A new text of the surrender parley in the Ford Motor Factory.

1968

Barber, Noel. *Sinister Twilight. The Fall and Rise Again of Singapore* (London: Collins). Portrays the atmosphere in Singapore through the lives of a group of individuals who have recorded their experiences.

Leasor, James, *Singapore. The Battle that Changed the World* (London: Hodder and Stoughton). Rather confusing, but one of the few authors to interview General Percival.

Barclay, C. N., 'The Fall of Singapore: a Reappraisal', *Army*, **18**(4), 44–53. A brief survey, which suggests that, even if certain possible reinforcements had been sent in 1941, defeat was likely.

1969

Swinson, Arthur, *Defeat in Malaya: the fall of Singapore* (London: Macdonald). A lavishly illustrated short narrative.

Connell, John, *Wavell: Supreme Commander 1941–1943* (London: Collins). Includes the texts of Wavell's main cables.

Ghosh, Kalyan Kumar, *The Indian National Army. Second Front of the Indian National Movement* (Meerut: Meenakshi Prakashan). The INA mainly from Indian sources, including the post-war trials.

1970

Simson, Ivan, *Singapore: too little, too late. Some aspects of the Malayan disaster in 1942* (London: Leo Cooper). An important book by the former Chief Engineer, Malaya Command, who tried to persuade Percival to prepare defence works on the Peninsula and the north shores of the Island.

1971

Kirby, S. Woodburn, *Singapore: The Chain of Disaster* (London: Cassell). The best book covering both the campaign and its background.

Smythe, John, *Percival and the Tragedy of Singapore* (London: Macdonald). Disappointing, but by a friend of Percival's, who has interesting material about his early career.

Lebra, Joyce C., *Jungle Alliance. Japan and the Indian National Army* (Singapore: Asia Pacific Press). Uses Japanese sources and interviews, but less good on the Indian sources.

McCarthy, John M., 'Singapore and Australian Defence 1921–1942', *Australian Outlook*, **25**(2), 165–80. One of the first accounts to use British inter-war archives opened in 1967. Critical of British policy and of Australia's participation in it.

1973

Hamill, Ian, 'An Australian Defence Policy?: the Singapore strategy and the defence of Australia 1919–1942', *A.N.U. Historical Journal*, **10** and **11**; 10–20. Covers similar ground to McCarthy but is more sympathetic to the dilemmas of British policy-makers and suggests there were no viable alternatives for Australia.

Bennett, Geoffrey, *The Loss of the Prince of Wales and Repulse* (London: Ian Allen). Brief narrative, with good photographs, battle plans and technical data.

1974

Callahan, Raymond, 'The Illusion of Security: Singapore 1919–42', *Journal of Contemporary History*, **9**, 69–92. A further step in the critical analysis of British policy following the opening of the archives, which stresses Britain's inability to fulfil all its commitments.

Caffrey, Kate, *Out in the Midday Sun. Singapore 1941–45* (London:

Andre Deutsch). The campaign and the captivity, seen through memoirs.

1975
Falk, Stanley L., *Seventy Days to Singapore. The Malayan Campaign 1941–42* (London: Hale). The best short account of the campaign itself. Had access to US intelligence summaries of 1941.

1976
Allen, Louis, 'Singapore', Ch. 12 in Noble Frankland and Christopher Dowling, *Decisive Battles of the Twentieth Century* (London: Sidgwick and Jackson). A very clear and balanced essay.

1977
Middlebrook, Martin and Mahoney, Patrick, *Battleship. The Loss of the Prince of Wales and the Repulse* (London: Allen Lane). A gripping account of the disaster based largely on the memories of hundreds of survivors and other participants.

Allen, Louis, *Singapore 1941–42* (London: Davis Poynter). A brief, up-to-date account of the Campaign (which includes material from Japanese sources), followed by an analysis of the judgements made about the Campaign by civil and military leaders. Rather confusing in organisation, but stimulating.

Callahan, Raymond, *The Worst Disaster: The Fall of Singapore* (Newark: University of Delaware Press; London: Associated University Presses). The best analysis of the impact of Churchill's strategy on the Far East.

(b) *Contemporary works and memoirs*

Agar, Augustus W. S., *Footprints in the Sea* (London: Evans Bros, 1959).

Agar, Augustus, W. S., *Showing the Flag* (London: Evans Bros, 1962).

Barber, Noel, *How Strong is Japan?* (London: Harrop, 1942).

Braddell, Roland, *The Legal Status of the Malay States* (Singapore: Malaya Publishing House, 1931).

Bryant, Arthur, *The Turn of the Tide, 1939–1943* (London: Collins, 1957).

Casey, Richard G., *Personal Experience 1939–46* (London: Constable, 1962).

Chatfield, A. E. M., *The Navy and Defence* (London: Heinemann, 1942).

Chatfield, A. E. M., *It Might Happen Again* (London: Heinemann, 1947).
Cornish, Vaughan, 'Singapore and Naval Geography', *United Empire* (1925) 500–12.
Craigie, Robert, *Behind the Japanese Mask* (London: Hutchinson, 1946).
Crosby, Josiah, *Siam: The Cross Roads* (London: Hollis & Carter, 1945).
Dreyer, Frederick C., *The Sea Heritage. A Study in Maritime Warfare* (London: Museum Press, 1955).
Guillemard, Lawrence, *Trivial Fond Records* (London: Methuen, 1937).
Gunther, John, 'Singapore: A Warning to Japan', *Saturday Evening Post*, June 1938, 10–11, 90–4.
Hornbeck, Stanley K., *The United States in the Far East* (Boston: World Peace Foundation, 1942).
Ishimaru, Tota, *Japan Must Fight Britain* (trans.) (London: Paternoster Library, 1936).
Ismay, Hastings, *The Memoirs of General the Lord Ismay* (London: Heinemann, 1960).
Hull, Cordell, *The Memoirs of Cordell Hull*. 2 vols (New York: Macmillan, 1948).
Longmore, Arthur M., *From Sea to Sky. 1910–1945* (London: Bles, 1946).
Massey, Vincent, *What's Past is Prologue: the Memoirs of the Right Honourable Vincent Massey, C. H.* (London: Macmillan, 1963).
Mlaker, Lieut-Col., 'Singapore-British Naval Base', *Military Review* (1941), **21**(82), 52–3.
Moran, Lord, *Winston Churchill. The Struggle for Survival 1940–65* (London: Constable, 1966).
Page, Earle, *Truant Surgeon. The Inside Story of Forty Years of Australian Political Life* (Sydney: Angus and Robertson, 1963).
Purcell, Victor, *The Memoirs of a Malayan Official* (London: Cassell, 1965).
Purcell, Victor, *Malaya: Communist or Free?* (London: Gollancz, 1954).
Richmond, Herbert R., *Statesmen and Sea-Power* (Oxford: University Press, 1946).
Roosevelt, Nicholas, 'The Strategy of Singapore', *Foreign Affairs* (1929), **7**(2), 317–22.

Slessor, John, *The Central Blue. Recollections and Reflections* (London: Cassell, 1956).
Stirling, Alfred, *Lord Bruce: The London Years* (Melbourne: Hawthorn Press, 1974).
Tedder, Arthur W., *With Prejudice. The War Memoirs of Marshal of the Royal Air Force Lord Tedder, G. C. B.* (London: Cassell, 1966).
Van Mook, H. J., *The Netherlands Indies and Japan. Their Relations 1940–4* (London: Allen and Unwin, 1944).

(c) *Other books and articles*

Ahmat, Sharom, 'The Political Structure of the State of Kedah, 1897–1905', *Journal of Southeast Asian History* (1970), **1**(2), 115–28.
Allen, James de V., 'The Elephant and the Mousedeer – A New Version: Anglo-Kedah Relations, 1905–1915', *Journal of the Malayan Branch of the Royal Asiatic Society* (1968), **40**(1), 59–64.
Anderson, Irvine H., 'The 1941 *De Facto* Embargo on Oil to Japan: A Bureaucratic Reflex', *Pacific Historical Review* (1975), 201–31.
Andrews, C. M., *Isolation and Appeasement in Australia. Reactions to the European Crisis, 1935–39* (Canberra: A.N.U. Press, 1970).
Bacon, Reginald H. S., *Life of John Rushworth, Earl of Jellicoe* (London: Cassell 1936).
Barclay, C. N., *On their Shoulders: British generalship in the lean years, 1939–1942* (London: Faber, 1964).
Barclay, Glen St. J., *The Empire is Marching. The Dominions and War, 1899–1945* (London: Weidenfeld and Nicolson, 1976).
Barnett, Correlli, *The Collapse of British Power* (London: Methuen, 1972).
Bassett, Reginald, *Nineteen Thirty-One. Political Crisis* (London: Macmillan, 1958).
Bassett, Reginald, *Democracy and Foreign Policy. A Case History. The Sino-Japanese Dispute, 1931–33* (London: Longmans, Green, 1952; Cass: 1968).
Boyle, Andrew, *Trenchard. Man of Vision* (London: Collins, 1962).
Braisted, William R., *The United States Navy in the Pacific, 1909–1922* (Austin and London: University of Texas Press, 1971).
Brice, Martin H., *The Royal Navy and the Sino-Japanese Incident, 1937–41* (London: Ian Allen, 1973).
Butler, J. R. M., *Lord Lothian, Philip Kerr, 1882–1940* (London: Macmillan, 1960).

Butow, Robert C., *Tojo. And the Coming of the War* (Princeton: University Press, 1961).
Carew, Tim, *The History of the Royal Norfolk Regiment* (London: Leo Cooper, 1967).
Carlton, David, *MacDonald versus Henderson. The Foreign Policy of the Second Labour Government* (London: Macmillan, 1970).
Carlton, David, 'The Anglo-French Compromise on Arms Limitation, 1928', *Journal of British Studies* (1969), **8**(2), 141–62.
Chai Hon Chan, *The Development of British Malaya 1896–1909* (Kuala Lumpur: Oxford-in-Asia, 1964).
Chalmers, W. S., *The Life and Letters of David, Earl Beatty* (London: Hodder and Stoughton, 1951).
Clifford, Nicholas, *Retreat from China: British Policy in the Far East, 1937–41* (London: Longmans, 1967).
Connell, John, *Wavell, Scholar and Soldier to June 1941* (London: Collins, 1964).
Cowan, Charles Donald, *Nineteenth Century Malaya: the Origins of British Political Control* (London: Oxford University Press, 1961).
Cowling, Maurice, *The Impact of Labour 1920–1924* (Cambridge: University Press, 1971).
Digman, Roger, *Power in the Pacific. The Origins of Naval Arms Limitation, 1914–1922* (Chicago and London: University of Chicago Press, 1976).
Dignan, Don K., 'Australia and British Relations with Japan 1914–1921', *Australian Outlook* (1967), **21**(2), 138–50.
Dignan, Don K., 'New Perspectives on British Far East Policy, 1913–1919', University of Queensland Papers (1969), **1**(5), 263–302.
Edwards, Cecil, *Bruce of Melbourne: Man of Two Worlds* (London: Heinemann, 1965).
Emerson, Rupert, *Malaysia. A Study of Direct and Indirect Rule* (New York: Macmillan, 1937; Kuala Lumpur: University of Malaya, 1970).
Feis, Herbert, *The Road to Pearl Harbor* (Princeton: U.P., 1950; New York: Atheneum, 1966).
Gibbs, Norman, H., *The Origins of Imperial Defence* (Oxford: Clarendon Press, 1955).
Gibbs, Norman H., *Grand Strategy*, vol. 1, *Rearmament Policy*. History of the Second World War. United Kingdom Military Series. (London: HMSO, 1976).

Gibbs, Norman H., 'British Strategic Doctrine 1918–39' in *Theory and Practice of War*. Essays presented to B. H. Liddell Hart on his 70th Birthday (New York: Praeger, 1966).

Gilbert, Martin, *Winston S. Churchill*, vol. 5, 1922–39 (London: Heinemann 1976).

Hasluck, Paul, *The Government and the People 1939–41*. Australia in the War of 1939–1945. Series 4 (Civil); vol. 1 (Canberra: Australian War Memorial, 1952).

Hasluck, Paul, *The Government and the People 1942–1945*, vol. 2 (Canberra: Australian War Memorial, 1970).

Higham, Robin, *Armed Forces in Peacetime: Britain 1918–1940* (London: Foulis, 1963).

Higham, Robin, *The Military Intellectuals in Britain 1918–1939* (New Brunswick: Rutgers University Press, 1966).

Howard, Michael, 'The Mediterranean in British Strategy in the Second World War', in *Studies in War and Peace* (London: Temple Smith, 1970).

Howard, Michael, *The Continental Commitment. The dilemma of British defence policy in the era of the two world wars* (London: Temple Smith, 1972).

Hyde, H. Montgomery, *British Air Policy Between the Wars, 1918–1939* (London: Heinemann, 1976).

Johnson, Franklyn Arthur, *Defence by Committee. The British Committee of Imperial Defence, 1885–1959* (London: Oxford University Press, 1960).

Lee, Bradford A., *Britain and the Sino-Japanese War, 1937–1939. A Study in the Dilemmas of British Decline* (London: Oxford University Press, 1973).

Leutze, James R., *Bargaining for Supremacy. Anglo-American Naval Collaboration 1937–1941* (Chapel Hill, N.C.: University of North Carolina Press, 1977).

Lissington, M. Patricia, *New Zealand and the United State 1840–1944* (Wellington: Government Printer, 1972).

Lissington, M. Patricia, *New Zealand and Japan 1900–1941* (Wellington: Government Printer, 1972).

Long, Gavin, *To Benghazi*, Australia in the war of 1939–1945, Series 1 (Army), vol. 1 (Canberra: Australian War Memorial, 1952).

Louis, William Roger, *British Strategy in the Far East, 1919–39* (Oxford: Clarendon Press, 1970).

Lowe, Peter, *Great Britain and Japan 1911–1919* (London: Macmillan, 1969).

Lowe, Peter, *Great Britain and the Origins of the Pacific War. A Study in British Policy in East Asia 1937–1941* (Oxford: Clarendon Press, 1977).

Lyman, Richard W., *The First Labour Government 1924* (London: Chapman and Hall, 1957).

McCarthy, John M., *Australia and Imperial Defence 1918–1939. A Study in Air and Sea Power* (St Lucia: University of Queensland Press, 1976).

McDonald, J. Kenneth, 'Lloyd George and the Search for a Post-War Naval Policy, 1919' in *Lloyd George: Twelve Essays*, A. J. P. Taylor (Ed.) (London: Hamish Hamilton, 1971).

MacGibbon, Ian, 'The Constitutional Implications of Lord Jellicoe's Influence of New Zealand Naval Policy, 1919–1930', *New Zealand Journal of History* (1972), **6**(1), 57–80.

McIntyre, W. David, 'The Strategic Significance of Singapore 1917–1942: The Naval Base and the Commonwealth', *Journal of Southeast Asian History* (1969), **10**(1), 69–94.

McIntyre, W. David, 'New Zealand and the Singapore Base between the Wars', *Journal of Southeast Asian Studies* (1971), **2**(1), 2–21.

Marder, Arthur J., *From the Dardanelles to Oran. Studies of the Royal Navy in War and Peace 1915–1940* (London: Oxford University Press, 1974).

Marder, Arthur J., *Portrait of an Admiral. The Life and Papers of Sir Herbert Richmond* (London: Cape, 1952).

Marquand, David, *Ramsay MacDonald* (London: Cape, 1976).

Maurice-Jones, K. W., *History of Coast Artillery in the British Army* (London: Royal Artillery Institution, 1959).

Medlicott, William N., *British Foreign Policy since Versailles 1919–1963* (London: Methuen, 1968).

Middlebrook, Martin and Mahoney, Patrick, *Battleship. The Loss of the Prince of Wales and the Repulse* (London: Allen Lane, 1977).

Middlemas, Keith, *The Diplomacy of Illusion. The British Government and Germany, 1937–1939* (London: Weidenfeld and Nicolson, 1972).

Morison, Samuel Eliot, *The Rising Sun in the Pacific, 1931–April 1942*, vol. 3 of History of the United States Naval Operations in World War II (Boston: Little, Brown, 1948).

Mowat, Charles L., *Britain between the Wars, 1918–1940* (London: Methuen, 1955).

Naylor, John F., *Labour's International Policy* (London: Weidenfeld and Nicolson, 1969).

Neatby, H. Blair, *William Lyon Mackenzie King, 1929–1932* (Toronto: University Press, 1963).
Nish, Ian H., *Alliance in Decline, 1908–1923* (London: Athlone Press, 1972).
Northedge, F. S., *The Troubled Giant. Britain among the Great Powers 1916–1939* (London: Bell, 1966).
O'Connor, Raymond G., *Perilous Equilibrium. The U.S. and the London Naval Conference of 1930* (New York: Greenwood, 1969).
Olssen, Erik, *John A. Lee* (Dunedin: University of Otago Press, 1977).
Ovendale, Ritchie, *'Appeasement' in the English-Speaking World* (Cardiff: University of Wales Press, 1975).
Owen, Roderic, *Tedder* (London: Collins, 1952).
Pelling, Henry, *Winston Churchill* (London: Macmillan, 1974).
Pelz, Stephen E., *Race to Pearl Harbor. The Failure of the Second London Naval Conference and the Onset of World War II* (Cambridge, Mass.: Harvard University Press, 1974).
Peters, G. W. N., *The Bedfordshire and Hertfordshire Regiment* (London: Leo Cooper, 1970).
Potter, John Deane, *A Soldier Must Hang. The Biography of an Oriental General [Yamashita]* (London: Muller, 1963).
Potter, John Deane, *Admiral of the Pacific. The Life of Yamamoto* (London: Heinemann, 1965).
Pratt, Lawrence R., 'The Anglo-American Naval Conversations in the Far East of January 1938', *International Affairs* (1971) **47**(4).
Pratt, Lawrence R., *East of Malta, West of Suez. Britain's Mediterranean Crisis, 1936–39* (Cambridge: University Press, 1975).
Preston, Richard A., *Canada and 'Imperial Defense'. A Study in the Origins of the British Commonwealth's defense organisation, 1887–1919* (Durham N.C.: Duke University Press, 1967).
Roff, William R., *The Origins of Malay Nationalism* (New Haven: Yale University Press, 1967).
Roskill, Stephen W., *Hankey. Man of Secrets*, 3 vols (London: Collins, 1970–74).
Roskill, Stephen W., *Naval Policy Between the Wars*, 2 vols (London: Collins, 1968–76).
Ross, J. M. S., *Royal New Zealand Air Force*. Official History of New Zealand in the Second World War 1939–45 (Wellington: War History Branch, Department of Internal Affairs, 1955).
Sinclair, Keith, 'The British Advance in Johore 1885–1914', *Journal of the Malayan Branch of the Royal Asiatic Society* (1967), **40**(1), 93–110.

Sinclair, Keith, *Walter Nash* (Auckland: University Press/OUP, 1976).
Skidelsky, Robert J. A., *Politicians and the Slump. The Labour Government of 1929–1931* (London: Macmillan, 1967).
Soenarno, Radin, 'Malay Nationalism 1896–1941', *Journal of Southeast Asian History* (1960), **1**(1), 1–33.
Soh Eng Lim, 'Tan Cheng Lock and the Leadership of the Malayan Chinese', *Journal of Southeast Asian History* (1960), **1**(1), 39–55.
Stacey, C. P., *Six Years of War. The Army in Canada, Britain and the Pacific* (Ottawa: Queen's Printer, 1966).
Tamshina, Rainer, 'In Search of Common Causes: The Imperial Conference of 1937', *Journal of Imperial and Commonwealth History* (1972), **1**(1), 79–100.
Taylor, A. J. P., *English History 1914–1945* (Oxford: Clarendon Press, 1965).
Thio, Eunice, *British Policy in the Malay Peninsula 1880–1910*, vol. 1. *The Southern and Central States, 1874–1895* (Kuala Lumpur: University of Malaya Press, 1968).
Thorne, Christopher, *The Limits of Foreign Policy. The West, the League and the Far Eastern Crisis of 1931–33* (London: Macmillan 1973).
Thorne, Christopher, 'The Shanghai Crisis of 1932: the basis of British policy', *American Historical Review* (1970), **70**(6), 1616–39.
Toland, John, *The Rising Sun. The Decline and Fall of the Japanese Empire 1939–1945* (London: Cassell, 1970).
Treat, P. J., 'Shanghai, Jan. 28, 1932', *Pacific Historical Review* (1940), **9**, 337–43.
Trotter, Ann, 'The Dominions and Imperial Defence. Hankey's Tour in 1934', *Journal of Imperial and Commonwealth History* (1974), **2**(3), 318–29.
Trotter, Ann, 'Tentative Steps towards an Anglo-Japanese rapprochement in 1934', *Modern Asian Studies* (1974), **8**(1), 59–83.
Trotter, Ann, *Britain and East Asia 1933–1937* (London: Cambridge University Press, 1975).
Turnbull, C. Mary, *Indian Presidency to Crown Colony. The Straits Settlements 1826–1867* (London: Athlone Press, 1971).
Turnbull, C. Mary, *A History of Singapore 1819–1975* (Kuala Lumpur: Oxford-in-Asia, 1977).
Vinson, John C., *The Parchment Peace. The United States Senate and the Washington Conference, 1921–22* (Athens, Ga.: University of Georgia Press, 1955).

Waters, S. D., *The Royal New Zealand Navy*. Official History of New Zealand in the Second World War 1939-45. (Wellington: War History Branch, Department of Internal Affairs, 1956).

Watt, Donald Cameron, *Personalities and Powers. Studies in the formulation of British Policy in the Twentieth Century* (London: Longmans, 1965).

Watts, A. J. and Gordon, B. G., *The Imperial Japanese Navy* (London: MacDonald, 1971).

Wheeler, Gerald E., *Prelude to Pearl Harbor. The United States Navy in the Far East, 1921-1931* (Columbia: University of Missouri Press, 1963).

Winton, John, *The Forgotten Fleet* (London: Michael Joseph, 1969).

Wood, F. L. W., *The New Zealand People at War. Political and External Affairs*. Official History of New Zealand in the Second World War, 1939-45 (Wellington: War History Branch, Department of Internal Affairs, 1958).

Notes

INTRODUCTION

1. The system is outlined in CID memo 313-C, 'Some General Principles of Imperial Defence', 12 Mar 1928 (CAB 5/7) which includes this definition: 'Except where otherwise stated, the word "Imperial" is used throughout this Memorandum as the adjectival form of the words "British Empire".'
2. See table of comparisons in Stephen W. Roskill, *Naval Policy Between the Wars*, vol. 1 (London: Collins, 1968), p. 71.
3. IWC, 4th and 5th days, 28 Mar and 30 Mar 1917. CAB 32/1 (I).
4. Memo GT 4571, 'Naval Defence of the British Empire', 17 May 1918. CAB 24/51; IWC, 21st mtg 27 June 1918. (CAB 23/41); Borden to Geddes, 15 Aug 1918. ADM 116/1831.
5. Draft, 30 Nov 1918, revised 17 Dec 1918 (ADM 116/1815). Approved by IWC, 18 Dec 1918. CAB 23/42.
6. Min. by Dewar, 28 Apr 1919 on 'British Imperial Naval Bases in the Pacific', Plans Division, 26 Apr 1919. ADM 1/8570/287.
7. Ibid, Min. by DCNS, 10 June 1919.
8. 'Post-war Naval Policy', 12 Aug 1919, sent to Hankey for Cabinet, 13 Aug. ADM 116/1774. On the issues involved see J. Kenneth McDonald, 'Lloyd George and the Search for a Postwar Naval Policy, 1919' in *Lloyd George: Twelve Essays*, Ed. A. J. P. Taylor (London: Hamish Hamilton, 1971).
9. War Cab., 15 Aug 1919 and Adm. Bd. Min., 18 Aug 1919. ADM 167/56. See also Norman H. Gibbs, *Grand Strategy*, vol. 1, *Rearmament Policy* (London: HMSO, 1976), pp. 2–6; Stephen W. Roskill, *Hankey, Man of Secrets*, 3 vols (London: Collins 1970–74), II, pp. 111–12.
10. Adm 1/8571/295.
11. Adm. Bd. Min. 958, 25 Sept 1919. ADM 167/56.
12. Debate discussed in Eugene H. Miller, *Strategy at Singapore* (New York: Macmillan, 1942), chs 3 & 4.
13. Min. by Pound, 12 June 1922, that Singapore, even when fully developed, would not be capable of dealing with all the repairs of the fleet. ADM 116/3165.
14. See Vincent T. Harlow, *The Founding of the Second British Empire, 1763–1793* (London: Longmans, 1952), vol. I.
15. See C. Mary Turnbull, *Indian Presidency to Crown Colony. The Straits Settlements, 1826–67* (London: Athlone Press, 1971) and *A History of Singapore* (Kuala Lumpur: Oxford-in-Asia, 1977); Soh Eng Lim, 'Tan Cheng Lock and the Leadership of the Malayan Chinese', *Journal of Southeast Asian History* (1960), **1**(1), 29–55; William

Robert Roff, 'The Malayo-Muslim World of Singapore at the Close of the Nineteenth Century', *Journal of Asian Studies* (1964), **24**(1), 75–90; Wong Lin Ken, 'Singapore; Its Growth as an Entrepot Port, 1819–1941', Ibid (1978), **9**(1), 50–84.

16. For nineteenth-century proposals see R. D. Jansen, 'The Idea of Singapore as a Naval Base and the Abandonment of that Idea 1885–1905' (Research Exercise in University of Singapore Library); Richard A. Preston, *Canada and 'Imperial Defense'. A Study of the Origins of the British Commonwealth's Defense Organisation, 1867–1919* (Durham, N.C.: Duke University Press, 1967), p. 399; 'Development of Imperial Defence Policy in the Far East', Memo by Hankey, 24 Mar 1925. CID 244-C. CAB 5/5.

17. See Rupert Emerson, *Malaysia. A Study in Direct and Indirect Rule* (New York: Macmillan, 1937; Kuala Lumpur: University of Malaya Press, 1970; Charles Donald Cowan, *Nineteenth Century Malaya: The Origins of British Political Control* (London: Oxford University Press, 1961); Eunice Thio, *British Policy in the Malay Peninsula, 1880–1910*, vol. I. *The Southern and Central States* (Singapore: University of Malaya Press, 1969); Emily Sadka, *The Protected Malay States, 1874–1895* (Kuala Lumpur: University of Malaya Press, 1968); Chai Hon Chan, *The Development of British Malaya, 1896–1909* (Kuala Lumpur: Oxford University Press, 1964).

18. See Keith Sinclair, 'The British Advance in Johore, 1885–1914', *Journal of the Malayan Branch of the Royal Asiatic Society* (1967), **40**(1), 93–110; Sharom Ahmat, 'The Political Structure of the State of Kedah, 1879–1905', *Journal of Southeast Asian Studies* (1970), **1**(2), 115–28; James de Vere Allen, 'The Elephant and the Mousedeer – A New Version: Anglo-Kedah Relations, 1905–1915', *Journal of the Malayan Branch of the Royal Asiatic Society* (1968), **40**(1), 59–94.

19. Victor Purcell, *The Memoirs of a Malayan Official* (London: Cassell, 1965), p. 292.

20. The classic work is William R. Roff, *The Origins of Malay Nationalism* (New Haven: Yale University Press, 1967).

21. Martin Middlebrook and Patrick Mahoney, *Battleship. The Loss of the Prince of Wales and the Repulse* (London: Allen Lane, 1977), p. 326.

22. 203rd mtg CID, 15 Oct 1925. CAB 2/4; Keith Sinclair, *Walter Nash* (Auckland: Auckland University Press/Oxford University Press, 1976), p. 148.

23. For the origins of the CID see Norman H. Gibbs, *The Origins of Imperial Defence* (Oxford: Clarendon Press, 1955); Nicholas d'Ombrain, *War Machinery and High Policy. Defence Administration in Peacetime Britain 1902–1914* (London: Oxford University Press, 1973) and Franklyn Arthur Johnson, *Defence by Committee. The British Committee of Imperial Defence 1885–1959* (London: Oxford University Press, 1960).

24. Gibbs, *Grand Strategy*, I, p. 769.

25. *The Diplomatic Diaries of Oliver Harvey, 1937–1940*, Ed. John Harvey (London: Collins, 1970), p. 229.

26. Note by Prof. P. Noel Baker and A. A. Ponsonby M. P., Labour Party Archives Transport House, London: LP/IAC/2/336, Apr 1925.

27. H. Blair Neatby, *William Lyon Mackenzie King 1929–1932*, (Toronto: University Press, 1963), pp. 41–2; Vincent Massey, *What's Past is Prologue: The Memoirs of the Right Honourable Vincent Massey, C. H.* (London: Macmillan, 1963), pp. 237–40.

28. Cecil Edwards, *Bruce of Melbourne: Man of Two Worlds* (London: Heinemann, 1965) ch. 29; see also Alfred Stirling, *Lord Bruce: The London Years* (Melbourne: Hawthorne Press, 1974).

CHAPTER I 'THE NAVAL KEY TO THE FAR EAST'

1. William Reynolds Braisted, *The United States Navy in the Pacific, 1909–1922* (Austin & London: University of Texas Press, 1971), pp. 40–2, 253–62.
2. On British suspicions about the Japanese see: D. K. Dignan, 'Australia and British Relations with Japan 1914–1921', *Australian Outlook* (1967), **21**(2), 138–50; P. Lowe, *Great Britain and Japan 1911–19* (London: Macmillan, 1969); Ian H. Nish, *Alliance in Decline, 1908–23* (London: Athlone Press, 1972).
3. 'Naval Situation in the Far East', 21 Oct 1919, sent to Sec. CID, 31 Oct 1919. ADM 1/8571/295.
4. Mins. by Capt. Frank Larken, Dir. Local Def. Div. 14 Oct 1919 and Brock, 17 Oct 1919. ADM 1/8570/287.
5. Min. by Adm. Wemyss, 31 Oct 1919. ADM 116/1815.
6. Jellicoe to Long, 2 May 1919. *The Jellicoe Papers*. Ed. A. Temple Patterson (London: Navy Records Society, 1968), vol. 2, p. 296. The Indian Report is in Jellicoe to Sec. Adm. 3 May 1919 (ADM 116/1831) in which he recommended converting the Royal Indian Marine into a Royal Indian Navy.
7. Gov. Gen. to SS Cols, 5 Sept 1919. CO 418/177.
8. *Jellicoe Papers*, II, p. 347.
9. Ibid, p. 329.
10. ADM 116/1831/487.
11. AJHR, 1919, A-4. Part of the Australian report was also published.
12. Min. by DDOP, 10 Jan 1920. ADM 116/1831/140.
13. Ibid, 242. Min. by Brock on Jellicoe to Sec. of Adm. 3 Feb 1920.
14. This document, which was enclosed in Adm. letter M. 00340, 20 Jan 1920, has not been found in London, Canberra or Wellington, but long excerpts are quoted in the Report of the Penang Flag Officers Conference, 13 Mar 1921. Australian Archives (AA), Canberra: A 981/350 (1) Sect. 3.
15. 134th and 135th mtgs CID, 14 and 23 Dec 1920. CAB 2/3.
16. Effect of the Anglo-Japanese Alliance upon Foreign Relationship', 28 Feb 1920. *Imperial Conference 1921*: E-1, p. 7.
17. Memo from Finance Committee, 25 Jan 1921. ADM 116/1775.
18. Summary of Adm. recommendations. ADM 1/8611/151.
19. W. G. Green (Adm) to U-Sec (CO), 15 Feb 1917. CO 273/462.
20. Mins. by Learmouth, 8 July; Larken, 31 Aug; Dickens, 30 Aug 1920. ADM 116/2100.
21. Ibid, Mins. by Larken, 12 Oct; Brock 25 Oct; Beatty, 26 Oct 1920; Adm. to CO. 27 Oct 1920.
22. Adm. to CO. 7 Mar 1921. CO 273/512.
23. Report by Cdr. Leonard Garbett, HMS *Merlin*, Feb 1921. ADM 116/2100.
24. See WO to Sec. Adm. 12 Mar 1921. ADM 116/2100.
25. 136th and 137th mtgs CID, 2 May and 6 May 1921. CAB 2/3; ODC 62, 3 May and 63, 5 May 1921. CAB 8/8.
26. See Adm. to U-Sec. WO, 12 Jan 1921. CO 273/512; SS Cols to Gov SS 20 Jan 1921 and Cdr Garbett's report, Feb 1921. ADM 116/2100.
27. 249th mtg ODC, 4 Mar 1920. CAB 7/9. See also 273rd mtg, ODC, 26 Nov 1926, when the CO representative suggested discrimination against Japanese buyers would encourage the use of dummies.

Notes

28. Report of Penang Naval Conference, 13 Mar 1921. Min. by Adm. Sec. noting arrival, 17 May 1921. ADM 116/3100.
29. 'Singapore. Development as a Naval Base', ODC paper 501M, CID paper 143C, Imperial Conf. 1921 paper E18, pp. 9–10; 257th mtg ODC, 7 June 1921. CAB 7/9.
30. 140th and 141st mtgs, CID, 10 and 13 June 1921. CAB 2/3.
31. Cab. Concl. 50/21 (3), 16 June 1921. CAB 23/286. p. 51.
32. 142nd mtg CID, 17 June 1921. CAB 2/3, p. 2.
33. Imp. Conf. 1921, 8th mtg, 28 June 1921, pp. 11–12. CAB 32/2.
34. Actg. Sec. CID to Sec. Adm. 22 Aug 1922. ADM 116/2100.
35. Domvile to Hydrographer, 19 July 1921. ADM 116/3170; 143rd and 144th mtgs CID, 22 and 28 July 1921. CAB 2/3.
36. Instr. to Committee, 22 Nov. 1921. ADM 116/2100.
37. Imp. Conf. 1921 14th and 15th mtgs, 4 and 5 July 1921. CAB 32/2, Part 2.
38. On the relationship between the Imperial Conference and the US invitation to the Washington Conference, see Braisted, *The United States Navy in the Pacific, 1909–1922*, pp. 563–4; Nish, *Alliance in Decline*, pp. 336–51.
39. Ibid, chs 21–23; See also Wm. Roger Louis, *British Strategy in the Far East 1919–1939* (Oxford: Clarendon Press, 1971). ch. 3.
40. CID paper 277-B. CAB 4/7, p. 206.
41. Min. by CNS, 22 Mar 1922 on Memo by DOP 'Strategical View of Naval Situation after Washington' 24 Feb 1922. ADM 116/3195.
42. Notes by Civil Engr-i-C, 3 July 1922 and Report of Comm. Mar 1922. ADM 116/3149. Printed as CID paper 170C. CAB 5/4, p. 146.
43. Note by DNI, 22 Aug 1922. ADM 116/3149.
44. CID paper 169C, 30 May 1922. CAB 5/4/139.
45. 159th mtg CID, 12 July 1922. CAB 2/3.
46. Ibid, 165th and 168th mtgs CID, 30 Nov and 14 Dec 1922.
47. Adm. Bd. Min. 1 Feb 1923. ADM 167/67.
48. *Hansard's Parliamentary Debates*, 5th Series, 1923, vol. 161, col. 1099.
49. 5 *Hansard*, 1923, 163; 1228.
50. Mins. by Pound 17 June and Beatty 7 July on CO to Adm. 13 June 1923. ADM 116/3149.
51. Tel. from Gov. Gen. NZ, 16 July 1923. CO 532/237.
52. AA Canberra: Imperial Conference paper, A981/330.
53. Min. by Hydrographer, 25 June 1923; Adm. Bd. Min. 13 Dec 1923. ADM 1/8653/262.
54. 'Liability of Suez Canal to Blocking Attack', memo by Amery, 24 July 1923. CID 438-B. CAB 4/10.
55. 'We have had no experience yet of the 15-inch in coast defence.' Admission by Sir Ronald Charles, Master-Gen. of Ordnance, to Coast Defence Subcommittee, 4th mtg, 10 Mar 1932, p. 19. CAB 16/105.
56. Mins. of Staff Conf. 15 May 1923. ADM 116/2397.
57. Brancker's reports, June–Aug 1923. WO 32/3622; Inter-departmental Conf. report, n.d. WO 32/3624.
58. J. A. Webster (AM) to Sec. WO, 4 Sept 1923. Copy in ADM 116/2394.
59. Min. by Pound, 11 Nov 1923. ADM 1/8948.
60. 6th mtg COS, 8 Jan 1924. Note by CIGS, 17 Jan 1924. CAB 53/1.

CHAPTER 2 'SOMETHING LESS THAN THE WHOLE'

1. W. S. Chalmers, *The Life and Letters of David, Earl Beatty* (London: Hodder and Stoughton, 1951), p. 394.
2. See Maurice Cowling, *The Impact of Labour 1920–1924* (Cambridge: At the University Press, 1971), pp. 365–81; John F. Naylor, *Labour's International Policy* (London: Weidenfeld and Nicolson, 1969), ch. 1; Richard W. Lyman, *The First Labour Government 1924* (London: Chapman and Hall, 1957) pp. 212–13.
3. 7th mtg COS, 31 Jan 1924. CAB 53/1.
4. 180th and 181st mtgs CID, 4 and 11 Feb 1924. CAB 2/4.
5. Cab. Concl. 14(24)1, 18 Feb 1924. CAB 23/47; SS Dom Aff to GG's Doms and India, 20 Feb 1924. Parl. Papers, 1924, 15, 184; 'Singapore Naval Base' [Cmd. 2083], p. 5.
6. Chalmers, *Beatty*, p. 397.
7. RS(24), 1st mtg, 27 Feb 1924. CAB 27/236.
8. Ibid, RS(24) 2nd mtg, 3 Mar 1924; excerpts printed in David Marquand, *Ramsay MacDonald* (London: Cape, 1976), pp. 315–16.
9. RS(24) 3rd mtg, 5 Mar 1924. CAB 27/236; Cab. 18(24)1. CAB 23/47; Cmd. 2083, pp. 5–6.
10. Draft in NZPM 455 7/1/1; printed (worded differently) in Cmd. 2083, pp. 13–15.
11. Ibid, p. 7.
12. Ibid, pp. 10–12.
13. Jellicoe to Massey, Nelson, 7 Mar 1924. NZPM 455/7/1, Part 1; see also Ian MacGibbon 'The Constitutional Implications of Lord Jellicoe's Influence on New Zealand Naval Policy, 1919–1930', *New Zealand Journal of History* (1972), **6**(1), 70–2.
14. Cmd. 2083, pp. 8–9.
15. Cab. 21(24)1, 14 Mar 1924. CAB 23/47; 5 Hansard, 1924, 171, cols 289 (Ammon), 319–21 (Macdonald's statement, which varies slightly from the text published afterwards).
16. Filed for pr. office, 19 Mar 1924. ADM 116/3149.
17. 183rd mtg CID, 3 Apr 1924. CAB 2/4; 263rd mtg ODC, 21 July 1924. CAB 7/9.
18. Air Staff Notes on the Effect of the Government Decision, 21 Mar 1924. AIR 9/38/1.
19. Wavell GSO1 (MO&I) to Maj. Harrison, GSO2 (Malaya) 15 Apr 1924. WO 32/3622. This file has Brancker's later reports. See passage from Wavell's 'Recollections' (1946) quoted in John Connell, *Wavell, Scholar and Soldier to June 1941* (London: Collins, 1964), pp. 151–2.
20. DOP, 23 June 1924. ADM 116/2416.
21. L. Guillemard, *Trivial Fond Records* (London: Methuen, 1937), p. 111; Cab. concl. 18(24)1f, 5 Mar 1924 CAB 23/47; 5 H, 1924, 171, col. 288.
22. CP 502(24) p. 76. CAB 24/169; Notes by Hankey, 20 Nov 1924. CAB 2/4/66.
23. Cab. 64(24) 3, 26 Nov 1924. CAB 23/49.
24. Gov. HK to SS Cols, 25 Nov and 16 Dec 1924. CO 129/485.
25. Churchill to Hoare, 12 Dec 1924. AIR 8/70, Part 1, file 4.
26. 193rd mtg CID, 5 Jan 1925. CAB 2/4.
27. SD(25), 1st mtg, 16 Jan 1925. CAB 16/63.

28. GOC, J. Fraser to DMO & I, 29 Nov 1924 and J. E. S. Brind to GOC, 12 Mar 1925. WO 32/3624.
29. SP(25) 2nd mtg, 5 Feb 1925. CAB 16/63.
30. Ibid, SP(25) 3rd mtg, 17 Feb 1925.
31. Ibid, SP(25) 4th mtg, 26 Feb 1925. Interim Report, CP 124(25), 27 Feb. CAB 16/63; Cab. 12(25)2, 2 Mar 1925. CAB 23/49.
32. NP(25), 1st mtg, 2 Mar 1925. CAB 27/273.
33. Ibid, NP (25) 2nd mtg, 2 Mar 1925.
34. 198th and 199th mtg, CID, 30 Mar and 2 Apr 1925. CAB 2/4; see Gibbs, *Grand Strategy*, I, pp. 50–1 and Roskill, *Naval Policy*, vol. 1, p. 450, where this is seen as a new application of the Ten Year Rule.
35. Ibid, p. 451.
36. Memo by DOP, 16 Apr 1926. ADM 116/2416.
37. Ibid, memo by Savile, 21 June 1926, Min. by Controller, 14 July 1926.
38. Adm. Bd. Min., 15 July 1926. ADM 167/73; See Adm. to Sec CID, 16 July 1926. ADM 116/2416.
39. Hankey to Trenchard, 23 June 1926. AIR 8/70, Part 1, file 2.
40. SP (25), 7th mtg, 20 July 1926. CAB 16/63.
41. 215th mtg, CID, 22 July 1926. CAB 2/4; Cab 50(26)1, 3 Aug 1926. CAB 23/52.

CHAPTER 3 'A BAIT TO CATCH SOME MONEY'

1. Summary of Adm. Recommendations, para. 10, encl. in Report of Committee on arrangements for Imp. Conf. 4 Feb 1921. ADM 1/8611/151.
2. 141st mtg, CID, 13 June 1921. CAB 2/3; Cab. 16 June 1921. CAB 23/286, p. 51.
3. Summary in Street to Hankey 11 July 1921, CAB 21/187.
4. *Imp. Conf. 1921.* 26th mtg; 19 July 1921. CAB 32/2, part 2.
5. Min. by Pound, 14 Mar 1923 on U.-Sec. Cols to Sec. Adm. 7 Mar 1923; Adm. to CO 16 Mar 1923. ADM 116/3149.
6. SS Cols to Govs. Gen. Doms(119) 27 Mar 1923. Copy in CAB 5/5.
7. Reported to 168th mtg, CID, 14 Dec 1922. CAB 2/3.
8. Adm. to CO, 21 Feb 1923; SS Cols to Gov. S. Setts 26 Feb 1923; Min. by Grindle, 26 Feb 1923. CO 273/524, pp. 4–6.
9. Min. by Gent, 3 May on Gov. S. Setts to SS Cols, 3 May 1923. CO 273/522, p. 111.
10. Note by Green on Adm. to WO 26 May 1923. CO 273/524.
11. *Proceedings of the Legislative Council of the Straits Settlements*, 1923, B-126, 3 Sept; B-160, 29 Oct; B-220, 17 Dec.
12. Mins. by Pound, 19 June, Beatty, 2 July 1923 on CO letter 13 June. ADM 116/3149.
13. Letter of protest from Sir Frank Swettenham, *The Times*, 19 July 1923, p. 8, and reply and regret from Linlithgow, 20 July 1923, p. 8.
14. E. K. Bowden (Def. Min) to Bruce 30 Apr 1923; CG Aust to SS Cols, 7 May 1923. Australian Archives, Canberra: A 981/350(II).
15. GG S.Af. to SS Cols 18 May 1923. Copy in CAB 5/5.
16. Min. by Jellicoe, 10 May 1923 on SS Cols to GG NZ, 27 Mar 1923. National Archives, Wellington, NA 10/2.

17. *Lyttelton Times*, 6 June 1923, p. 6; *New Zealand Parliamentary Debates* (NZPD), 1923, 200, p. 599; Jellicoe to SS Cols 16 July 1923, CO 532/237.
18. *Imp. Conf. 1921* 11th mtg, 22 Oct 1923, p. 8; Amery to Massey, 22 Dec 1923. Copy in ADM 116/3149.
19. *Commonwealth Parliamentary Debates*, 27 Mar 1924, 106, p. 73.
20. Paul Hasluck, *The Government and the People 1939–41* (Canberra: Australian War Memorial, 1952), p. 30.
21. Gov. HK to SS Cols, 25 Nov 1924. CO 129/485 file 55247.
22. Ibid, Amery to Bridgeman, 2 Dec 1924; Bridgeman to Amery, 5 Dec 1924.
23. Min. by Grindle, 17 Dec 1924 on Gov. HK to SS Cols, 16 Dec 1924. CO 129/485.
24. Treas, to CO 22 Dec; W-Evans to Amery 23 Dec 1924. CO 129/485; WO to CO 9 Feb 1925. Grindle to WO, 16 Feb 1925. CO 129/491.
25. Note by Bell, 6 Dec 1924 with SS Cols to GGNZ 4 Dec 1924. NZPM 455/7/1/1.
26. Beatty to Lady Beatty, 1 Feb 1925. Chalmers, *Life and Letters*, p. 405.
27. 'Invitation to India to help in creating of the Singapore Dockyard', India Office Records: Financial Collections 2, Adm. file 3, F/6476/1923.
28. *India Legislative Assembly Debates*, 1925, vol. 5, part 1, no. 432; vol. 6, part 1, no. 80; 1926, vol. 7, part 1, no. 76. See also summary in Sir Stuart Brown (IO) to Lt. Col. Macready (CID) 10 Oct 1930. CAB 21/335.
29. 5 *Hansard* 1926, vol. 192, cols. 57–8.
30. Maxwell to Guillemard, 27 Feb 1926, encl. *Malay Mail*, 25 Feb CO 717/48, file C8496.
31. Ibid, Guillemard to Lee, 9 Mar 1926.
32. Amery to Bridgeman 24 Mar; Bridgeman to Amery 25 Mar 1926. CO 717/52.
33. Ibid, Mins. by Clutterbuck 22 Mar, Grindle 23 Mar, Wilson 24 Mar on Guillemard's tel. 21 Mar 1926; Amery to Guillemard 1 Apr 1926.
34. Wilson to Murray, Sec. Adm. 30 Apr 1926. CO 717/48.
35. *Proceedings of the Federal Council of the Federated Malay States*, 1926, 23 June, B36–7.
36. Guillemard to Amery, 28 July 1926. CO 717/53.
37. Adm. Bd. Mins. 15 July 1926. ADM 167/73; Sec. Adm. to Sec. CID, 16 July 1926. ADM 116/2416.
38. *Imp. Conf. 1926*. 1st mtg, 19 Oct 1926, p. 6.
39. Ibid, 9th mtg, 26 Oct 1926, p. 10.
40. W-Evans to Amery 8 July 1926; Amery to W-Evans 3 Aug 1926. WO 32/4568.
41. Min. by Beckett, 30 Sept 1926 on WO to CO 20 Sep 1926. CO 717/53, file CF 17859.
42. U.-Sec. CO to U.-Sec. WO 13 Oct 1926. WO 32/4568.
43. W-Evans to Amery 27 Oct 1926; Guillemard to Amery, 16 Dec 1926. CO 717/53, file CF 17859.
44. Amery to W-Evans 20 Jan 1927. WO 32/4568.
45. Plans Div. memo 19 Oct 1926 on DO to Adm. 12 Aug 1926. ADM 116/2247.
46. Undated notes with Hotham's submissions. NZPM 87/2/1 Part I.
47. Ibid, Churchill to Coates 13 Dec 1926; Coates to Churchill 15 Dec 1926.
48. *The Press*, Christchurch, 26 Apr 1927, p. 13.
49. John A. Lee; *NZPD*, 1927, 214, p. 257.
50. Ibid, Harry Holland, pp. 259–64, Ward pp. 274–6, Jones, p. 284, Henry Holland, p. 286.

51. Treas. to CO, 22 Apr 1927. Copy in DO 35/24, p. 465.
52. Specification issued to companies for completion of Tenders, Nov 1927. ADM 1/8967.
53. Parr to PM, 12 Dec 1927. NZPM 455/7/1 Part 1.
54. 236th mtg, CID 5 July 1928, CAB 2/5; Cab. 18 July 1928 printed as CID 896-B, CAB 4/17; Gibbs, *Grand Strategy*, I, p. 58.
55. Parr to Coates, Confid. 13 July 1928. NZPM 455/7/1 Part II; Ryrie to Bruce. Pers. and Secret 19 July 1928. AA: A 981/331 (I).
56. Discussion in SP (25) 8th mtg, 10 July 1928. Decision in SP (25) 22. CAB 16/63.
57. 239th mtg, CID, 13 Dec 1928. CAB 2/5. Cab. Concl. 58(28) 13, 1928. CAB 23/59.

CHAPTER 4 'GUNS V AIR'

1. Memo, 15 July 1925. AIR 8/70, Part 1, file 1.
2. SP (25) 6th mtg, 15 Oct 1925. CAB 16/63; 34th COS, 22 June 1926. CAB 53/1.
3. H. Montgomery Hyde, *British Air Policy Between the Wars 1918–1939* (London: Heinemann, 1976), p. 73.
4. 'Aerial Defence of New Zealand', by A. Vere Bettington, 5 June 1919, p. 3 (National Archives, Wellington).
5. Hyde, *Air Policy*, p. 64.
6. 'Handbook dealing with the Military Aspects of Imperial Defence', May 1921. CID 142-C. CAB 5/4.
7. 'The Part of the Air Force in the future of Imperial Defence', Mar 1921. CID 135-C. CAB 5/4.
8. Ibid, 'Air Defence and suggested lines of Development for Dominion Air Forces', Feb 1921. CID 132-C.
9. 'Singapore. Development of a Naval Base', 7 June 1921. ODC 501M, also as *Imp. Conf. 1921*, E.18, p. 9.
10. Sec. WO to Sec. Adm., 3 Sep 1921. ADM 116/2100.
11. 261st mtg ODC, 30 Nov 1922. CAB 7/9; CID 182-C, 7 Dec 1922. CAB 5/5.
12. 167th mtg CID, 6 Dec 1922. CAB 2/3.
13. Ibid, 168th mtg CID, 14 Dec 1922.
14. U.-Sec. WO to Sec. Adm. 14 June 1923. ADM 116/2397.
15. Mins. of Naval Staff conference, 15 May 1923; Sec. Adm. to Sec. WO, 21 Nov 1923. ADM 116/2349.
16. Cab. 21 Feb 1923. CAB 23/45.
17. CID 169-C, 30 May 1922. CAB 5/4.
18. Pieced together from: Camberley Exercise, Mar 1923. ADM 116/2394; Notes on the Defence of Singapore, Dec 1923. AIR 9/38/5; Singapore. Summary of Actions as regards air defence, May 1924. AIR 9/38/6; Sec. WO to Sec. ODC [n.d.] WO 32/3624; 263rd mtg ODC, 21 July 1924. CAB 7/9; ODC 132, 17 June 1924. CAB 8/9.
19. Air Min. to WO 4 Sept 1923 (copy). ADM 116/2394; 'Aircraft in the Far East', by T. R. Cave, Apl 1924. AIR 9/38/3.
20. Churchill to Hoare, 12 Dec 1924. AIR 8/70, Part 1, file 4.
21. Trenchard to Hoare, 23 Dec and 31 Dec 1924. AIR 8/70, Part 2, file 10.

22. Notes on the Composition of the Singapore Garrison, 23 Dec 1924. AIR 9/38.
23. 16th mtg COS, 24 Feb 1925; 18th mtg COS, 5 May; 19th mtg COS, 19 May; 20th mtg COS, 23 June; 21st mtg COS 3 July 1925. CAB 53/1.
24. Memo for PM, 15 July 1925. AIR 8/70, Part 1, file 1.
25. SP (25) 5th mtg, 27 July 1925; 6th mtg, 15 Oct 1925. CAB 16/63. Hyde, *Air Policy*, pp. 156-7, following Andrew Boyle, *Trenchard. Man of Vision*. (London: Collins, 1962), pp. 552-4, puts the meeting at mid-July, which was when Trenchard wrote his memorandum.
26. See exchange of letters between Beatty and Trenchard, Mar 1926. AIR 8/70, Part 1, file 5.
27. Memo by Trenchard, 12 May 1926. Printed in CAB 5/6; Min. by Wing Cdr. Portal, 26 May 1926. AIR 8/70, Part 1, file 4.
28. Ibid, including map. See also Boyle, *Trenchard*, pp. 555-7.
29. 34th mtg COS, 22 June 1926. CAB 53/1. The plan clearly did not go 'undebated', as Boyle (p. 557) suggests. On Trenchard's failure to guarantee the presence of his squadrons, see Sir John Slessor, *The Central Blue. Recollections and Reflections*. (London: Cassell, 1956) pp. 74-5.
30. Hankey to Trenchard. Personal, 23 June 1926. AIR 8/70, Part 1, file 2.
31. 35th mtg COS, 6 July 1926. CAB 53/1.
32. Boyle, *Trenchard*, p. 557.
33. Admitted later at 62nd mtg COS, 24 Nov 1927. CAB 53/2.
34. Singapore. Defences. CID 304-C. CAB 5/6.
35. Roskill, *Hankey*, II, p. 446; 62nd mtg COS, 24 Nov 1927. CAB 53/2.
36. Singapore. Scale of Attack, 7 Mar 1928. CID 312-C. CAB 5/7; after draft discussed at 66th mtg COS, 1 Mar 1928. CAB 53/2.
37. Interim Report of results of Coast Defence practices held in 1928. Appdx to 78th mtg COS, 11 June 1929. CAB 53/2.
38. 239th mtg CID, 13 Dec 1928. CAB 2/15; Cab. 19 Dec 1928. CAB 23/59.
39. 78th mtg COS, 11 June 1929. CAB 53/2. MacDonald did not attend the full meeting, only met the COS subcommittee and told them to continue in existence.
40. Hankey to Trenchard 11 June 1929; min. by Slessor, 13 June; Trenchard to Hankey 13 June. AIR 8/102/8.
41. On Trenchard's 'swan song' and the ill-will it generated among the services, see Hyde, *Air Policy*, pp. 230-1; Slessor, *Central Blue*, pp. 70-5, and Roskill, *Hankey*, II, p. 448.

CHAPTER 5 'SLOWED DOWN AS MUCH AS POSSIBLE'

1. Opening address, *The Times*, 13 May 1929, p. 10; Baldwin at Plymouth, Ibid, 14 May, p. 9; MacDonald at Newcastle, Ibid, 29 May, p. 9.
2. Ibid, 31 May 1930, p. 12.
3. Marquand, *Ramsay MacDonald*, pp. 499-509. See below pp. 93-5.
4. Adm. Bd. Min. 2589, 3 June 1929. ADM 167/79.
5. Memo by First Lord, 21 June 1929. CP 162(29). CAB 24/204.
6. FS (29) 2nd mtg, 28 June 1929 (a heading only). CAB 27/407.
7. 1st Report of FS Comm., 6 July 1929. CP 195(29). CAB 24/204.
8. Batterbee to Vansittart, 8 July 1929, PREM 1/67; Circular tel. A27, 7 July 1929, to Gov. Gen. NZ in NZPM 455/7/1/2; to Gov. Gen. Aust. in AA. A981/350 (III).

Notes 259

9. Ibid, Decode of tel. from Casey, 8 July 1929.
10. Memo, 9 July enclosed in Hankey to MacDonald, 8 July 1929. CAB 21/335.
11. Notes on Hankey's memo of 8 July in PREM 1/67.
12. Noted in 'Defence of Singapore', 15 July 1929. CID 336-C, CAB 5/7.
13. 79th mtg, COS, 16 July 1929. CAB 53/5.
14. Decode of tel. from Casey, 17 July 1929. AA: A 981/350 (III).
15. Circular B 95, 19 July 1925, to PM Aust. Ibid., and to Gov. Gen. NZ NZPM 455/7/1/2.
16. Decode of tel. from Casey, 20 July 1929. AA: A981/350 (III).
17. Parr to PM, 23 July 1929. NZPM 455/7/1/Part 2.
18. 244th mtg CID, 25 July 1929. CAB 2/5.
19. Memo for Gov. Gen., 9 Aug 1929. NZPM 455/7/1/2.
20. Adm. Memo, 16 Sept 1929. C.P.243(29). CAB 24/205; Cab. 25 Sept CAB 23/61.
21. 2nd Report of FS Comm., 22 Oct 1929. CP 291(29). CAB 24/206; Cab., 6 Nov 1929. CAB 23/62; 5 *Hansard*, 1929–30, 231, vol. 2012.
22. SSDA to Gov. Gen. NZ 12 Nov 1929; Memo by Wilford for Gov. Gen. 13 Nov. NZPM 455/7/1/3; Cab. 13 Nov. CAB 23/62.
23. Memo by Wilford for Gov. Gen. 14 Nov 1929. PMNZ 455/7/1/3.
24. Decode of tel. from Casey, 15 Nov 1929. AA: A981/350 (III).
25. Min. of Adm. Conf., 18 Nov 1929. WO 32/3631. Details of work affected in Adm. Conf. 11 Feb 1932. ADM 116/3615.
26. Nicols to Dixon, 28 Nov 1929. CP 16(30). CAB 24/209.
27. *Commonwealth Parliamentary Debates*, 1929, 122, p. 67.
28. 5 *Hansard*, 1929–30, 232, Col. 35.
29. See David Carlton, *MacDonald versus Henderson. The Foreign Policy of the Second Labour Government* (London: Macmillan, 1970), chs 5 and 6; Raymond G. O'Connor, *Perilous Equilibrium. The United States and the London Naval Conference of 1930* (New York: Greenwood, 1969), chs 4 and 5; Roskill, *Naval Policy*, II, pp. 37–50; Roskill, *Hankey*, II, pp. 510–19.
30. Text in O'Connor, pp. 129–44.
31. Memo for PM, 4 Aug 1930, 'Disarmament Conferences – Washington (1921–22) to London (1930), p. 21. NZ Archives: Navy NA 22/4/13, Part 1.
32. Memo by Lord President, 14 May 1930 C.P. 165(30). CAB 24/212.
33. Passfield to PM, 20 May 1930. PREM 1/152.
34. FS (29) 10th mtg, 22 May 1930. CAB 27/407; Report, 23 May. CP 173(30). CAB 24/212; Cab. 28 May 1930. CAB 23/64.
35. Casey to Scullin, 5 June 1930. AA: A981/331 (II).
36. 'The Singapore Base', 4 June 1930. CID 346-C. CAB 5/7; Duff to PM 20 June, Duff to Hankey 23 June, Hankey to Duff 25 June, and Note by MacDonald, 27 June. PREM 1/152; Roskill, *Hankey*, II, pp. 497–8.
37. Waterfield to K. Lyon (WO), 31 July 1930. WO 32/3632.
38. Ibid, Waterfield to J. B. Crosland, 25 Sept 1930.
39. Min. of Def. Council, 11 Apl 1930. Copy in *Imperial Conference 1930*, memos for Delegates AA: A 981/126, file 9.
40. Ibid, *Imp. Conf. 1930*. 'Singapore – The Need for an Empire Naval Base.'
41. Tel. read out 26 Feb 1930 at International Subcommittee of the Executive Council. Mins of International Subcommittee. Transport House.
42. Comm. Comdg. NZ Station to Naval Sec. 16 June 1930. NZ Archives:

NZ 22/4/13; Memo for Min. of Def., 8 Aug 1930. NZPM 455/7/1/3.
43. Cab., 15 Oct 1930. CAB 23/65.
44. E(S.B.) 1st mtg, 16 Oct 1930. NZPM 455/7/1/Part 3. Report of Committee on Singapore, 27 Oct 1930. CID 354-C. CAB 5/7.
45. Hankey to Thomson, 27 Oct; Hankey to Batterbee (DO), 27 Oct; Hankey to PM, 28 Oct 1930. CAB 21/414.
46. 251st mtg CID 28 Nov 1930. CAB 2/5.
47. 94th mtg COS 22 Oct 1930. CAB 53/3.
48. Ibid, 95th mtg COS 4 Dec 1930.
49. COS 262/CID 358-C, 11 Mar 1931. CAB 5/7.
50. Sec. of State to Gov. Fergusson, 5 Nov 1929; Maj-Gen Sinclair-Burgess to Min. of Def. 21 Feb 1930; Cab. Min. 14 Aug 1930. NZPM 86/5/1-Part 1.
51. Gen Milne to 89th mtg COS, 1 May 1930. CAB 53/3; Appreciation of General Naval Situation in 1931, 10 Apr 1930. CAB 24/220; CID 1048-B, 27 Apr 1931. CAB 4/21.

CHAPTER 6 'THE WRITING ON THE WALL'

1. See R. Bassett, *Nineteen Thirty-One. Political Crisis* (London: Macmillan, 1958); Robert J. A. Skidelsky, *Politicians and the Slump. The Labour Government of 1929–31* (London: Macmillan, 1967); Marquand, *MacDonald*, chs 25–6.
2. Draft terms of ref. in CAB 21/358; appointed at 259th mtg CID, 7 Dec 1931.
3. Adm. Bd. Min., 10 Dec 1931. ADM 167/83.
4. See especially Christopher Thorne, *The Limits of Foreign Policy. The West, the League and the Far Eastern Crisis of 1931–1933* (London: Macmillan, 1972). See also R. Bassett, *Democracy and Foreign Policy. A Case History. The Sino-Japanese Dispute, 1931–33*. (London: Longmans, Greene, 1952; Cass, 1968), and Louis, *British Strategy in the Far East*, ch. 6.
5. Clementi to SS Cols 18 Oct 1931; Stephenson (DO) to Macready (CID), 11 Jan 1932. CAB 21/402.
6. Thorne, *Limits of Foreign Policy*, pp. 206–10; Louis, *British Strategy*, pp. 184–5.
7. 101st mtg COS, 4 Feb 1932. CAB 53/4.
8. Memo by First Lord, 5 Feb 1932. CP 64 (32). CAB 24/228; Thorne, pp. 241–2.
9. Cab. 10 Feb 1932. CAB 23/70.
10. DCOS 1/COS 295 (DC), 22 Feb 1932. CAB 53/22; considered at 102nd mtg COS, 29 Feb 1932. CAB 53/4; circulated as CID 1084-B. CAB 4/21.
11. COS Annual Review. CID 1082-B, 23 Feb 1932. CAB 4/21.
12. Ibid, CID 1087-B, 11 Mar 1932.
13. Cab. 23 Mar 1932. CAB 23/70; see also Gibbs, *Grand Strategy*, I, pp. 80–2. Roskill, *Hankey*, II, 537–8, argues that the Ten Year Rule did not lapse until Nov 1933, but the Cabinet agreed, in sending the reports to the Ministerial Committee on the Disarmament Conference, 'That in considering the Reports the Committee could assume the abandonment' of the 10 year rule. CAB 23/70, p. 392.
14. Mins. by Hunter, 11 Feb 1932; Backhouse 13 Feb 1932. ADM 116/3615.
15. Adm. Bd. Min, 2929, 17 Mar 1932. ADM 167/85.
16. Mins. by Savile, 14 Apl 1932 and Cunningham 20 Apl 1932. ADM 116/3615.
17. CD, 2nd mtg, 25 Feb 1932, and 6th mtg, 25 Apl 1932. CAB 16/105.
18. Ibid, 3rd mtg, 3 Mar 1932.

54. Roskill, *War at Sea*, I, p. 557; Gwyer, *Grand Strategy*, vol. IV, Part I, p. 273.
55. Bernard Ash, *Someone had Blundered. The Story of the 'Repulse' and the 'Prince of Wales'* (London: Michael Joseph, 1960), p. 152. It also had the war correspondents 'sizzling with rage'. Cecil Brown, *Suez to Singapore* (New York: Random House, 1942), p. 277.
56. Roskill, *War at Sea*, I, ch. 26; Gwyer, *Grand Strategy*, III, Part I, p. 274.

CHAPTER 10 'A CLOSE RUN THING'

1. Ivan Simson, *Singapore: Too Little, Too Late. Some Aspects of the Malayan Disaster* (London: Leo Cooper, 1970), ch. 3.
2. See Nobutaka Ike (Ed.) *Japan's Decision for War. Records of the 1941 Policy Conferences*, (Stanford: U.P. 1967); Stephen E. Pelz, *Race to Pearl Harbor. The Failure of the Second London Naval Conference and the Onset of World War II* (Cambridge, Mass; Harvard U.P., 1974); Robert J. C. Butow, *Tojo and the Coming of the War* (Princeton: U.P., 1961); Feis, *Road to Pearl Harbor*.
3. Pelz, *Race to Pearl Harbor*, p. 173.
4. John Deane Potter, *Admiral of the Pacific. The Life of Yamamoto* (London: Heinemann, 1965), ch. 6.
5. Pelz, *Race to Pearl Harbor*, p. 224.
6. Ike, *Japan's Decision*, p. 133.
7. Ibid, p. 238. General Tojo: 'We have some uneasiness about a protracted war. But how can we let the United States continue to do as she pleases, even though there is some uneasiness?'
8. Feis, *Road to Pearl Harbor*, p. 332.
9. Churchill, *Second World War*, III, pp. 538–40.
10. Ibid, p. 547.
11. C-in-C Far East to WO (108) 13 Dec 1941. (CAB 105/20) lists 166 planes; Douglas Gillison, *Royal Australian Air Force 1939–1942* (Canberra: Australian War Memorial, 1962), pp. 204–5 puts it at 164; the most commonly cited figure is 158 aircraft: e.g., Brooke-Popham's despatch, 28 May 1942. Supp. to *London Gazette*, 20 Jan 1948 [38183] p. 574; Churchill, *Second World War*, IV, p. 858; Kirby, *War Against Japan*, p. 511. The difference arises because Gillison counts the photo-recce. *Beaufort* at Kota Bahru, and 2 photo-recce *Buffaloes* and 3 Dutch *Catalinas* at Singapore. There were 86 reserve planes. Gen. Percival (who also includes spotter bi-planes) in a rough list gives the total as 141. Desp., 25 Apr 1946. Supp. to *London Gazette*, 26 Feb 1948 [38215], para. 108.
12. Gillison, p. 224, gives 534 as the Japanese total; Kirby, p. 524, gives 560, and Masanobu Tsuji, *Singapore, the Japanese Version* (Sydney: Ure Smith, 1960), p. 38, gives 617.
13. Kirby, p. 163, lists 31 battalions (which is arrived at by counting one battn. of the Malay Regiment, but not five units of Indian State Forces or forces from the Unfederated Malay States). Lieut. General Pownall in Appendix D of Churchill's *Second World War*, IV, p. 838 gives 32 battalions. He probably counted the second battn. of the Malay Regiment, which was formed in 1941.
14. See D. Ramli, 'History of the Malay Regiment, 1933–1942, *Journal of the Malayan Branch of the Royal Asiatic Society* (1965), **38**(1), 199–243.

15. John Smythe, *Percival and the Tragedy of Singapore* (London: Macdonald, 1971), p. 80.
16. Kirby, *Singapore: Chain of Disaster*, p. 131. See also H. Gordon Bennett, *Why Singapore Fell* (Sydney: Angus and Robertson, 1944), p. 19.
17. A. E. Percival, supp. to *London Gazette*, 26 Feb 1948 [38215], para 114 and *The War in Malaya* (London: Eyre & Spottiswoode, 1949), p. 101. He may have borrowed the idea from Bennett; See *Why Singapore Fell*, pp. 45-6.
18. This figure is from Louis Allen, *Singapore 1941-1942* (London: Davis-Poynter, 1977), p. 120. Kirby, *War Against Japan*, I, p. 527 says 17,230 combat troops came ashore in the 'first flight' at Singora, Patani and Kota Bahru.
19. Tsuji, *Singapore, the Japanese Version*, pp. 36-7, 183. Allen in 'Singapore', ch. 12, Noble Frankland and Christopher Dowling, *Decisive Battles of the Twentieth Century* (London: Sidgwick Jackson, 1976), p. 156, uses the figure 62,200. Kirby, *War Against Japan*, I, p. 527 gives a figure of 67,660 combat troops at the outset of the assault on Singapore Island, but 110,660 if service troops and air forces are added.
20. Charles McCormac, *You'll Die at Singapore* (London: Robert Hale, 1954) p. 21.
21. Kirby, *War Against Japan*, I, 518-19.
22. Report of CNS on visit to Singapore circulated 22 Dec 1941. NA 22/4/46. (National Archives, Wellington.)
23. The fullest discussion of the Thailand issue is in Allen, *Singapore 1941-1942*, chs 4-6.
24. FE (41) 5th mtg, 30 Jan 1941. CAB 96/2.
25. Ibid, FE (41) 9th mtg, 27 Feb 1941.
26. JP (41) 3 Aug 1941, considered by COS, 5 Aug 1941. CAB 79/13.
27. COS (41) 324th mtg, 16 Sept 1941. CAB 79/14.
28. The fullest account is K. D. Bhargava and K. N. V. Sastri, *Campaigns in South-East Asia 1941-2* (Combined Inter-Services Historical Section India and Pakistan, 1960), pp. 121-38. Tsuji, *Singapore, the Japanese Version*, p. 96, calls it 'one of the most violent actions of the Malayan campaign'.
29. See the moving account in Martin Middlebrook and Patrick Mahoney, *Battleship: the Loss of the 'Prince of Wales' and 'Repulse'* (London: Allen Lane, 1977).
30. C-in-C Far East to WO (for COS Committee), 8 Dec 1941. CAB 105/20.
31. For the best account of the air war see Gillison, *RAAF 1939-1942*, pp. 208-24.
32. Tsuji, *Singapore, the Japanese Version*, pp. 125-8.
33. A. O. Robinson, 'The Malayan Campaign in the Light of the Principles of War', *Journal of the R. United Service Institution* (1964), **109**(635), 232.
34. COS (40) 412th and 413th mtgs, 8 Dec 1941. CAB 79/16.
35. Ibid, Ismay at COS (41) 421st mtg, 13 Dec 1941.
36. Tels. C-in-C Far East to WO (108) 13 Dec; (158) 17 Dec 1941. CAB 105/20.
37. Copy of Conf. report, 18 Dec 1941. NA/22/4/25. (National Archives, Wellington.)
38. C-in-C E. Fleet to Adm., (100) 13 Dec; Adm. to C-in-C E. Fleet (118) 14 Dec 1941. CAB 105/20.
39. COS (41) 422nd mtg, 15 Dec 1941. CAB 79/16.
40. 'Future British Naval Strategy', 14 Dec 1941. COS (41) 277(o) and COS (41) 280(o), 20 Dec 1941. CAB 80/60. Discussed at COS (41) 429th mtg, 20 Dec 1941. CAB 79/16.
41. Wigmore, *Japanese Thrust*, p. 154; Hasluck, *Government and People*, II, p. 28; Churchill, *Second World War*, III, p. 565; COS (41) 429th mtg, 20 Dec 1941. CAB 79/16.

25. Memo by Butler 23 Nov; FE Committee 10th mtg, 28 Nov 1940. CAB 96/1.
26. Alexander to Pound, 27 Nov 1940. ADM 1/10865.
27. PM Aust. to PM NZ, 1 Dec 1940; 37th mtg, NZ COS Committee, 6 Dec 1940. NA 22/4/43. (National Archives, Wellington.)
28. Combined Far East Appreciation, 13 Feb 1941. Australian War Memorial, 243/5/36; Advisory War Council, 14 Feb 1941. Hasluck, *Government and the People 1939–41*, pp. 328–9; Gill, *Royal Australian Navy, 1939–42*, p. 425. On Brooke-Popham, see Lowe, *Britain and the Origins of the Pacific War*, p. 187 and Callahan, *Worst Disaster*, pp. 66–8.
29. Report of Anglo-Dutch-Australian Conference, Singapore, 22–5 Feb 1941. AIR 2/5308 and NZPM 81/10/13 Part 1; Hasluck, *Government and People 1934–41*, p. 329; Lowe, pp. 201–2.
30. Hasluck, p. 296.
31. ABC, 1st session, 31 Jan 1941. CAB 99/5; Lowe, pp. 191–7.
32. ABC, 3 Feb 1941 and 10 Feb 1941. CAB 99/5.
33. Leutze, *Bargaining for Supremacy*, pp. 241–2.
34. BUS (J) 13, para 2. Discussed at ABC, 26 Feb 1941. CAB 99/5.
35. ABC-1, Report, 27 Mar 1941. CAB 99/8.
36. DO (41) 12th mtg, 9 Apr 1941; 20th mtg, 29 Apr 1941. CAB 69/2.
37. JP(41)288, 13 Apr; COS(41) 133rd mtg, 14 Apr 1941. CAB 79/10.
38. Ibid, JP(41)291, 14 Apr; COS (41) 137th mtg, 17 Apr 1941.
39. ADB Report, 27 Apr 1941. NZPM 81/10/13, Part 2; see also JP(41) 371 on telegraphic summary of Conference, 13 May 1941. CAB 79/11; Morison, *Rising Sun*, pp. 53–5; Lowe, *Britain and the Origins of the Pacific War*, pp. 203–6.
40. BD Report, 27 Apr 1941. NZPM 81/10/13, Part 2; Plans for Employment of Naval and Air Force of Associated Powers in Eastern Theatre (PLENAPS), 27 Apr 1941, Copy in AIR 23/1873; Gill, *Royal Australian Navy 1939–42*, p. 431; Lowe, pp. 206–7.
41. JP(41)441, 9 June 1941. CAB 79/12.
42. Ibid, JP(41)444, 14 June 1941, discussed at COS(41)213d mtg, 16 June 1941.
43. Herbert Feis, *The Road to Pearl Harbor* (Princeton: University Press, 1950; New York: Atheneum, 1966), pp. 236–9; Irvine J. Anderson, 'The 1941 De Facto Embargo on Oil to Japan: A Bureaucratic Reflex', *Pacific Historical Review* (1975), pp. 201–31.
44. Feis, *Road to Pearl Harbour*, pp. 257–8.
45. Pound's memo, 25 Jan 1942 on loss of *Prince of Wales* and *Repulse*. PREM 3/163/2, a survey of correspondence; Stephen W. Roskill, *The War at Sea 1939–45*, vol. I (London: HMSO, 1954), pp. 554–5; Gill, *Royal Australian Navy 1939–42*, pp. 442–3.
46. The correspondence is in PREM 3/163/3.
47. C-in-C Far East to WO, 1 Oct 1941. At COS(41)348 the mtg, 9 Oct 1941. CAB 79/14; Page, *Truant Surgeon*, p. 302.
48. Ibid, p. 306. Page says here he was told of the despatch of the *Prince of Wales* and *Repulse*, but the decision had not yet been taken.
49. DO (41) 65th mtg, 17 Oct 1941. CAB 69/8.
50. DO (41) 66th mtg, 20 Oct 1941. CAB 69/8.
51. Churchill to PMNZ, 2 Nov 1941. PREM 3/163/3.
52. War Cab. 5 Nov 1941. 109(41)2. CAB 65/20.
53. Ibid, War Cab. 12 Nov 1941 112(41)1.

43. Leutze, *Bargaining for Supremacy*, pp. 129–30.
44. War Cab. 17 and 18 Apr 1940. CAB 65/6.
45. War Cab. 13 June 1940. CAB 65/7.
46. Circular Z 106, 14 June, para 8. *New Zealand War Documents*, III, p. 206.

CHAPTER 9 'KITH AND KIN'

1. For the background to the Japanese moves, see below pp. 189–92.
2. NZ *Documents*, III, pp. 206–7.
3. 'Immediate Measures Required in the Far East' 25 June 1940. COS (40) 493/WP(40) 222, and draft cable. CAB 69/9.
4. War Cab. 26 June 1940. 183(40)13. CAB 65/7.
5. Hollis to Ismay, 3 July 1940; Ismay to Bruce 3/4 July 1940. CAB 21/893. Discussed at 209th mtg COS, 5 July 1940 CAB 79/5.
6. War Cab. 22 July 1940. 209(40)5. CAB 65/8. For Japanese trade demands see H. J. van Mook, *The Netherlands Indies and Japan. Their Relations, 1940–1941* (London: Allen & Unwin, 1944), pp. 27–37.
7. Gort at 226th mtg COS, 22 Dec 1937. CAB 53/8.
8. COS memo (4) 568/WP(40) 289, 27 July 1940. CAB 66/10; War Cab. 29 July 1940, 214(40)7. CAB 65/8.
9. 'The Situation in the Far East in the Event of Japanese intervention against us', 31 July 1940. COS(40)592. CAB 66/10.
10. Ibid, COS covering note, 31 July 1940; Note by Sec. of Cab., 5 Aug 1940.
11. Ibid, Annex I to 'Assistance to the Dutch in the Event of Japanese Aggression', COS(40)605/WP(40)308, 7 Aug 1940.
12. War Cab. 8 Aug. 1940. 222(4)4. Confid. annex. CAB 65/14.
13. Tel. to PM Aust. and PM NZ (copy to Smuts) 11 Aug 1940. CAB 65/14. There are various versions of this sentence, e.g. Churchill, *Second World War*, III, pp. 385–6; Butler, *Grand Strategy*, II, p. 334.
14. Hasluck, *Government and the People 1939–1941*, p. 224.
15. Comment on British Far East Appreciation, COS 51, 3 Sep 1940. NZPM 81/4/3 Part 2.
16. Churchill, *Second World War*, II, pp. 591–2.
17. WP(40) 364, 9 Sep 1940. CAB 66/11.
18. Decypher of tel. from Casey, 14 Oct 1940. AA: A981/331 Part III; Leutze, *Bargaining for Supremacy*, pp. 165–6.
19. FE(40) 1st mtg, 5 Oct 1940. Committee set up by War Cab. 2 Oct 1940. CAB 96/1.
20. 'Singapore Defence Conference, 1940', 31 Oct 1940. ADM 1/11183. See also Lowe, *Britain and the Origins of the Pacific War*, pp. 180–2.
21. Samuel Eliot Morison, *History of the United States Naval Operations in World War II*, Vol. III, *The Rising Sun in the Pacific 1931–April 1942* (Boston: Little, Brown, 1948), p. 53; Leutze, *Bargaining for Supremacy*, p. 172.
22. Tel. from C-in-C China, 28 Nov 1940. COS (40), 410th mtg, 30 Nov 1940. CAB 79/8.
23. Leutze, *Bargaining for Supremacy*, pp. 186–8; War Cab. 6 Nov 1940. 283(40)3. CAB 65/10.
24. Hasluck, *Government and the People 1939–41*, pp. 296, 298.

19. Ibid, 4th mtg, 10 Mar 1932.
20. Ibid, CD 20/CID 370-C, 24 May 1932.
21. Note by MacDonald, n.d. on Hankey to PM, 27 May 1932. CAB 21/358.
22. 103rd mtg, COS, 2 June 1932. CAB 53/4.
23. 256th mtg CID, 9 June 1932. CAB 2/5.
24. Eyres-Monsell to Hankey, 13 June 1932; Hankey to E-Monsell, 14 June 1932. ADM 116/3615.
25. Notes by Warren Fisher (Treas) 28 Jul 1932 and MacDonald, n.d. with 'Notes on the Singapore Naval Base'. PREM 1/152; Cab. 11 Oct 1932. CAB 23/72.
26. Arthur J. Marder, *From the Dardanelles to Oran* (London: Oxford University Press, 1974), p. 75.
27. 107th mtg COS, 28 Feb 1933. CAB 53/4.
28. Ibid, 108th mtg COS, 27 Mar 1933.
29. COS 305/CID 1103-B, 31 Mar 1932. CAB 53/25, CAB 4/22.
30. Note for PM by Hankey, 5 Apr 1933. PREM 1/152, CAB 21/402.
31. Cab. 12 Apl 1933. CAB 23/75.
32. The evolution of *War Memo. (E)* is pieced together from: Report of Penang Conf. 1921. ADM 116/3100; *War Memo. (E)*, Aug 1924. ADM 116/3125; Memo on Passage of the Fleet to the Far East. ADM 116/3123; C-in-C E. Indies to Sec. Adm. 3 Sep 1925. ADM 116/2394; Revised *War Memo. (E)*, July 1931. ADM 116/3118; Revised *War Memo. (E)*, 1933. ADM 116/3475.
33. Corrigenda to *War Memo*, 10 Aug 1927. ADM 116/3125.
34. C-in-C China to Sec. Adm. 11 Jan 1928; Adm. to C-in-C China 3 May 1928. ADM 116/3126.
35. C-in-C E. Indies to Sec.'Adm. 3 Sep 1925. ADM 116/2394.
36. C-in-C China to Sec. Adm. 27 Jan 1932. ADM 116/3112.
37. Tels to C-in-C China 24 and 25 Apl 1933; Memo on Naval Dispositions in the Far East, 26 Apl 1933. ADM 116/2472.
38. Dreyer to Chatfield, 12 Dec 1933. National Maritime Museum. CHT/4/4.
39. Notes on 1934 Singapore Conf. by Adm. Dreyer, 29 Jan 1934. ADM 116/3121.
40. 111th mtg COS, 20 June 1933. CAB 53/4.
41. Annual Review. COS 310/CID 1113-B, 12 Oct 1933. CAB 4/22.
42. 261st mtg CID, 9 Nov 1933. CAB 2/6/(i); Hankey to PM 9 Nov 1933. CAB 21/434; Gibbs, *Grand Strategy*, 1, p. 86.
43. Cab., 15 Nov 1933. CAB 23/77. See also *Chief of Staff. The Diaries of Lieutenant-General Sir Henry Pownall*, Ed. Brian Bond, vol. I (London: Leo Cooper, 1972), pp. 24-5.
44. 3rd mtg, DRC, 4 Dec 1933. CAB 16/109. Fisher did the 'big thing' and withdrew an anti-American addendum he had contemplated, when Hankey persuaded him against it. Fisher to Hankey 17 Feb; Hankey to COS 17 Feb; and Hankey to Fisher 17 Feb 1934. CAB 21/432; Pownall, *Chief of Staff*, I, p. 36.
45. 1st Defence Requirements report. CID 1147-B, 28 Feb 1934. CAB 4/23.
46. DC(M) 32. The debate is here summarised from mtgs of 3 May, 25 June, 26 June, 24 July 1934. CAB 27/507. The Treasury view was outlined in DC(M) (32) 120, 20 June 1934. CAB 16/111.
47. Hankey to Lord Pres. 30 July and aide-memoire initialled S.B., 31 July 1934. CAB 63/66 and CAB 21/398. Hankey said his fears were roused at 'Friday's proceedings at the Ministerial Committee'. This would be 27 July, but no minutes seem to have been kept. Text of *aide-mémoire* in Ann Trotter, 'The Dominions and

Imperial Defence: Hankey's Tour in 1934', *J. of Imperial and Commonwealth History* (1974), **2**(3), 323, who implies that Chamberlain also initialled the paper. But Hankey to Chamberlain 1 Aug 1934 encloses a copy, which he said had been initialled by Baldwin, CAB 21/398.
48. Annual Review, 29 Apr 1935. COS 372/CID 1181-B para. 19. CAB 4/23.
49. Noted at 268th mtg CID, 25 Feb. 1935, CAB 2/6(1). This rare case of a Crown Colony legislature defeating the War Office can be followed in *Proc. of the Legis. Council of the Straits Setts.*, 1927–34, WO 32/4568–9, CO 717/53, CO 273/537, 546, 557, 560, 576, 580, 581, and CP 298(27). CAB 23/55.
50. Ibrahim to Windstedt, 27 Apl 1935. CO 717/112, file 51575.
51. Ibid, High Commissr. to SS Cols, 2 May 1935; Wigram to SS Cols, 1 May 1935; Tel. to High Commissr. 2 May 1935.
52. 146th mtg COS, 5 July 1935. CAB 53/5.
53. For details of the guns by an Australian officer, who was involved in the ordering and siting, see L. E. Beavis, 'The Defences of Singapore', *Stand-To* [Canberra] (1963), **8**(2), 7–9. The pair installed at Changi with the Sultan's gift was called the 'Johore Battery'.
54. 3rd mtg DPR, 18 July 1935. CAB 16/136; Cab. 24 July 1935. CAB 23/82.
55. JDC 222/COS 400/DPR 38, 1 Oct 1935. CAB 16/139.
56. 151st mtg COS, 4 Oct 1935. CAB 53/5.

CHAPTER 7 'THREATS AT BOTH ENDS OF THE EMPIRE'

1. Quoted in Marder, *Dardanelles to Oran*, p. 84.
2. For a good analysis of Chatfield's approach, see Lawrence R. Pratt, *East of Malta, West of Suez. Britain's Mediterranean Crisis, 1936–1939* (Cambridge: Cambridge University Press, 1975), pp. 22–4.
3. CID 1113-B, 12 Oct 1933, para 29. CAB 4/22.
4. NCM (35)1, 23 Mar 1934, para 3. CAB 29/148 and 16/111.
5. Ibid, para 11, in italic in original; a large part of the text is published in Gibbs, *Grand Strategy*, I, pp. 118–20.
6. Ibid, p. 259.
7. The 3rd DRC report, 21 Nov 1935 (CAB 16/139) notes: 'Since 1932 the standard of naval strength has, for practical purposes been based on . . .' the formula quoted. The Adm. memo 'A New Standard of Naval Strength', 26 Apl 1937, (ADM 1/9081) also refers to 'the 1932 standard'.
8. See admission of Lawrence Burgis quoted in Roskill, *Hankey*, III, p. 21. I would endorse Gibb's comment (*Grand Strategy*, I, p. 371, n. 30): 'I have not . . . discovered the original statement of 1932 – if one was made'.
9. CID 1181-B, 29 Apl 1935, para 18. CAB 4/23.
10. Gibbs, *Grand Strategy*, I, p. 167.
11. Chatfield to Fisher (C-in-C Med), 25 Aug 1935. Quoted in Marder, *Dardanelles to Oran*, p. 83.
12. 149th mtg COS 6 Sep 1935. CAB 53/5, p. 178.
13. Marder, p. 99. See also Pratt, *East of Malta, West of Suez*, ch. 2.
14. DRC 17th mtg 10 Oct 1935. CAB 16/112.
15. Ibid, 18th mtg 14 Oct 1935.
16. DRC 37/DPR 52, 3rd report of DRC subcommittee, 21 Nov 1935, para 34.

CAB 16/139. The version suggested by Chatfield on 14 Oct was slightly less strongly worded.
17. 200th mtg COS, 5 Mar 1937. CAB 53/7.
18. 174th mtg COS, 13 May 1936, CAB 53/6.
19. Adm. Bd. Min. 26 Apr 1937. ADM 1/9081, and DP (P) 3, Memo by First Lord, 29 Apr 1937. CAB 16/182; See also Gibbs, *Grand Strategy*, I, pp. 339-43.
20. Hankey to Harding, 28 Nov 1934. CAB 63/70; Diary of Visits. CAB 63/67.
21. Report by Sir Maurice Hankey on certain aspects of Australian Defence, 15 Nov 1934 (PREM 1/174); Memos by Bruche, 5 Mar, and Laverack, 14 Mar 1935 in CAB 21/397; H. D. Wynter, 'Defence of Australia and its Relation to Imperial Defence', 1935, typescript in Nat. Lib. of Australia, Canberra. One para is common to Bruche and Wynter.
22. Debate on defence estimates, H. of Rep. 17 Sep 1936 *C.P.D.*, 1936, 151, p. 265.
23. Hankey to Dill, 2 Dec 1934. CAB 63/78.
24. Sinclair-Burgess to Hankey, 11 Feb 1936 and tel. 8 Aug 1936 (CAB 21/414) Gov. Gen. NZ to SSDA 1 June 1936 in SSDA to Inskip 8 June 1936. CAB 64/28. See also E. Olssen, *John A. Lee* (Dunedin: Univ. of Otago Press, 1977), pp. 87-8. Lee was a member of the committee.
25. Sinclair-Burgess to Min. of Def., 15 Dec 1936. NZPM 153/8/1-1.
26. Darvall's report on Visit to Far East, 27 Dec 1936. AIR 23/1971.
27. Report of AOC, Far East, 6 Mar 1937. AIR 9/38/68 and Air Staff comments, AIR 2/1886.
28. Suggested at 195th mtg COS, 5 Feb 1937. CAB 53/6; Para 17(i) of the Review in *Imp. Conf.* 1937 E(37)1.
29. Ibid, from paras 79-81.
30. 201st mtg COS, 16 Mar 1937. CAB 53/7.
31. Ibid, 204th mtg, COS, 6 May 1937.
32. Mins of DP(P) 2nd mtg 11 May 1937. CAB 16/181.
33. 207th mtg COS, 18 May 1937. CAB 53/7.
34. A brief analysis in R. Tamchina, 'In Search of Common Causes. The Imperial Conference of 1937', *J. of Imperial and Commonwealth Hist.* (1972), **1**(1), 79-105.
35. *Imp. Conf. 1937* E(P.D.) (37). 5th and 6th mtgs 24 and 25 May 1937.
36. Ibid, 7th mtg 26 May 1937. Printed in *Documents on Australian Foreign Policy 1937-49*, vol. I, *1937-38*, Ed. R. G. Neale (Canberra: Australian Government Publishing Service, 1975), pp. 84-90.
37. 208th mtg COS, 26 May 1937. CAB 53/7.
38. Far East Appreciation, COS 596, 14 June 1937. CAB 53/32 and 16/182. The paper began as COS 579(JP); the version given to the Aust, NZ and Indian delegates was COS 590.
39. Questions raised by NZ Delegates, COS 594, 4 June 1937. CAB 53/32; mins. of 209th mtg, COS, 1 June 1937. (CAB 53/7); printed in Neale, *Documents*, I, pp. 101-16; Questions raised by NZ Delegates, Report, 4 June 1937. CAB 53/32.
40. 211st mtg COS, 7 June 1937. CAB 53/7; The Strategic Importance of the Pacific Islands, 28 May 1937. COS 586/CID 1327-B discussed at the CID 17 June 1937. CAB 2/6 (2).
41. Questions raised by the Australian Delegates, Report, 9 June 1937, COS 595. CAB 53/32; 212th mtg, COS, 21 June 1937. CAB 53/7.
42. 296th mtg CID, 5 July 1937. CAB 2/6(2).
43. Chatfield to Backhouse, 8 Oct 1937. CHT/4/1. For the China War see: Peter

Lowe, *Great Britain and the Origins of the Pacific War. A Study in British Policy in East Asia 1937–1941* (Oxford: Clarendon Press, 1977); Bradford A. Lee, *Britain and the Sino-Japanese War, 1937–1939. A Study in the Dilemmas of British Decline* (London: Oxford University Press, 1973) and Nicholas Clifford, *Retreat from China: British Policy in the Far East 1937–41* (London: Longmans, 1967).

44. 312th CID, 4 Mar 1938. CAB 2/7. The earlier discussions were at 194th COS, 22 Jan 1937 (CAB 53/6), 200th COS, 5 Mar 1937. (CAB 53/7) and 292nd CID, 15 Apl 1937. CAB 2/6(2).

45. The Ingersoll-Phillips conversations were the first in the series of staff talks, which culminated in the ABC-1 agreement of 1941. See James R. Leutze, *Bargaining for Supremacy. Anglo-American Naval Collaboration 1937–1941* (Chapel Hill, N. C.: University of N. Carolina Press, 1977), pp. 23–5. For the record of the talks see L. Pratt, 'The Anglo-American Naval Conversations on the Far East of January 1938', *International Affairs* (1971), **47**(4), 757.

46. The Adm. file of correspondence on the arrangements 1937–38 in ADM 116/3664; *The Times*, 14 Feb 1938, pp. 11–14; Naval Base Supplement, *Singapore Free Press*, 14 Feb 1938. When Curtin (the ALP leader) asked in the Australian Parliament about the 18″ gun story, the Min. of Def. replied that the calibre of guns was secret information. *CPD*, 1938, 155, p. 569. The rumour arose, perhaps, because of the presence of the monitor HMS *Terror*, which had 15″ guns, but three monitors had, in fact, mounted 18″ guns in 1918.

47. Min. by Danckwerts, 22 Dec 1938. Exercise Reports in C-in-C China to Sec. Adm. 15 July 1938. ADM 1/9903.

48. Raymond Callahan, *The Worst Disaster. The Fall of Singapore* (Newark: University of Delaware Press; London: Associated University Presses, 1977), p. 70. 9 out of 18 completed or started radar stations were operational in Dec 1941. Sir Paul Maltby's despatch, 26 July 1947. Supp. to *London Gazette*, 26 Feb 1948 [28216], p. 1414.

49. A. W. S. Agar, *Footprints in the Sea* (London: Evans, 1959), p. 225. Agar says the exercise was solely to test the shore but not the air defences, but this is not supported by the exercise scenario and reports.

50. A. W. Tedder, *With Prejudice. The War Memoirs of Marshal of the Royal Air Force Lord Tedder G. C. B.* (London: Cassell, 1966) p. 7.

51. Arthur E. Percival, *The War in Malaya* (London: Eyre & Spottiswoode, 1949), pp. 17, 44; Kirby, *Singapore, the chain of Disaster*, p. 31; Louis Allen, *Singapore, 1941–42* (London: Davis-Poynter), p. 45.

52. Dobbie to Sec, WO 27 Jan 1938; GOC to WO, tel. 27 Oct 1938; GOC to WO 29 Oct and 2 Dec 1938. WO 32/9366.

53. 264th mtg COS, 14 Dec. 1938. CAB 53/10.

54. See C. M. Andrews, *Isolation and Appeasement in Australia. Reactions to the European Crisis, 1935–39* (Canberra: ANU Press, 1970); Ritchie Ovendale '*Appeasement*' *and the English-Speaking World* (Cardiff: University of Wales Press, 1975).

55. Hasluck, *Government and the People 1939–41*, pp. 102–3.

56. Australian Cooperation: Imperial Defence, 31 Mar 1938 JP 281/COS 703 (JP); New Zealand Cooperation in Imperial Defence, 31 Mar 1938. JP 282/COS 704 (JP). CAB 53/37; Day to Berendsen, 10 Mar 1938. NZPM 455/7/1/3.

57. 236th mtg COS, 13 Apr 1938. CAB 53/9.

58. Sir Cyril Newall to 267th mtg COS, 13 Jan 1939. CAB 53/10. In his memoirs Page said Chamberlain promised 4 battleships would be stationed at Singapore

within 90 days of war. (E. Page, *Truant Surgeon. The Inside Story of Forty Years of Australian Political Life* (Sydney: Angus and Robertson, 1963), p. 258), but COS 595, 9 June 1937, para 20 (CAB 53/32) included the figures from the *Far East Appreciation*: 1937/38–10, 1938/39–8, 1939/40–10, the actual capital ships being named. Chamberlain was probably referring to the planned arrival of the 1st battle squadron from the Mediterranean.
59. Chatfield to Page, 3 June 1939. Neale, *Documents*, I, pp. 368–9.
60. Speech on 27 Apl 1938. *C.P.D.*, 1938, vol. 155, p. 544. Copy in Acting UK High Commissioner to SSDA, 28 Apl 1938. DO 35/576.
61. Information given by Sir Roger Backhouse to 267th mtg COS, 13 Jan 1939. CAB 53/10.
62. Tel. Bruce to Lyons, 1 Nov 1938. Neale, *Documents*, I, p. 511. The 7 ships mentioned were *Nelson, Rodney* and 5 *Royal Sovereigns*.
63. Ibid, p. 512. Bruce to Lyons, 7 Nov 1938.
64. Whiskard to Harding, 28 Nov 1938. Copy enl. in Ismay to Newall, 22 Dec 1938. AIR 9/56/58.
65. Ibid, pp. 534–5. Stanhope to Bruce, 2 Dec 1938. Backhouse to Sec. CID 20 Dec 1938. COS 813, 22 Dec 1938. CAB 53/43.
66. 267th mtg COS, 13 Jan 1939. CAB 53/10.
67. The Strategic Importance of the Pacific Islands, 13 July 1938. COS 748, CAB 53/40; 244th COS, 20 July 1938. CAB 53/9; 331st CID, 27 July, CAB 2/7 and 33rd CID, 6 Oct 1938. CAB 2/8.
68. Gov. Gen. NZ to SSDA tel. 24 Dec 1938 in COS 818, 3 Jan 1939. CAB 53/43.
69. 271st mtg COS, 27 Jan 1939. CAB 53/10.
70. COS 818, 3 Jan 1939. CAB 53/43.
71. COS 832, 1 Feb 1939. CAB 53/44, paras 11 and 23. Italics added.

CHAPTER 8 'SO MANY VARIABLE FACTORS'

1. Min. by Phillips, 15 Jan 1938 on Ismay to Sec. Adm. 28 July 1937. ADM 116/3863; *War Memo. (E)*, 'Passage of the Fleet' (Feb 1939). ADM 116/4393.
2. Backhouse to Ismay, 20 Dec 1938, with COS 813, 22 Dec 1938. CAB 53/43; Backhouse to Ismay 29 Dec 1938. Copy in AIR 9/56/38.
3. Ibid, Gort to Ismay, Dec 1938; Note by Peirse, Jan 1939.
4. 267th mtg COS, 13 Jan; 276th mtg COS, 15 Feb 1939. CAB 53/10.
5. DP(P) 44/COS 843, 20 Feb 1939. CAB 53/45. See also Gibbs, *Grand Strategy*, I, pp. 657–666.
6. 348th mtg CID, 24 Feb 1939. CAB 2/8; Pownall, *Chief of Staff*, I, p. 190.
7. SAC 4, 28 Feb: SAC, 1st mtg, 1 Mar 1939. CAB 16/209.
8. Ibid, SAC, 2nd mtg, 13 Mar 1939.
9. Colvin to Backhouse, 14 Mar 1939 and Backhouse to Colvin, 17 Mar 1939. *Documents on Australian Foreign Policy 1937–49*, Ed. R. G. Neale (Canberra: Australian Government Publishing Service, 1976), vol. II, p. 60.
10. Ibid, pp. 69–73. Note by J. S. Duncan, 17 Mar 1939 and Note by Ismay, 18 Mar 1939. (Ismay's date is probably incorrect as he refers to an SAC meeting 'this morning', which was on the 17th. See 3rd mtg SAC, 17 Mar. CAB 16/209.) The episode is not mentioned in Alfred Stirling's memoir, *Lord Bruce: The London Years* (Melbourne: Hawthorne Press, 1974).

11. Chamberlain to PM Aust., 20 Mar 1939. CAB 21/893.
12. At meeting in DO 1 July 1939. CAB 2/9.
13. CNS's Sec. to Ismay, 23 Mar 1939. CAB 21/893.
14. SAC, 16, Memo by DCNS, 5 Apr 1939. CAB 16/209. See also Gibbs, *Grand Strategy*, I, p. 425; F. L. W. Wood, *The New Zealand People at War* (Wellington: Government Printer, 1958), p. 77.
15. 6th mtg SAC, 17 Apr 1939. CAB 16/209; Memo by Chatfield, 19 Apr 1939. CAB 16/183(A).
16. AFC(J) 17, 20 Apr 1939. CAB 29/160.
17. Ibid, AFC(J) 45, 25 Apr 1939.
18. Ibid, AFC(J) 53, 4 May 1939. In the subsequent COS memo JP 408/COS 905(JP), 16 May 1939 it became 'will not be lightly undertaken'. CAB 53/49.
19. Pacific Defence Conf. Papers of NZ Delegation, 1 Mar 1939. ADM 116/3803.
20. NZ COS 22, 4 Apr 1939. NZPM 81/4/3, Part 1.
21. *War Memo. (E)*, revisions of Feb 1939. ADM 118/4393.
22. Summarised from NZPM 86/27/10, Part 1.
23. Report of Pacific Defence Conf. National Archives, Wellington, AD 12/22; British copy entitled 'New Zealand Defence Conference', COS 910, 22 May 1939. CAB 53/49.
24. A. Longmore, *From Sea to Sky* (London: Bles, 1946) pp. 203–6; Batterbee to Inskip, 26 Apr 1939. Copy in ADM 116/3803.
25. 298th mtg COS, 25 May 1939. CAB 53/11.
26. 355th mtg CID (no Dominion representatives) 2 May 1939. CAB 2/8.
27. Report of meeting on 14 June 1939. ADM 116/3922, pp. 155–6. See also Leutze, *Bargaining for Supremacy*, pp. 37–40 and Lowe, *Britain and the Origins of the Pacific War*, pp. 97–8.
28. Min. by Danckwerts, 3 May 1939 on Revised Sec. XVIII of *War Memo. (E)*. ADM 116/3863.
29. 300th mtg COS, 16 June 1939. CAB 53/11; Cab. 21 June 1939. CAB 23/100.
30. 362nd mtg CID, 26 June 1939. CAB 2/9.
31. Ibid, Mins. of meeting in PM's rooms at House of Commons, 28 June 1939. Neale, *Documents*, II, pp. 140–3.
32. Ibid, Mins. of meeting in DO 11 July 1939, pp. 150–3.
33. Franco-British Staff Conf. Singapore, 27 June 1939 COS 941. CAB 53/52; HQ RAF Far East to Air Min., 30 June 1939. AIR 2/4128.
34. Ibid, Babington to Slessor, 16 Aug 1939.
35. COS(39) 7th mtg, 8 Sep 1939; 32nd mtg, 29 Sep 1939. CAB 79/1.
36. War Cab. 19 Oct 1939. CAB 65/1.
37. War Cab. 2 Nov 1939. CAB 65/2.
38. Memo by Churchill, DMV (39) 3, 17 Nov 1939. (CAB 99/1). Summary in Casey to Menzies, 17 Nov 1939. Neale, *Documents*, II, pp. 417–19.
39. Notes by Ismay with WP (39) 125. CAB 21/893.
40. War Cab. 20 Nov 1939. CAB 65/2.
41. DMV, 8th mtg, 20 Nov 1939. CAB 99/1.
42. Australian and New Zealand Defence (Winter 1939), DMV (39) 4, 21 Nov 1939. CAB 99/1. Full text also in *Documents Relating to New Zealand's Participation in the Second World War*, III (Wellington: Dept of Internal Affairs, 1963), pp. 535–7. See also J. R. M. Butler, *Grand Strategy*, vol. II, (London: HMSO, 1957), pp. 356–60.

42. 'Fighter Reinforcement Plan', in AIR 8/942.
43. DO (41), 75th mtg, 27 Dec 1941. CAB 69/2.
44. Churchill, *Second World War*, IV, p. 26-7.
45. C-in-C Far East to WO (203), 21 Dec; C-in-C E. Fleet to Adm. (212), 21 Dec 1941. CAB 105/20.
46. Slessor, *Central Blue*, p. 40.
47. C-in-C Far East to WO (personal for CIGS 10), 27 Dec 1941. CAB 105/21. See also Diary entry, 30 Dec 1941. Pownall, *Chief of Staff*, II, p. 70.
48. C-in-C Far East to WO 29 Dec 1941. CAB 105/21.
49. Hasluck, *Government and People*, II, p. 32.
50. C-in-C Far East to WO (Wavell to COS 141) 8 Jan 1942. CAB 105/21.
51. John Deane Potter, *A Soldier Must Hang, The Biography of an Oriental General* (London: Muller, 1963), pp. 64-5.
52. John Connell, *Wavell, Supreme Commander 1941-3* (London: Collins, 1969), pp. 88 and 95.
53. Abdacom to WO and Comb. COS Wash., 12 Jan 1942. CAB 105/21.
54. Discussion on situation in ABDA area, 11 Jan 1942, in Report of Arcadia, Washington, Conf. 13 Feb 1942. COS (42) 81. CAB 99/77.
55. Described in Wigmore, *Japanese Thrust*, pp. 212-20 and A. W. Penfold *et al.*, *Calleghan's Greyhounds. The Story of the 2/30th Australian Infantry Battalion, 22 November 1940-10 October 1945* (Sydney: 2/30th AIF Assoc., 1949), chs 3-6.
56. Abdacom to WO (235 Wavell to PM). 19 Jan 1942. CAB 105/21.
57. Air Vice-Mar. Maltby's desp. Supp. to *London Gazette*, 26 Feb 1948 [38216], para 347. Gillison, *RAAF*, pp. 339-40 and Kirby, *War Against Japan*, I, pp. 233-4 give quite different accounts of this.
58. J. M. S. Ross, *Royal New Zealand Air Force* (Wellington: Department of Internal Affairs, 1955), pp. 99-100.
59. J. O. C. Haynes (naval liaison officer) quoted in Ian Mac A. Stewart, *History of the Argyll & Sutherland Highlanders (The Thin Red Line). Malayan Campaign 1941-42* (London: Nelson, 1947), p. 133.
60. DO (42) 4th mtg, 21 Jan 1942. CAB 69/4. See also Churchill, *Second World War*, IV, 42-4.
61. Simson, *Singapore: Too Little, Too Late*, p. 69.
62. Percival's despatch, 25 Apr 1946. Supp. to *London Gazette*, 26 Feb 1948 [38215], para 536; Tsuji, *Singapore, the Japanese Version*, p. 254; Falk, *Seventy Days to Singapore*, pp. 2-3, 245-6.
63. Convoy timetables in COS (41) 437, 27 Dec 1941. CAB 79/16; Adm. to C-in-C Far East (25), 28 Dec 1941. CAB 105/21; 'Convoys to Far East', AIR 8/942. The arrivals were not all on time.
64. PM Aust. tel. 24 Jan 1942. WP(42)4. CAB 65/29; War Cab. 26 Jan 1942. CAB 65/25. Churchill, *Second World War*, IV, 51.
65. Ibid, p. 87-8. PM to Wavell 10 Feb 1942.
66. Smyth, *Percival and the tragedy of Singapore*, p. 228.
67. Connell, *Wavell, Supreme Commander*, pp. 158-9.
68. Potter, *A Soldier Must Hang*, p. 92; Tsuji, *Singapore, the Japanese Version*, p. 260.
69. Percival to Wavell, 13 Feb 1942. Connell, *Wavell*, p. 165.
70. JIC (42) 47(0), 12 Feb 1942. COS (42) 49th mtg, 13 Feb 1942. CAB 79/18. See also Arthur Bryant, *The Turn of the Tide 1939-1943* (London: Collins, 1957), p. 304.
71. Arthur Percival, *The War in Malaya*, p. 287.

72. War Cab. 21(42)2, 16 Feb 1942. CAB 65/25; Points made summarised in CAB 65/20, p. 91.
73. Churchill, *Second World War*, IV, p. 81.

POST-MORTEM

1. 5 *Hansard*, 1941–2, vol. 377, cols. 1674, 1676.
2. Ibid, vol. 378, cols. 45–7.
3. Churchill, *Second World War*, IV, p. 61.
4. Ibid, III, p. 551.
5. Lord Moran, *Winston Churchill. The Struggle for Survival 1940–65* (London: Constable, 1966), pp. 101 and 27.
6. Churchill, *Second World War*, IV, p. 81.
7. Introd. Dec. 1958 to Kenneth Attiwill, *The Singapore Story* (London: Miller, 1959), p. 14.
8. 5 *Hansard*, 1941–42, vol. 378. col. 69.
9. Allen, *Singapore 1941–42*, pp. 50, 118.
10. Callahan, *Worst Disaster*, p. 271.
11. Kirby, *Singapore: The Chain of Disaster*, chs 10, 11, 18; Simson, *Singapore, Too Little, Too Late*, ch. 7; George Maxwell, *The Civil Defence of Malaya* (London: Hutchinson, 1947).
12. Callahan, *Worst Disaster*, pp. 116–18.
13. Allen, 'Singapore' in Frankland and Dowling, *Decisive Battles of the Twentieth Century*, p. 168.
14. Allen, *Singapore 1941–1942*, p. 186. Ian Morrison *Malayan Postscript* (Sydney: Argus and Robertson, 1943), p. 185, suggests two months would have made all the difference.
15. Churchill, *Second World War*, IV, p. 61.
16. Herbert R. Richmond, 'Singapore, *The Fortnightly*, March 1942, 151, p. 243; *Statesmen and Sea-Power* (Oxford: University Press, 1946), p. 328; See also Arther J. Marder, *Portrait of an Admiral. The Life and Papers of Sir Herbert Richmond* (London: Cape, 1952).
17. Ian Hamill, 'An Australian Defence Policy: the Singapore Strategy and the defence of Australia 1919–1942', *ANU Historical Journal* (1973–74), **10** and **11**, 18.
18. R. Callahan, 'The Illusion of Security: Singapore 1919–42, *Journal of Contemporary History* (1974), **9**, 91. and McIntyre 'The Strategic Significance of Singapore 1917–1942: The Naval Base and the Commonwealth', *Journal of Southeast Asian History* (1969), **10**(1), 104.
19. Stanley L. Falk, *Seventy Days to Singapore. The Malayan Campaign 1941–42* (London: Robert Hale, 1975), p. 9.
20. Roskill, *Naval Policy*, II, p. 347.
21. Ibid, p. 456.
22. John McCarthy, *Australia and Imperial Defence 1918–39: A Study in Air and Sea Power* (St. Lucia: University of Queensland Press, 1976), p. 131.
23. Gibbs, *Grand Strategy*, I, p. 775.
24. Roskill, *Naval Policy*, II, pp. 347–9.
25. Callahan, *Worst Disaster*, p. 272.
26. Memo by First Lord, for Finance Committee, 25 Jan 1921. ADM 116/1775.

27. CID 161st mtg, 28 July 1922. CAB 2/3.
28. Roskill, *Naval Policy*, II, p. 353.
29. Quoted by CBS correspondent Cecil Brown, *Suez to Singapore*, p. 240. *The Times* correspondent, Ian Morrison, said: Singapore 'gave its inhabitants the illusion of security'. *Malayan Postcript* (Sydney: Angus and Robertson, 1943), p. 1. See also F. Spencer Chapman, *The Jungle is Neutral* (London: Chatto & Windus, 1949), p. 13.
30. Liability of Suez Canal to Blocking Attack. Memo by First Lord, 24 July 1923. CID 438-B. CAB 4/10.
31. Military Policy in Egypt. Air Staff Memo, Nov. 1923 CID 462-B. CAB 4/10.
32. Moran, *Churchill*, p. 27.
33. Churchill, *Second World War*, IV, p. 43.
34. Percival's despatch. Supp. to *London Gazette*, 26 Feb 1948 [38215] paras 433, 536.
35. Tedder, *With Prejudice*, pp. 209–10.
36. Slessor, *The Central Blue*, p. 347.
37. Richard G. Casey, *Personal Experience 1939–46* (London: Constable, 1962), pp. 31, 40, 50, 61.
38. See John Winton, *The Forgotten Fleet* (London: Michael Joseph, 1969), p. 284.
39. Churchill, *Second World War*, IV, 14.
40. Pownall, *Chief of Staff*, II, p. 92.
41. G. Sansom, 'The Story of Singapore', *Foreign Affairs* [New York] (1944), **22**(2), 279. See also Bennett, *Why Singapore Fell*, p. 230.
42. B. H. Liddell Hart, *History of the Second World War* (London: Cassell, 1970), p. 233.
43. Louis, *British Strategy in the Far East*, pp. 1–2; Allen, *Singapore 1941–42*, ch. 11; Callahan, *Worst Disaster*, pp. 115–17, but not mentioned in Lowe, *Britain and the Origins of the Pacific War* (1977). See Prime Minister Tojo's promise: 'I will be careful to avoid the war's becoming a racial war'. Ike, *Japan's Decision for War*, p. 239.
44. Final report of Naval Mission to India and the Dominions, enclosed in Jellicoe to Sec. of Adm. 3 Feb 1920. ADM 116/1831.
45. Confid. annex. to War Cab., 222(40)4. 8 Aug 1940. CAB 65/14.
46. Statement, received 20 Feb 1920, with memo. in Conversations with Japanese Foreign Office, 13 Jan 1920. Piesse Papers, MS 882/5 p. 64. Australian National Library.
47. Tota Ishimaru, *Japan Must Fight Britain* (London: Paternoster Library, 1936), pp. 84, 150, 271.
48. Pownall, *Chief of Staff*, II, p. 73; Victor Purcell, *Malaya: Communist or Free?* (London: Gollanz, 1954), p. 12.
49. Note on Military Policy in Malaya, 27 Sept 1927 encl. in GOC Malaya to Sec. WO 22 Mar 1928. WO 32/3625.
50. D. Ramli, 'History of the Malay Regiment 1933–1942', *JMBRAS* (1965), **38**, 199–243.
51. Memo Fighting Value of the Races in Malaya, 25 Nov 1930, in GOC to U.-Sec. WO 15 Dec 1930. WO 32/3617.
52. W. Somerset Maugham, *Ah King: Six Stories* (London: Heinemann, 1933).
53. Ramli, 'History of the Malay Regiment', p. 228.
54. The Dutch guerrillas were referred to in C-in-C Far East to WO 21 Dec 1941. CAB 105/20; Brooke-Popham's despatch. Supp. to *London Gazette*, 22 Jan 1948

[38183], para 149, and Percival's despatch. Supp. to *London Gazette*, 26 Feb 1948 [38215], para 333.
55. Chapman, *The Jungle is Neutral*, pp. 91-2.
56. Anthony Short, *The Communist Insurrection in Malaya 1948-1960* (London: Muller, 1975), p. 22.
57. Morison, *Malayan Postscript*, p. 168. See also Turnbull, *History of Singapore*, pp. 177-8, 181, 185, 188, 'the final battle for Singapore showed of what stuff her people were made'.
58. Ramli, 'History of the Malay Regiment', pp. 228-41.
59. Radin Soenarno, 'Malay Nationalism 1896-1941', *Journal of Southeast Asian History* (1960), **1**(1), 6.
60. On the fascinating story of the INA see Kalyan Kumar Ghosh, *The Indian National Army Second Front of the Indian Independence Movement* (Meerut: Meenakshi Prakashan, 1969) and Joyce C. Lebra, *Jungle Alliance: Japan and the Indian National Army* (Singapore: Asia Pacific Press, 1971).
61. Ike, *Japan's Decision For War*, pp. 201-2.
62. Ibid, p. 207.
63. Quoted in Feis, *Road to Pearl Harbor*, p. 293.
64. SAC 1st mtg, 1 Mar 1939. CAB 16/209. Compare Pownall's diary, 20 Dec 1941. *Chief of Staff*, II, p. 67: 'Singapore has *got* to be held, for to lose it may well mean losing Australia, if not New Zealand. I don't mean losing them to the Japanese, but to the Empire . . .'
65. Ibid, SAC 2nd mtg, 13 Mar 1939.

Index

Abdacom, 206
Abu Bakar, Sultan of Johore, 11
Achilles, HMS, 130, 160; HMNZS, 196
Addison, Vice-Admiral, 107
Addu Attol, 31, 113, Map 7
Aden, 101, 125, 183–4
Admiralty: 14, 44; cruiser programme, 48–9; truncated scheme, 50–1; requests Empire sharing, 54; FMS gift, 63; New Zealand policy, 64–6; big guns for Singapore, 72; slowed-down policy, 92–3; base restarted, 106–8; Australian fears considered, 140–1; Singapore unsafe, 204
Admiralty Board, 6, 87
Adventure, HMS, 111
Advisers, Unfederated Malay States, 11
Advisory War Council, Australia, 175, 184
Air Defences, Singapore: first proposals, 37, 71–2; 1923 Staff College Exercise, 74; Drummond alternatives, 75–6; truncated scheme, 78–80; 1930 trials, 108–9; Stage I approved, 110; finalised, 122; Anzac Squadrons mooted, 139; 1940 Appreciation, 169; opening of Pacific War, 194–5, 269 n11
Air Ministry, 14, 72, 84, 122
Air power: substitution theory, 14, 69–71; northern Malaya, 137; decisive importance, 195; role of Egypt, 217
Air reconnaissance, Pacific Islands, 141, 155
Aircraft carriers: Jellicoe reports, 22; 1923 Staff College Exercise, 37; Japanese, 74, 77; 1929 goal, 87; 1937 goal, 127; one for Ceylon, 170, 173, 175; one for Far East, 183–7, 205; Taranto, 191
Airfield Construction Unit, RNZAF, 176, 194, 207
Albania, 144, 160, 217
Alexander, A. V., 88, 92, 175, 185
Alexandria, 217
Allen, Captain Archer, USN, 176
Allen, Louis, 212, 213
Alor Star, 78, 194, 202, 228
Amboina, 177
American-British-Canadian talks, A-B-C-1 (1941), 177–80, 221
American-Dutch-British conference, A-D-B (1941), 181–2
Amery, L. S.: Under-secretary for Colonies, 25; First Lord, 35, 56; Secretary of State for Colonies, 57, 58, 60, 62; Straits Settlements military contribution, 63–4, 66; guns v. air, 80; War Cabinet, 181
Ammon, Charles, 44
Anglo-Dutch-Australian conference, A-D-A (1941), 176–7
Anglo-German Naval Agreement (1934), 125
Anglo-Italian Agreements: of 1937, 126; of 1938, 138
Anglo-Japanese Alliance, 20, 22, 24, 29, 30–1; talk of renewal in 1930s, 116, 117
Annual Review, Chiefs of Staff: of 1932, 106–7; of 1933, 116, 124; of 1935, 125; of 1937, 129–32, 140, 143, 145
Anti-submarine booms, 74, 78, 105, 107, 115
Arafura Sea, 174
Arcadia Conference, 205
Army Council, 81, 84

275

Index

Army in Malaya, 195, 224–5
Artillery: 15″ guns, Plates 3, 9, 10; 1923 proposals, 36–7, 71–2; 15″ and 9.2″ on all round traverse, 47; Stage I, 51; 1928 gunnery trials, 67–8, 83; Trenchard's attitude, 77–85; Gillman Committee, 81–4; 1932 situation, 107; Coastal Defence Committee, 108–9; Stage II, 120–2; Johore Battery, 120–2; final layout, 121; rumour about 18″ guns, 136, 264 n46; opening ceremony, first turret, 137; use during siege, 208; high explosive ammunition, 218
Ashwin, Bernard, 152, 154
Asiatic Fleet, USN, 174, 178, 180, 181, 186
Atlantic War, 175, 178
Attlee, Clement, 168, 181
Australia: separate navy, 3; vulnerable, 6; founding, 7; External Affairs Liaison Officer, 17; Jellicoe mission, 21–2; Washington Treaty, 31; contribution requested, 35, 56, 61; 1924 cancellation, 43, 56; cruiser programme, 56–7; Casey cables, 88–93; Labor Government of 1929, 97; 1930 Singapore Subcommittee, 98–9; help with island garrisons, 100; China Squadron, 114; Hankey visit, 119; Ethiopian crisis, 125; doubts about Imperial defence, 127–8; 1937 Imperial Conference, 130–5; plan for Pacific Pact, 131; Munich, 138–9, 140–1; *European Appreciation 1939–40*, 147; Tientsin silver crisis, 157; German war, 160; DMV meetings, 160–2; division requested for Malaya, 169; 1940 *Far East Appreciation*, 171; Advisory War Council, 175; 8th Division, 176, 195; capital ship plan, 183–7; Pearl Harbor, 193; seige of Singapore, 208–9
Australia, HMAS, 139
Australian Imperial Force (AIF), 163, 195, 205, 206
Australian Labor Party, 128
Austria occupied, 138, 217

Axis Pact, 165

Babington, Air Vice-Marshal, 159, 173, 176
Backhouse, Admiral Sir Roger, 140–1, 145, 146, 147, 148, 158
Baker, Philip Noel, 16
Baldwin, Stanley: second ministry, 45; FMS gift, 52, 62; Jackson contract, 67; 1929 election, 86, 87; Shanghai crisis, 105; Coastal Defence Committee, 108–9; attitude to Japan, 110; Defence Requirements report, 119; end of premiership, 131–2
Balfour, Lord, 29, 30, 215
Barstow, Sir George, 35, 55
Bartholomew, Major-General W. H.: DMO, 35; deputy COS committee, 105–6; COS India, 133
Batterbee, Sir Harry, 143, 152
Battle-cruisers: Beatty plan for squadron, 47, 101, 113; dropped, 82, 221; one for Ceylon, 170, 173, 175; *see also* Capital ships
Battleships, *see* Capital ships
Beatty, Admiral of the Fleet, David, Lord: CNS, 23, 26, 31; Washington treaty, 32; defences for base, 34; Labour Government, 39; Curzon Committee, 45–8; battle-cruiser squadron, 47, 101, 113, 221, Plate 4; Baldwin Government, 58; air power, 70, 76, 78, 215
Beaufort, Photo-reconnaissance, 194
Beckett, Harold, 63
Bell, Sir Francis Dillon, 58
Bellairs, Rear-Admiral, 178
Bennett, Major-General H. Gordon, 196, 206; Plate 39
Berendsen, Carl, 133, 152–3
Betting Kusah battery, 121
Bettington, Colonel Vere, 69–70
Big guns, *see* Artillery
Birkenhead, Lord, 48
Bismarck, 183
Blakang Mati, 26, 107, 208; Maps 6, 12; Plate 11
Blake, Commodore Geoffrey, 97

Index

Blenheim bomber, 194, 203; night fighter, 194
Bombay, naval base, 54
Bombers, *see Blenheim, Horsley, Hudson, Vildebeeste*
Bond, Lieutenant-General, 173, 176
Borden, Sir Robert, 3
Borneo, 8, 116, 174, 179, 202–3
Bostock, Air Commodore, 173, 176
Brancker, Lieutenant-Colonel, 36–7, 44
Brennan, Frank, 98
Bridgeman, W. C., 45, 57, 60, 66
Brink, Lieutenant-Colonel, 176
Britain: 1921 naval tonnage, 32; 1930 naval tonnage, 94–5; financial contribution to base, 96; battleships, 1932, 117; 1936 naval Conference, 126; 1937 naval programme, 127; 40,000-ton battleships, 144; 1940 naval strength, 170; freezes Japanese assets, 182
British Commonwealth Pacific Fleet, 221
British Empire Pacific Fleet, 10, 22
Brock, Vice-Admiral Sir Osmond, 20, 26
Brooke-Popham, Air Chief Marshal, 176, 181, 184, 198–9, 202, 203, 205, 216; Plate 35
Bruce, Stanley M.: High Commissioner in London, 17; Prime Minister of Australia, 43, 56, 88–90; after Shanghai crisis, 112; fears of Germany and Japan, 117; Munich, 140–1, 145, 147–8; Tientsin silver crisis, 157–9; 1940 conference, 166–7; Defence Committee, 1941, 205
Bruche, Major-General, 128
Brunei, 13
Buffalo fighters, 194, 201
Bukit Timah, 208–9
Buona Vista Battery, 121
Burdon, Sir Ernest, 59
Burges-Watson, Rear-Admiral, 115
Burma Rifles, 226
Burma Road, 165, 167
Burnett, Air Vice-Marshal, 105
Burnett, Captain J., 173

Butler, R. A., 172, 175

Cabinet, UK: Ten Year Rule, 21; Clynes Committee, 40–1; FMS gift, 51, 62; Fighting Services Committee, 88–9, 91; Shanghai crisis, 106; Coastal Defence Committee, 108–9; Tientsin silver crisis, 157; War Cabinet, 160; DMV meetings, 161–3; attitude to Netherlands East Indies, 168; Australian representative, 1941, 184–6; surrender at Singapore, 209
Calcutta, 113
Callahan, Raymond, 212, 214
Cam Ranh Bay, 144–5, 172, 182, 191
Canada: separate navy, 3; attitude to CID, 17; Jellicoe report, 22; 1921 Imperial Conference, 31; Singapore base, 35; 1924 cancellation, 42; brigade to Hong Kong, 202–3
Canton, 105
Cape of Good Hope, 7, 8, 31, 178, 181, 204
Cape Town, 186; *see also* Simonstown
Capital ships: anti-torpedo bulges, 1; docking, 10; two for Pacific, 29; anchorages, 31; 1922 Washington treaty, 32; 1929 Admiralty policy, 87; 1930 London treaty, 94–5; timetable for move East, 113; treaty totals, 117; New Naval Standard, 126–7; *King George V* class, 127, 141; 1937 *Far East Appreciation*, 133; possible Australian battleship, 139–40, 147–8; *Lion* class, 144; two for Singapore, 147; British weakness, 149; 1939 totals, 156; Japan and Britain, 1940, 170; Menzies' request for, 175; Admiralty plans, 1941, 183–7; peak of Japanese strength, 190; Commonwealth Pacific Fleet and US Fleet, 221
Casey, Richard G.: External Affairs Liaison Officer, 88–90, 95, 96, 98, 220–1; Minister of Supply, 161–2; Australian Minister, Washington, 167, Plate 16
Catalina flying boat, 188, 194

Index

Causeway, Johore Strait, 10, 25–6, 207, 209
Cavan, General the Earl of, 37–8, 47, 71, 76–7, Plate 5
Ceylon, 7, 8, 175, 227
Chamberlain, Austen, 46
Chamberlain, Neville: 1932 Annual Review, 106; 1933 Review, 117; Defence Requirements Report, 118–19; Prime Minister, 131; assurances to Australia, 148; Tientsin silver crisis, 157; DMV meetings, 161–2; resigned, 163
Changi, 107, 208
Chapei, 104
Chapman, Spencer, 227
Charles, Lieutenant-General Sir Ronald, 108
Chatfield, Admiral Sir Ernle: Controller, 51; CNS, 110; China Squadron orders, 115; Defence Requirements Committee, 117–19; Ethiopian crisis, 122–3; Two Power Standard, 124–5; 1937 Imperial Conference, 130–5, Sino-Japanese War, 134; *European Appreciation 1939–40*, 146–7; Tientsin silver crisis, 157–8; DMV meetings, 162, 215, 219; fatalism, 229–30; Plate 20
Chauvel, General Sir Harry, 97
Chelmsford, Lord, 40
Chief of Air Staff: Trenchard, 34; Salmond, 104; Newall, 143
Chief of Naval Staff: Fergusson, 5; Beatty, 23; Madden, 82; Field, 108; Chatfield, 110; Backhouse, 145; Pound, 168
Chief of the Imperial General Staff: Cavan, 37–8, 47, 71, 76–7; Wilson, 70; Milne, 80; Montgomery-Massingberd, 116; Gort, 144; Dill, 168
Chiefs of Staff subcommittee, CID: 15; Singapore defence plan, 37–8; guns v. air, 76–7; 1926 compromise, 80–1; Gillman Committee, 82–4; New Zealand defence paper, 100–2; 1932 Annual Review, 104–7, 106–7; deputy COS subcommittee, 105–6;
Latham's visit, 109; appeal to warrant, 111; 1933 Review, 116; 1937 Imperial Conference, 129–35; Johore defences, 138; Australian and New Zealand fears, 1938, 141–2; Longmore's report, 155; attitude to Netherlands East Indies, 168; accepts Stark's strategy, 175; reinforcements for Malaya, 203–5; assumes loss of Singapore, 209; few illusions, 215–16, 217
China Squadron RN, 106, 111, 114–15, 125, 196
China: trade, 7; 21 Demands, 20; Shanghai incident, 104–5; war with Japan, 134, 153, 217; Tientsin silver crisis, 156–7; Japan's move south, 165; British garrisons withdrawn, 167, 169; Japan's aims, 190–1
Chinese, Malayan, 13, 195, 225–7
Chins, 226
Christmas Island, 141
Churchill, Winston: 17; Secretary of State for War and Air, 24, 69, 70; Chancellor of the Exchequer, 45–9, 65–6; air substitution debate, 75, 77; First Lord of the Admiralty, 160; DMV meetings, 161–2; Prime Minister, 163–4; 1940 *Far East Appreciation*, 170–1; accepts Stark's strategy, 175; attitude to ABC-1, 178–9; meets Roosevelt at Placentia Bay, 182; capital ships for Far East, 183–7; Mediterranean priority, 188–9, 212–13; Pearl Harbor, 193; visits Washington, 1941, 205; fall of Singapore, 208–9, 210–11; loss of *Prince of Wales* and *Repulse*, 218; US protector of Dominions, 164, 223
Civil Engineer-in-Chief, Admiralty, 14, 107–8
Clarke, Captain A. W., RN, 174
Clark Field, Philippines, 193
Clutterbuck, Alexander, 61
Clynes, Lord, 40–1
Coastal Defence Artillery, *see* Artillery
Coastal Defence Committee, 108–9
Coates, Gordon, 64–6
Cochrane, Group-Captain R., 130, 139

Index

Colombo, 47, 186, 203
Colonial Office: and Straits Settlements, 9, 14; told of dockyard, 26–7; sites, 55; FMS gift, 61–2; Johore gift, 122
Colvin, Vice-Admiral R., 147, 152–3, 181
Committee of Imperial Defence: 6; background, 15–16; Anglo-American relations, 24; Singapore base plan, 27; port defences, 34; Curzon Committee, 46; cruiser programme, 49; truncated scheme, 50–1; 1928 gunnery trials, 68, 84; Labour Government, 1929, 90–1; 1930 Imperial Conference, 100; Shanghai crisis, 106; Latham's visit, 109; Stage I of defences, 110; 1933 Review, 117; Mediterranean and Ethiopian crisis, 134; 1937 Imperial Conference, 134–5; *European Appreciation 1939–40*, 146–7; leak of information to Australians, 148; Tientsin silver crisis, 157
Commonwealth Defence Council, Australian, 35–6
Connaught Battery, 121
Cook Islands, 141–2
Cook, Sir Joseph, 4
Cooper, Duff, 184, 203
Craigie-Arita formula, 159
Cruisers: replacement programme, 48–9; disarmament fails, 1927, 93; MacDonald reduces total, 93–4
Cunliffe-Lister, Sir Philip, 108–9
Cunningham, Captain J. H. D., RN, 107
Cunningham, Vice-Admiral Andrew, 149, 150, 155, 164
Curtin, John, 128, 140, 175, 184, 185, 222
Curzon, Lord, 24, 45, 47
Cyprus, 126
Czech crisis, 138, 160, 217

Dalley, Lieutenant-Colonel J., 227
Danckwerts, Captain Victor, RN, 137, 150, 156, 178–9, 220
Darvall, Squadron-Leader L., 128–9

Dawes, General, 87
Defence Committee (Ops), 181, 184–5, 208
Defence contributions, Crown Colonies, 53; *see also* Hong Kong, Straits Settlements
Defence Policy and Requirements subcommittee, 16
Defence Policy (Plans) Committee, 16, 131
Defence Requirements Committee, 16, 117–19, 125–6
Deutschland class, 116
Dewar, Captain Kenneth, RN, 5
Dickens, Captain Gerald, RN, 26
Diego Garcia, 31; Map 7
Dill, Field Marshal, 168, 207
Director of Dockyards, 31
Disarmament, 39, 93, 117
Dixon, Sir Charles, 142
Dobbie, General, 137–8
Dockyard: plans, 25–7, 32–3; site preparations, 45; truncated scheme, 50–1; slowed down and possible commercial use, 91; restarted, 106–8; N. Chamberlain queries role, 119; opening of graving dock, 135–6; US interest in, 163; completion of wharves, 172; *Prince of Wales* and *Repulse* arrive, 186–7; unsafe for ships, 203; oil stores fired, 207
Dominions: Singapore base decision, 29–30; help requested, 46; air power, 70–1; and second Labour Government, 88–93; 1930 London Naval Conference, 94–5; joint battleship and brigade of guards, 127; 1937 Imperial Conference, 129–35; help in Pacific, 139; promises to, queried by Chamberlain, 146–7; not told of Washington staff talks, 156; DMV meetings, 160–2, 167; war with Italy, 164; 1940 *Far East Appreciation*, 170–1; freezing of Japanese assets, 182; self-reliance, 216; Chatfield and Britain's pledge, 230
Dominions Office, 14
Domvile, Captain Barry, RN, 22, 30
Dorsetshire, HMS, 136

Dreyer, Rear-Admiral: deputy COS committee, 105-6; C.-in-C. China, 115, 219
Drummond, Squadron-Leader, 76
Duff, Patrick, 96
Duff, Vice-Admiral, 28
Duigan, Major-General, 173
Duke of York, HMS, 183
Dunbar-Nasmith, Vice-Admiral, 115
Duncan, John S., 148
Dutch strength, East Indies: air, 176-7; naval, 182, 196

Eagle, HMS, 136; Plate 26
East Anglian Territorial Division, 18th, 203-4, 207, 208-9
East India Company, 7
East Indies, *see* Netherlands East Indies
East Indies Station, 114, 213
Eastern Department, Colonial Office, 55, 61, 62
Eastern Fleet, 186-8, 196, 200-3, 221
Eden, Anthony, 184-5
Egerton, Captain Wilfred, RN, 50
Egypt, 101, 134, 217
Eight: Eight fleets, 22
Ellington, Air-Marshal Sir Edward, 117
Endau, 206, 207
Ethiopian crisis, 15, 122-3, 131
European Appreciation 1939-40, 146-7, 229
Exeter, HMS, 196
External Affairs Liaison Officer, Australian, 17, 88-90
Eyres-Monsell, Sir Bolton, 35, 119

Fadden, Arthur, 184
Fanning Island, 101, 139, 141, 155, 160; Map 9
Far East Appreciations: of 1937, 129-35, 140-1, 143, 145, 162, 265 n58; of 1940, 166-71, 173-4, 188, 194, 223
Far East interdepartmental committee, 172, 175
Federated Malay States: naval subsidy, 3; origins, 10-12; railways, 25; £2 million gift, 51-2, 59-63, 87; Volunteers, 195

Fergusson, Rear-Admiral Sir James, 5
Field, Admiral Sir Frederick, 65, 104, 108
Fifteen-inch guns, *see* Artillery
Fighters, *see Blenheim, Buffalo, Hurricane, Zero*
Fighting Services subcommittee, 88-90, 95
Fiji: annexation, 8; possible threat to New Zealand, 141-3; reinforcements, 155, 169; defence needs, 173
Fisher, Sir Warren, 117-18, 261 n44
FitzMaurice, Sir Maurice, 27
Five Power Naval Limitation Treaty, 1922, 32
Fleet Air Arm, 71, 82, 136, 221
Fleet anchorage, 6, 26-8, 30, 31, 33
Floating dock: decision, 1923, 36, 49, 58; at Singapore, 1928, 86-7, 113; Plates 19, 23, 27, 30, 31, 32
Forbes, George, 98, 100
Force Z, 201-3, 212
Foreign Office, 24, 77, 117
Fortress troops, 196-7
Four Power Treaty, 1921, 31
Fraser, Peter, 152, 184
Freezing of Japanese assets, 182, 192
Fuel oil, *see* Oil fuel
Fuelling anchorages: Red Sea and Indian Ocean, 31; South China Sea, 144; Maps 7, 10
Fujiwara, Colonel, 228
France: ally, 5; no plans against, 117, 129; 1939 London staff talks, 144, 146, 149-50; Singapore staff talks, 159; alliance with, 160; collapse of, 164
Franco-Thai War, 1940-1, 182

Gemas, 207
Geneva Disarmament Conference, 1932-4, 16, 110, 123
Gent, Edward, 55, 122
German Navy, 116, 124, 130, 141, 146, 161, 166, 183
Germany: not a rival, 5; main danger, 118; Naval Agreement, 1934, 125; reoccupation of Rhineland, 126; battleship total, 127; Munich, 138;

Index

Prague, 144, 148; war, 160; Axis Pact, 165, invades Russia, 182, 217
Germany-First strategy, 177–80
Ghormley, Admiral, USN, 156
Gibbs, Norman, 214
Gibraltar, 125, 170, 181, 217
Gilbert Islands, 141
Gillman, Lieutenant-General Webb, 81–5; Plate 17
Gilmour, Sir John, 108–9
Gneisenau, 185, 210
Gong Kedah, 194
Gort, General, 145, 147
Grace, Rear-Admiral, 176
Graving docks: Keppel Harbour, 10, 114; Pearl Harbor, 19; Singapore base proposals, 33, 36; truncated scheme, 50–1; Jackson contract, 66–8; slowed down, 92; restarted, 107–8; *see also* King George VI Graving Dock
Greater East Asia Co-prosperity Sphere, 190–1
Green, John F. N., 55
Grindle, Sir Gilbert, 55, 58, 61, 63
Guam, 174, 193
Guerillas, 227
Guillemard, Sir Lawrence, 45, 55, 60, 62
Gulf of Siam, 188
Guns, *see* Artillery
Gurkhas, 195, 212

Hainan, 144, 169, 199, Map 10
Haldane, Lord, 39
Halifax, Earl of, 155, 157, 166
Hamill, Ian, 214
Hampton, Commander T. C., RN, 156
Hanihara Masanao, 223
Hankey, Sir Maurice: secretary of CID, 15, 17; FMS gift, 51, 62; air power, 77; 1926 guns v. air compromise, 80; Gillman Committee, 82; excluded from Fighting Services Committee, 88; relations with MacDonald, 89, 96, 111; 1930 Singapore subcommittee, 99; a New Zealand CID, 99–100; Coastal Defence Committee, 109; Defence Requirements Committee, 117–19, 125–6; Neville Chamberlain's heretical ideas, 119; Australian visit, 127–8; 1937 COS' Review, 129; retires from Cabinet secretaryship, 142; Plate 13
Harding, President, 32
Hart, Admiral, USN, 186–7, 196
Hart, Basil Liddell, 222
Hawaii, 163, 191
Heath, Lieutenant-General Sir Lewis, 195
Henderson, Arthur, 88, 98–9
Hewlett, Wing-Commander, 31, 71
Higher Command Far East, 28
Hitler, 116, 138, 143, 215
Hoare, Sir Samuel, 75, 132
Holiday, Battleship construction, 94–5
Holland, Harry, 65
Holland, Henry, 66
Hollis, Colonel Leslie, 167
Hong Kong: future of dockyard, 4, 5; vulnerable, 6, 7, 31; annexed, 8; prestige, 20; gift for Singapore base, 45–6, 57–8, 61; submarine base, 82, 217; slowed down policy, 98; Anzac help to, mooted, 100–1, 139; Shanghai incident, 104–5; advance base, 112–13, 114, 115; supply route to China, 165; threat to, 173, 179; Japanese air raid, 193; destroyers escape, 196; Canadian brigade, 202–3; surrender, 203
Hydrographer, Admiralty, 25, 36
Hood, HMS, 21, 105, 215
Hoover, President, 86–7, 91, 93
Hore-Belisha, Leslie, 135
Hornbeck, Stanley, 172, 220
Horsburgh Attol, 31; Map 7
Horsley torpedo-bomber, 78, 84, 116; Plate 6
Hotham, Vice-Admiral Alan, 64–5
House of Representatives: Australian, 56, 93; New Zealand, 65–6
Hudson, reconnaissance bomber, 188, 194, 203, 212
Hull, Cordell, 167
Hunter, T. B.. 107
Hurricanes, 181, 203, 205, 207, 212, 220

Ibrahim, Sultan of Johore: reign, 11–12; consulted about base, 28; Jubilee gift and Johore Battery, 120–2; Plate 21

Imperial Conferences: 15, 16; of 1921, 25, 28, 30, 70; of 1923, 35–6, 56; of 1925, 50, 64–6, 78; of 1930, 95–9; Singapore subcommittees, 98–9; Jubilee, 1935, 125; of 1937, 129–35, 214; DMV meetings, 1939, 160–3, 167

Imperial defence: definition, 2, 250 n1; Dominion's naval subsidies, 3; Australian and New Zealand doubts, 127–8, 129, 132–5, 138–43. *See also* Committee of Imperial Defence, Dominions

Imperial Naval Authority, 3

Imperial War Cabinet, 3

Imperialism, 13, 229

'Impregnable fortress', 28, 136, 208

India: air and land reinforcements, 5, 76, 188; Jellicoe reports, 21–2; 1921 Imperial Conference, 29; no Singapore contribution from, 35, 59; Royal Indian Navy, 54; unrest, 83; New Zealand battalion mooted for, 100, 128; Shanghai crisis, 105; timing of reinforcements, 113, 203; garrison in Malaya, 195; State Forces from, 195

India Office, 14

Indian Legislative Assembly, 59

Indian National Army, 228

Indian Ocean, 174, 177, 183, 221

Indians in Malaya, 225–7

Indo-China, 165, 169, 172, 175, 182, 192, 202, 203

Indomitable, HMS, 205

Inskip, Sir Thomas (Viscount Caldecote), 131–3, 155, 167; Plate 22

Invergordon naval dockyard, 31

Iraq, 76, 78, 105, 113, 139

Irish Free State, 42

Ismay, General Hastings, 141, 161, 167, 168

Isthmus of Kra, 11, 177, 194, 195, 198–9, 219

Italy: no plans against, 117, 125, 129; invades Ethiopia, 122–3; Anglo-Italian Agreement, 1937, 126; Anglo-Italian Agreement, 1938, 138; occupied Albania, 144; *European Appreciation* 1939–40, 146, 229; at war, 164; Axis Pact, 165; to knock-out first, 169

Jackson, Sir Arthur, Plate 18

Jackson, Sir John (Singapore Ltd): contract for docks, 67, 86, 88; under review, 90; continues, 98, 102; graving dock completed, 135–6

Japan: naval rival, 2, 5, 6; 1914–18 war, 20; potential enemy, 25; land holdings in Johore, 28, 33; Washington Conference, 32; air power, 74; Foreign Office concern about, 89; 1930 London Naval Conference, 94–5; Manchuria, 102; Shanghai, 103–5; rumours of Singapore plans, 110; British fleet plans, 114; battleship totals, 117, 127; 1936 London Naval Conference, 126; war with China, 134, 153; Australian fears of, 140–1; Tientsin silver crisis, 156–7; encroachments south, 165; Axis Pact, 165; 1940 naval strength, 170; in Indo-China, 182; attack on Malaya, 188; war plans, 184–92, peak of naval strength, 191; air superiority, 195; landings, 199; assault on Singapore, 208–9; British and US Fleets off coast of, 221; race feelings, 223; 1941 fatalism, 229

Jellicoe, Admiral of the Fleet Lord: naval mission, 4, 21–2, 133; Governor-General of New Zealand, 43, 56, 222

Jervois, Sir William, 9

Jitra, 195, 199, 202

Johore: position of, 11, 27; defence perimeter in, 36; possible help from, 60; 1935 Jubilee gift, 120–2; 1937 defence plan, 138, 219; State Forces, 195, 226; attempt to hold, 206–7; failure to concentrate in, 212; Indonesian guerillas, 227

Johore Bahru, 27, 208

Johore Battery, 121
Johore Strait, *see* Old Strait
Joint Planning subcommittee, 15, 139, 181, 198
Jones, David, 66
Jones, Frederick, 152
Jones, Wing Commander G., 152
Jordan, William, 157, 162
Jurong, 71; Map 6

Kachins, 226
Kallang Civil Airport, 121
Kamaran Bay, Red Sea, 31, 113; Map 7
Kedah, 11, 193, 195, 202, 227, 228
Kelantan, 11, 193, 195, 202
Kelly, Admiral, 115
Keppel Harbour, 10, 26, 47, 48, 107–8, 114
Kerr, Rear-Admiral Munro, 97
King George V, 122
King George V, HMS, 127, 140–1, 144, 183
King George VI Graving Dock: 1938 opening, 135–6; 1975 new dock alongside, 230; Plates 24–8
Kirby, Major-General S. Woodburn, xii, 212, 240
Kirk, Captain Alan, USN, 163
Kluang, 207
Koepang, 177
Kongo class battleship, 201
Korea, 5, 6, 189
Kota Bahru, 188, 193, 194, 195, 199, 202, 212
Kowloon, 57
Kra, *see* Isthmus of Kra
Kuala Lumpur, 11, 59, 62, 78, 206, 207, 227
Kuantan, 194, 201, 202
Kuomintang, 225–6, 227

Labor Party, Australian, 128
Labour Governments: Britain, of 1924, 39–45, 74; of 1929, 86–102; Australia, of 1929, 93; of 1941, 184; New Zealand, of 1935, 128
Labour Party, New Zealand, 65, 97, 128

Labrador Battery, 121
Labuan, 8, 13
Larken, Captain Frank, RN, 25
Latham, Sir John, 109
Laverack, Colonel J. D., 128
Law, Bonar, 24, 34
Layton, Vice-Admiral, 173, 176, 203, 205
League of Nations, 39, 42, 43, 125, 134, 189
Leahy, Admiral, USN, 156
Leander, HMS, 130, 160
Learmouth, Rear-Admiral, Sir Frederick, 25, 31, 47
Lee of Fareham, Lord, 54, 59–61
Legislative Council, Straits Settlements, 9, 64, 120
Leveson, Admiral, 47
Lindsay, Parkinson and Co., 167
Line Islands, 142
Linlithgow, Lord, 55
Llewellan, Colonel J. T., 136
Lloyd George, David, 24, 34
Lloyd, Lord, 166
Local Defence Division, Admiralty, 22, 25
Lock, Colonel R. F., 81
London Naval Conferences, *see* Naval limitation conferences
Longmore, Air Vice-Marshal, 152–5
Lothian, Lord, 167
Luke, Sir Harry, 152
Lyons, Joseph, 128, 138–9, 140, 145, 148, 152

McCarthy, John, 214
McLean, Sir Donald, 108–9
MacDonald, Malcolm, 133, 157
MacDonald, Ramsay, 39, 41, 84; relations with USA, 86–7, 91; slowed down policy, 88–102; 1930 Imperial Conference, 96; Shanghai crisis, 106; Stage I of the defences, 109–10; Hankey's presses, 111; Defence Requirements report, 119; Johore gift, 122
Machang, 194
Mackesy, General, 152, 154
Mad Mullah, 70

Madden, Admiral Sir Charles, 82, 88–9
Madras, 113
Malacca, 9, 27
Malan, Colonel L. N., 81
Malay barrier, US strategy for, 178–9
Malay Regiment, 195, 225, 227
Malay Rulers, 28, 136, 225, 226
Malaya: 5, 6; British expansion in, 10–13; overland threat, 169; 1940 *Far East Appreciation*, 169–71; defence deficiencies, 173–4; campaign, 193–207; Volunteers, 224–7; population percentages, 226; garrison, 269 n13
Malaya, HMS, 59, 62
Malayan Civil Service, 13
Malayan Communist Party, 226–7
Malayan Peoples' Anti-Japanese Army, 227
Malayan Volunteer Air Force, 226
Malays, 13, 195, 224–7
Malta, 1, 19, 50, 54, 83, 217
Manchukuo, 189–90
Manchurian crisis, 1, 15, 102, 103, 215
Manila, 163, 174, 178, 187, 193, 200
Marks, Walter M., 56
Marshall Islands, 178
Massey, William F., 3, 30, 43–4, 54, 56, 58
Matador, *see* Operation Matador
Maxwell, Sir George, 59, 62
Mediterranean: 1924 exercises, 80; main fleet stationed, 87; Ethiopian crisis, 122–3, 125–6; reliance in France, 130; 1937 discussions, 134; Anglo-French staff talks, 1939, 149–50; guarantees to Greece, Rumania and Turkey, 155; Tientsin silver crisis, 159; DMV meetings, 161–2; Italian war, 163–4; naval strength, 1940, 170; US attitude to, 175; Churchill's priorities, 188–9, 214
Memphis, USS, 136
Menzies, Robert: Attorney-General, 140; Prime Minister, 157, 175; to visit London, 177; in London, 1941, 180–1, 183–4; resigned, 184; Plate 16
Merlin, HMS, 26
Middle East, 125, 188, 203, 205, 206, 210, 211, 213, 220

Military contribution, Crown Colonies: Straits Settlements, 9, 63–4, 120; Hong Kong, 57–8
Military Operations Directorate, War Office, 34–5, 44, 71, 120
Millar, E. W. H., 29
Milne, Field Marshal Sir George, 80, 84, 100, 104, 108
Milwaukee, USS, 136
Ministerial Committee on Defence Requirements, 16, 118–19
Ministerial Committee on Disarmament, 16
Ministerial Fighting Services Committee, 16
Mobile naval base, 6
Monash, General, 36
Monitor, 15″ gun, 111, 115–16, 121–2, 264 n46
Montagu, Edwin, 54, 59
Montgomery-Massingberd, Field Marshal, 116, 117–19
Morris, Colonel Edwin, 139
Muar, 206
Muckden, 102
Munich crisis, 15, 217
Murray, Sir Oswyn, 4

Nagano, Admiral, 229
Nagumo, Admiral, 221
Nancowry Harbour, 79, 113
Nash, Walter, 130, 133, 152–5
National Government, 103
Nauru, 155
Naval Estimates: of 1923, 35; of 1937, 127
Naval limitation conferences: Washington, 1921–2, 31; Geneva, 1927, 93; London, 1930, 92, 94–5, 123; London, 1936, 126
Naval Staff, UK: 14; post-war policy, 1919, 19–20; attitude to Jellicoe reports, 22–3; sites, 25–6; effect of Washington treaty, 32; truncated scheme, 50–1; defence of base, 72; *War Memo. (E)*, 112–14; Australian anxieties, 141; 1939 as 'worst year'; for, 144; Far East Priority queried by, 146–9; 1941 *Appreciation*, 204

Index

Nazis, 1, 106, 116
Nelson, HMS, 183, 184, 215
Netherlands East Indies: 7; importance of, 134, 168–70; US fears about, 163; Japanese trade pressure on, 165; Cabinet disagreement about, 175, 181; freezes Japanese assets, 182; Japan's aims, 190–2; AIF divisions for, 206
New Caledonia, 177
New Guinea, 8, 155, 174, 177, 217
New Hebrides, 155
New naval standard, 123, 126–7, 130, 262 n7
New Zealand: 3, 6, 8; Jellicoe report, 22; Washington treaty, 31; contributions requested, 35, 61; protest, 1924, 43–4; support for base, 54, 56; £1 million gift, 64–8; air power, 69–70; demands consultation, 91–3; 1930 Imperial Conference, 97–9; Col. Thoms and the COS, 100–1; contribution reduced, 110; China Squadron, 114; Ethiopian crisis, 125; idea of joint battleship or brigade of guards, 127; idea of battalion for India, 128; doubts about Imperial defence, 128; 1937 Imperial Conference, 130–5; cruisers retained, 139; offers help in Pacific, 141–3; Pacific Defence Conference, 151–5; Tientsin silver crisis, 157; DMV meetings, 160–2; effect of Italian war, 164, 166; brigade for Fiji, 169; 1940 *Far East Appreciation*, 171; airfield construction unit, RNZAF, 176; capital ship plan, 183–7; Pearl Harbor, 193
New Zealand Division of the RN, 58, 64
New Zealand, HMS, 4
Newall, Air Chief Marshal Sir Arthur, 82, 143, 168
Newfoundland, 3, 42, 182
Nicols, Philip, 93
Nine-point-two inch guns, *see* Artillery
Niue, 141
Norfolk, HMS, 136–7; Plate 30
Norfolk Island, 155
Normanton oil fuel depot: Map 8; Plate 2
North Borneo, 13
Norton Griffiths, Co., 67
Northcott, Major-General, 173, 176

Odend'hal, Vice-Admiral Jean, 150
Oil fuel: one year's supply, 30, 31; Red Sea and Indian Ocean anchorages, 31; reserves, 32; Normanton depot, Map 8; US freezing order, 182; Japan's needs, 190–1
Old Strait, 26–8, 30, 48, 86, 115
Olivier, Lord, 40
One power standard, 24, 223
Operation Matador, 198–9, 212
Ottawa, 17
Overseas Defence subcommittee: 15; Singapore defences referred to, 27; reports, 29; requests delay, 30; Labour Government, 1924, 44; role of services, 71; Labour Government, 1930, 96; Stage II of defences, 120; provisioning needs, 135

Pacific Defence Conference, 1939, 142–4, 151–5, 161
Pacific Islands: vulnerability, 6; New Zealand's concern, 133; offers help, 139, 141–3; Pacific Defence Conference, 151–5; air reconnaissance system, 155; effect of Pearl Harbor on, 193
Pacific Naval Intelligence Centre, 29
Pacific Ocean, 2, 4, 7
Pacific Pact, Australian plan for, 131
Pacific War begins, 188
Page, Sir Earle, 140, 184, 186, 209
Pahang, 11, 194, 227
Palestine, 134, 217
Parkhill, Sir Archdale, 130–4
Parmoor, Lord, 95
Parr, Sir James, 66, 91
Parry, Captain, RN, 196
Pasir Laba Battery, 121
Patani, 193, 199
Pearce, Sir George, 127
Pearl Harbor, 192–3, 210
Peirse, Air Vice-Marshal, 146

Penang: British acquisition, 8–9; importance, 10, 27, 47; 1921 staff conference, 28; reinforcement route, 113; loss of, 202
Penggerang Battery, 121
Perak, 10, 202, 206; *see also* Sultan of Perak
Perak Malay Volunteer Infantry, 225
Percival, Lieutenant-General Arthur, 41, 137, 195, 196, 202, 206, 208–9, 219; Plates 38, 40
Period before relief: in 1920 is 90 days, 29, 113; in 1921 is 42 days, 31, 35, 78, 101; in 1924 is 28 days (or 42 in bad weather), 113, 135; in 1938 is 70 days, 135; in 1939 extension to 90 days, 154, 158; 120 days suggested by Americans, 156; extended to 180 days on outbreak of war, 159
Perlis, 11
Persian Gulf oilfields, 101
Perth, HMAS, 160
Philippines, 31, 163, 177, 179, 192–3, 205
Phillips, Admiral Sir Tom: Director of Plans, 133, 139; Vice-CNS, 155, 163, 185–7; C-in-C Eastern Fleet, 186–8, 196; Force Z, 200–204, 219; Plate 36
Piesse, Major E. L., 223
Placentia Bay, 182
Plan Dog, 175
Plans Division, Naval Staff, 14, 37, 64, 107
Pocket battleships, 11" gun, 116, 146
Ponsonby, Arthur, 16
Poorten, General H.ter, 176
Port defences, 34, 72
Portsmouth gun trials, 83
Pound, Admiral Sir Dudley: Director of Plans, 35, 37, 44–5, 54, 55, 74; Assistant CNS, 82; CNS, 168, 181; capital ships for Far East, 183–7, 219
Pountney, Arthur, M., 59
Power, Sir Lawrence, 31, 47
Pownall, Sir Henry: Secretary Defence Requirements Committee, 117, 219; C-in-C Far East, 205, 222, 224
Prince of Wales, HMS, 127, 184–7, 193, 201–3, 218; Plate 33

Pritchard, Major-General H. L., 225
Pulau Blakang Mati, *see* Blakang Mati
Pulau Tekong Battery, 121
Pulau Ubin, 115
Pulford, Air Vice-Marshal, 209
Purnell, Captain William, USN, 174, 176, 181

Queen Mary, troopship, 195

Race, 222–8
Radar, 137, 264 n48
RAF bases, *see* Alor Star, Gong Kedah, Kuantan, Machang, Sembawang, Sungei Patani
Raffles, 7, 8, 36
Railways, strategic, 70
Ramilles, HMS, 183, 186
Rearmament: 1932 COS review, 106–7; 1933 review, 117; Defence Requirements Committee, 117–19; shipbuilding programme, 127
Red Sea, 31, 113, 134
Reinforcements policy, 1941, 203–5, 207
Renown, HMS, 183, 186
Repulse, HMS, 105, 183–7, 193, 200, 201–3, 218; Plate 34
Residents, Malay States, 11
Resolution, HMS, 183, 186
Revenge, HMS, 183, 186
Rhineland, 126, 217
Richmond, Sir Herbert, 114–15, 188, 213
Rodney, HMS, 183, 185, 215
Roosevelt, President: cruisers for Singapore, 1938, 136; Bruce visits, 158; Singapore facilities offered to, 163; reassures Casey, 167; 1940 Election, 172; meets Churchill, Placentia Bay, 182; Churchill tells of *Prince of Wales* and *Repulse*, 185; Atlantic war preparations, 190, 216; Pearl Harbor, 193; Arcadia Conference, 205
Roskill, Stephen, 214
Royal Air Force, 69–70
Royal Australian Navy, 113, 221
Royal Canadian Navy, 221

Royal Malay Army, 227
Royal Sovereign, HMS, 183, 186
Royle, Vice-Admiral Sir Guy, 196
Russia, 165, 182, 190, 210, 211, 213
Ryrie, Sir Granville, 66, 91

Saigon, 172, 182
Salmond, Air Marshal Sir John, 104, 108-9
Sansom, Sir George, 222
Sarangong Harbour, 71; Map 6
Sarawak, 13, 116, 122, 203
Saunders, Group Captain, 173, 181
Savage, Michael Joseph, 131-3, 152, 162, 164
Savile, Sir Leopold, 31, 50, 108; Plate 14
Scharnhorst, 185, 210
Scullin, James, 93, 95, 98-9
Selangor, 10; *see also* Sultan of Selangor
Selat Sinki, 6
Seletar, 33, 35, 71, 121, 137
Self-reliance, Australian, 128
Sembawang, 32, 35, 36, 47, 188; air base, 121; *see also* Dockyard
Sembawang Shipyard Ltd., 230
Serapong Battery, 121
Shanghai crisis, 1, 104-5, 105-6, 215
Shanghai, treaty port of, 9, 193
Shaw, Tom, 88
Sidey, Thomas, 98
Silingsing Battery, 121
Siloso Battery, 121
Silver Jubilee, George V's, 120-2, 125
Simon, Sir John, 119
Simonstown Base, 67, 183-4
Simson, Brigadier Ivan, 212
Sinclair-Burgess, Major-General, 128
Singapore: strategic position of, 5, 6; annexation, 8; early defence, 9-10; assembly point, main fleet, 20; Jellicoe proposals, 22-3; decision to build base, 29-30; Washington treaty excludes, 32; dockyard layout, 33; 1924 Labour Government, 40-5; site drainage, 45; site purchase, 55, 61; Straits military contribution, 63-4, 67; Gillman Committee, 81-4; idea of new New Zealand battalion for, 103-4; Shanghai incident, 104-5; air reconnaissance, 116; New Zealand battalion, 128; keystone to security, 130; graving dock opened, 135-6; 1938 exercise, 136-8; Anzac help mooted, 139; Pacific Defence Conference discussed, 151-5; US fleet, 156; defensive net sought, 166; Japanese at Saigon, 183; air defences of, 1940, 169; Defence Conference, October 1940, 173-4; Anglo-Dutch conversations, 174; Stark rejects sending US fleet, 175; Anglo-Dutch-Australian Conference, 1941, 176-7; A-B-C 1 disagreement about, 177-80; Anglo-Dutch-British Conference, April 1941, 181-2; capital ships for, 183-7; *Prince of Wales* and *Repulse* arrive at, 186-7; Japanese air raid, 193; surrender of, 209; Volunteers, 224-7; Malay Regiment, 227; Sembawang Shipyard Ltd, 230
Singapore Harbour Board, 10
Singora, 193, 198-9, 201, 206
Slessor, Sir John: Plans Division, Air Ministry, 84; Director of Plans, 139, 159; A-B-C 1 talks, 177, 220
Slim River, 206
Smuts, General Jan, 42, 56
Snowden, Philip, 40, 88, 98-9
Socotra, 113
Solomon Islands, 155
South Africa, Union of, 17, 22, 35, 127
South China Sea, 8, 14, 116
South Pacific, *see* Pacific Islands
Southby, Sir Archibald, 211
Special Training Schools, 226-7
Sphinx Battery, 121
Spotter planes, 37, 75-6, 116
Spratly Islands, 143-5
Staff College Exercises, 36, 37, 74
Stage II defences, 51, 80-1, 83-4, 109, 118
Standing Defence Subcommittee, CID, 29
Stanhope, Lord, 67, 140, 155, 158
Stark, Admiral, USN, 172, 174-5, 180, 207
Stay-behind parties, 226-7

Steel, Air Commodore, 74
Stirling, Alfred, 148
Stores basin, 33, 51; Plates 31–2
Straits of Malacca, 7, 113
Straits Settlements: founding of, 8, 9, 11; gift of land, 35, 55, 61; military contributions of, 63–4, 67, 120; opening of dockyard, escorts from, 136; Volunteers, 195, 224–7
Stalin, 185
Status quo area, Washington treaty, 32
Strategic Appreciations Committee, 16, 146–7, 155, 229
Strategy: for Pacific, 1919, 4–5, 6, 19; Jellicoe reports, 21–3; 1921 Imperial Conference, 30; *see also* Malay barrier, *War Memorandum (Eastern)*
Straubenzee, Brigadier-General, 224
Stubbs, Governor Sir Edward, 57
Sturdee, Colonel, 152
Submarines, 75–6, 82, 94, 119, 217
Substitution, Air Staff doctrine of, 14, 75–7
Suez Canal: opened, 1869, 9; eastern route, 31, 178; fear of blockship in, 36, 101, 217
Sullivan, Dan, 154
Sultan of Perak, 60, 62, 122
Sultan of Selangor, 62
Sungei Patani, 194, 202
Sungei Ujong, 10
Surrender, 15 Feb. 1942, 209; Plates 40, 41
Sydney, 5, 7, 27

Tamils, 13, 226
Tanks, 138, 174, 205, 206, 207, 211
Taranto, 191
Tedder, Air Vice-Marshal Arthur, 129, 137, 220; Plate 8
Ten Year Rule: made in 1919, 5–6, 16, 21; extended, 1928, 66; reaffirmed, 102, 103; ending urged, 1932, 105–7, 215, 260 n13
Tengah air base, 121, 137, 208
Terror, HMS, 111, 115–16, 121–2, 264 n46
Thailand: Malay States, 11; possible attack route, 137; Japanese pressure on, 165, 169, 172, 182, 190–1; British interest in, 175, 177; Japanese landings, 193; Operation Matador, 198–9
Third Indian Corps, 195, 199, 202, 205, 206, 228
Thomas, Commander A. C., USN, 173, 176
Thomas, J. H., 40–1, 119
Thomas, Sir Shenton, 128, 166, 212
Thoms, Lieutenant-Colonel, N.W.B.B., 100
Thomson, Frank D., 65, 99, 100
Thomson, Lord, 40–1, 88
Three Power Standard, 127
Thwaites, General Sir William, 34
Tientsin silver crisis, 156–7, 160, 217
Timetable, Fleet movements, 113–14
Timor, 173, 174, 177
Tin mining, 13
Tirpitz, 183–5
Tojo, General, 229
Tonga, 142, 155, 173
Tonkin, 172
Topham, Jones, Railton, Co., 67
Torpedo bombers: 51, 75–8; *Horsley*, 78, 84, 116, Plate 6; *Vildebeeste*, 194, 212, Plate 11; 36 Squadron, 85, 89
Treasury, UK: 14; opposed base, 29, 35; and Straits Settlements gift, 55; and Hong Kong gift, 58; and FMS gift, 61, 62; Straits Settlements military contribution controversy, 64, 120; slowed down policy, 96; Shanghai crisis, view, 106; rearmament, 117
Trenchard, Marshal of the Royal Air Force, Sir Hugh: port defences, 34; FMS gift, 51; artillery trials, 68; air power, 69; proposal for Singapore, 75–8; 1926 compromise, 80–1; 36 Squadron moved, 84–5; Plate 7
Trengganu, 11
Trenton, USS, 136
Trincomalee, 7, 46, 101, 105, 113, 139
Truncated scheme, 50–1, 78, 87, 107, 122
Tsuji Masanobu, 196

Index

Turner, Rear-Admiral Kelly, USN, 178, 180
Two Power Standard, 2, 124, 127, 213, 215, 223
Tyrwhitt, Vice-Admiral, 114

Unfederated Malay States, 11–12
United Australia Party, 128
USA: naval rival, 2, 5, 6, 20; 1916 naval programme of, 21; in Pacific, 24; Anglo-Japanese Alliance, attitude to, 31–2; Washington Conference, 32; London Naval Conference, 1930, 93–5; no war plans against, 117, 129; London Naval Conference, 1936, 126; no commitments by, 134; three cruisers to Singapore dock opening, 136; Britain admits weakness to, 1939, 147, 155; Staff talks, Washington, 1939, 156; Tientsin silver crisis, 158; alliance with crucial, 160; Dominions look to protection to, 163–4; Casey, Australian Minister to, 167; attitude to Japan, 167–8; importance for Netherlands East Indies, 168; naval staff and Singapore base, 172; Plan Dog, 175; Anglo-Dutch-Australian conference, 1941, observers at, 176–7; A-B-C 1 talks, 177–80; American-Dutch-British conference, 1941, 181–2; freezes Japanese assets, 182; negotiations with Japan, 1941, 186, 215; security pact, 216; Pacific Fleet, 221

Vansittart, Sir Robert, 117
Vichy Government, 165, 171, 182
Victoria Point, Burma, 78, 199
Vildebeeste torpedo bomber, 194, 212; Plate 11
Volunteers, 188, 195, 224–7

Wake Island, 193
Walsh, Stephen, 40
War Cabinet, *see* Cabinet, UK
War Memorandum (Eastern): written, 1920, 23, 28; details and revisions, 112–13; Richmond criticises, 114–15; 1933 revisions, 115, 153, 219; 1939 revisions, 155, 156; 1941 revisions, 183; Pacific War changes, 204
War Office: 14; first defence plans, 27, 36–7; 1924 cancellation, 44; Hong Kong gift, attitude to, 58; seeks free land, Singapore, 63–4, 67; railways, plans for, 70; big guns, 71–2; Johore gift, use of, 122
Ward, Sir Joseph, 3, 65, 91
Warren, Sir William, 42
Warship construction, 5, 127, 144
Washington: naval conference, 31; MacDonald's US-Japanese negotiations, 91; 1941, 186; Churchill's visit, Dec. 1941, 205
Washington treaties, 31–2, 34, 40, 65, 87, 116–17, 124
Waterfield, Percival, 96
Wavell, General Sir Archibald: War Office, 44, 218–19; Supreme Commander, ABDA, 206; authorised Percival to surrender, 209, 218; Plate 37
Weihaiwei, 9
Wellington, *see* Pacific Defence Conference
Wemyss, Admiral Sir Rosslyn, 3
Western Samoa, 141–2
Wharf walls, 51; Plates 23, 29, 30
Whiskard, Sir Geoffrey, 140
Wilford, Sir Thomas, 92
Williams, Air Vice-Marshal Richard, 97, 136; Plate 8
Wilson, Sir Henry, 70
Wilson, Sir Samuel, 61
Winterton, Lord, 59, 210
Wood, Sir Kingsley, 146
Worthington-Evans, Sir Laming, 58, 63–4, 68, 83–4
Wynter, Colonel H. D., 128

Yamashita, Lieutenant-General, 196, 206, 209; Plates 40, 41
Yamoto class battleships, 190
Young Malay Union, 227
Yu Lin Bay, Hainan, 144–5

Zero fighters, 207

SOUTHEASTERN MASSACHUSETTS UNIVERSITY
VA459.S5 M32 1979b
The rise and fall of the Singapore Naval

3 2922 00070 173 7

241063